Flash Builder and Flash Catalyst

The New Workflow

Steven Peeters

friendsof

DESIGNER TO DESIGNER™

an Apress® company

Flash Builder and Flash Catalyst
The New Workflow

Copyright © 2010 by Steven Peeters

ISBN-13 (pbk): 978-1-4302-2835-6

ISBN-13 (electronic): 978-1-4302-2836-3

Printed and bound in the United States of America 9 8 7 6 5 4 3 2 1

Trademarked names may appear in this book. Rather than use a trademark symbol with every occurrence of a trademarked name, we use the names only in an editorial fashion and to the benefit of the trademark owner, with no intention of infringement of the trademark.

Distributed to the book trade worldwide by Springer-Verlag New York, Inc., 233 Spring Street, 6th Floor, New York, NY 10013. Phone 1-800-SPRINGER, fax 201-348-4505, e-mail orders-ny@springer-sbm.com, or visit www.springeronline.com.

For information on translations, please e-mail rights@apress.com, or visit www.apress.com.

Apress and friends of ED books may be purchased in bulk for academic, corporate, or promotional use. eBook versions and licenses are also available for most titles. For more information, reference our Special Bulk Sales–eBook Licensing web page at www.apress.com/info/bulksales.

The information in this book is distributed on an "as is" basis, without warranty. Although every precaution has been taken in the preparation of this work, neither the author(s) nor Apress shall have any liability to any person or entity with respect to any loss or damage caused or alleged to be caused directly or indirectly by the information contained in this work.

Credits

Publisher and President:
Paul Manning

Lead Editor:
Ben Renow-Clarke

Technical Reviewer:
Peter Elst

Editorial Board:
Clay Andres, Steve Anglin, Mark Beckner, Ewan Buckingham, Gary Cornell, Jonathan Gennick, Jonathan Hassell, Michelle Lowman, Matthew Moodie, Duncan Parkes, Jeffrey Pepper, Frank Pohlmann, Douglas Pundick, Ben Renow-Clarke, Dominic Shakeshaft, Matt Wade, Tom Welsh

Coordinating Editor:
Laurin Becker

Copy Editor:
Mary Behr, Sharon Terdeman

Compositor:
Bronkella Publishing LLC

Indexer:
BIM Indexing & Proofreading Services

Artist:
April Milne

Cover Designer:
Anna Ishchenko

Photo Credit:
Steven Peeters

Contents at a Glance

Contents

About the Author

Steven Peeters is an Adobe Certified Instructor who works for multimediacollege (Adobe Authorised Training Center in Belgium and Luxembourg) and has 10+ years of development experience with different companies and technologies such as C, C++, Java, Flex, AIR, etc. He is passionate about all things related to Flex, AIR and ColdFusion and he teaches courses on those topics on a regular basis. In between teaching courses he also manages and works on technically complex projects to keep improving his skills.

As a Belgian ColdFusion User Group manager, Steven is also dedicated to the community and he also shares his knowledge regularly on his own website http://www.flexpert.be and on his company's blog http://www.multimediacollege.be/blog.

When he's not behind the computer you can find Steven spending quality time with his family or catching up on articles from about all areas in the science world.

CERTIFIED INSTRUCTOR

USER GROUP MANAGER

About the Technical Reviewer

 **Peter Elst** is a freelance Flash Platform consultant and Founding Partner of Project Cocoon Multimedia, based in Belgium and India. As an Adobe Community Professional, author, and speaker at various international conferences, Peter is a well known and respected member of the Flash Community. Whenever he has the time you'll find him posting on his personal blog: www.peterelst.com

Acknowledgments

First and foremost I would like to thank my loving wife Mieke and my two little boys Ilyan and Rhune for allowing me the time and space to write this book. I know it's been a long journey and I haven't been able to spend as much time as I wanted with you, but I promise I'll make it up to you all.

I also like to thank my colleagues Frederik, Alwyn and Marije for inspiring me to write this book and for helping me out with the designs I've made.

Next, I would like to thank some people from Adobe: Andrew Shorten, Ryan Stewart, Steven Heintz and Tim Buntel (who is no longer a part of the Adobe team unfortunately). All of you helped me out a lot in gaining in-depth insight in these new products.

Of course I mustn't forget Peter Elst who did a wonderful job in reviewing the technicalities of this book. Your comments and remarks have been very helpful.

And finally I would like to thank the Friends of ED team for their wonderful assistance and for allowing me the opportunity to write this book.

Introduction

Hello and welcome to *Flash Builder and Flash Catalyst: the New Workflow*. I've written this book to guide you through the process of deciding how to tackle a new project.

As you probably know, developing a Rich Internet Application is not always an easy task to do. There are several aspects to keep in mind. One of the key aspects is the project workflow. Not every application will have the same workflow applied to it during its creation. A lot of it depends on the size of the project, whether or not you need to connect your application to some kind of back end technology, how many people you are working with and, let's not forget this one, how the application is designed.

If you have been developing RIAs in the past you are likely to have spoken unspeakable words when receiving the final design for the application from the designer on your team, especially if the designer is not familiar with the capabilities and limits of the technology that is used for actually developing the application. Or maybe you had to redo a couple of days work because of some "minor" design changes. You will no doubt have had a couple of frustrating moments in your life due to these kinds of problems.

Most of these problems, however, are based on the fact that designer and developers speak totally different languages. You may think they speak English or Dutch or even Swahili, but in fact, designers are talking in colors and pixels, while the developers speak in view states, loops and variables. With the arrival of Flash Catalyst the two profiles can now speak the same language and understand what they are trying to do. Designers can create basic Flex applications by working only with pixels and colors, whereas developers can now simply take those applications and extend them with a database connection, for example.

This is what this book is about. The first 4 chapters will guide you through the basics and new features of Flex 4, Flash Builder 4 and Flash Catalyst so you're up-to-speed on the capabilities and limits of those products. In chapters 5 and 6 I will take you on a tutorial based tour of the various possible workflows you can have for your applications. These chapters will help you understand how these products work together and how they improve the interaction between designers, interaction designers and developers when creating Rich Internet Applications. Choosing the best workflow will make your development process much more efficient and will help you use the available resources to their maximum potential.

In the last parts of this book I will explain to you the best practices in creating RIAs. These best practices come not only from official sources such as Adobe related articles. Most of them come from my own experience as a developer and project manager. One of the best practices, depending on the size of your project of course, is the usage of application frameworks. They will help you to collaborate with other developers and maximize extensibility, scalability and maintainability for your application. I've dedicated an entire chapter to the application frameworks, explaining the differences and similarities between the ones that are most commonly used by Flex developers.

Layout conventions

To keep this book as clear and easy to follow as possible, the following text conventions are used throughout.

Important words or concepts are normally highlighted on the first appearance in **bold type**.

Code is presented in `fixed-width font`.

New or changed code is normally presented in **`bold fixed-width font`**.

Pseudo-code and variable input are written in *`italic fixed-width font`*.

Menu commands are written in the form **Menu ➤ Submenu ➤ Submenu**.

Where we want to draw your attention to something, We've highlighted it like this:

> *Ahem, don't say I didn't warn you.*

Sometimes code won't fit on a single line in a book. Where this happens, we use an arrow like this: ➥.

```
This is a very, very long section of code that should be written all on the same ➥
line without a break.
```

Chapter 1

Flex and AIR: Taking RIAs to the Next Level

In this chapter I'll explain a little about creating Rich Internet Applications (RIAs) and desktop applications using Internet technology, where the technology came from and how it is used today. I'll try to provide some basic understanding of Adobe Flex for the novice user. I will also look briefly at how Flash Catalyst changes that workflow and how it can make you more productive when creating Rich Internet Applications. Finally, I'll present a brief overview of some of the technologies that are commonly used for connecting a Flex application to a back end, because I'm going to be using different kinds of back-end technologies in the examples throughout this book.

Taking Advantage of Flash Technology

Let's start with a brief overview of where the technology comes from and what we have already accomplished, as shown in Figure 1-1.

Mainframe

A very long time ago, the interactive programming business started out on a **mainframe**. Who hasn't seen the famous black screens with green or orange letters on them? In fact, some mainframe programs are still out there doing their jobs. Even today there are still new programs being written for a mainframe environment.

In this type of environment, applications run on a central machine and you need a direct line to that machine to be able to access the program. Users access programs using a computer known as a *thin client,* which relies on the mainframe for processing and storage, and are of little use in stand-alone mode. The problem is, this means that only the employees of the company, or of other companies that have a leased-line connection have access. It also means that most of the programs are written only for internal use, though that actually has a couple of advantages for the configuration: there are typically not that many simultaneous connections, security is tight, and downtimes are manageable because you know which users are currently using the application.

Client-Server

Early in the nineties, things started changing. The price of a personal computer (PC) had dropped enough to get companies interested in distributed environments. This type of environment came to be known as **client-server**, because it involves a centrally located server that users access from client machines (their PCs) to run their programs. This may sound similar to what I just described, but don't be fooled. There are some similarities but there are also some major differences. The similarities lie in the fact that a server is placed at a central location and that server is necessary to run certain programs. But in the mainframe era, users were equipped with what is called a *thin client*. This is a computer that is of little use in a stand-alone mode. It always needs a mainframe to connect to. In a client-server setup it is assumed the user has tasks to do that don't require a connection to a server. Just think about writing analyses and reports, creating flowcharts or other everyday tasks. The PC, with its own hard drive and memory, enabled the user to work without having to acquire server access. Many of the programs used every day are installed on every computer, and most of the time, some services and databases are all that is located on the server.

This architecture also has benefits, in particular the fact that servers can be clustered to provide better performance and availability. Clustering is useful when one or more applications on the server may need to have a lot of simultaneous connections available.

By using the Internet as a global network between the company branches, the server could be located halfway across the globe, while the nice-looking applications could run on their local machines, with no lag in performance due to network latency issues while going to another screen or calling a dialog box, because this was all done using the local machine's capabilities.

A huge step forward during this time was the development of an attractive Graphical User Interface (GUI). All of a sudden, those monotone screens were disappearing and making way for appealing, easier-to-use interfaces for programs that need to be used every day by the same users. The way people interact with an application determines how they experience it. *User friendly* became the new buzzword and the whole user experience was given a boost.

However, these advantages came at a cost. Every time a new version of a program had to be installed, it had to be installed on all the connected computers individually. Although programs were later developed that could do this automatically (e.g. overnight), the process was often quite labor-intensive and not always practical. Examples of this type of software are *Remote Installer* from Emco Software (http://www.emco.is/products/remote-installer/features.php) and Desktop Central produced by Manage Engine (http://www.manageengine.com/products/desktop-central/windows-software-installation.html).

Web Applications

In the mid-nineties, the World Wide Web was coming out of the shadows and more and more people were connecting to the wonderful global network that was the Internet. Suddenly, the whole world was connected. Initially, almost all of the content that was available was in text format, basically some text on a page with maybe a few images. Interactivity essentially meant the user clicking on some part of the text and a new page being loaded. Animations were scarce and consisted mainly of animated GIF (Graphics Interchange Format) images.

Even though this was a step back from the client-server technology, because there was no way to build a rich GUI experience, companies recognized an opportunity to reach a much broader audience. The first **web applications** were born as companies opened up these services to everybody and the race towards globalization made a gigantic leap. Suddenly, the whole world could become a client.

Web applications accessed through the Internet have an advantage, one that was common to all mainframe applications. Since the application resides on a shared server, you only have to install or update the application once! The next time the user visited your web application, he would automatically be working with the latest version.

Rich Internet Applications

Meanwhile, web sites continued to develop, adding a variety of elements and functionality. Flash technology was growing from being a way to add animations to a web site, to being a tool to add interactivity to the web application. Some web sites were built entirely in Flash; others used only small bits and pieces of Flash on their web sites. But interest in Flash kept growing until in 2004, Macromedia, which was acquired by Adobe Systems Inc. in 2005, launched a new technology called Flex. This technology is actually an extension of the existing Flash platform in the sense that it uses the same basic functionality. But Flex is a framework with a Software Development Kit (SDK); it uses the existing ActionScript language to create library components that can be used *out of the box*. Over time, more and more library components became available and they also became more elaborate in their functionality. The applications built with this technology became known as **Rich Internet Applications (RIAs)**. I'm not saying that there weren't any RIAs existing before Flex emerged. It is just that around this time Adobe launched the term, which is now widely accepted to indicate these kinds of applications.

The *rich* part refers to the fact that the technology allows attractive, user-friendly applications to be built. The design for such applications, however, was quite challenging in the past for Flex developers, because it is not always easy to programmatically re-create a nifty design. But with the arrival of Flash Catalyst, the process has been made a lot easier. Flash Catalyst lets you start developing your application directly from the Photoshop or Illustrator design file, creating a much closer connection between the design and development team.

The *Internet* part of the term refers to the reach of these applications. Since the applications are accessible via the Internet, they are available to every computer in the world that has been connected to the internet. All any user needs to run a Flex application is a proper version of the Flash Player. Which version is required will be discussed in the next section.

With rich Internet applications, you get the *best of both worlds*, because you have the power to create a graphical, fully interactive application with the ease of having to install or update it only once on the server, while still reaching to the ends of the world.

Of course, there are some competitors like OpenLazlo, Silverlight, and Ajax (and I'm probably forgetting a few others), but they all seem to be copying a lot of the Flex functionality. This is not necessarily a bad thing, because copying and improving capabilities is often the way technologies are advanced. The competition results in better components, smaller file sizes, reduced development times, and improved tools.

These factors have contributed to the development of Flex. Today, Flex is widely adopted by lots of companies all over the world. It has been used both in simple administrative programs as well as for real-time and mission-critical applications. In fact, I've worked at the Port of Antwerp for a couple of years and during my time there, we went from traditional client-server development to using Flex as a front end to the existing back end, as well as creating completely new applications to replace old mainframe applications. Those new applications needed to work in real-time, to monitor the traffic in the harbor, for example.

Another big company that has adopted Flex as their development tool is Coggno. (This is a company that specializes in providing a platform for e-learning. So, you can develop your online content, upload it to the Coggno site, and they will take care of licensing and secure payments for you, so you don't have to go through all of that development yourself. And they use Flex as the tool to allow you to create and manage your online content. The fact that Adobe thrives in a worldwide community also lets that community suggest new or improved features. If the community shouts loud enough, Adobe listens and starts working on those issues, which is why we are already using the fourth release of the Flex SDK.

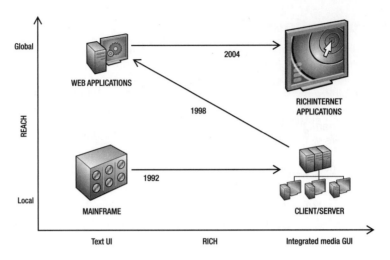

Figure 1-1. A schematic overview of applications types over time

Why Should You Use the Flash Platform?

To install a rich Internet application, you can choose from a number of technologies: Flash Player, Java plug-in, Shockwave (which is a plug-in for Director), Silverlight plug-in, and more. An important factor to take into account is the worldwide installation numbers, and even though the numbers in Figure 1-2 have been taken from the Flash Player web site, they have been gathered from a representational sample and extrapolated to the entire Internet-connected population.

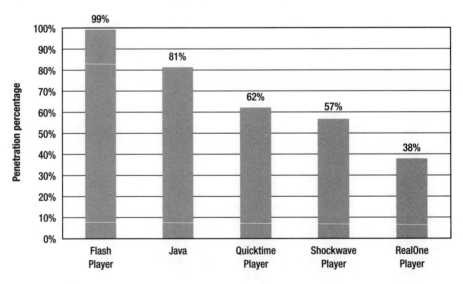

Figure 1-2. Interactive plug-in penetration statistics (December 2009)

Now, what we can learn from these statistics is that the Flash player is the most widely distributed plug-in for interactive content, not surprising since it has been around for over 15 years. (Unfortunately, at the moment of writing, no statistics were available for the Silverlight plug-in.) If you dig a little deeper into the version penetration of the Flash Player, you can see just how fast a new version of this player is adopted. The latest major version was released in October 2008 and it has already been adopted by almost 95% of all mature markets. I'm sure this number will continue to climb toward 99%, just like version 9 of the player.

Version 9.0.0 is all it takes to develop and run Flex 3 projects, but for Flex 4 you must target version 10 of the Flash Player. This means that in theory your business could be missing out on up to 5% of its client potential because of users who don't have the required version installed. But most Flash web sites and web applications have a detection mechanism that gives the user the option to automatically install the latest version before continuing. This doesn't always do the trick because some companies make it impossible for a user to install a new version, and there's not much a developer can do about that. However, the June 2009 statistics for enterprise penetration of Flash player 10 show that almost 75% of enterprises are already running this version. As this number continues to grow, the threshold for implementing Flex 4 applications will gradually disappear.

Adobe is also putting great effort in getting the Flash Player on the mobile platform. With the release of version 10.1, the company promises the player will run on several different mobile operating systems. You used to have a Flash Player version for the PC and a Flash Lite version for the mobile devices. Now, while the PC version continued to develop quite rapidly, Flash Lite could be compared to having Flash Player 7 on the device. That was a huge difference in performance, let alone the fact that you can't use ActionScript 3.0 in that version. But as I said, the new 10.1 release synchronizes the two platforms, so you should be able to create Flex 4 applications for mobile devices. To do that, though, you won't use the ordinary version of the Flex SDK. At the moment of writing this book Adobe is currently working on a special "mobile optimized" version of the Flex framework, with the working name of "Slider." This version will reflect the constraints of a mobile platform, such as limited memory, less powerful CPUs, and different input mechanisms. The first edition of the mobile Adobe Flex SDK is expected to be available in 2010. If you want to know more about Slider, take a look at the white paper "Flex and mobile: a vision for building contextual applications," available at `http://download.macromedia.com/pub/labs/flex/mobile/flexmobile_whitepaper.pdf`.

Where is Flex Used?

Since I'm talking about the use of the Flash Player for both companies and individuals, let's take a closer look at where Flex applications are being used. The usage of this technology can be divided into two large groups: web applications that are generally available to the public, and business applications. Let's take a closer look.

Flex on the Web

Don't get me wrong here. A lot of business applications are available through the Internet. Just think about **e-commerce sites**. That is basically the first category I'd like to talk about.

When these kinds of applications are brought to the Web using Flex, they have a couple of advantages over standard HTML web sites. A major benefit is that through use of the Flash technology, visitors can be turned into buyers more easily. Now, you may think "What does Flash have to do with the content I'm offering?" Well, the short answer is "nothing." But if you know Flash technology and what it can do, you know the effect it can have on the way a user experiences your site. It's fairly easy to make some kind of promotional article stand out from the crowd using an animation for example. In other words, you draw the attention of the visitor to a certain item you want to sell. I am not pretending to know a lot about marketing, but I do know this is exactly how you can persuade a visitor to actually buy something from your site.

Another fairly common application type is the **tracking system**. If you've ever ordered something from a major e-commerce site, you probably know what I'm talking about. After your purchase, you generally receive a confirmation mail that includes a link to some transport company's web site where you can track your order. You can see where it's at and sometimes even where it's going next and how it's going to get there—by plane, train or delivery truck. Whenever a key transport step is finished, the information is updated. And sometimes this even happens in real-time, which means that the web site is updated as soon as the package information is updated on the server. I'll talk a bit more about real-time possibilities when I discuss LiveCycle Data Services.

Besides the advantage of having real-time communication possibilities, tracking web sites created with Flex have another advantage over traditional HTML-based sites. With the latter, whenever you refresh the data on the tracking page, the entire page needs to be regenerated and sent over the Internet in its entirety. This means that even elements that haven't changed, such as images, headers, footers, and so forth, are also sent, increasing the network load and consuming unnecessary bandwidth. When using Flex, only the actual data that has been changed will be sent over the network connection. So, in this way, you are actually conserving bandwidth.

Flex is also great for creating **widgets,** small tools that are added to the user interface, typically to provide some specific functionality, such as weather forecasts, stock values, live tennis scores, mortgage simulators, and so on. You can use Flash technology to create interesting animations between different values. And of course you can combine these animations with real-time server-side pushed data to create eye-catching interactive widgets.

Flex can also be used to build **a complete web site.** It can be quite useful when you require some kind of data table, for example, since Flex has a Datagrid component built-in. But I've tried this myself a couple of times and found that inevitably you end up with a web application instead of merely an informative web site. This is because the Flex SDK was developed for creating applications and almost all of its components are geared toward that goal. Of course, there are some good Flex web sites out there. I'm thinking of Adobe TV (http://tv.adobe.com), which contains a nice set of technical video tutorials, and Parleys (http://www.parleys.com), which contains a lot of recorded presentations and even has an offline version. Still, if you want a Flash-based web site, you're better off just using Flash, even if you have the need for some minor back-end communication.

Flex in the Enterprise

When we take a closer look at how Flex is used in the enterprise, it's not all that different, but still there are some very big differences. E-commerce and tracking sites can be considered enterprise applications, but the type I'd like to discuss are the ones that are not available to the general public. These are business-to-business (B2B) applications or tools that are intended only for internal use.

Here are examples of some of the kinds of enterprise applications I've worked on:

- A document management system. This application was essentially a tool to keep all project-related files together on a central server. Project folders were created and contained everything from the analysis and design to zipped project source code and build script. The tool let you search across projects for certain file names and allowed for versioning of the uploaded files.
- A real-time ship-tracking system for a harbor. Barge captains, terminal operators, agents, garbage collectors, and customs authorities could all access certain parts of the same Flex applications to organize the entire path of a barge from the point it enters the harbor until it leaves again.

- An application for gathering statistical data. This one allowed neurologists to enter an initial diagnosis and keep track of their patients' progress for a certain treatment. All the data is then gathered in a central location for statistical analysis concerning these treatments.

- A building maintenance application. This tool allowed users to register certain malfunctions or structural problems in a building. The problems were directed to the proper areas and assigned to an appropriate worker. The person requesting the fix was able to keep track of the progress on his request.

Of course this is not an exhaustive list of possibilities, but it gives you an example of what's out there, because most of the time, such applications are not visible to the public.

Testing Flex applications

As you know, testing is an important part of application development, and so it is with Flex applications, especially in the enterprise. You have to run tests on different levels: locally, combined with other team members' changes, and acceptance testing. The first two levels of testing are done iteratively for every change and for every release to another level. During this iterative testing it is imperative that you perform regression tests as well. So, with every design change, with every code change, you should test not only your changes, but also the surrounding components to see whether your changes have introduced any unwanted side effects. For acceptance testing, the application runs in an environment that is supposed to resemble its intended environment; this is done just before going into production.

Of course, testing an application is not something you do only with an enterprise application. Even for the simplest of applications, I urge you to test everything thoroughly before even thinking about deploying it or handing it over to your client. But I will talk more about how you can test your applications properly later on in this book.

Connecting Applications to a Back End

Since the kinds of applications we'll be discussing will need some kind of back-end communication, let me introduce to you a few methods of communication with a certain kind of back end. In the examples throughout the book, I'll use several of these back end types, so it's important that you understand their differences and similarities when implementing them in a Flex application. Later in this book I will discuss in detail how Flash Builder 4 will make your life as a developer a lot easier than it used to be with Flex 3. The new version of the product has extensive built-in capabilities to help you connect to different kinds of back-end technologies. Add the drag-and-drop binding features and you are set for some real rapid development.

I'm not going to list all the possible technologies you could use to connect your Flex application, but I'll try to give you an overview and some example code for the most common ones. All of these have advantages and disadvantages, just as with any other technology. So you will have to decide which technology best suits your needs for a certain project.

Sometimes deciding which technology to use is difficult, because you have to make a decision which you can't really base on anything when this client-server workflow is completely new to you. Sometimes it's quite easy to make that decision because you already have developers experienced in ColdFusion, PHP, or Java on your staff. You should take advantage of that experience and choose the back-end technology they are comfortable with. And sometimes, of course, you don't even have a choice, because you need to use the existing back end and you have to adopt the communication type that can work with that particular technology.

AMFPHP

AMFPHP is a free, open source PHP implementation of the Action Message Format (AMF) that allows you to connect Flash and Flex applications to a PHP back end. It can't be compared to LiveCycle Data Services (LCDS) or BlazeDS (which I'll both discuss in a bit) because it only has support for using the `<mx:RemoteObject>` tag. And even though it hasn't been updated in ages, it still performs beautifully.

AMFPHP does have some things going for it. First of all, BlazeDS and LCDS don't allow you to use PHP as your back-end technology. Moreover, as a kind of middleware layer between Flex and the back-end code, it is very lightweight. In fact, I think it's the most lightweight solution out there at this time, mainly because AMFPHP doesn't include or impose any development framework. You are free to choose the one you want to use, or you can simply not use a specific framework at all. AMFPHP also lets you map your ActionScript classes directly to your PHP classes. This works much the same as in LCDS and BlazeDS. The only difference is that in your PHP class you have to explicitly state the fully qualified class name in a property called `$_explicitType`. This property is then mapped to the `[RemoteClass]` metadata tag in your ActionScript class definition.

Let me give you a small example of how this would look with some basic classes. Assume we have to fetch a list of people (such as registrations via a website) to display them in some kind of grid. The basic PHP `PersonDTO` class might look like this:

```php
<?php
  class PersonDTO {
    var $id;
    var $firstname;
    var $lastname;
    var $phone;
    var $email;

    var $_explicitType = "com.domain.project.valueObjects.PersonDTO";
  }
?>
```

In this example, the `PersonDTO.php` file should be located in a package (which is basically a directory) on the server called `com.domain.project.valueObjects`. Now, where does this package structure start from? Let's take a look at the installation procedure for AMFPHP, which is pretty straightforward. All you need to do is go to the download section of the AMFPHP site (`http://www.amfphp.org`), which will redirect you to SourceForge. There you can find and download the latest version—1.9 beta2. (Or you go directly to `http://sourceforge.net/projects/amfphp/files/amfphp/amfphp%201.9%20beta2/amfphp-1.9.beta.20080120.zip/download`.) Just unzip this file into the web root of your server (htdocs for Apache servers). All this does is install a separate directory into which you can place your services and valueObjects, as you can see in Figure 1-3.

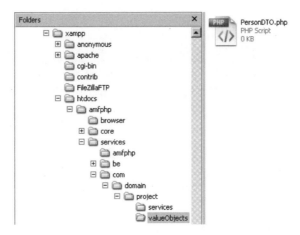

Figure 1-3. Directory structure in amfphp when installed in xampp (the Apache server package)

Now, we still have to link our ActionScript class to that PHP class. To make it easy on myself here, I'm going to use publicly accessible attributes in the class. Normally, you shouldn't do this; you should declare all properties `private` and create some implicit getters and setters for them. These implicit getters and setters are specific ActionScript implementations that differ from other programming languages in both their notation and usage. Instead of defining the getter as `getProperty()`, you need to put a space between the words, creating a `get property()` method. The advantage is that you can still use the dot-notation when working with these properties as if they were public properties. But you are still in fact executing a method, so additional calculations or other functionality will be executed when setting a value, for example. Occasionally, however, it can be handy to use these `public` properties for quickly testing something, which is why I'll show this in the first example. The other examples will use `private` properties.

```
package com.domain.project.valueObjects {
  [Bindable]
  [RemoteClass(alias="com.domain.project.valueObjects.PersonDTO")]
  public class PersonDTO {
    public var id:Number;
    public var fistname:String;
    public var lastname:String;
    public var phone:String;
    public var email:String;
  }
}
```

Notice that the `[RemoteClass]` metadata tag contains an `alias` property that is set to the exact same value as the `$_explicitType` property of the PHP class. This is necessary for the system to work properly. I'll explain more about this tag and its purpose in the section on Flash Remoting with LiveCycle Data Services.

In your back-end method that retrieves this list of people, you have to create an `array()` and fill it with `PersonDTO` objects. The AMFPHP middleware layer will make sure that this list is then converted to an `Array` of `PersonDTO` objects in ActionScript.

> Please note that the return value from such a PHP method is an Array and not an ArrayCollection. If you wish to use the result in a binding expression (e.g. dataProvider in a DataGrid) you still have to convert it to an ArrayCollection. You can't just cast it to an ArrayCollection, so you have to convert it like this:
>
> var arr:ArrayCollection = new ArrayCollection(event.result as Array);

The really great feature of AMFPHP is its browser. This is a Flex application that allows you to browse through the different services you've created. An introspection module generates a list of LinkButton components for each method in the selected service. By clicking on this button, you can fill out any necessary parameters and make the actual function call. In this way, you can verify that you don't have any errors in your code, because you will get compilation errors from your PHP code. You can also check the result value for the function because it is displayed in the same browser application. So, all in all, AMFPHP is a great tool to verify your back-end functionality apart from your Flex application, which can be very helpful for locating bugs or errors.

Zend AMF

Zend AMF is another way of communicating between Flex or Flash and PHP in a back-end environment. It is quite similar to AMFPHP in the sense that it uses the Action Message Format (AMF) protocol, but ZendAMF is essentially the new implementation and is officially supported by both Adobe and Zend.

ZendAMF is part of the Zend framework, so you'll need to download the framework from http://frameswork.zend.com/download/latest. If you're using Flash Builder 4, you have the option of installing the framework on your server automatically when using the Data/Services panel. Thus, I won't go into too much detail here; I'm just going to explain briefly how ZendAMF works without Flash Builder. We'll get to the practical details in Chapter 3, where I'll explain more on how to use the framework from within Flash Builder 4.

After installing the Zend framework on your web server, you need to create a bootstrap file. This file is like the gateway.php file used with AMFPHP. It is the endpoint you'll be connecting to from Flash or Flex. This file should include the Server.php file you'll find in the Zend framework directory. This class will actually be doing most of the work for us when calling a back-end method. Assuming the framework is located in a directory next to the browser root (the htdocs folder on Apache), the bootstrap file might look like this:

```php
<?php
  // Turn on the error reporting. This should be turned off in a
  // production environment.
  error_reporting(E_ALL|E_STRICT);
  ini_set("display_errors", "on");

  // Extend the include path to include the framework directory
  ini_set("include_path", ini_get("include_path") . ":../frameworks");

  // Include the server classes we are going to use
  require_once "Zend/Amf/Server.php";
  require_once "PersonServices.php";
```

```php
  // Initialize the server object and tell it which service class it wants to
expose.
  // You can expose multiple classes by repeating the setClass() method call for
each
  // class.
  $server = new Zend_Amf_Server();
  $server->setClass("PersonServices");
?>
```

The `PersonServices.php` file that is included in this file defines the functionality made available to the Flash and Flex applications. Let's assume that this services class contains a method available to retrieve all the people from the database.

```php
<?php
  class PersonServices {
    public function __construct() {
      // Set up the connection details
      mysql_connect("localhost", "root", "");
      mysql_select_db("flex4");
    }

    public function getAllPersons() {
      $result = mysql_query("SELECT * FROM person");
      $arr = array();
      while($row = mysql_fetch_assoc($result)) {
        // Just attach the associative row object to the end of the array
        array_push($arr, $row);
      }

      return $arr;
    }
  }
```

> You may have noticed that I did not include the closing PHP tag. Because of potential problems with whitespace characters in class files, Zend actually recommends leaving out this closing tag as a best practice.

Just as with AMFPHP, you need to create a `services-config.xml` file that contains the destination to which you want to connect. However, this file is a little bit different for ZendAMF since you're not connecting to the `gateway.php` file anymore. Instead, you're connecting to the bootstrap file you just created. Everything else stays the same.

```xml
<?xml version="1.0" encoding="UTF-8"?>
<services-config>
  <services>
    <service id="amfphp-flashremoting-service"
             class="flex.messaging.services.RemotingService"
             messageTypes="flex.messaging.messages.RemotingMessage">
      <destination id="zend">
```

```
        <channels>
          <channelref="my-zend"/>
        </channels>
        <properties>
          <source>*</source>
        </properties>
      </destination>
    </service>
  </services>
  <channels>
    <channel-definition id="my-zend"class="mx.messaging.channels.AMFChannel">
      <endpoint uri="http://localhost/zendamf_remote/"
                class="flex.messaging.endpoints.AMFEndpoint"/>
    </channel-definition>
  </channels>
</services-config>
```

Once you've created this `config` file, you need to include it in the compiler settings of your Flex project. From that point on, all you need to do is create an `<mx:RemoteObject>` in your Flex application with the `zend` destination and call the `getAllPersons` method of the back-end class, as shown in the code example below. The results of this call will be transferred back to the Flex front end in the form of a `result` event, while potential faults will be returned as a `fault` event.

```
<mx:Script>
  private function resultHandler(event:Resultevent):void {
    for(var i:uint = 0; i < event.result.length; i++) {
      // Just print out the firstname and lastname fields concatenated
      trace(event.result[i].firstname + " " + event.result[i].lastname);
    }
  }

  private function faultHandler(event:FaultEvent):void {
    Alert.show(event.fault.faultString, event.fault.faultCode);
  }
</mx:Script>

<mx:RemoteObject id="service" destination="zend"
                result="resultHandler(event)"
                fault="faultHandler(event)"/>
```

What I've just shown you is a tiny example of how to use the ZendAMF implementation of the AMF protocol for connecting to a PHP back end. This is only a small part of the entire Zend framework, so I suggest you take a closer look at the rest of the framework as it is very useful if you're working with a PHP back end. You'll find the documentation at `http://framework.zend.com/docs/overview`.

LiveCycle Data Services

LiveCycle Data Services is the main way of connecting your back end to a Flex application if you want to use Adobe technology. It offers a lot of possibilities and features, as you can see in Figure 1-4.

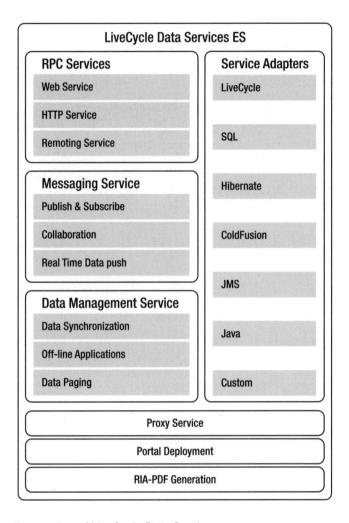

Figure 1-4. A schematic overview of LiveCycle Data Services

Proxy Service

The first feature I'd like to take a closer look at is the solution to **cross-domain issues**. Let me first explain the problem. The Flash Player has a few security restrictions, including the fact that you can't just access any file on any sever using a Flash (or Flex) application. Your web application is located on your web server and the Flash player only allows you to access remote files located on the same server as your application. If you want to access a file on another server, you'll get a "Security error accessing URL."

There are two solutions to this problem. The first is rather simple: you just have to place (or modify) a crossdomain.xml file on the root of the web server you're trying to access. The content of this cross-domain file is:

```
<cross-domain-policy>
  <allow-access-fromdomain="IP Address or range" />
</cross-domain-policy>
```

The problem with this solution is that this file needs to be located on the remote server and unless this is a server you control, you probably won't have access to that location. I'm sure you can imagine the security risks if you at company X would have access to the web root of company Y, which could be a competitor, the Department of Defense or even NASA.

That's why there's a second solution—the **ProxyService**. This is really just a work-around for the problem, but it's a good one. The main configuration file for LiveCycle Data Services is services-config.xml, and it includes a proxy-config.xml configuration file in which you can define a destination to be used when accessing a remote file. Here's an example of a proxy-config.xml file.

LCDSIntro ➤ *lcds-config* ➤ *proxy-config.xml*

```
<?xml version="1.0" encoding="UTF-8"?>
<service id="proxy-service"
         class="flex.messaging.services.HTTPProxyService"
         messageTypes="flex.messaging.messages.HTTPMessage,
                       flex.messaging.messages.SOAPMessage">
  <properties>
    <connection-manager>
      <max-total-connections>100</max-total-connections>
      <default-max-connections-per-host>2</default-max-connections-per-host>
    </connection-manager>
    <allow-lax-ssl>true</allow-lax-ssl>
  </properties>

  <adapters>
    <adapter-definition id="http-proxy"
                        class="flex.messaging.services.http.HTTPProxyAdapter"
                        default="true"/>
    <adapter-definition id="soap-proxy"
                        class="flex.messaging.services.http.SOAPProxyAdapter"/>
  </adapters>

  <default-channels>
    <channel ref="my-http"/>
  </default-channels>

  <!--Default destination using a dynamic URL-->
  <destination id="DefaultHTTP">
    <properties>
      <dynamic-url>
        http://remote-machine:port-number/*
      </dynamic-url>
    </properties>
  </destination>

  <!--Named destination using a fixed URL-->
```

```
<destination id="myProxy">
  <properties>
    <url>
      http://remote-machine:post-number/file.xml
    </url>
  </properties>
</destination>
</service>
```

When you use a ProxyService like this, it is actually the server that hosts the LiveCycle Data Services that will fetch the file and then send it back to your application. So, no more cross-domain issues, because the fetching happens outside of the Flash Player. If you use the first destination in the example, you are allowed to access any file on any subdirectory starting from the root of the defined remote web server. But you still have to specify the actual URL of the file you wish to access.

If you use the named proxy destination from the example, you don't have to specify the URL of the remote file anymore, because it is explicitly defined in the destination. This has a nice benefit in that you can use the LiveCycle Data Services configuration on different deployment levels, so the actual Flex application remains the same, but the file you wish to access can be placed in different locations for development, acceptance, and production environments. It saves you the trouble of having to recompile the application or using an external parameter file you'd have to read dynamically at startup.

Web-Tier Compiler

LiveCycle Data Services allows your code be compiled by the application server. The advantage is that your application is always built on the same server, using the same SDK, namely the one that is available on the server. This can be quite useful if the developers at your company work with different operating systems, such as Mac OS or Windows, which can lead to the resulting application SWFs having different sizes. It also means you could limit the number of professional licenses for Flex Builder if, for example, you are going to introduce some charts in your application. Since locally, you can use the watermarked standard version, when you put it into production the professional license is used and the watermark is removed.

This is actually how the first versions of Flex worked, with applications being compiled on the server. There is a small drawback, however. Since you actually compile the application on the server, the first time somebody visits your web application, the compilation will be triggered and that person will have to wait for the compilation to complete before the resulting SWF file is downloaded to his browser. After this compilation, the SWF file is available and will simply be downloaded to anyone visiting the site. That is, until you upload some updates. Then the server compiler will detect some changes and will start a new compilation that will have to complete before the visitor receives the SWF file. However, this increased waiting time which happens occasionally, can be solved simply by you (or a colleague) being the first one to go to the application when new source files are placed on the server.

Flash Remoting

One of the key features in LCDS is the ability to easily connect to a Java back end. This is done by using the `<mx:RemoteObject>` tag in Flex and specifying a destination for that remote object in the `remoting-config.xml` file on the server. By using this tag, you can talk directly to a Java class as if it were an ActionScript class. Most of the time, this Java back-end class will be an Assembler class, which is part of a design pattern commonly used with the Data Access Object pattern and ValueObjects or Data Transfer Objects (DTO). If you'd like to read about this, here are some excellent resources:

- Data Transfer Object pattern: http://java.sun.com/blueprints/corej2eepatterns/ Patterns/TransferObject.html
- Data Access Object pattern: http://java.sun.com/blueprints/corej2eepatterns/ Patterns/DataAccessObject.html
- Transfer Object Assembler pattern: http://java.sun.com/blueprints/corej2eepatterns/ Patterns/TransferObjectAssembler.html

Another great feature of this remoting is the fact that you can have strongly typed communication between Flex and Java. This means that the Java DTOs can be directly typed as ActionScript classes. I'll demonstrate this in a small example. Imagine you have a PersonDTO class in the back end like this.

LCDSIntro_java ➤ *com* ➤ *domain* ➤ *project* ➤ *valueObjects* ➤ *PersonDTO.java*

```java
package com.domain.project.valueObjects;
public class PersonDTO {
  private int id;
  private String firstname;
  private String lastname;
  private String phone;
  private String email;

  public PersonDTO() {}

  public void setId(int id) {
    this.id = id;
  }
  public int getId() {
    return id;
  }
  public void setFirstname(String firstname) {
    this.firstname = firstname;
  }
  public String getFirstname() {
    return firstname;
  }
  public void setLastname(String lastname) {
    this.lastname = lastname;
  }
  public String getLastname() {
    return lastname;
  }
  public void setPhone(String phone) {
    this.phone = phone;
  }
  public String getPhone() {
    return phone;
  }
  public void setEmail(String email) {
    this.email = email;
```

```
  }
  public String getEmail() {
    return email;
  }
}
```

If you want to transfer this class to the Flex front end, you have to let the application somehow know that the ActionScript class is actually the same as the Java class you've just defined. For this purpose, we'll use the [RemoteClass] metadata tag. With this tag, you have to provide a property called alias that contains the fully qualified class name for the corresponding Java class. In most cases, you'll also want to make this class [Bindable], which means you can use the properties in binding expressions. So, you'll end up with this ActionScript class.

LCDSIntro ➤ *com* ➤ *domain* ➤ *project* ➤ *valueObjects* ➤ *PersonDTO.as*

```
package com.domain.project.valueObjects {
  [Bindable]
  [RemoteClass(alias="com.domain.project.valueObjects.PersonDTO")]
  public class PersonDTO {
    private var _id:Number;
    private var _fistname:String;
    private var _lastname:String;
    private var _phone:String;
    private var _email:String;

    public function PersontDTO() {}

    public function set id(v:Number):void {
      _id = v;
    }
    public function get id():Number {
      return _id;
    }
    public function set firstname(v:String):void {
      _firstname = v;
    }
    public function get firstname():String {
      return _firstname;
    }
    public function set lastname(v:String):void {
      _lastname = v;
    }
    public function get lastname():String {
      return _lastname;
    }
    public function set phone(v:String):void {
      _phone = v;
    }
    public function get phone():String {
      return _phone;
```

```
    }
    public function set email(v:String):void {
      _email = v;
    }
    public function get email():String {
      return _email;
    }
  }
}
```

For the linking between ActionScript and Java classes to work, you must place the Java classes in the **classes** folder of your LiveCycle Data Services installation folder on the server, since that location is where the [RemoteClass] metadata tag starts searching for that fully qualified class name.

This means that when you request a list of persons from the database, you will not get just a list of objects returned from the back end call; the objects in the list will be typed as PersonDTO objects, as you can seen in Figure 1-5. In this way, you get strongly typed arguments and results passing between ActionScript and Java, which allows you to benefit from code completion and compile-time type checking without having to use type casting all the time.

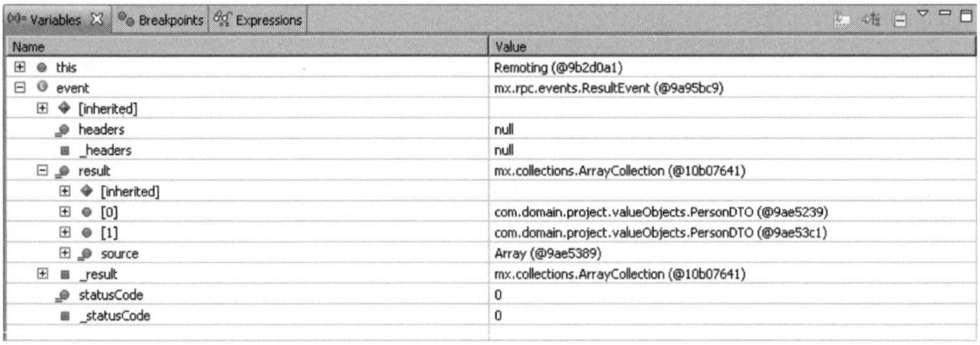

Name	Value
⊞ ● this	Remoting (@9b2d0a1)
⊟ ◐ event	mx.rpc.events.ResultEvent (@9a95bc9)
⊞ ◆ [inherited]	
🔎 headers	null
▦ _headers	null
⊟ 🔎 result	mx.collections.ArrayCollection (@10b07641)
⊞ ◆ [inherited]	
⊞ ● [0]	com.domain.project.valueObjects.PersonDTO (@9ae5239)
⊞ ● [1]	com.domain.project.valueObjects.PersonDTO (@9ae53c1)
⊞ 🔎 source	Array (@9ae5389)
⊞ ▦ _result	mx.collections.ArrayCollection (@10b07641)
🔎 statusCode	0
▦ _statusCode	0

Figure 1-5. The debug window shows strongly typed objects being returned as PersonDTO classes.

Data Management

Data Management is "la pièce de résistance" of LiveCycle Data Services. It can take advantage of the Real-Time Messaging Protocol (RTMP) as the channel to use in connecting to your back end. This gives you a real-time connection that is kept open for each client, which means you can also push data from the server to the client. And if you use it in an AIR application (discussed later in this chapter), you can even use online/offline synchronization of your data. Let's take a closer look.

Reduce Written Code

When you use the Data Management Service, changes to data at the Flex client are automatically batched and sent to the Data Management Service running in your application server. The Data Management Service then passes the changes to your business layer or directly to your persistence layer; you can use data access objects (DAOs) with straight JDBC calls, Hibernate, Java Persistence API (JPA), or any other solution.

Depending on the type of application you are building, the Data Management Service can save you from writing a great deal of client-side code in the following scenarios:

- Keeping track of all the items created, updated, and deleted by the user at the client side. This means that you can keep on creating, updating, and deleting items (if the autoCommit property is set to false, of course), even when you are temporarily disconnected from the server. We will take this one step further when I talk about AIR applications later on in this chapter.

- Keeping track of the original value of the data as initially retrieved by the client. The persistence layer often needs the original value to implement optimistic locking, which allows for easy and correct enabling of buttons or other functionality based on whether you have changed a value. If you change the value back again to the original, the Data Management Service will detect this and will no longer consider that value to be changed.

- Making a series of RPC calls to send changes (creates, updates, deletes) to the middle tier. What actually happens when you call the commit() method on the Data Management Service is that the back-end code will receive a list of changes, not the entire list of items in your record set. So, if you have changed one item, only one record will be sent over the network connection to your back end. If you have changed 10 records, the Data Management Service will automatically send only those 10 records and you as a programmer don't have to worry about that.

- Handling the conflicts that arise during the data synchronization process. Of course, once in a while you encounter a situation where two people are committing their changes on the same data at virtually the same time. This can lead to conflicts in the sense that one user may try to do an update on an item while the other has just deleted it. This results in a database conflict, and it is detectable in the backend since you get some sort of exception thrown (depending on the programming language used). The Data Management Service allows you to throw a specific type of exception to the client and the client gets a conflict message, which you can then capture and act upon, allowing you to easily handle concurrency issues.

Tracking Changes

The Data Management Service often uses the Data TransferObject pattern to convey data between the client and the server. This is no different from the way a <mx:RemoteObject> communicates. In this case, however, the client doesn't have to request new data. Instead, the server pushes data to the client, and the client needs to be able to detect any changes that have been pushed. For that reason, the client ActionScript version of the DTO will not just be made [Bindable], but instead will be set [Managed].

Having a [Managed] DTO is the same as setting it [Bindable], but with one big difference. In addition to making all publicly accessible properties available for use in binding expressions, the Data Management Service will intercept the get and set property operations on the DTO to perform on-demand loading, deleting, and updating features.

Another great feature of a [Managed] ArrayCollection is that you don't even need to call a back-end method anymore. You just add, change, or delete items in the ArrayCollection and because it is managed by the Data Management Service, automatically, upon committing your changes, the service will detect what has changed and will call the synchronization method in the back end with the proper records and an indication of which action needs to occur. Changes are made and the result, which is a list of only the changes, is sent to every client that is connected to the same destination. So the changes are actually pushed from the server to all the connected clients.

Assume you have the same `PersonDTO` object that needs to be transferred between ActionScript and Java. With the Data Management Service, that `DTO` class remains exactly the same on the Java side, but on the Flex side of the application, it will look like this:

LCDSIntro ➤ *com* ➤ *domain* ➤ *project* ➤ *valueObjects* ➤ *PersonDTO.as*

```
package com.domain.project.valueObjects {
  [Managed]
  [RemoteClass(alias="com.domain.project.valueObjects.PersonDTO")]
  public class PersonDTO {
    private var _id:Number;
    private var _fistname:String;
    private var _lastname:String;
    private var _phone:String;
    private var _email:String;

    public function PersontDTO() {}

    public function set id(v:Number):void {
      _id = v;
    }
    public function get id():Number {
      return _id;
    }
    public function set firstname(v:String):void {
      _firstname = v;
    }
    public function get firstname():String {
      return _firstname;
    }
    public function set lastname(v:String):void {
      _lastname = v;
    }
    public function get lastname():String {
      return _lastname;
    }
    public function set phone(v:String):void {
      _phone = v;
    }
    public function get phone():String {
      return _phone;
    }
    public function set email(v:String):void {
      _email = v;
    }
    public function get email():String {
      return _email;
    }
  }
}
```

Differences with Remote Procedure Calls (RPC services)

So far, nothing much has changed if we compare this Data Management Service with `Flash Remoting`. The biggest difference is that with an `<mx:RemoteObject>`, you need to call the back-end method and handle the result using a `resultHandler()` event listener. With the Data Management Service, you don't have to worry about this. Well, that's not entirely true, but it has become a lot simpler. Let me explain how it works.

I mentioned that you don't have to call a back-end method anymore, but you still have to let LiveCycle Data Services know you want to convey some data to the back end. For that purpose, the Data Management Service has four methods available:

- **fill-method**: This method takes an `ArrayCollection` as the first parameter, along with some optional extra parameters for the back-end method. It returns a list of objects—usually a list of Data Transfer Objects—to fill out the provided `ArrayCollection`. The method is executed by calling the `dataservice.fill()` method.
- **get-method**: This method fetches a single object, also usually a single DTO, from the back-end. It takes a single parameter, which is a `Map` (in the case of Java) of the values that make up the identity of the object to retrieve. This method is executed when calling the `dataservice.getItem()` method in the ActionScript code.
- **sync-method**: This method is executed when you call the `dataservice.commit()` function in ActionScript or when the property `autoCommit` is set to `true`, which is the default setting for an `<mx:DataService>` communication class. The Flex class will automatically detect which items from the managed `ArrayCollection` have actually been changed, so only those records are sent to the back-end method. Furthermore, the `DataService` also detects if the change is a create, update, or delete action. What the back-end method receives is a list of `ChangeObject` objects, which have the methods `isCreate()`, `isUpdate()` and `isDelete()`. The Data Management Service calls one back-end method and you have to split it up into the different operations.
- **count-method**: This method is executed by calling the `dataservice.count()` method in ActionScript. It returns an integer value, representing a number of records to be retrieved with the `fill-method`. You can use this method, for example, when using the paging option to retrieve large amounts of data in chunks and you want to display a message like "Showing records 50-100 of 2150."

Now, this is all nice, but when you call `dataservice.fill()` in your Flex application, how does LiveCycle Data Services know what back-end method to call? The answer again is in the server configuration files. This time you have to use the `data-management-config.xml` file. The file is located in the same place as the `remoting-config.xml` file, but the content of the file itself is a little bit different. You don't only have to specify where to find the `Assembler` class and what scope it needs to reside in on the server, you also have to specify the four specific methods I described above and the properties that make up the unique identity an object. Here's an example of such a file that is used with an application that manages simple `PersonDTO` objects.

LCDSIntro ➤ *lcds-config* ➤ *data-management-config.xml*

```
<?xml version="1.0" encoding="UTF-8"?>
<service id="data-service" class="flex.data.DataService">
```

```
<adapters>
  <adapter-definition id="ActionScript" class="flex.data.adapters.ASObjectAdapter"/>
  <adapter-definition id="java-dao" class="flex.data.adapters.JavaAdapter"
                      default="true"/>
</adapters>

<default-channels>
  <channelref="my-rtmp"/>
</default-channels>

<destination id="DMPersonServices">
  <properties>
    <source>com.domain.project.assemblers.DMPersonAssembler</source>
    <scope>application</scope>

    <metadata>
      <identity property="id"/>
    </metadata>

    <server>
      <fill-method>
        <name>getAllPersons</name>
      </fill-method>
      <fill-method>
        <name>getAllPersons</name>
        <params>java.lang.String</params>
      </fill-method>
      <sync-method>
        <name>syncPersons</name>
      </sync-method>
    </server>
  </properties>
</destination>
</service>
```

In this file you place the link between the fixed names for the ActionScript methods and the actual back-end methods that need to be executed. As you can see in this example configuration file, you can even use function overloading, which is not possible with the remoting. The reason for that is that the ActionScript language doesn't allow for function overloading, and in the remoting service you are calling the back-end method directly. So if you were to use overloading here, Flex wouldn't know which function to call. But with the Data Management Service, the actual function you call is defined in the configuration file, which is not bound by the ActionScript language restrictions. Now, let's take a look at a small application that uses the Data Management Service to update the person records in the database.

LCDSIntro ➤ *DataManagement.mxml*

```
<?xml version="1.0" encoding="utf-8"?>
<s:Application xmlns:fx="http://ns.adobe.com/mxml/2009"
               xmlns:s="library://ns.adobe.com/flex/spark"
               xmlns:mx="library://ns.adobe.com/flex/halo"
```

```
                creationComplete="personServices.fill(personsList)">
<s:layout>
  <s:VerticalLayout horizontalAlign="center" paddingTop="10"/>
</s:layout>
<fx:Script>
  <![CDATA[
    import com.domain.project.valueObjects.PersonDTO;
    import mx.collections.ArrayCollection;
    import mx.controls.Alert;
    import mx.rpc.events.FaultEvent;

    [Bindable]
    private var personsList:ArrayCollection = new ArrayCollection;

    [Bindable]
    private var selectedPerson:PersonDTO;

    protected function personServices_faultHandler(event:FaultEvent):void{
      Alert.show(event.fault.faultString, event.fault.faultCode);
    }

    protected function btnNew_clickHandler(event:MouseEvent):void{
      personsList.addItem(new PersonDTO());
      grid.selectedIndex = personsList.length - 1;
      selectedPerson = grid.selectedItem as PersonDTO;
    }

    protected function btnDelete_clickHandler(event:MouseEvent):void{
      personsList.removeItemAt(grid.selectedIndex);
      selectedPerson = null;
    }
  ]]>
</fx:Script>
<fx:Declarations>
  <s:DataService id="personServices" destination="DMPersonServices"
                 fault="personServices_faultHandler(event)"
                 autoCommit="false"/>
</fx:Declarations>

<fx:Binding source="fname.text" destination="selectedPerson.firstname"/>
<fx:Binding source="lname.text" destination="selectedPerson.lastname"/>
<fx:Binding source="phone.text" destination="selectedPerson.phone"/>
<fx:Binding source="email.text" destination="selectedPerson.email"/>

<mx:DataGrid id="grid" x="10" y="10" dataProvider="{personsList}"
             change="selectedPerson = grid.selectedItem as PersonDTO">
  <mx:columns>
    <mx:DataGridColumn headerText="ID" dataField="id" width="30"/>
    <mx:DataGridColumn headerText="First name" dataField="firstname" width="100"/>
```

```
          <mx:DataGridColumn headerText="Last name" dataField="lastname" width="100"/>
          <mx:DataGridColumn headerText="Phone" dataField="phone" width="100"/>
          <mx:DataGridColumn headerText="Email" dataField="email" width="200"/>
        </mx:columns>
      </mx:DataGrid>
      <mx:Form>
        <mx:FormItem label="First name">
          <s:TextInput id="fname" width="200" text="{selectedPerson.firstname}"/>
        </mx:FormItem>
        <mx:FormItem label="Last name">
          <s:TextInput id="lname" width="200" text="{selectedPerson.lastname}"/>
        </mx:FormItem>
        <mx:FormItem label="Phone">
          <s:TextInput id="phone" width="200" text="{selectedPerson.phone}"/>
        </mx:FormItem>
        <mx:FormItem label="Email">
          <s:TextInput id="email" width="200" text="{selectedPerson.email}"/>
        </mx:FormItem>
      </mx:Form>
      <mx:HBox>
        <s:Button id="btnNew" label="New"click="btnNew_clickHandler(event)"/>
        <s:Button id="btnDelete" label="Delete"click="btnDelete_clickHandler(event)"
                  enabled="{grid.selectedIndex > -1}"/>
        <s:Button id="btnSave" label="Save"click="personServices.commit()"
                  enabled="{personServices.commitRequired}"/>
        <s:Button id="btnCancel" label="Cancel"click="personServices.revertChanges()"
                  enabled="{personServices.commitRequired}"/>
      </mx:HBox>
    </s:Application>
```

> *This is just the basic form of an application using a DataService. As I discuss the new Flash Builder 4 features in Chapter 3, I'll be looking at the new way of connecting to this kind of back end using the Data /Services panel.*

Now, what you can clearly see in this application is that I never use any of the synchronization methods like createItem() or deleteItem(). This is because the PersonDTO objects in the ArrayCollection are actually set to [Managed] and are therefore being monitored by the DataService class. All I need to do is to call the commit() method to start up the back-end communication where only the created, altered, and deleted objects are transmitted. Or you can call the revertChanges() method to undo any changes you've made since you last committed or fetched the data.

This example also shows you a very useful feature—the commitRequired property. This property indicates whether or not the managed collection of objects has been changed. Now, I've often written something like this to disable the save button until some value changes. You capture the change event and set the button to enabled. But what if you type a backspace? Or you select the initial value in a list or combo box again? Well, you usually don't want to compare every value of your input form with the original one to make sure you only allow the save action to occur when something has actually been changed. Fortunately, the commitRequired property keeps track of this for you—and it does so very efficiently. When I've used it, it wasn't noticeable at all with regard to memory or processing time.

Fiber

The new Fiber data modeling features in LiveCycle Data Services ES2 version 3 allow you to use model-driven development to take advantage of advanced Data Management Service features without writing Java code or configuring services on the server. This is achieved by letting the Fiber Modeler tool and the Fiber Assembler generate both client and server side code.

You can also choose to generate the initial model from an existing SQL database, edit it in the Modeler tool, and then deploy it to both Flash Builder and the LiveCycle Data Services or the BlazeDS server. Optionally, you can build a model in the Modeler tool and then deploy it to the server to generate new database tables based on the model.

Since this book is not a complete reference for the Flash Builder product, going deeper into this new and wonderful plug-in would take us too far outside of this book's scope. But there are a lot of good references, articles, and blog posts about how to use it. Please refer to the reference list in this book for more information.

BlazeDS

Because LiveCycle Data Services comes with a price tag and because you don't always need that real-time data push technology, Adobe offers another solution that is completely free of charge. BlazeDS is the open-source version of LCDS. You can download the latest version at `http://opensource.adobe.com/wiki/display/blazeds/BlazeDS`, where you can also find the installation instructions and the documentation.

Businesses often refrain from using open source products because they are typically community-built and have zero support. In the case of BlazeDS, however, Adobe allows the community to contribute, but each contribution is screened and tested before becoming a part of the next release. This means that Adobe actually has certified builds and therefore provides enterprise support.

If you take a look at the overviews of LiveCycle Data Services (Figure 1-4) and BlazeDS (Figure 1-6), you can clearly see that the basic features are the same. The major difference is in the use of the RTMP (Real-Time Messaging Protocol) channel, which is not available in BlazeDS. However, there is an alternative called **Streaming AMF and HTTP channels**. This way of implementing the data push technology is called a Comet-like data push.

> In web development, **Comet** is a neologism to describe a web application model in which a long-held HTTP request allows a web server to push data to a browser, without the browser explicitly requesting it. Comet is an umbrella term for multiple techniques for achieving this interaction. All these methods rely on features included by default in browsers, such as JavaScript, rather than on non-default plug-ins.
>
> In theory, the Comet approach differs from the original model of the web, in which a browser requests a complete web page or chunks of data to update a web page. However in practice, Comet applications typically use Ajax with long polling to detect new information on the server. The concept predates the coining of the neologism, and is known by several other names, including Ajax Push, Reverse Ajax, Two-way-web, HTTP Streaming and HTTP among others.
>
> Wikipedia, http://en.wikipedia.org/wiki/Comet_(programming)

This capability is supported for HTTP 1.1, but is not available for HTTP 1.0. There are a number of proxy servers still in use that are not compliant with HTTP 1.1. When using a streaming channel, make sure that the channel has `connect-timeout-seconds` defined and the channel set has a channel to fall back to, such as an AMF polling channel.

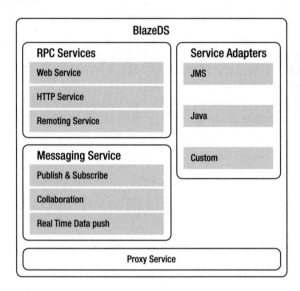

Figure 1-6. A schematic overview of BlazeDS

Using streaming AMF or HTTP channels/endpoints is like setting a long polling interval on a standard AMF or HTTP channel/endpoint, but the connection is never closed, even after the server pushes the data to the client. By keeping a dedicated connection for server updates open, network latency is greatly reduced because the client and the server do not continuously open and close the connection, unlike polling channels. Of course, these streaming channels can also use a secure connection over HTTPS, which provides tighter security in sending sensitive data over the Internet.

Since the channel definitions for BlazeDS are also located in the `services-config.xml` file on your server, the definitions will look something like this:

```
<!-- AMF with streaming -->
<channel-definition id="my-amf-stream"
                    class="mx.messaging.channels.StreamingAMFChannel">
  <endpoint url="http://servername:2080/myapp/messagebroker/streamingamf"
            class="flex.messaging.endpoints.StreamingAMFEndpoint"/>
</channel-definition>

<!-- Secure AMF with streaming -->
<channel-definition id="my-secure-amf-stream"
                    class="mx.messaging.channels.SecureStreamingAMFChannel">
  <endpoint url="http://servername:2080/myapp/messagebroker/securestreamingamf"
            class="flex.messaging.endpoints.SecureStreamingAMFEndpoint"/>
</channel-definition>
```

```
<!-- HTTP with streaming -->
<channel-definition id="my-http-stream"
                    class="mx.messaging.channels.StreamingHTTPChannel">
  <endpoint url="http://servername:2080/myapp/messagebroker/streaminghttp"
            class="flex.messaging.endpoints.StreamingHTTPEndpoint"/>
</channel-definition>

<!-- Secure HTTP with streaming -->
<channel-definition id="my-secure-http-stream"
                    class="mx.messaging.channels.SecureStreamingHTTPChannel">
  <endpoint url="http://servername:2080/myapp/messagebroker/securestreaminghttp"
            class="flex.messaging.endpoints.SecureStreamingHTTPEndpoint"/>
</channel-definition>
```

The most significant feature of BlazeDS is the remoting with Java. Just as with LiveCycle Data Services, you use the `remoting-config.xml` file to define the endpoints to your Java back end classes. On the Flex side of the story, everything stays the same as well. You still use `<mx:RemoteObject>` with the destination set to the one defined in the `remoting-config.xml` file. You still call a back-end method as if it were an ActionScript method, and you still use the same result and fault handlers. The only thing that is actually different is that you don't need to install LCDS.

This means that BlazeDS has another nice advantage. Since LiveCycle Data Services is licensed per CPU and/or per number of users, you can use BlazeDS on central development and acceptance servers, but for the actual production version of your application, you install only LCDS on your production server and deploy the same web application with the same configuration files, and this will work just fine. If your application requires using RTMP, for example, you can also use BlazeDS on the local testing servers by **creating a failover structure** in the channels you use. This might be a good idea when you are not sure whether the channel is blocked on the firewall; different channels use different port numbers and these ports have to be allowed by the firewall in order to be used in your application. Creating such a failover is fairly simple: you just declare two channels for your destination (or in the `<default-channels>` section, you set the RTMP channel as the first one in the list).

```
<default-channels>
  <channelref="my-rtmp" />
  <channelref="my-amf" />
</default-channels>
```

What happens then is that the application first tries to connect to the RTMP channel on your server. If that connection doesn't succeed, it will try the AMF channel. But this is also the Achilles heel of the system. The RTMP connection attempt must actually get a timeout before trying to connect to the second channel. Depending on the timeout settings, this could take a few seconds. So that could mean that back-end calls would take significantly more time and performance might drop to an inacceptable level. Now, you can argue that on a development server, this is not a big issue, since you're aware of this side effect and you know it is going to be fixed in the production version. But what about acceptance testing? This typically involves a group of actual users and they will complain about the slow response times. They will not accept the promise that in production it will be solved. There's no way to guarantee it for them.

A better solution in my opinion is to employ custom build scripts using tools like Maven and Ant. With this approach, you can specify build settings for the different levels of deployment (development, acceptance, and production) and set only one channel definition, depending on the intended deployment of the application build. In that way, you don't ever have to wait for a connection timeout before attempting another channel since you already know that the RTMP channel is not going to be available.

Unfortunately, with BlazeDS you can't use a direct connection to Hibernate in your back end. Hibernate is a framework that maps Java classes to SQL database table and frees you from having to write any SQL statements, because the framework generates them for you. This makes your application database independent, because it allows you to simply ask for a list of objects. Hibernate will perform the database operation and convert the results into the requested list. So if you're using that way of connecting your back end, you will have to deploy LiveCycle Data Services on each level of deployment and on your local development machine. This last one poses no problems, because LCDS is free of charge for the development version.

However, you do have the option of using ColdFusion as your back-end technology, using its built-in Flash Remoting or LiveCycle Data Services features; but more about that later in this chapter.

GraniteDS

Granite Data Services is another open source alternative to LiveCycle Data Services. You can find the latest version of this technology on `http://www.graniteds.org`. GraniteDS allows for use of the `RemoteObject` class, just like BlazeDS. And just like BlazeDS, it allows near-real-time communication by using a Comet-like data push implementation over the HTTP channel.

Dedicated service factories, which are framework classes that allow you to connect to a specific type of class in the back end (see Figure 1-7), are available for:

- EJB 3 (session beans that return entity beans)
- Seam (with identity security and conversation/task support)
- Spring (with Acegi/Spring security and entity beans support)
- Guice/Warp (with entity beans support)
- Simple Java classes (Plain Old Java Object or POJO) interactions

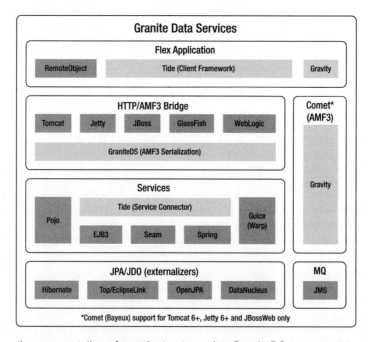

Figure 1-7. Schematic representation of a project setup using GraniteDS to connect to a Java back end

In essence, GraniteDS works in the same way BlazeDS does, so it runs on several Java-enabled applications servers like Tomcat, WebSphere, and so forth, and it supports full AMF3 back end communication using the `<mx:RemoteObject>` class. Also the configuration of the available services is much the same. So, for connecting to a simple POJO (Plain Old Java Object) class, your `services-config.xml` might look like this:

```xml
<?xml version="1.0" encoding="UTF-8"?>
<services-config>
  <services>
    <service id="granite-service"
             class="flex.messaging.services.RemotingService"
             messageTypes="flex.messaging.messages.RemotingMessage">
      <destination id="helloWorldService">
        <channels>
          <channel ref="my-graniteamf"/>
        </channels>
        <properties>
          <scope>application</scope>
          <source>com.domain.project.assemblers.PersonAssembler</source>
        </properties>
      </destination>
    </service>
  </services>

  <channels>
    <channel-definition id="my-graniteamf" class="mx.messaging.channels.AMFChannel">
      <endpoint uri="http://{server.name}:{server.port}/{context.root}/graniteamf/amf"
                class="flex.messaging.endpoints.AMFEndpoint"/>
    </channel-definition>
  </channels>
</services-config>
```

In this example, both the channel and the destination are defined in the same file. Of course, you can split this up into several parts, using a `<service-include file-path="`*services file*`">` *tag.* The variables {`server.name`}, {`server.port`}, and {`context.root`} will be filled out during compilation depending on the settings in the Apache ANT (`http://ant.apache.org/`) task. For those of you who are unfamiliar with Ant, it's a build tool that is extended using Java classes, rather than extending shell-based commands like most build tools (make, nmake, jam, and so on). Instead of writing shell commands, the build configuration is located in an XML file that contains several build targets. So, as an example for different tasks, you can specify a separate deploy task for the different deployment levels (e.g. development, acceptance and production). Tasks can call one another, so reusability is also available in this configuration file. Since this is not a book about Ant, I won't really cover it; I'll just present a small example for compiling a Flex application. This example has two build tasks: main and clean. The main target compiles the *Main.mxml* file into a SWF file. The clean target deletes the output of the main target.

```xml
<?xml version="1.0" encoding="utf-8"?>
<project name="My App Builder" basedir=".">
  <taskdef resource="flexTasks.tasks"
➥classpath="${basedir}/flexTasks/lib/flexTasks.jar" />
  <property name="FLEX_HOME" value="C:/flex/sdk"/>
  <property name="APP_ROOT" value="apps"/>
```

```
<property name="DEPLOY_DIR" value="c:/lcds/tomcat/webapps/"/>
<target name="main">
  <mxmlc file="${APP_ROOT}/Main.mxml"
         output="${DEPLOY_DIR}/Main.swf"
         ActionScript-file-encoding="UTF-8"
         keep-generated-ActionScript="true"
         incremental="true">
    <!-- Get default compiler options. -->
    <load-config filename="${FLEX_HOME}/frameworks/flex-config.xml"/>

    <!-- List of path elements that form the roots of ActionScript
         class hierarchies. -->
    <source-path path-element="${FLEX_HOME}/frameworks"/>

    <!-- List of SWC files or directories that contain SWC files. -->
    <compiler.library-path dir="${FLEX_HOME}/frameworks" append="true">
      <include name="libs" />
      <include name="../bundles/{locale}" />
    </compiler.library-path>

    <!-- Set size of output SWF file. -->
    <default-size width="500" height="600" />
  </mxmlc>
</target>
<target name="clean">
  <delete dir="${APP_ROOT}/generated"/>
  <delete>
    <fileset dir="${DEPLOY_DIR}" includes="Main.swf"/>
  </delete>
</target>
</project>
```

This way of compiling applications is also supported for the other means of communication. After all, it is just a compilation. You just have to provide the right commands and settings for each target. What's the advantage of using Ant instead of just the Flash Builder compilation? Well, for one, with Ant you don't really need Flash Builder since you can code Flex applications in a simple text editor. The Ant task will then compile your code into an application. Of course, Flash Builder is an excellent code editor for Flex, especially the latest version, as we'll discuss in the chapter about Flash Builder. But my point is that you don't really need Flash Builder (or Flex Builder, as it used to be called) to write and compile a Flex application.

A second advantage of using Ant build tasks to compile your application is that you can combine several build tasks into one major task. So, for example, you can create a build-deploy task in the build.xml file to compile your SWF file and your Java code, then package it into a WAR file and place it on the server to deploy the application. All of this with just one command.

Code Generation

Another feature of Granite Data Services is that it can generate ActionScript classes from Java classes. For this it uses the Gas3 code generator to create ActionScript 3 objects that represent the Java data objects. Essentially, Granite DS will take your Java Data Transfer Objects (DTOs) and convert them to ActionScript 3 objects.

The Gas3 code generator is implemented as an Eclipse Builder plug-in and as an Ant task. This Ant task is packaged as an Eclipse 3.2+ Ant plug-in but may also be used outside of Eclipse for command-line Ant calls. A common problem with code generators is that you can lose all your manual changes after regeneration of the code. Either the file can be generated only once and you make some manual changes, or the file is generated over and over again and you don't make any changes at all.

Gas 3 makes use of base classes, which are generated over and over again, and derived classes, which are generated only when they have not yet been created. So you can generate all the classes the first time and then apply your changes to the derived class. In this way, the back-end Java class can be regenerated without having to worry about manual changes that have been made on the ActionScript side of the application. Of course, sometimes there will be conflicts, depending on the changes you've made. For example, if you've added a calculated field to your ActionScript derived class that uses certain properties from the base class, you're going to run into problems when you delete one of those properties, because your calculation will no longer be possible. In this case, you still have to enter your changes manually to suit the available class properties.

ColdFusion Data Services

Although ColdFusion is a very elaborate and easy to understand back end technology, maybe you've never even heard of it. A lot of the time Flex and Flash back ends are written in Java or PHP, but there are a lot of other options out there which I haven't discussed in this chapter (.NET, Ruby on Rails, etc.). I would like to take a few moments and tell you about ColdFusion, because it has some great features when used in combination with a Flex front end.

Let me start by explaining what it actually is. ColdFusion is a development platform with a tag-based language called ColdFusion Markup Language (CFML) that has been around since 1995 and it is usually used for building dynamic web applications. You can write an entire web site in ColdFusion, like you would in any other dynamic server language such as PHP, ASP.NET or CGI, to name a few. As a tag-based language, it is similar to HTML but of course it has a specific syntax. You could also compare it to Flex, which also has a tag library and a scripting language. ColdFusion tags (CFML) can be used in combination with ordinary HTML tags to create dynamic web pages. There's also a scripting language called CFScript that is similar to JavaScript or server-side ActionScript.

Now, you may think "great, another server scripting language to choose from! Why should I use this one?" Well, ColdFusion offers some significant functionality, including:

- Easy database connection with virtually any database engine
- Conversion from HTML to PDF or FlashPaper
- Easy interaction with PDF documents (filling out forms, adding watermarks, and so forth)
- Simple WebService implementation
- Full-text search capabilities using the Verity K2 (which is now officially deprecated) or SOLR (`http://lucene.apache.org/solr/`) search engines

These are only a few of ColdFusion's standard features. But the chapter is not about the ColdFusion language, so let's focus on how you can use this server technology to interact with your Flex front-end application. Again, I'm going to use the same example of a MySQL database with one table called person; I want to retrieve all the persons in that table and display them in an `<mx:DataGrid>` in my application. What do we need to do in both ColdFusion and Flex to get this to work?

Well, first of all we need to connect to the database. As I mentioned in my small list of great features, ColdFusion allows easy access to almost any database. So, you start off in your ColdFusion Administrator, which you can find at `http://localhost:8500/CFIDE/administrator/`, assuming your server is running on the default port 8500. When you log in and you go to **Data Services** ➤ **Data Sources**, you'll see an overview of the available database connections. At the top of this page, you can add a new name and select the database type to create a new database connection. When you indicate a MySQL database, you get the form shown in Figure 1-8 to fill out.

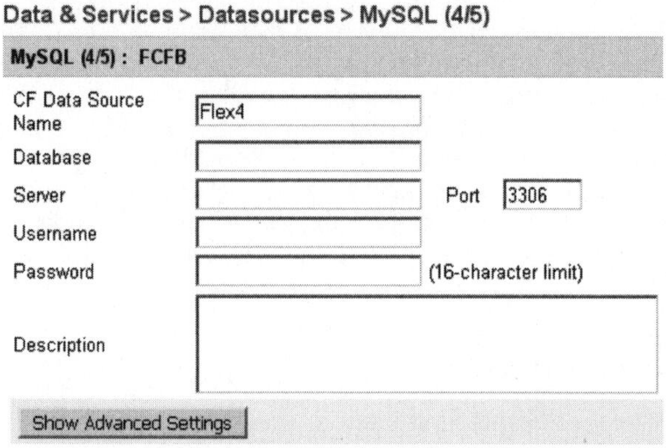

Data & Services > Datasources > MySQL (4/5)

MySQL (4/5) : FCFB		
CF Data Source Name	Flex4	
Database		
Server		Port 3306
Username		
Password		(16-character limit)
Description		

Show Advanced Settings

Figure 1-8. The creation properties for a new MySQL database connection

These input fields are all you need to create a new data source in ColdFusion. You can, of course, click on the Show Advanced Settings button to add a little more security by granting access rights and setting timeouts etc. Now, let me show you how easy it is to actually use this connection in a ColdFusion Component (CFC). A component is what you'll be using when communicating with a Flex application. If you compare it with a Java back end using design patterns, your assembler or services class would be a CFC. If the CFC is used only to retrieve data, it would look something like this:

CFIntro_cf ➤ com ➤ domain ➤ project ➤ services ➤ PersonServices.cfc

```
<cfcomponent output="no">
  <cffunction name="getAllPersons" displayname="getAllPersons"
              description="Retrieve all the persons from the database"
              access="remote" output="no"
              returntype="com.domain.project.valueObjects.PersonDTO[]">
    <cfquery name="qPersons" datasource="Flex4" >
      SELECT * FROM person
    </cfquery>

    <cfset myArr = arrayNew(1)/>
    <cfset var obj=""/>

    <cfloop query="qPersons">
      <cfscript>
        obj = createObject("component", ➥
"com.domain.project.valueObjects.PersonDTO").init();
        obj.setId(qPersons.id);
        obj.setFirstname(qPersons.firstname);
```

```
        obj.setLastname(qPersons.lastname);
        obj.setPhone(qPersons.phone);
        obj.setEmail(qPersons.email);
        ArrayAppend(myArr, obj);
      </cfscript>
    </cfloop>

    <cfreturn myArr>
  </cffunction>
</cfcomponent>
```

So now we have a component with a remote accessible method `getAllPersons()`. As you can see in the function declaration, it returns an array of `PersonDTO` objects. So, just like with the other back-end technologies that I've discussed in this chapter, with ColdFusion you also have the possibility of conveying strongly typed objects between the client and the server. And just like before, such a strongly typed object is going to be a separate class, which in this case translates into a new CFC.

CFIntro_cf ➤ *com* ➤ *domain* ➤ *project* ➤ *valueObjects* ➤ *personDTO.cfc*

```
<cfcomponent output="false" alias="com.domain.project.valueObjects.PersonDTO">
  <cfproperty name="id" type="numeric" default="0">
  <cfproperty name="firstname" type="string" default="">
  <cfproperty name="lastname" type="string" default="">
  <cfproperty name="phone" type="string" default="">
  <cfproperty name="email" type="string" default="">

  <cfscript>
    //Initialize the CFC with the default properties values.
    variables.id = 0;
    variables.firstname = "";
    variables.lastname = "";
    variables.phone = "";
    variables.email = "";
  </cfscript>

  <cffunction name="init" output="false" returntype="PersonDTO">
    <cfreturn this>
  </cffunction>

  <cffunction name="getId" output="false" access="public" returntype="any">
    <cfreturn variables.id>
  </cffunction>
  <cffunction name="setId" output="false" access="public" returntype="void">
    <cfargument name="val" required="true">
    <cfif (IsNumeric(arguments.val)) OR (arguments.val EQ "")>
      <cfset variables.id = arguments.val>
    <cfelse>
      <cfthrow message="'#arguments.val#' is not a valid numeric"/>
    </cfif>
  </cffunction>
```

```
<cffunction name="getFirstname" output="false" access="public" returntype="any">
  <cfreturn variables.firstname>
</cffunction>
<cffunction name="setFirstname" output="false" access="public" returntype="void">
  <cfargument name="val" required="true">
  <cfset variables.firstname = arguments.val>
</cffunction>

<cffunction name="getLastname" output="false" access="public" returntype="any">
  <cfreturn variables.lastname>
</cffunction>
<cffunction name="setLastname" output="false" access="public" returntype="void">
  <cfargument name="val" required="true">
  <cfset variables.lastname = arguments.val>
</cffunction>

<cffunction name="getPhone" output="false" access="public" returntype="any">
  <cfreturn variables.phone>
</cffunction>
<cffunction name="setPhone" output="false" access="public" returntype="void">
  <cfargument name="val" required="true">
  <cfset variables.phone = arguments.val>
</cffunction>

<cffunction name="getEmail" output="false" access="public" returntype="any">
  <cfreturn variables.email>
</cffunction>
<cffunction name="setEmail" output="false" access="public" returntype="void">
  <cfargument name="val" required="true">
  <cfset variables.email = arguments.val>
</cffunction>
</cfcomponent>
```

> *Don't forget to set the alias to the fully qualified class name of your component or the strong typing between this CFC and the ActionScript DTO class will not work properly.*

As you can see, the notation is a little different from what you may be used to, but the principles of the class are still clearly visible in the ColdFusion Component. You get some private properties, a constructor, and publicly accessible getters and setters. And our ActionScript class is going to be exactly the same as the one I described in the section on Flash Remoting with LiveCycle Data Services. Even the application remains exactly the same, with an <mx:DataGrid> being filled out using an <mx:RemoteObject> class to connect to our ColdFusion back end.

Be sure to create an instance of the PersonDTO ActionScript class or you will end up with an array of basic object classes and the strong typing will not have worked. This is due to the fact that the ActionScript compiler actually optimizes the generated SWF file by not including classes that are not used. So, if you never use a class in your entire project, the class is not included in the SWF file. Even a cast expression like obj = result[i] as PersonDTO will not be enough to include the class. I've seen this happen often in generic methods, so I hope this tip saves you some time in debugging this type of error, because it will eventually result in a runtime class casting error.

In the example, I use ColdFusion Flash Remoting, which is one of the options you have in connecting your Flex application with the server. You could also opt for BlazeDS or LiveCycle Data Services communication with ColdFusion as well.

Now that we have our back-end ColdFusion Components, our ActionScript value objects mapped to the CFC value objects, and our calling application, all that is left is the server configuration of the destination we can connect to using the <mx:RemoteObject> tag. Just as with BlazeDS or LCDS, there are a couple of configuration files that get shipped with the ColdFusion server. You can find these in the web root of your server, under the directory **WEB-INF ➤ flex**. The configuration file I'm interested in for this example is remoting-config.xml, which is not unlike the one I've already discussed in the sections on LiveCycle Data Services and BlazeDS.

CFIntro ➤ cf-config ➤ remoting-config.xml

```
<?xml version="1.0" encoding="UTF-8"?>
<service id="remoting-service" class="flex.messaging.services.RemotingService" ➥
        messageTypes="flex.messaging.messages.RemotingMessage">
  <adapters>
    <adapter-definition id="cf-object"
                        class="coldfusion.flash.messaging.ColdFusionAdapter"
                        default="true"/>
    <adapter-definition id="java-object"
class="flex.messaging.services.remoting.adapters.JavaAdapter"/>
  </adapters>

  <default-channels>
    <channel ref="my-cfamf"/>
  </default-channels>

  <destination id="ColdFusion">
    <channels>
      <channel ref="my-cfamf"/>
    </channels>
    <properties>
      <source>*</source>
    </properties>
  </destination>

  <destination id="personServices">
    <properties>
```

```
      <source>com.domain.project.services.PersonServices</source>
      <scope>application</scope>
    </properties>
  </destination>
</service>
```

Now this is just a basic configuration file. There are many other options, like access policy and timeout settings, that I'm not going to discuss in this chapter. If you are interested in a more detailed destination configuration, I suggest you read up on the ColdFusion documentation, which you can find at http://www.adobe.com/support/documentation/en/coldfusion/.

Adobe AIR: Why Do We Want Desktop RIAs?

At the moment it is becoming increasingly important to spread your application or information as widely as possible. The Internet is the ideal means for achieving this. Unfortunately, web applications still require a browser to display that information or interact with it. What if you could leverage the power of the technology to move away from the browser? You could deploy your applications on PDAs, cell phones, desktop computers, interactive television, and many other devices.

Moreover, users want to be able to work offline. Users don't have access to the internet at all times and in all places. So you have to make sure that, to have a broader reach, the user has to be able to take his application away from the Internet, outside of the browser. Users need to be able to run your application both online and offline. These hybrid applications are the next step companies are now beginning to explore.

With the Adobe Integrated Runtime (AIR), the technology has become available to create these kinds of applications. Since AIR basically runs on top of a stand-alone Flash Player, you still have the advantage of the cross-platform capabilities. And, a Flex application can easily be converted into an AIR application. Well, at least most of the time. Just take a look at Parley's, which exists both as a web application (http://www.parleys.com) and as an AIR application that you can install by clicking the install badge in the web application. But this doesn't work the other way around. Because the Flash Player has a rather tight security sandbox, you can't have both local file-system access and network access (though this has improved a bit with the release of Flash Player 10, where you can have file access using the FileReference class to either load or upload certain files. Since AIR applications are stand-alone versions, system access is not restricted. In fact, with the release of AIR 2.0, you will even get notifications of USB devices being connected to the computer. But that's not all that is different in AIR:

- Local encrypted SQLite database, which is a lightweight database.
- Online/offline detection, either on the HTTP level or via a socket connection.
- Automatic updating framework, letting you push application updates from the server.
- Local/remote data synchronization using LiveCycle Data Services' caching feature.
- Encrypted Locale Store, which you can use to store all kinds of data (such as passwords).
- Chromeless windows, allowing you to create custom, innovative user experiences.
- Starting native windows and interacting with them.
- Microphone access to record sound.
- Opening external documents with the default program associated with them.

All of these features make AIR a great technology to take your web applications out of the browser to reach an even larger audience. You'll definitely want to look into it if you're planning to create a Rich Internet Application.

Summary

The Flash platform has been around for many years now. Flex, as an addition to that platform, has been around for a while and it has been widely adopted by businesses as a very useful development platform. Flash Builder and Flash Catalyst are two additions to that same platform. Especially with the latest versions of these products, developer productivity has increased substantially by making it much easier to integrate complex designs and a variety of back-end technologies.

In the next chapters I will guide you through the basic functionality of both Flash Builder and Flash Catalyst to help you understand the features I'll use when discussing the different types of workflows between designers and developers later on in this book. But before we start on that you need to have an understanding of the differences between Flex 3 and Flex 4, because that will be important to thoroughly understand what Flash Builder and Flash Catalyst have to offer in view of the designer-developer workflow. Chapter 2 looks at these differences.

Chapter 2

Flex 4 SDK: Overview of the New Features

In this chapter we'll delve into the new Flex 4 SDK. Where applicable, I'll point to some problems with the Flex 3 SDK and demonstrate how you solve them with Flex 4. Remember, as I noted in Chapter 1, Flex 4 projects can only target Flash Player 10 and higher. Since the December 2009 Flash player statistics indicate that version 10 has already reached an adoption rate of almost 95% of Internet connected computers all around the world in just one year after its initial release, there should be no holding back on moving on to the next version of the Flex SDK.

You need to know about the features of Flex 4 because when you import a project that has been created in Flash Catalyst, the components and styling are all created using the Flex 4 SDK. This chapter will help you understand the code that gets generated and it will show you how to make changes to the code using only Flash Builder, avoiding a roundtrip to Flash Catalyst with all of the attendant consequences, like having to merge the changes manually.

Understanding the new features and syntax of Flex 4 not only helps you to make small changes to the generated code, it also enables you to write entire Flex 4 applications from scratch, as I'll demonstrate when I look at the different workflow types later in this book.

Component Architecture

The Flex 4 SDK brings a new namespace associated with the new **Spark** components that supersede the old Flex 3 Halo components. Throughout this chapter, we'll examine the architecture and new features of the Spark components—and you'll find the improvements to be quite substantial.

The Flex 4 components are designed to coexist with Flex 3 components. They can do so because Flex 4's new component architecture subclasses the UIComponent class, the base class for visual components in Flex 3. The result is that you can mix and match Flex 3 and Flex 4 components in a single application, providing for incremental upgrading of existing code.

The new and main Flex 4 base class is a subclass of UIComponent called SkinnableComponent. All the visual (and therefore skinnable) components in the new Spark architecture extend from this base class. However, not all Flex 3 components are available in the Spark namespace (e.g. Form, FormItem,

DataGrid, and more). You'll find an almost complete list of Flex 3 components that don't have a Flex 4 equivalent at `http://www.adobe.com/devnet/flex/articles/flex3and4_differences_04.html`.

`Group` is another `UIComponent` subclass in the Flex 4 SDK and is designed for components that don't have associated skin classes—typically containers and layouts for other components. In Flex 3, you'd use these containers inside your custom component. So, for example, you might have a component that would contain an `HBox` to organize the layout. Changing this layout at runtime would be quite difficult, since it would mean removing the components and reattaching them to the new layout container. With Flex 4's `Group` layout component, in contrast, you can change the layout using the `layout` property. Moreover, this property can be changed at runtime and, as a result, can to be used, for example, in view states to have the component layout set dynamically. Let me demonstrate the impact of this new layout component architecture in a small comparison of Flex 3 and Flex 4. Let's start with the Flex 3 version.

Flex3 ➤ *Flex3_Components.mxml*

```
<?xml version="1.0" encoding="utf-8"?>
<mx:Application xmlns:mx="http://www.adobe.com/2006/mxml" layout="absolute">
  <mx:Script>
    <![CDATA[
      protected function btn1_clickHandler(event:MouseEvent):void {
        if((currentState == null) || (currentState == "")) {
          currentState = "newLayout";
        } else {
          currentState = "";
        }
      }
    ]]>
  </mx:Script>

  <mx:states>
    <mx:State name="newLayout">
      <mx:AddChild>
        <mx:VBox id="vbox"/>
      </mx:AddChild>
      <mx:RemoveChild target="{lbl1}"/>
      <mx:AddChild relativeTo="{vbox}" position="lastChild" target="{lbl1}"/>
      <mx:RemoveChild target="{btn1}"/>
      <mx:AddChild relativeTo="{vbox}" position="lastChild" target="{btn1}"/>
      <mx:RemoveChild target="{hbox}"/>
    </mx:State>
  </mx:states>

  <mx:HBox id="hbox">
    <mx:Label id="lbl1" text="Click on this button to change the layout"/>
    <mx:Button id="btn1" label="Change layout" click="btn1_clickHandler(event)"/>
  </mx:HBox>
</mx:Application>
```

This is a Flex 3 example of *reparenting*, where the parent component is a layout container. Reparenting is simply taking a component from a certain container and attaching it to another container. To do this in Flex 3, you need to remove all the components from the display list and add them again to the proper parent, in this case an `<mx:VBox>` container. To add a component that already exists in another state on which the new state is based, you use the `target` property to refer to that component in the `<mx:AddChild>` tag. In Flex 4, the same functionality looks like this.

Flex4 ➤ *Flex4_Components.mxml*

```
<?xml version="1.0" encoding="utf-8"?>
<s:Application xmlns:fx="http://ns.adobe.com/mxml/2009"
               xmlns:s="library://ns.adobe.com/flex/spark"
               xmlns:mx="library://ns.adobe.com/flex/mx">

  <fx:Script>
    <![CDATA[
      protected function btn1_clickHandler(event:MouseEvent):void {
        if(currentState == "default") {
          currentState = "newLayout";
        } else {
          currentState = "default";
        }
      }
    ]]>
  </fx:Script>

  <s:states>
    <s:State name="default"/>
    <s:State name="newLayout"/>
  </s:states>

  <s:Group id="group">
    <s:layout.newLayout>
      <s:HorizontalLayout/>
    </s:layout.newLayout>
    <s:layout.default>
      <s:VerticalLayout/>
    </s:layout.default>

    <s:Label id="lbl1" text="Click on this button to change the layout"/>
    <s:Button id="btn1" label="Change layout" click="btn1_clickHandler(event)"/>
  </s:Group>
</s:Application>
```

In this example, you can already see the changes in using view states. We'll go into more detail about the new view state syntax in the next section of this chapter.

Note that I didn't use any skinning is this example. The components just have their default look and feel. However, that doesn't mean they don't have a skin. Take a look at the official documentation for the `<s:Button>` tag at http://help.adobe.com/en_US/FlashPlatform/reference/actionscript/3/spark/components/Button.html. There you'll find it has a default skin, which is a separate file with the fully qualified class name of `spark.skins.spark.ButtonSkin`. Because the component and the skin are two different files, each has its own distinct view state. So a button skin file contains its up, over, down and disabled state, while the component file will, for example, add an icon when requested. The MXML tags in the skin file use the new Flash XML Graphics (FXG) language (which I'll also explain in more detail later in this chapter). Those tags are compiled into ActionScript classes that directly use the Flash Player 10 rendering and graphics primitives, which make them very efficient.

The separation between the layout, graphical representation, and functionality actually makes it simpler in Flex 4 to extend existing components. So you can easily extend a component to include a new layout and leave the functionality as is, or you could do it the other way around and extend the functionality, but leave the layout alone. You'll find that both approaches are important when you work with Flash Catalyst to create a basic application. As you'll see in Chapter 5, Flash Catalyst can create a Flex application with some very complex design elements, and you can import your project into Flash Builder to add extra functionality. You can also take components generated by Flash Catalyst and put them in a library project. That way, you have an external library you can include in your own project to extend components from to do exactly what I've just described here. Another advantage of using such a library is also the fact that, since you're extending those components, you can change the library components to look and behave differently without having to touch your code. This makes the integration of design changes far easier.

View States

The new Flex SDK also comes with a new way of working with view states, one that I've been waiting for ever since I started using view states a couple of years ago. I love view states and their ease of use. They're also fun to work with when you have to create some basic animations as you're moving from one state to another. But in Flex 3, they do have some drawbacks.

If you've used view states in Flex 3, chances are you've encountered these drawbacks. View states have a property called basedOn that lets you create a kind of inheritance structure. Basically, any state you create is based on the default state—which is your basic layout—without having to do anything specific. You just enter <mx:State name="*yourStateName*"> and automatically the state is based on the default application or component layout. Adding this basedOn property to another state allows you to base the new state on the previously defined one, like this:

<mx:State name="*anotherState*" basedOn="*yourStateName*">

Now that's really great, because you can create entire inheritance structures. Figure 2-1 shows a graphical representation of what could be the hierarchy of view states in a component.

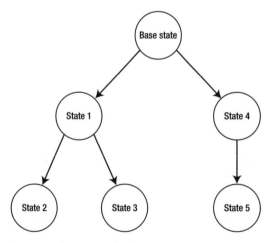

Figure 2-1. A visual representation of Flex 3 view states

What is striking in this picture is that only single inheritance is used. Single inheritance in Object Oriented Programming (OOP) indicates that a class can extend functionality only from one other class, as shown in Figure 2-2. If you have come from a Java or .NET background, you may not be familiar with the concept, but there is a thing called **multiple inheritance**. This is also an OOP concept, but this time a single class extends the functionality of (typically) two classes in order to combine the functionality, as shown in Figure 2-3. I know about multiple inheritance from my days as a C++ programmer and I loved it, mainly because it enabled some very clever class constructions that could save you a whole lot of time developing applications. But, I admit, it has a downside. You really have to know what you are doing and how this type of inheritance works internally to be able to fully use its power and not be caught by the pitfalls.

Why would we want to apply multiple inheritance to Flex view states? Picture this: an application has a few multiple choice questions . Let's call them A, B and C for convenience. Now suppose that if a certain selection is made for question A, the question will need to be expanded to include question A1. This is also true for question C, so you'd get a question C1. If you think of this in terms of view states, you can see it as a form of multiple inheritance because A1 and C1 can exist separately, but they may also have to be shown at the same time. That means that you may find yourself in the situation where the user has made the selections in questions A and C where the both need to show their extended state (respectively A1 and C1), since questions A and C are totally independent. Coding this possibility in Flex 3 might look like this:

Flex3 ➤ *ViewStates.mxml*

```
<?xml version="1.0" encoding="utf-8"?>
<mx:Applicationxmlns:mx="http://www.adobe.com/2006/mxml" layout="vertical">
  <mx:Script>
    <![CDATA[
      import mx.events.ItemClickEvent;
      protected function firstGroup_itemClickHandler(event:ItemClickEvent):void {
        if(event.label == "Yes") {
          if(currentState == "state2") {
            currentState = "state3";
          } else {
            currentState = "state1";
          }
        } else {
          if(currentState == "state3") {
            currentState = "state2";
          } else {
            currentState = "";
          }
        }
      }

      protected function thirdGroup_itemClickHandler(event:ItemClickEvent):void {
        if(event.label == "Yes") {
          if(currentState == "state1") {
            currentState = "state3";
          } else {
            currentState = "state2";
          }
        } else {
          if(currentState == "state3") {
```

```
                    currentState = "state1";
              } else {
                    currentState = "";
              }
           }
        }
    ]]>
  </mx:Script>

  <mx:states>
    <mx:State name="state1">
      <mx:AddChild position="after" relativeTo="{box1}">
        <mx:HBox id="box4">
          <mx:Label text="Do you see the second question now?"width="300"/>
          <mx:RadioButtonGroup id="fourthGroup"/>
          <mx:RadioButton label="Yes"group="{fourthGroup}"/>
          <mx:RadioButton label="No"group="{fourthGroup}"/>
        </mx:HBox>
      </mx:AddChild>
    </mx:State>
    <mx:State name="state2">
      <mx:AddChild position="after" relativeTo="{box3}">
        <mx:HBox id="box5">
          <mx:Label text="Do you see the fifth question now?" width="300"/>
          <mx:RadioButtonGroup id="fifthGroup"/>
          <mx:RadioButton label="Yes"group="{fifthGroup}"/>
          <mx:RadioButton label="No"group="{fifthGroup}"/>
        </mx:HBox>
      </mx:AddChild>
    </mx:State>
    <mx:State name="state3" basedOn="state1">
      <mx:AddChild position="after" relativeTo="{box3}">
        <mx:HBox id="box6">
          <mx:Label text="Do you see the fifth question now?" width="300"/>
          <mx:RadioButtonGroup id="sixthGroup"/>
          <mx:RadioButton label="Yes"group="{sixthGroup}"/>
          <mx:RadioButton label="No"group="{sixthGroup}"/>
        </mx:HBox>
      </mx:AddChild>
    </mx:State>
  </mx:states>

  <mx:HBox id="box1">
    <mx:Label text="Do you want to show the second question?" width="300"/>
    <mx:RadioButtonGroup id="firstGroup"
                          itemClick="firstGroup_itemClickHandler(event)"/>
    <mx:RadioButton label="Yes"group="{firstGroup}"/>
    <mx:RadioButton label="No"group="{firstGroup}"/>
  </mx:HBox>
```

```
<mx:HBox id="box2">
   <mx:Label text="Is this is the third question?" width="300"/>
   <mx:RadioButtonGroup id="secondGroup"/>
   <mx:RadioButton label="Yes"group="{secondGroup}"/>
   <mx:RadioButton label="No"group="{secondGroup}"/>
</mx:HBox>
<mx:HBox id="box3">
   <mx:Label text="Do you want to show the fifth question?" width="300"/>
   <mx:RadioButtonGroup id="thirdGroup"
                        itemClick="thirdGroup_itemClickHandler(event)"/>
   <mx:RadioButton label="Yes"group="{thirdGroup}"/>
   <mx:RadioButton label="No"group="{thirdGroup}"/>
</mx:HBox>
</mx:Application>
```

This code creates three different view states for the application. The first one, called state1, shows just the extra question for the first item on screen. The second state shows only the extra question for the third element on screen. The last state, called state3, inherits from state1, which means the first question will be in the extended state. But it also adds the extra question for the third item again, so now both the first and third item will shows the extra questions. As you can see, this takes a whole lot of coding to get this to work. In fact, the code isn't even complete yet, because if you run it and you have to switch from state2 to state3, you have to copy the values from box5 to box6, then do the reverse when returning to state2. This is because you're working with two different variables to indicate the same thing, so synchronization and reading out the results require additional code. With multiple inheritance, you wouldn't have this duplicate item and the extra coding wouldn't be necessary, as I'll show in the Flex 4 version of the same example. However, a possible solution in Flex 3 could be to create a custom component for such a question and have two view states for the question, so you could reuse those components and not have any duplicates. If we put this into a graphical representation of the view states, you'll get something like Figure 2-2.

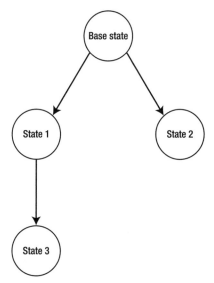

Figure 2-2. No multiple-state inheritence is possible with Flex 3 view states.

In Flex 4, however, such difficulties are a thing of the past because of the new view state syntax, which enables a certain form of multiple view state inheritance and makes constructions like this a piece of cake. I don't mean that either ActionScript or MXML actually supports real multiple inheritance, but you can base a certain view state on more than one other state, which is a similar concept. Take a close look at the code below, which has the same functionality as the Flex 3 example above.

Flex4 ➤ *ViewStates.mxml*

```
<?xml version="1.0" encoding="utf-8"?>
<s:Application xmlns:fx="http://ns.adobe.com/mxml/2009"
               xmlns:s="library://ns.adobe.com/flex/spark"
               xmlns:mx="library://ns.adobe.com/flex/mx">
  <s:layout>
    <s:VerticalLayout/>
  </s:layout>
  <fx:Script>
    <![CDATA[
      importmx.events.ItemClickEvent;

      protected function firstGroup_itemClickHandler(event:ItemClickEvent):void {
        if(event.label == "Yes") {
          if(currentState == "state2") {
            currentState = "state3";
          } else {
            currentState = "state1";
          }
        } else {
          if(currentState == "state3") {
            currentState = "state2";
          } else {
            currentState = "";
          }
        }
      }

      protected function thirdGroup_itemClickHandler(event:ItemClickEvent):void {
        if(event.label == "Yes") {
          if(currentState == "state1") {
            currentState = "state3";
          } else {
            currentState = "state2";
          }
        } else {
          if(currentState == "state3") {
            currentState = "state1";
          } else {
            currentState = "";
          }
        }
      }
```

```
        ]]>
    </fx:Script>

    <fx:Declarations>
        <s:RadioButtonGroup id="firstGroup"
                            itemClick="firstGroup_itemClickHandler(event)"/>
        <s:RadioButtonGroup id="secondGroup"/>
        <s:RadioButtonGroup id="thirdGroup"
                            itemClick="thirdGroup_itemClickHandler(event)"/>
        <s:RadioButtonGroup id="fourthGroup"/>
        <s:RadioButtonGroup id="fifthGroup"/>
    </fx:Declarations>

    <mx:states>
        <s:State name="default"/>
        <s:State name="state1"/>
        <s:State name="state2"/>
        <s:State name="state3"/>
    </mx:states>

    <s:Group id="box1">
        <s:layout>
            <s:HorizontalLayout/>
        </s:layout>
        <s:Label text="Do you want to show the second question?"width="300"/>
        <s:RadioButton label="Yes" group="{firstGroup}"/>
        <s:RadioButton label="No" group="{firstGroup}"/>
    </s:Group>
    <s:Group id="box2"includeIn="state1, state3">
        <s:layout>
            <s:HorizontalLayout/>
        </s:layout>
        <s:Label text="Do you see the second question now?" width="300"/>
        <s:RadioButton label="Yes" group="{fourthGroup}"/>
        <s:RadioButton label="No" group="{fourthGroup}"/>
    </s:Group>
    <s:Group id="box3">
        <s:layout>
            <s:HorizontalLayout/>
        </s:layout>
        <s:Label text="Is this is the third question?" width="300"/>
        <s:RadioButton label="Yes" group="{secondGroup}"/>
        <s:RadioButton label="No" group="{secondGroup}"/>
    </s:Group>
    <s:Group id="box4">
        <s:layout>
            <s:HorizontalLayout/>
        </s:layout>
        <s:Label text="Do you want to show the fifth question?" width="300"/>
```

```
    <s:RadioButton label="Yes" group="{thirdGroup}"/>
    <s:RadioButton label="No" group="{thirdGroup}"/>
  </s:Group>
  <s:Group id="box5"includeIn="state2, state3">
    <s:layout>
      <s:HorizontalLayout/>
    </s:layout>
    <s:Label text="Do you see the fifth question now?" width="300"/>
    <s:RadioButton label="Yes" group="{fifthGroup}"/>
    <s:RadioButton label="No" group="{fifthGroup}"/>
  </s:Group>
</s:Application>
```

Let's start by looking at the similarities between these two versions. Setting the new state uses exactly the same code—you just have to set the `currentState` property to the desired value. You also have to specifically define the available view states, but that's where the similarities end because in the definition of the view states, you don't specify any layout or content anymore. It's just a definition. In the general layout part of the application (or component), you have to specify the most complete layout, which means in our example both questions are expanded to include the additional questions. However, to indicate in which state these additional questions should be shown, you can use two new properties called `includeIn` and `excludeFrom`. The first property includes the components and layout only in the defined states, while the latter includes them in the default state and removes them from the defined states. So, there is still more than one way to write your view states. Which one is best depends on the specific layout of your application or component. To represent the Flex 4 version graphically, it would look something like Figure 2-3.

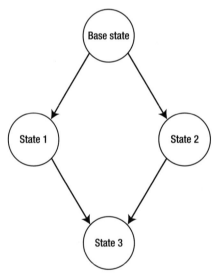

Figure 2-3. Multiple view state inheritance in Flex 4

It's clear that with the Flex 4 view states, multiple view state inheritance *is* actually possible. This is mainly because you don't specify components in the actual view states themselves, but in the general layout of your application or component. The `includeIn` and `excludeFrom` properties also allow you to specify multiple states, with the result that components can exist in separate and combined states as in our example.

FXG

FXG is the short notation for Flash XMLGraphics, a new XML-based graphical representation language, and it's probably the most visible change that has been made to the new SDK. FXG is part of the MXML syntax and contains tags such as `<Rect>`, `<Ellipse>` and `<Path>`, as well as tags and attributes for filling and stroking those shapes with different colors, gradients or bitmaps, and support for filters, masks, alphas, and blend modes on FXG elements. This means you can create both simple components and components that are graphically challenging using FXG. And since the graphical code is located in a different file from the functional code, changing the design of your application should be easier.

FXG also functions as the interchange format between Flash Catalyst and Flash Builder 4. This means that understanding the new graphical format is crucial not only to understanding the workflow between these two products, but also for understanding the new workflow you'll use in your Flex-based web applications—as well as desktop and mobile applications. Since a general best-practice rule is to use the tools you have at hand to do the job they are meant to do, lots of applications will be created first within Flash Catalyst and are then imported into Flash Builder to attach the back-end or other functionality. But understanding FXG allows you to start coding some nifty graphical representations directly in Flash Builder. So, if you're familiar with the syntax and there are only one or two complex graphical elements in the application, why not do it directly in Flash Builder? In that case, you don't need to involve the interaction designer who would normally use Flash Catalyst, so you simplify the workflow.

Let me give you a couple of examples to show you how to use FXG in a Flex 4 application and how it makes changing things much easier.

Excerpt from the Spark Button skin

```
<s:SparkSkin xmlns:fx="http://ns.adobe.com/mxml/2009"
             xmlns:s="library://ns.adobe.com/flex/spark"
             minWidth="21" minHeight="21"
             alpha.disabled="0.5">

  <fx:Metadata>
    <![CDATA[
      [HostComponent("spark.components.Button")]
    ]]>
  </fx:Metadata>
  ...
  <s:states>
    <s:State name="up"/>
    <s:State name="over">
    <s:State name="down"/>
    <s:State name="disabled"/>
  </s:states>

  <s:Rect left="-1" right="-1" top="-1" bottom="-1" radiusX="2" radiusY="2">
    <s:fill>
      <s:LinearGradient rotation="90">
        <s:GradientEntry color="0x000000"
```

```
                        color.down="0xFFFFFF"
                        alpha="0.01"
                        alpha.down="0"/>
        <s:GradientEntry color="0x000000"
                        color.down="0xFFFFFF"
                        alpha="0.07"
                        alpha.down="0.5"/>
        </s:LinearGradient>
      </s:fill>
   </s:Rect>
   ...
   <s:SimpleText id="labelElement"
                textAlign="center"
                verticalAlign="middle"
                lineBreak="toFit"
                truncation="1"
                horizontalCenter="0"
                verticalCenter="1"
                left="10" right="10" top="2" bottom="2">
   </s:SimpleText>
</s:SparkSkin>
```

Flex 4 ➤*com.domain.project.components.SkinnedComponent.mxml*

```
<?xml version="1.0" encoding="utf-8"?>
<s:Graphic xmlns:fx="http://ns.adobe.com/mxml/2009"
           xmlns:mx="library://ns.adobe.com/flex/mx"
           xmlns:s="library://ns.adobe.com/flex/spark" >
  <s:Rect id="rect1" width="200" height="200" >
    <s:fill>
      <s:SolidColor color="0xFFFFCC" />
    </s:fill>
    <s:stroke>
      <s:SolidColorStroke color="0x660099" weight="2" />
    </s:stroke>
  </s:Rect>
</s:Graphic>
```

Figure 2-4. A simple skinned component

Notice that the component in Figure 2-4 is just a simple yellow rectangle with a bluish border and no dynamic features. In this case, the component *is* the skin. Of course, this is just a small demonstration of how the FXG language is used. In more complex examples, the FXG part can become quite large, as it defines the entire look and feel of the component in all its states. Note that the FXG tags in the code have nothing to do with binding, layout, or event handlers. This example very simply defines only a rectangle with a fill color and stroke color, and there's nothing about placement or event handling. This is because the graphical representation of the component is completely separate from its functionality, allowing you to change the look and feel without having to rewrite a bunch of ActionScript code. Changing the look and feel can either be done by coding the FXG for the component or by merging the existing component with a new version created by the interaction designer using Flash Catalyst.

Spark-ling Effects

One of the advantages of using a technology like Flex is that you can incorporate animations in your application. It's fairly easy to do so and the possibilities are almost endless. A word of caution to the pure developers out there: don't overdo it! Animations are a great tool to draw a user's attention to a certain part of your web site or application. However, too much animation or animations that take too long can have the opposite effect, because the user gets distracted and doesn't pay any attention to the real content. But, depending on the type of application you're building, this may not always be a concern for the developer since Flash Catalyst lets the interaction designer create and trigger all of the effects he wants to incorporate into the application. In such cases, developers don't have to worry about animation. Of course, you can always start building applications from scratch using just Flash Builder, in which case you do have to pay attention to the design. You may be used to working on Flex projects in just this way, but later on in this book you will see just how valuable Flash Catalyst is to the new workflow between designers and developers.

Flex 3 has a lot of nice little effects you could use to help your application become more user-friendly. You could incorporate effects and transitions to add small animations using tags like `<mx:Fade>`, `<mx:Rotate>` and `<mx:Zoom>`. You could even combine your animations to run in sequence or all at the same time using the `<mx:Sequence>` and `<mx:Parallel>` tags respectively.

Sometimes combining the effects gave you weird and unwanted side effects, however, because some effects change the x and y position of the component. If you combine these with a similar effect or with a fixed position in the application, they tend to counteract each other and you can get some flickering as a result. The following code shows an example of these effects going wrong.

Flex3 ➤ *SideEffects.mxml*

```
<?xml version="1.0" encoding="utf-8"?>
<mx:Application xmlns:mx="http://www.adobe.com/2006/mxml"
                layout="absolute"
                minWidth="1024" minHeight="768">
  <mx:Rotate id="rotate" angleFrom="0" angleTo="360" duration="3000"/>

  <mx:Panel width="300" height="300"
            horizontalCenter="0" verticalCenter="0"
            creationCompleteEffect="{rotate}">
    <mx:Text width="100%"
             text="Loremipsum dolor sit amet, consecteturadipiscingelit. ➡
Vestibulumquisleo at ligulaimperdietsagittis id convallisneque. Duisnisl."/>
  </mx:Panel>
</mx:Application>
```

In this application we have a panel that is centered on the stage. As soon as the panel is created, a rotation effect is played that turns the panel 360 degrees. This changes the x and y position of the panel continuously, because the rotation action happens around the center point of the component. The diagonal size of a square, for example, is bigger than its sides, so to keep the center point in the same location, the x and y positions need to change constantly, because they refer to the upper left corner of the component's bounding box. But the panel is set fixed to the center of the stage by using the horizontalCenter and verticalCenter properties, resulting in a conflict. The result is a flickering effect during the rotation. Just run the example code and you'll see what I mean.

Another problem we encounter in this application is that the text disappears as soon as the effect starts playing. However, this has nothing to do with the actual effect; it's the result of the Flash Player not being able to animate non-embedded fonts. You can easily solve the problem by using CSS to embed the font.

If we take the example into Flex 4, the code looks like this:

Flex4 ➤ SideEffects.mxml

```
<?xml version="1.0" encoding="utf-8"?>
<s:Application xmlns:fx="http://ns.adobe.com/mxml/2009"
               xmlns:s="library://ns.adobe.com/flex/spark"
               xmlns:mx="library://ns.adobe.com/flex/mx">
  <fx:Declarations>
    <s:Rotate id="rotate" angleFrom="0" angleTo="360" duration="3000"/>
  </fx:Declarations>

  <s:Panel width="300" height="300"
           horizontalCenter="0" verticalCenter="0"
           creationCompleteEffect="{rotate}">
    <mx:Text width="100%"
             text="Loremipsum dolor sit amet, consecteturadipiscingelit. ➥
Vestibulumquisleo at ligulaimperdietsagittis id convallisneque. Duisnisl."/>
  </s:Panel>
</s:Application>
```

If you run this code, you will see that the application initializes properly and the rotation effect executes flawlessly due to the new way of working with effects. In Flex 4, multiple effects aren't played separately at the same time. Instead, the new Flex 4 effect classes—and, more specifically, combinations of effects—are compiled into a single effect to be played, resulting in smoother animations and fewer errors.

> *If you want to know more about how to include fonts in your Flex application, check my blog post at http://www.flexpert.be/flex/embedding-fonts-in-flex-air-and-actionscript-projects/. This post covers font embedding only when working in Flash Builder 4. However, you can include font subsets directly from within Flash Catalyst as well when publishing the application, as I'll discuss in Chapter 4.*

As my blog post mentions, one of the possibilities for embedding fonts is to use Flash Professional to create an SWF file that limits the number of characters or glyphs in the embedded font. Flash Professional CS5 gives you some very nifty options for embedding fonts in your SWF file.

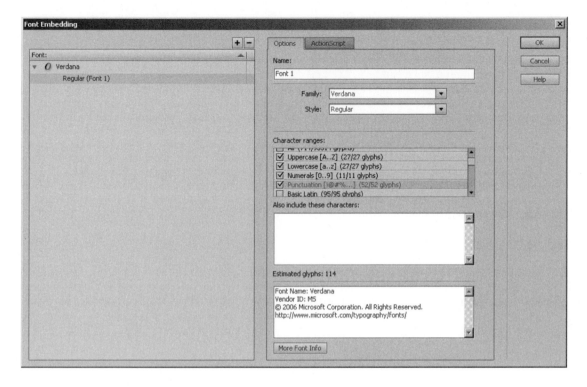

Figure 2-5. The `Font Embedding` dialog in Flash Professional CS5

As you can see in Figure 2-5, this dialog lets you easily manage the fonts and the glyphs to embed for a certain font. Naturally, you can add multiple fonts in the same SWF file.

As we'll see, many other effects have also been enhanced in the new Flex version, including:

- Property effects
- Transform effects
- 3D effects
- Pixel-shader effects (created by PixelBender)
- Filter effects

All of these effects can be applied to either Spark or Halo components. So, even though you may still be using some Halo components in your Flex 4 applications, you can still take advantage of the improved effects.

Property Effects

As the name suggests, this kind of effect is played on a specific property. Each effect is based on the `Animate` class, which can animate any property on a component. There are also a number of more specific animation classes, such as `Fade`, `Resize`, `AnimateColor`, and so forth. The `AnimateColor` class is something special, because it can animate a color property, not by just changing the hexadecimal code, but by interpreting the beginning and end colors. This means that colors are animated using the color wheel. Colors are interpreted and the most logical way is followed to get to the destination color, allowing for smooth color transitions.

Note that you can't just add any decimal number to the color value, because the colors will be messed up. Let me explain this with a small example. Assume you want to lighten a certain gray value from #999999 to #C0C0C0. If you write a loop to increase the value sequentially, you have to take into account that the hexadecimal value actually represents the three separate color channels: Red, Green and Blue. So increasing the numbers first increases just the Blue channel, then the Green channel, followed by the Blue channel again for every increase in that Green channel. And as the last one, the Red channel will be adjusted, with the Green and Blue channels being looped for every increase in that Red channel. And finally you reach the light gray color. But even though you reach the color you wanted, you will have gone through an entire range of colors to get there when what you'd expect is that the gray color would just lighten up. To see a nice color transition without going through a lot of (apparently) bright colors during the animation, just run the example code in the file Flex4 ➤ AnimateColor.mxml in the example projects downloadable from the friendsofED web site.

Transform Effects

Transform effects are those that include some kind of movement, including Move, Rotate, Scale, or Zoom (which has now been deprecated in favor of Scale). What is new for the transform effects? Again, these effects are also based on the Animate base class, so using an <mx:Parallel> on these effects will combine them into a single effect, just as in the example I gave earlier, which you can find in the application file Flex4 ➤ SideEffects.mxml

3D Effects

Ever since Flash animations were produced by means of ActionScript programming using tweening libraries, developers have tried to create semi-3D effects using the Z-order and scaling the component or image to make it look as if there were an actual 3D animation going on, when in fact it was only an optical illusion. Sometimes this kind of 3D animation is called 2.5D (two and a half D). This worked pretty well in some examples, but you could never shed the feeling that it was still only a 2D animation.

Then Flash Player 10 came along with native 2.5D support. By this I mean that Flash Player 10 has support for 3D effects, but it does not automatically add the third dimension (depth) when rotating a component. Version 10 comes with hardware access to the Graphics Processing Unit (GPU), so you can now create amazing 3D effects without overloading the CPU, utilizing the extreme powers of the latest 3D graphic cards. Since Flex 4 also targets at least Flash Player 10, it can add some specific 3D effects that leverage the new capabilities, such as Rotate3D, Move3D and Scale3D. All of these are quite similar to their transform equivalents, but they add another dimension to the movement.

Pixel-Shader Effects

Pixel-shader effects are of a different kind nowadays. You may be familiar with WipeLeft, WipeUp, WipeRight, and WipeDown effects from Flex 3, and perhaps you've played around with a CrossFade effect in Flex 4. But there's also a fairly new tool called Pixel Bender. It allows you to create virtually any kind of effect using a scripting language to create a PBJ file, which contains the Pixel Bender byte code. You can use Pixel Bender filters in Flex to create a ShaderFilter effect. The following example is a Pixel Bender script that applies a grayscale effect on a photograph.

Flex4 ➤ assets ➤ grayscale.pbk

```
<language : 1.0;>
kernel Grayscale
```

```
<namespace: "Your namespace";
 vendor: "Your vendor";
 version: 1;
 description: "Your description";>
{
  input image4 src;
  output pixel4 dst;

  void evaluatePixel()  {
    dst = sampleNearest(src, outCoord());
    dst.r = dst.g = dst.b = (dts.r + dst.g + dst.b) / 3.0;
  }
}
```

This filter simply loops through every pixel in an image from top-left to bottom-right and converts the pixel value to a grayscale value by calculating the average value of the three color channels. This is a very basic filter. Of course you can elaborate on this and create very complex filters that you can use in your Flex applications. To do so, you need to export your filter as a PBJ file and import it into your Flex application.

Flex4 ➤ *PixelBenderEffect.mxml*

```
<?xml version="1.0" encoding="utf-8"?>
<s:Application xmlns:fx="http://ns.adobe.com/mxml/2009"
               xmlns:s="library://ns.adobe.com/flex/spark"
               xmlns:mx="library://ns.adobe.com/flex/mx">
  <fx:Script>
    <![CDATA[
      import flash.filters.ShaderFilter;

      // Define the PBJ asset
      [Embed(source="../assets/grayscale.pbj", mimeType="application/octet-stream")]
      private var pbj:Class;
      // Define a Shader based on the loader Pixel Bender asset.
      private var shader:Shader = newShader (newpbj() asByteArray);
      // Create a ShaderFilter, based on the Shader object we just created.
      private var filter:ShaderFilter = newShaderFilter(shader);

      private function convertTograyScale():void {
        if((img.filters == null) || (img.filters.length == 0)) {
          img.filters = [filter];
          btn.label = "Reset to full color";
        } else {
          img.filters = null;
          btn.label = "Convert to grayscale";
        }
      }
    ]]>
  </fx:Script>
```

```
  <s:GrouphorizontalCenter="0" verticalCenter="0">
    <s:layout>
      <s:VerticalLayouthorizontalAlign="center"/>
    </s:layout>

    <mx:Image id="img" source="../assets/waterfall.jpg"/>
    <s:Button id="btn" label="Convert to grayscale" click="convertTograyScale()"/>
  </s:Group>
</s:Application>
```

This small program takes a picture and converts it to grayscale when you click a button. When the image is grayscale and you click the button again, the image reverts to full color. Again, this is only a basic filter. You can create very complex effects, and you can even use parameters so you can animate them using the Flex animation classes.

Filter Effects

The Flex 3 filter effects like `Blur`, `DropShadow`, and `Glow` are still available. The Flex 4 equivalents haven't really been modified but are preferred since these are the versions Flash Catalyst will generate, and you won't be able to read Flex 3 filters into Flash Catalyst once roundtripping has been enabled between Flash Builder and Flash Catalyst. *Roundtripping* refers to the process of importing a Flash Catalyst project into Flash Builder and after some coding modification (like tying the project to a back end), importing the project back into Flash Catalyst to make some design or interaction changes. Although this is not yet possible in the first version of Flash Catalyst, it will be in the near future, and it will further improve the designer-developer workflow because developers won't have to manually merge the design changes anymore.

Advanced CSS Selectors

In this section I will discuss the new CSS capabilities and give you some examples of how to use them. If you are used to HTML CSS, you will find a lot of similarities but also a few differences. This CSS will be generated by Flash Catalyst as well. Thus, when you import a project into Flash Builder, you need to know how the CSS is applied to certain components in order to understand the impact of changes you may want to make to the CSS file.

> *As long as you are not writing the style properties in MXML code directly, you can use both the ActionScript (titlecase) and HTML (with a dash in between words) notations for your style elements. Using the HTML style notation gives you the advantage of being able to use code completion for the style properties.*

Use of Namespaces

As I noted earlier, the new Spark namespace in Flex 4 lets the new components coexist with the older Flex 3 components. This can pose some problems in styling these components, however, since now you have two Button classes available. You need to be able to style the buttons differently—you can't just use a simple class selector when you want to use both namespaces at the same time. Instead, you must indicate the namespace for the button component type for which you want to specify some styling attributes. If you're upgrading an existing Flex 3 application to Flex 4 and you're using the new namespaces but forgot to include them in the CSS file, you will get warnings about the CSS code not being correctly applied to the components.

How do you specify such a namespace for styling a component? You declare the namespace using the `@namespace` keyword followed by a name for the namespace, and then you add the URI where the definitions for that namespace can be found. You use the defined name for that namespace followed by a pipe symbol and the component class name to start creating styles on a component level. The result for the Button class using the Spark namespace is something like this: `s|Button`. The following code styles a Spark button and a Halo button using their respective namespaces.

Flex4 ➤ CSS_Namespaces.mxml

```
<?xml version="1.0" encoding="utf-8"?>
<s:Application xmlns:fx="http://ns.adobe.com/mxml/2009"
               xmlns:s="library://ns.adobe.com/flex/spark"
               xmlns:mx="library://ns.adobe.com/flex/mx">
  <fx:Style>
    @namespace s "library://ns.adobe.com/flex/spark";
    @namespacemx "library://ns.adobe.com/flex/mx";

    mx|Button, s|Button {
      baseColor: #666666;
      color: #CCCCCC;
      focusColor: #666666;
    }
  </fx:Style>

  <s:Group horizontalCenter="0" verticalCenter="0">
    <s:layout>
      <s:VerticalLayout/>
    </s:layout>
    <mx:Button label="This is a Halo button"/>
    <s:Button label="This is a Spark button"/>
  </s:Group>
</s:Application>
```

Now, if you execute this code and you hover over both buttons, you will see a slight difference in the color of the label on the button. On the Spark component it remains the same as in the up state, whereas in the Halo component, the text color has changed, as you can clearly see in Figure 2-6.

Figure 2-6. The rollover colors for a Halo button (left) and a Spark button (right)

So, even if you have specified the same CSS code, keep in mind that the result can be different, depending on whether you use a Halo component or a Spark component.

Now, you can use these namespaces not only for making a distinction between Halo and Spark components, but also to distinguish between Flex components and components from your own custom library. To assign a namespace to a library, you specify a manifest file for the library that indicates the link between the component's name and its physical location in the library package structure. This lets you use just one namespace for every single component in your library as the namespace refers to that manifest file.

If you want to know more about making Flex libraries, read the livedocs and search for the term "Creating Libraries." This will guide you to the documentation you need for creating static libraries and, of course, Runtime Shared Libraries (RSLs). But you could even attach a CSS namespace to the components in your project; this would work similarly to the namespaces in your MXML code. If the components reside in a components package in your project structure, the code for defining the namespace in CSS would be `@namespace co "com.domain.project.components.*"`.

Type Selector

Type selectors in Flex 4 follow the Flex 3 CSS specifications. They work the same as in HTML, so you just type the name of the component as the selector, and every style that is defined inside of that selector is applied to all instances of that component. So, for example, you can use a single set of styling properties to adjust the look of one or more components anywhere in your application, without having to alter anything in your code, because these type selectors are automatically applied to the specified component types.

Flex4 ➤ *CSS_Types.mxml*

```
<?xml version="1.0" encoding="utf-8"?>
<s:Application xmlns:fx="http://ns.adobe.com/mxml/2009"
               xmlns:s="library://ns.adobe.com/flex/spark"
               xmlns:mx="library://ns.adobe.com/flex/mx">
  <fx:Style>
    @namespace s "library://ns.adobe.com/flex/spark";
    @namespace mx "library://ns.adobe.com/flex/mx";

    s|Button {
      baseColor: #333333;
      color: #CCCCCC;
      focusColor: #666666;
      fontFamily: Verdana;
      fontSize: 14;
      fontStyle: italic;
    }
  </fx:Style>

  <s:Group horizontalCenter="0" verticalCenter="0">
    <s:layout>
      <s:VerticalLayout/>
    </s:layout>
    <s:Button label="This is a button"/>
    <s:Button label="This is another button"/>
  </s:Group>
</s:Application>
```

Even though only one type is specified, both instances of the `Button` component are styled using the type selector properties, as you can see in Figure 2-7 below.

Figure 2-7. Two buttons are styled with a single type selector.

Class Selector

The CSS notation for class selectors has received an upgrade since Flex 3. They still function the same, which means you have to type a "." (period) before the selector name to specify the styles. You can choose the name for the selector freely, but I advise you not to use the same name as any of the Flex components, or even any custom components as this can only cause confusion with type selectors.

A class selector is not applied automatically when you define it; you still have to manually apply it to individual components using the `styleName` property. When you do that, you don't specify the dot before the name; just the name is enough. The styles defined in the selector are applied only to that specific component.

What's new in Flex 4 is that you can combine class selectors with type selectors. You do this by specifying the type name in front of the class selector name as in the example below.

Flex4 ➤ *CSS_Classes.mxml*

```
<?xml version="1.0" encoding="utf-8"?>
<s:Application xmlns:fx="http://ns.adobe.com/mxml/2009"
               xmlns:s="library://ns.adobe.com/flex/spark"
               xmlns:mx="library://ns.adobe.com/flex/mx">
  <fx:Style>
    @namespace s "library://ns.adobe.com/flex/spark";
    @namespace mx "library://ns.adobe.com/flex/mx";

    s|Button.myStyleName {
      baseColor: #333333;
      color: #CCCCCC;
      focusColor: #666666;
      fontFamily: Verdana;
      fontSize: 14;
      fontStyle: italic;
    }

    s|Label.myStyleName {
      color: #000099;
      fontWeight: bold;
    }
  </fx:Style>

  <s:Group horizontalCenter="0" verticalCenter="0">
    <s:layout>
      <s:VerticalLayout/>
```

```
      </s:layout>
      <s:Button styleName="myStyleName"label="This is a styled button"/>
      <s:Button label="This is button with default styling"/>
      <s:Label styleName="myStyleName" text="This is a styled label"/>
   </s:Group>
</s:Application>
```

In this example there are two buttons, but only one button is styled by setting the styleName property. The nice thing about this feature is that you can reuse the same class selector for multiple components. In the example code I created a second class selector with the same name, but for a different component—a Label in this case. See Figure 2-8.

Figure 2-8. A class selector is only applied to components with the styleName property set.

Even though the names are the same, only the styles for that specific class selector are applied to the Label in the application. The styles for the button are never applied to any other component than a Button or a component that inherits from the Button component.

Universal Selector

If you have already created some Flex projects, you've probably already used the global selector in your CSS. This selector is used for defining non-inheritable styles or for setting application-wide styles, like the font family or text color. These are examples of what you'd typically include in the selector, but of course it's not mandatory. You could also rely on the inheritance of styles to define them on the proper level. How is this inheritance processed? It's only slightly different from how it works for CSS in HTML pages. Here's the order of precedence:

1. The style defined by any inline style
2. The style defined by any class style
3. The style defined by any type style
4. The style defined inline for a parent container
5. The style defined by a class for the parent container
6. The style defined by a type selector for the parent container
7. A globally defined style

The global selector works very well in Flex and it is a handy feature, but sometimes you need to deviate from these settings, but on a container level. Here's an example.

Assume you have an application that's all in the same style and text color, except that for one component, perhaps a tooltip window, you want the text color to be different. You may think this is as simple as setting the color style for the Text component, but what if you have other components in that container, like a button, a label, or even some kind of form header. In that case, you'd need to set the color property for each of the subcomponents inside your container. Because of the descendant selectors in Flex 4, which I'll discuss later in this chapter, you could limit the effect of the CSS for these components to only the components in your container. But it would be so much more convenient to not have to care about which components reside in your custom container, especially for the maintainability and reusability of that container. That's exactly what the universal selector does for you: it behaves like the global selector, but on a deeper level in your application.

To apply a universal selector, you just use a type selector and append an asterisk to the end. This means that every component inside that specific type will have the styles that follow applied.

Flex4 ➤ *CSS_Universal.mxml*

```
<?xml version="1.0" encoding="utf-8"?>
<s:Application xmlns:fx="http://ns.adobe.com/mxml/2009"
               xmlns:s="library://ns.adobe.com/flex/spark"
               xmlns:mx="library://ns.adobe.com/flex/mx">

  <fx:Style>
    @namespace s "library://ns.adobe.com/flex/spark";
    @namespace mx "library://ns.adobe.com/flex/mx";

    global {
      font-family: Verdana;
      color: #333333;
    }

    s|Panel * {
      color: #000099;
    }
  </fx:Style>

  <s:Group horizontalCenter="0" verticalCenter="0">
    <s:layout>
      <s:VerticalLayout/>
    </s:layout>
    <s:Label text="This text is affected by the global selector"/>
    <s:Panel height="200" title="Panel container">
      <s:layout>
        <s:VerticalLayout paddingLeft="10" paddingTop="10" paddingRight="10"/>
      </s:layout>
      <s:Label text="This text is affected by the universal selector"/>
    </s:Panel>
  </s:Group>
</s:Application>
```

When you run this application, you'll see that the first `Label` component receives the styling from the `global` selector while the label inside the `Panel` container receives the styling from the universal selector. You will also notice that not only is the label color different inside the `Panel` container, but also the title is displayed in blue, due to the fact that the universal selector applies to all subcomponents inside the specified container.

ID Selector

Every once in a while you come across a situation where you have to style just one single component instance, and that's what the ID selector lets you do. You could, of course, create a class selector for that purpose and attach it to the specific component as I described earlier in this chapter. So you might think "What's the use of this ID selector then?" Well, one benefit is that you don't have to specifically attach it to the component, since the ID of that component is used to search for the CSS styles that need to be applied. To specify the ID selector, you simply prefix the component's ID with a "#" (hash sign), like this:

```
#componentID {
    color: #333333;
    paddingLeft: 10;
    paddingRight: 10;
}
```

Another advantage of using this type of selector is that you can reuse the same IDs over and over again. All of the components with the same ID will automatically get the styles defined by the ID selector. So, when you apply some kind of naming convention for a certain type of component and you don't need to style them all, but just a few instances in different components, you can opt for the ID selector and give all the instances that do need styling the same ID.

That being said, you'd still probably want to use the class selector. Let me clarify this further with an example.

Flex4 ➤ *CSS_Id.mxml*

```
<?xml version="1.0" encoding="utf-8"?>
<s:Application xmlns:fx="http://ns.adobe.com/mxml/2009"
               xmlns:s="library://ns.adobe.com/flex/spark"
               xmlns:mx="library://ns.adobe.com/flex/mx"
               xmlns:co="com.domain.project.controls.*">
  <fx:Style>
    #firstButton{
      baseColor: #333333;
      color: #CCCCCC;
      focusColor: #666666;
      fontFamily: Verdana;
      fontSize: 14;
      fontStyle: italic;
    }
  </fx:Style>

  <s:Group horizontalCenter="0" verticalCenter="0">
    <s:layout>
      <s:VerticalLayout/>
    </s:layout>
    <s:Button id="firstButton" label="This is the first button"/>
    <s:Button id="SecondButton" label="This is another button"/>
    <co:MyCustomDataGrid id="grid"/>
  </s:Group>
</s:Application>
```

Flex4 ➤ *com* ➤ *domain* ➤ *project* ➤ *controls* ➤ *MyCustomDataGrid.mxml*

```
<?xml version="1.0" encoding="utf-8"?>
```

```
<s:Group xmlns:fx="http://ns.adobe.com/mxml/2009"
         xmlns:s="library://ns.adobe.com/flex/spark"
         xmlns:mx="library://ns.adobe.com/flex/mx">
  <s:layout>
    <s:VerticalLayout/>
  </s:layout>

  <fx:Declarations>
    <s:ArrayCollection id="ac">
      <fx:Object podium="1 - Gold medal"/>
      <fx:Object podium="2 - Silver medal"/>
      <fx:Object podium="3 - Bronze medal"/>
    </s:ArrayCollection>
  </fx:Declarations>

  <s:Button id="firstButton" label="Display data" click="grid.dataProvider=ac"/>
  <mx:DataGrid id="grid"/>
</s:Group>
```

In this example, there are two different components: the application and `MyCustomDataGrid`. Both have a button with exactly the same ID. Because there is an ID selector for those buttons in the application, both buttons are styled, even though the external component doesn't have any styling defined. (See Figure 2-9.) This is the power of the ID selector.

Figure 2-9. Only two of the three buttons are styled, because they use the ID selector.

This power can reach even further when you combine an ID selector with a type selector, resulting in something like `s|Button#componentId`. In this case, you can even use the same ID for different types of components, but only those of the type `Button` or that inherit from it will be affected.

Descendant Selector

The descendant selector in CSS is also a new feature in Flex 4. It allows you to create a hierarchical structure to specify styling for certain components within a particular container. So, for example, when you have a `Button` component in a `Panel` container that you wish to apply some styling to, you can specify the styling using the descendant selector. You just have to set the `Panel` type in front of the `Button` type to indicate that only `Button` components inside a `Panel` container should receive the specified styling. The button doesn't even have to be on the top level in the container. The styling is applied to buttons on all levels within that container.

There are, however, a couple of things to keep in mind when using this type of CSS selector. The first is that you can mix a descendant selector with a class or ID selector to further drill down to a specific component. Also, you can only specify parent components or containers that reside in the display list. So, reparenting components using view states when the styled parent is defined only in a certain state can have nasty side effects, as the container is not always present in the display list.

Flex4 ➤ CSS_Descendant.mxml

```xml
<?xml version="1.0" encoding="utf-8"?>
<s:Application xmlns:fx="http://ns.adobe.com/mxml/2009"
               xmlns:s="library://ns.adobe.com/flex/spark"
               xmlns:mx="library://ns.adobe.com/flex/mx"
               xmlns:co="com.domain.project.controls.*">
  <fx:Style>
    @namespace s "library://ns.adobe.com/flex/spark";
    @namespace mx "library://ns.adobe.com/flex/mx";
    @namespace co "com.domain.project.controls.*";

    co|MyCustomDataGrids|Button{
      baseColor: #333333;
      color: #CCCCCC;
      focusColor: #666666;
      fontFamily: Verdana;
      fontSize: 14;
      fontStyle: italic;
    }
  </fx:Style>

  <s:Group horizontalCenter="0" verticalCenter="0">
    <s:layout>
      <s:VerticalLayout/>
    </s:layout>
    <s:Button id="firstButton" label="This is the first button"/>
    <s:Button id="SecondButton" label="This is another button"/>
    <co:MyCustomDataGrid id="grid"/>
  </s:Group>
</s:Application>
```

The component `MyCustomDataGrid` remains exactly the same as the one I used in the previous section. What's notable in the CSS this time is that we need to specify a custom namespace for the controls in order to style the components in that package. By placing that component in front of the `Button` type selector, only the buttons inside of the custom component will be styled, as you can see in Figure 2-10.

Figure 2-10. The descendant selector styles only the button inside the custom component.

Pseudo Selector

Sometimes you want the styling to be dynamically applied to certain components based on one or more criteria, perhaps related to exception handling. Flex has a standard way of handling errors by using the `Validator` classes. There are a couple of validators available out of the box, like `NumberValidator`, `EmailValidator`, `CreditCardValidator` and `RegExpValidator` (you can check almost anything with this last one if you're good at regular expressions). But you can also create your own validators by extending one of the existing ones. When the validator fails, the input field that failed its validation gets a red bounding rectangle and a red tooltip with an error message when you hover over it.

This has become widely accepted as a sort of standard in rich internet applications. But sometimes this way of showing errors is not sufficient, because red is a dangerous color if you're partially color blind with a condition called deuteranomaly, which means you have the inability to see the color red. In some applications in Belgium it is also very important, if not necessary, to adhere to the specifications of the AnySurfer label (`http://www.anysurfer.be/en/`). For the US there is the "section 508" (`http://www.section508.gov/`), and some other countries have similar guidelines. This is a quality label that indicates that your site can be viewed by the visually impaired. Other reasons for deviating from the standard could involve company design standards, coding standards, or even user input.

The pseudo selector is designed specifically for Flex, because it handles different styling in different view states. For example, you could define special styling for the various states of a button. Or you can change the style when a component gets errors, or is in expanded or contracted mode. These are situations where you usually use view states. To apply CSS styling to a particular state of a component, you have to put a ":" (colon) between the selector and the specific state name. Now, I explicitly wrote *selector*, not just component, because you can again combine this with class selectors, ID selectors, and descendant selectors to restrict the styling as needed. Just take a look at this simple example.

Flex4 ➤ *com* ➤ *domain* ➤ *project* ➤ *controls* ➤ *MyCustomTextInput.mxml*

```
<?xml version="1.0" encoding="utf-8"?>
<s:TextInput xmlns:fx="http://ns.adobe.com/mxml/2009"
             xmlns:s="library://ns.adobe.com/flex/spark"
             xmlns:mx="library://ns.adobe.com/flex/mx">
  <fx:Script>
    <![CDATA[
      override public function set errorString(value:String):void {
        if((value != null) && (value.length> 0)) {
```

```
            currentState = "error";
        } else {
            currentState = "default";
        }
    }
  ]]>
</fx:Script>

<s:states>
  <s:State name="default"/>
  <s:State name="error"/>
</s:states>
</s:TextInput>
```

In this custom component I've defined only one extra state beside the default state in order to apply my view state-specific CSS styling from the main application file. Setting the proper view state in this component is done by overriding the setter for the errorString property. This is the property that sets the red bounding rectangle when filled out. The value will be the text shown in the fly-over hint. So, when it is filled out, I set the component to the error view state. If the component has no error, I reset it to its default state.

> *Remember, this is merely a simple example to illustrate the use of pseudo selectors. In real-life applications, such a component would have more functionality in the error state.*

Flex4 ➤ CSS_Pseudo.mxml

```
<?xml version="1.0" encoding="utf-8"?>
<s:Application xmlns:fx="http://ns.adobe.com/mxml/2009"
               xmlns:s="library://ns.adobe.com/flex/spark"
               xmlns:mx="library://ns.adobe.com/flex/mx"
               xmlns:co="com.domain.project.controls.*">
  <fx:Style>
    @namespace co "com.domain.project.controls.*";

    co|MyCustomTextInput:default{
      contentBackgroundColor: #FFFFFF;
      color: #333333;
    }

    co|MyCustomTextInput:error{
      contentBackgroundColor: #CC0000;
      color: #FFFFFF;
    }
  </fx:Style>

  <fx:Declarations>
    <mx:StringValidator id="vUsername" triggerEvent=""
                        source="{username}" property="text"/>
    <mx:StringValidator id="vPassword" triggerEvent=""
```

```
                          source="{password}" property="text"/>
    </fx:Declarations>

    <mx:Form defaultButton="{btnLogin}" horizontalCenter="0" verticalCenter="0">
      <mx:FormHeading label="Login to application"/>
      <mx:FormItem label="Username:" required="true">
        <co:MyCustomTextInput id="username" width="200"/>
      </mx:FormItem>
      <mx:FormItem label="Password:" required="true">
        <co:MyCustomTextInput id="password" width="200" displayAsPassword="true"/>
      </mx:FormItem>
      <mx:FormItem direction="horizontal" width="100%" horizontalAlign="right">
        <s:Button id="btnLogin" label="Login"
                  click="mx.validators.Validator.validateAll([vUsername,
vPassword])"/>
        <s:Button id="btnCancel" label="Cancel"/>
      </mx:FormItem>
    </mx:Form>
</s:Application>
```

If you run this example and press the login button, you'll see that the erroneous fields will be colored red and if you type something in the red field, the text color will be white for better readability. You could do the same thing by setting the state on a property, as I discussed in the section on view states in this chapter. But now this functionality is in CSS, and you can put the CSS in a separate, external file that you can read at runtime. You can also use multiple CSS files, depending on your users' or customers' needs. This means that you don't have to recompile your application just because the error indication needs to have a different styling.

Two-Way Binding

Two-way binding has been substantially improved in the latest version of the Flex SDK. Of course, this feature was available in Flex 3, but it was a bit of a hassle to get it right. Let me demonstrate what I mean.

Assume you have a master-detail application that has a grid with a couple of records inside. When you select one of the records, the application should show a detail form with all the fields. Those fields would be editable and you would have a save button of some sort. To make sure that the detail form follows the selection, you would use binding. Here's the Flex 3 example code for the form.

Flex3 ➤ *Detail.mxml*

```
<mx:Form xmlns:mx="http://www.adobe.com/2006/mxml">
  <mx:Script>
    <![CDATA[
      [Bindable]
      public var person:Object;

      protected function btnSave_clickHandler(event:MouseEvent):void {
        lblFname.text = "First name = " + person.firstname;
        lblLname.text = "Last name = " + person.lastname;
      }
```

```
      protected function btnCancel_clickHandler(event:MouseEvent):void {
        lblFname.text = "";
        lblLname.text = "";
      }
    ]]>
  </mx:Script>

  <mx:FormHeading label="Person details"/>
  <mx:FormItem label="ID">
    <mx:Label text="{person.index}"/>
  </mx:FormItem>
  <mx:FormItem label="Firstname">
    <mx:TextInput id="fname" text="{person.firstname}"/>
  </mx:FormItem>
  <mx:FormItem label="Lastname">
    <mx:TextInput id="lname" text="{person.lastname}"/>
  </mx:FormItem>
  <mx:FormItem direction="horizontal">
    <mx:Button id="btnSave" label="Save" click="btnSave_clickHandler(event)"/>
    <mx:Button id="btnCancel" label="Cancel" click="btnCancel_clickHandler(event)"/>
  </mx:FormItem>

  <mx:Spacer height="50"/>

  <mx:FormItem label="Results after change">
    <mx:Label id="lblFname"/>
    <mx:Label id="lblLname"/>
  </mx:FormItem>
</mx:Form>
```

In this very simplistic example, there's a public person property that will be filled out by the master component. This property is then bound to the form items to show the data. The problem is that when you change the values in the TextInput fields, the original object is not changed in any way. When you click the save button, the values will be manually set to a couple of labels and you'll see that the old values are still in the public property. This is because the binding of a value only occurs in one direction: from the property to the visual representation (in this case). If you were to implement two-way binding in this code, you would have to use the <mx:Binding> tag to accomplish binding in the other direction. The code you'd need to add would be this:

```
<mx:Binding source="fname.text" destination="person.firstname"/>
<mx:Binding source="lname.text" destination="person.lastname"/>
```

Just these two lines of extra code and you have two-way binding in your Flex 3 application or component! However, you'd have to create such an <mx:Binding> tag for each and every property you want bound to that property again. In this case, we need only two lines because it is a very basic example. But in real applications, a single form can easily contain more than ten form items. And the detail information may be split up into several forms. That could lead to dozens of these extra statements.

That's why Adobe integrated two-way binding in the Flex 4 SDK, and made it very easy to use. You start by creating the form in the same way, but this time using the Spark components as much as possible. For each binding expression you use with the curly braces, you type an extra "@" sign in front of those braces to indicate you want to use two-way binding.

Flex 4 ➤ Detail.mxml

```
<?xml version="1.0" encoding="utf-8"?>
<mx:Form xmlns:fx="http://ns.adobe.com/mxml/2009"
         xmlns:s="library://ns.adobe.com/flex/spark"
         xmlns:mx="library://ns.adobe.com/flex/mx">
  <fx:Script>
    <![CDATA[
      [Bindable]
      public var person:Object;

      protected function btnSave_clickHandler(event:MouseEvent):void {
        lblFname.text = "Firstname = " + person.firstname;
        lblLname.text = "Lastname = " + person.lastname;
      }

      protected function btnCancel_clickHandler(event:MouseEvent):void {
        lblFname.text = "";
        lblLname.text = "";
      }
    ]]>
  </fx:Script>

  <mx:FormHeading label="Person details"/>
  <mx:FormItem label="ID">
    <mx:Label text="{person.index}"/>
  </mx:FormItem>
  <mx:FormItem label="Firstname">
    <s:TextInput id="fname" text="@{person.firstname}"/>
  </mx:FormItem>
  <mx:FormItem label="Lastname">
    <s:TextInput id="lname" text="@{person.lastname}"/>
  </mx:FormItem>
  <mx:FormItem direction="horizontal">
    <s:Button id="btnSave" label="Save" click="btnSave_clickHandler(event)"/>
    <s:Button id="btnCancel" label="Cancel" click="btnCancel_clickHandler(event)"/>
  </mx:FormItem>

  <mx:Spacer height="50"/>

  <mx:FormItem label="Results after change">
    <mx:Label id="lblFname"/>
    <mx:Label id="lblLname"/>
  </mx:FormItem>
</mx:Form>
```

So, just by putting the "@" sign in front of the curly braces, you get two-way binding automatically enabled and applied. You can see this by changing something and then clicking the save button. The new values will be reflected in the labels because now the person object is actually changed when you type something in the input fields.

Personally, I believe this to be one of the more productive features they've put into the new version of the Flex SDK as I know a lot of developers, myself included, have been asking for this feature a very long time. And now we've finally gotten the proper answer, along with lots of other useful goodies in the new SDK.

Summary

The Flex 4 SDK has been significantly improved over the previous version in terms of productivity, maintainability, and extensibility. Keeping the functional code completely separate from the design code makes it easier to change the design without breaking your existing code. And when roundtripping between Flash Catalyst and Flash Builder is enabled, the design can be updated just by importing the existing project back into Flash Catalyst.

But for now, you're stuck with having to merge the new design elements manually. Luckily, Flash Builder has a great comparison tool to facilitate this merge operation, which I will talk about in the next chapter. But you still have to know what exactly has to be merged and what needs to remain the same. That's why it is important to understand the code that has been generated by Flash Catalyst.

Chapter 3

Flash Builder 4: The programming environment

Now that we are up-to-date on the new features of the SDK, let's take a closer look at how the programming environment has changed since the last version. We'll start by taking a look at the IDE (Integrated Development Environment) and explore the product from there. Remember that this is not intended to be a book about Flash Builder—I'll just provide an overview of some of the great new features that were not available in Flex Builder 3.

What is Flash Builder 4?

Flash Builder 4 is a development tool that's closely based on the well-known Eclipse IDE (http://www.eclipse.org). You might be familiar with Eclipse if you've done any Java or even ColdFusion development using the CFEclipse plug-in. Or maybe you've used it to create web sites or PHP or ASP pages. That's all possible since Eclipse is a plug-in based tool. As long as you have the proper plug-ins installed, there's a whole lot of development you can do using this environment. And, of course, that's also the case with Flash Builder. What's even better is that a lot of these plug-ins are open source or freeware licensed, so you can just download and use them in a commercial production environment.

Now, Flash Builder comes in two versions: stand-alone and plug-in. Each is an installable executable you'll find on the Adobe website (http://www.adobe.com/products/flex). Since the stand-alone version is basically a stripped-down version of Eclipse with the Flash Builder plug-in, you can use either one. But as a developer, I strongly suggest you use the plug-in version, because then you already have the whole Eclipse environment set up correctly for Java or PHP or other back-end technology to connect to your Flex application. Of course, you can start out from the stand-alone installation and add the necessary plug-ins for your back-end development. I've tried this, though, and found it a lot harder to get the configuration right.

Moreover, Adobe has also released a similar product for ColdFusion, aptly named ColdFusion Builder. The beta version of this product was made available at the same time ColdFusion 9, the new server version, was released. And just as with Flash Builder, ColdFusion Builder is available as a stand-alone version or as a plug-in for Eclipse. I guess you can see where I'm heading here: if you always choose to install the plug-in versions, your front-end and back-end tool is exactly the same. That means you can create the front-end and back-end project parts using the same IDE, which is especially helpful if you are working on both parts. It also means you can usually use the same debugger session to take your front-end problem all the way into the back end by stepping through it or placing breakpoints. You just need to be able to start the server from within the IDE to be able to do that. But in most cases, that is not a problem at all. I've done it several times with both Tomcat and ColdFusion servers for my back-end code.

And the good stuff doesn't stop there. When you have the Web Tools Platform (WTP) plug-in installed in your Eclipse environment, you can opt to create combined Flex projects. You can find this additional plug-in on the Eclipse download site at `http://www.eclipse.org/webtools/`. What does this mean? Well, it means you don't have to create a separate Flex and LiveCycle project for instance. If you choose to create a combined project, the Java code for your back end can be written in the same project. So you end up with one project, which is even compiled in one build command. That makes your work very easy and convenient: one environment, one project, one build, one application! I'm sure you understand that this means that front-end and back-end developers need to work more closely. Obviously, it makes some kind of versioning tool necessary to avoid conflict by working on the same source files at the same time. And it requires a new way of collaborating. No one is on an island anymore.

What Happened to Flex Builder?

I've been talking a lot about Flash Builder, but you may be wondering what has happened to Flex Builder—has it disappeared in favor of this new tool? Not really. In fact, Flash Builder is just a new name for the same product; hence the fact that the product launched as version 4. (The previous version of Flex Builder was 3.0.2, which included a couple of hot fixes for version 3.)

Why has the name of the product changed? It's all part of a "master plan" by Adobe to initiate a re-branding of certain products. The Flash Professional authoring tool never had a decent coding environment and had remained more of a designer tool. A few years ago, however, developers started to get into Flash and Flash applications became increasingly popular. Since the tool wasn't really made for that, developers sought alternatives, with decent code completion and such, to write their code. A couple of open source products emerged, like Flash Develop, together with licensed alternatives, such as FDT (`http://fdt.powerflasher.com`), an Eclipse plug-in.. But then Adobe came along with Flex Builder, which also allowed for ActionScript 3 code completion, syntax checking, and integrated help functionality. Developers could use this product to code their Flash applications and so they did. So now, with the new version, Adobe acknowledges this use and has renamed it to Flash Builder.

Another reason for this rebranding is that Adobe is working very hard to get all of their products to work together. And the common technology for most of those tools is Flash. Let me give you a couple of examples to clarify what I mean:

- Flash Professional produces SWF files.

- Flex is compiled into an SWF file.

- Bridge allows you to create a slide show in SWF format with just one click.

- Photoshop, Illustrator, and Fireworks can be imported into Flash Catalyst, which produces Flex code, which in turn generates an SWF file.

- SWF files can be included in PDF documents to create rich, interactive documents.

- Captivate creates and uses SWF files to create SCORM-compliant interactive e-learning content and quizzes.

These are only a few examples of the collaboration possibilities among all of those products. But it shows the importance of the Flash technology in the entire product range.

The New Features

Of course, with a new version of the product, there are also some new and improved features available. With Flash Builder 4, the focus has been on developer productivity, and a lot of features are geared toward exactly that.

Backward Compatibility

You may well be wondering whether you can maintain your existing applications with the new version. The short answer is "yes", but there's a "but." Adobe has a history of supporting only two versions of a product in their development tools: the current one and the previous one. As a result, you will only be able to create Flex 3 and Flex 4 applications with the Flash Builder IDE. So, any Flex 2 applications still out there can't be maintained using Flash Builder 4. But don't worry, your Flex Builder 3 license will remain valid. Both versions can be run concurrently, though only one version can be installed as a plug-in. So, if you have to support Flex 2 projects, you can still do that.

With Flash Builder, you also have the option in the project settings to define new SDKs for compiling your application. You might think this could be the solution to your problem, because you can add the Flex SDK 2.0.1 hotfix 3 to the compiler options. Unfortunately, when you try to do this, you get an error like the one in Figure 3-1.

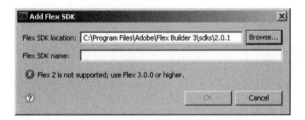

Figure 3-1. Flex SDK 2.0.1 is no longer supported in Flash Builder.

What are your options then? Can you just recompile to a higher SDK version? Do you have to rewrite the entire project? Well, I started out in Flex 1.5 and had to migrate some projects to version 2 of the Flex SDK. Adobe had a migration guide that was about seven pages long—and at the end of those 7 pages, it still wouldn't work. And this was still in ActionScript 2. Eventually, I had to rewrite the entire project. And just when Flex 2 projects were becoming numerous, Adobe released Flex 3 at the beginning of March of 2008. I was promised by the support team and all those evangelists that migrating wouldn't be such a hassle anymore. And you know what? They were right! It still wasn't just a recompilation for the more complex projects. But it was certainly doable. One feature I altered in the converted projects was the use of `ResourceBundle` classes for the localization of the labels and messages in the Flex applications. You *could* still use it like that, but it was deemed deprecated, so I decided it would be best to change that part. But I can honestly say migrating was much easier.

Is the migration to Flex 4 going to be even more straightforward or are we back to the seven-page migration document? Since the Halo components still exist and can still be used in a Flex 4 project (although the Spark components are preferred), I've had no problems recompiling and running small Flex 3 applications using the Flex 4 SDK. However, should you run into problems with larger applications, there is another new feature in the project settings that might be of help—**Flex 4 has a Flex 3 compatibility mode** that you can enable (see Figure 3-2).

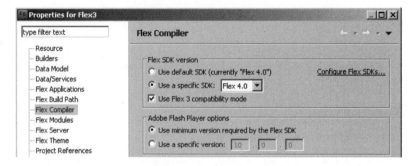

Figure 3-2. You can enable Flex 3 compatibility mode.

If that still doesn't do the trick, then, unfortunately, it's up to you to figure out what the compatibility issue is and adjust the code accordingly. This setting will make sure that the MX library locations are untouched and you can still reap the benefits of using the Flash Builder 4 compiler, which is faster and has better optimizations for the resulting SWF file.

Improved Project Properties

Since we're talking about the project **Properties** panel, let's take a closer look at what else has changed in those properties. First up is that you can now attach Flex SDK themes (and custom ones, too, of course) through the project settings. There is an option called **Flex Theme** that allows you to select one from a list, including the following that are available by default:

- Spark: This is the default look and feel for Flex 4 applications.

- Wireframe: This one just shows the outlines and has virtually no styling.

- Halo: This is from Flex 3 applications, which is still available.

- AeonGraphical: This is the graphical version of the default Halo theme.

You can also download other themes and load them into Flash Builder, either your own or those you can find by clicking on the hyperlink in the Flex Theme properties panel, which takes you to http://www.adobe.com/go/getflextheme. Clicking on the Import theme… button gives you a dialog that lets you select a theme from your local hard drive or network drive.

Another great feature that has been added is the ability to **change your application's back-end technology**. I've worked on several projects where you start out with a very simple project with, for example, a PHP back end. You set up the project structure, create your configuration files, create your back-end functionality in PHP—and all of a sudden the project specifications get adjusted. You find out you have to implement a feature you can't implement in PHP, like data push over RTMP (Real-Time Messaging Protocol). Or maybe the company has decided to move all back-end programming to Java or ColdFusion, and you're stuck with a project that is set up for PHP. In Flex Builder 3, you didn't really have any other option than to re-create the project with the proper back-end settings, copy your sources to the new project, and pray that it all still worked. This is because you could only set the project's server connection settings in the Create Project wizard.

In Flash Builder 4, however, Adobe lets you change these settings after creation. So now you can change the application's back end without having to re-create the project. To change the settings, go to the `Flex Server` panel.

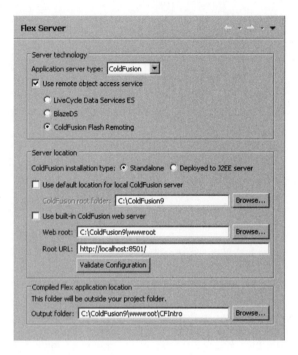

Figure 3-3. The Flex Server properties panel

As you can see in Figure 3-3, at the top of the `Flex Server` properties panel you can change the `Application Server Type`, even after having created the project. The new settings will be applied after validation of the new server settings.

You can also **change your application type**. In the past, I've created a couple of Flex projects that had to be web applications, as requested by the client. But then, for example, the client saw a demonstration of AIR and decided it would be great to have the project as an AIR application, with all of the extra features like automatic updates.

In the first versions of AIR, it used to be quite simple to turn a Flex application into an AIR application—all you needed to do was change the `<mx:Application>` into `<mx:WindowedApplication>` and you were set to go. I know this was not really the clean way to go, but it worked. But as of AIR version 1.5, this stopped working and you had to create a separate AIR project and copy the code from the Flex application to the new project. Usually this would work, if you also copied the project settings (libraries, configuration files, and so forth). But you couldn't just copy the settings files. You had to fix the settings manually and sometimes you'd forget to configure something and your project would fail its build or even create runtime exceptions.

Fortunately, In Flash Builder 4 you now have the option to change the application type from `Web application` to `Desktop application` by right-clicking the project and then selecting the `Add/Change Project Type`, as you can see in Figure 3-4.

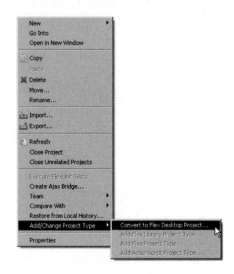

Figure 3-4. Changing the application type has become easy.

Package Explorer

Flash Builder 4 has a view that is called the Package Explorer. In the previous version, you used the Flex Navigator view to walk through the structure of your project and to create new folders. In Flex, these folders are exactly the same as package names. The Package Explorer is the new and improved version of the Navigator. It structures the project into packages instead of folders, but in the background the packages are still the folders. You just don't see any excess folders that contribute only to the structure and don't contain any classes themselves.

Furthermore, you can use the Package Explorer to browse through external CSS files, just as if you were browsing through a folder structure. You can even drill down to the level of the styles, as you can see in Figure 3-5.

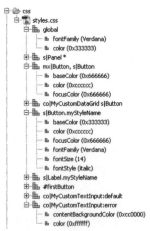

Figure 3-5. You can now browse through the CSS files.

Package Explorer goes even further in its exploring capabilities. Flex and AIR projects always have a `libs` folder that's used to incorporate external libraries into a project. This folder is automatically included in the class path, so just placing an SWC (an ActionScript library) in that folder allows you to use the components inside of it. SWC file are essentially ZIP files that include a manifest file, a compiled SWF, and some other files as well. Because the SWC file only contains the compiled version of the code, in the previous version of Flex Builder, there was no way of knowing the components in a library, except by reading the documentation (if available) or by decompiling the SWC file, which in a lot of cases would probably be illegal. But the Flash Builder 4 Package Explorer has a feature called *introspection* that lets you browse through the package structure of a library to see which components are available. At the same time, you also know the package they are located in, so you can figure out the import statements to write. To be honest, though, I don't think I've ever written an import statement in a Flex or AIR project myself. Usually I let Flex Builder (or Flash Builder from now on) generate those statements by using the code completion feature (which, by the way, has also been improved. But I'll talk more on that later on in this chapter.).

Now, browsing through a library project is already great for figuring out the components, but the Package Explorer goes even a little bit further because you can even browse the components themselves. This means you can see what methods, properties, and constants a component has available. And these are depicted just as in the outline view when you're coding in ActionScript. So, for example, you get a green dot in front of a public method and a red square for a private one. Since the Flex framework also consists of several SWC files, like the `playerglobal.swc`, `textlayout.swc` (which includes the new text layout framework), `spark.swc` (which contains the new Spark components), you can actually browse through the entire Flex framework, as you can see in Figure 3-6. So now you can investigate those libraries and even discover classes and features you may have never heard of before.

Figure 3-6. Browsing through the Flex 4 SDK using the `Package Explorer`

Code Generation

In the latest version of the IDE, Adobe's development team also added support for code generation on a couple of different levels:

- Generation of getters and setters

- Event-handler generation

- Changing variable scope

Let's start with the first one: **the generation of getter and setter methods**. In Eclipse, there has always been support for this when coding in Java. You just had to select the private class members, then right-click and choose the `Source` ➤ `Generate Getters and Setters`…You'd end up with a confirmation dialog that would also let you select the class members for which you wanted the generation. This is a very nice feature that was lacking in Flex Builder. Instead, you had to write them all yourself, which can be time-consuming if, for example, you have a Data Transfer Object with some 20 class members. Now, in Flash Builder 4, there is support for this kind of code generation. It is not yet as elaborate as I had hoped it would be, but it's definitely an improvement worth mentioning.

What I mean by not being as elaborate is the fact that you can't select multiple class members at the same time to generate the getters and setters all at once. You're stuck with generating the code one variable at a time. This is something that still needs to be improved in the next upgrades to the product, but I'm already quite happy with what's there now. I've even used the beta version of Flash Builder 4 on sources of Flex 3 projects, just to use this generation feature for my DTOs.

Another generation feature that has been added is automatic suggestion for event handlers. This means that when you want to add an event handler for an MXML component, Flash Builder 4 will suggest a name for that event handler. The name consists of the component ID, which is also potentially generated by the Flex framework if you don't specify one yourself, followed by an "_" (underscore), then the name of the event, and finally the word "Handler" is appended. So, for example, if you have a button with an ID of `btnSave` and you let Flash Builder generate the event handler, it will be called `btnSave_clickHandler(event:MouseEvent):void`. Now, the actual name of the event handler is not visible in the code completion; it just suggests "Generate Click Handler" as you can see in Figure 3-7.

Figure 3-7. Automatic event handler generation in Flash Builder 4

The last generation feature I'd like discuss involves changing the scope for a certain class member. This is new for Flash Builder 4 and has been long requested by ActionScript developers. Imagine a situation where you have created some kind of public property on a certain component. (I know this is not really the proper way to code, but sometimes it's more appropriate than creating overhead with the implicit get and set methods that do nothing but return the private value.) Or suppose you've done so to create a "quick and dirty" solution. In any event, you've been using this public class member in binding expressions in other components and now the original component needs to change. The project demands that the property should always be in uppercase, no matter what. Well, this is a classic example for the use of getters and setters. In our case, these methods will be implicit getters and setters.

In previous version of Flex builder, you'd have to create a `get` and `set` method, make the property private, make sure you don't have the "`Duplicate variable definition`" error and change all occurrences of that public property to use the implicit get and set method. Now, this last step could be facilitated by letting the name of the implicit getters and setters match the name of the public property, since these methods will be used as if you were just accessing public class members. But still, there was work involved.

In Flash Builder 4, there is now actual support to do this. To enable this support, you'll again generate implicit getter and setter methods. What you need to do is to select a public class member, right-click, and choose Source ➤ Generate Getter/Setter. You get the same dialog as before, but with a small difference. This time the first part of the dialog is enabled, as you can see in Figure 3-8.

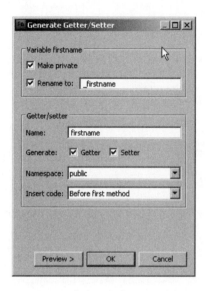

Figure 3-8. Automatic scope-changing while creating implicit getter and setter methods

As you can see, you now have the extra option of changing the scope of the class member from public to private with just one click of the button. And the feature automatically suggests putting an "_" (underscore) in front of the private property, as ActionScript naming convention dictates. (More on naming and coding conventions later in this book.) And just as with the ordinary generation of the getter and setter, you have a few options as to where to place the generated methods:

- Before first method, meaning right after the variable definitions.

- After last method, meaning at the end of the file.

- After variable declaration, meaning right after the definition and in between other variable definitions.

I prefer to use the After last method option because I like having my variables all grouped together at the top of my class definition. But if you take a closer look at some of the Flex SDK classes, you'll see that these class member declarations often occur throughout the entire class structure. In large classes, with perhaps hundreds of lines of code, I can agree it might seem more logical to group the variable definition together with its accessor methods. So all the options are valid and it's just a matter of convention and preference as to what to choose.

Refactoring Support

The next interesting feature I'd like to talk about is the ability to refactor certain parts of your code. *Refactoring* means you are going to rewrite or rework certain parts for better readability, optimization, maintainability, etc. If you're used to working with Eclipse on Java projects, you probably know what I'm talking about here. If not, well, let me explain.

There are two types of refactoring you usually have to perform at one point or another in the course of a project:

- Renaming class members

- Changing the location or package name of a certain component

Previous versions of Flex Builder had some support for **refactoring the names of class members** that resembled a find-and-replace strategy. When you chose Refactor ➤ Rename... you'd get the option to preview your changes before actually committing them. When you selected an implicit getter or setter method to rename, the dialog even got an extra checkbox that let you refactor its counterpart as well (see Figure 3-9).

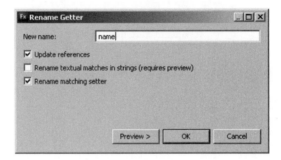

Figure 3-9. Renaming an implicit getter automatically suggests doing the same to the implicit setter.

However, if you selected a private class member and tried to rename it, the getters and setters were not automatically changed with them, and the new version of Flash Builder doesn't change this, so for now there is no improvement on the refactoring support.

However, Flash Builder 4 does add support to easily **change the location/package name of a certain component**. Suppose you've written some components and placed them in a certain package in your project. Later you decide it's best to create a new package and move a couple of components to that new package. In earlier versions, this was usually resolved by copying the source to the new location, changing the package definition in the source, and then recompiling the project to see where the component had been used, because that would generate some compilation errors. In some cases you could just change the import statement or the namespace definition in the MXML files. But sometimes you were still using other components from the old package and you had to create a new namespace definition.

Flash Builder 4 has a new feature that can be accessed by right-clicking the class name in a source file and selecting Refactor ➤ Move... in the menu. In the dialog that follows you can then select the package to which you want to move the class. You can also change any textual references. This is useful when you are moving a class that is used as an item renderer, for example, because in that case you will have a textual reference in the itemRenderer property in your MXML code that needs to be adjusted.

If you change the package for the class and then press the Preview button, you can look at all the changes that will be made and decide whether to go through with them. Another dialog will then appear with a list of all the changes and a comparison editor to indicate each change in the code so you can review it, as shown in Figure 3-10.

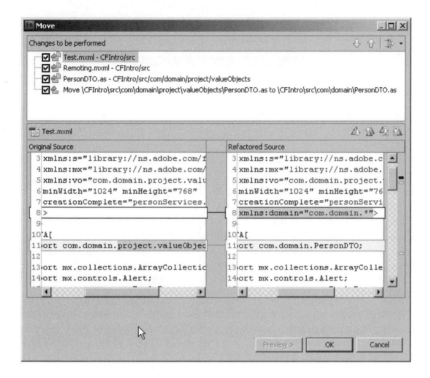

Figure 3-10. Previewing the changes when moving a class to a different package

As you can see, in my Test.mxml file there was a reference to the class using a namespace. In the comparison editor at line 5, it is clear that the vo namespace will still be available after the changes have been made, which is important because I may still be using other components or classes that reside in that package. However, a new namespace has been added called domain that refers to the new location for my class. In this example it's the package com.domain; which is also the name for the new namespace. The MXML instance of that specific component will also be changed to use the new namespace, so your code will compile perfectly after having relocated the component.

View States in Source Mode

As I mentioned in Chapter 3, view states have always been a key feature in Flex. A lot has changed in Flash Builder 4 in terms of implementing view states, and working with them is also a lot easier when it comes to debugging and maintaining your code. Not everything has changed, however.

Let's first take a look at what has remained the same, which will take us into the design view of an application or component. Let's examine an application I built to explore the differences in view states between Flex 3 and Flex 4. You can find the sources in the projects under Flex3 ➤ ViewStates.mxml and Flex4 ➤ ViewStates.mxml.

Let's start with the Flex 3 version of the application, which has three view states on top of the base state. In design mode, you can open the States panel (if it is not already open) by selecting it from the Window menu. Those three states are then displayed in a hierarchical structure, based on their inheritance structure (see Figure 3-11).

Figure 3-11. The States panel in the Flex 3 ViewStates application.

In this panel, you can clearly see that state3 is inheriting from state1 and that state2 is a completely different state. By selecting one of the states, as I've done with state3 in this particular case, the design editor will show you exactly what is going to be placed on the screen for that selected state. This allows you to browse through your states, seeing what they accomplish and whether they depict the application exactly as you imagined they would. This is a great tool to see if your view states are correct without having to implement the controlling part and without having to run your code.

What if you are working on a separate component that is not yet implemented in the application? In that case, there is no way of knowing whether your view states do what you want them to do except by writing a test application and immediately integrating it, or by using the design view in Flex Builder. I'd choose the latter as the other would take me some time to implement.

In Flash Builder 4 the States panel exists and functions much in the same way. The big difference is that there is no hierarchy anymore (see Figure 3-12). This is basically because the inheritance structure no longer exists. Remember that I talked about multiple view-state inheritance in Flex 4? Well, because of that feature and because you can now set a list of states in which the component needs to be present or absent, the hierarchical structure is no longer straightforward.

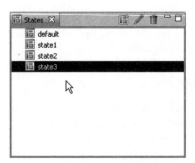

Figure 3-12: The States panel in the Flex 4 ViewStates application

So the major difference here is that you no longer see an inheritance tree to tell you what state inherits from what other state. But everything else stays the same and when you select a certain state, only the components that belong in that state will be shown in the design editor. As an alternative, to select a particular view state you could use the combo box at the top of the main panel, as shown in Figure 3-13.

This also contains all the possible view states for your component or application. Selecting a state in that combo box has the same effect as selecting a state in the States panel.

The reason I'm mentioning this alternate way of browsing through your view states is because this combo box has snuck into the source view in the latest version of Flash Builder. But wait a minute. Does that mean that you can use that combo box as a means to browse through your view states in source mode? Yes, amazingly, it does! This is a really great feature because sometimes you have an issue with one of the view states and you look at it in design mode (or in your application at runtime). You debug a little and finally you see what is actually wrong in your visual representation. If it's an easy fix, you can take care of it immediately in design mode, but sometimes it's more complicated and you have to dig into your source code to actually fix the problem. And that means you have to find out where the error is located. Now, from my Flex 3 experience, I never really used design mode a lot. I was used to deciphering the code and wrote a lot of view states directly in code. But I know developers who love using design mode to create their view states. And for them, digging into the code can be tricky sometimes.

But now, when you browse through your view states in source mode, everything that is not related to the view state you selected in that combo box is grayed out. So, instead of having to go through all the code trying to figure out what part of the code belongs to a certain view state, there's now a visual cue. This means that the relevant code is easier to identify, and errors concerning components not being visible in a certain component when they should be (or vice versa) can be identified quickly. This can save you time debugging your application. And once you get the hang of working with this view state-specific code, it's a tool you'll grow to rely on.

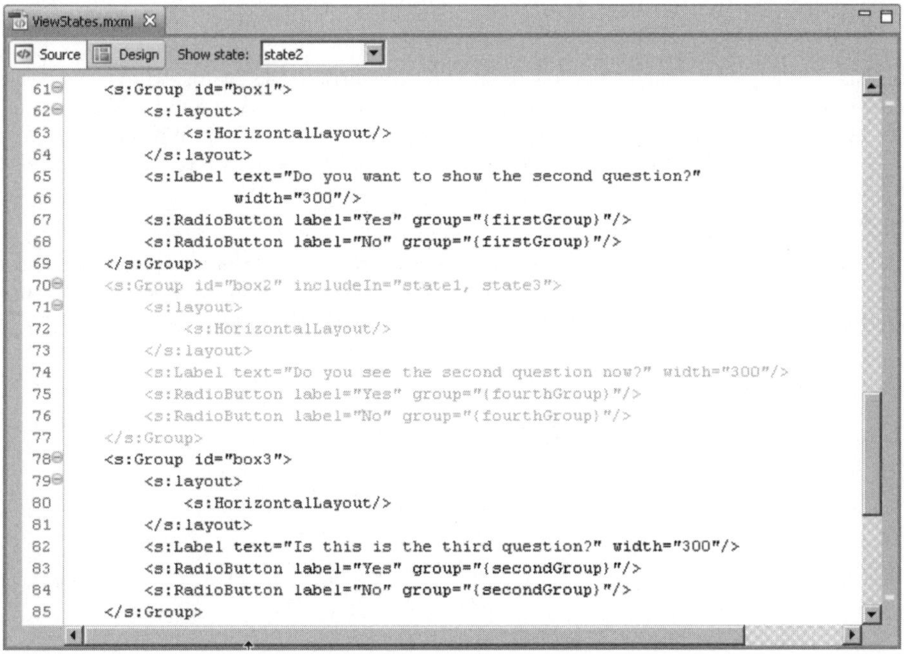

Figure 3-13. Selecting a view state in source mode grays out all irrelevant code.

Improved Design Editor

Now let's take a look at the new features of the design editor. As you may have guessed by now, I'm more of a pure coder with an extensive background in C and C++, and usually I'm not very fond of creating applications using the drag-and-drop features of the IDE (e.g., dragging a data list component into another component in Design View). I do know you can do some pretty amazing stuff without writing a lot of code, so maybe it's just an old habit lingering in my mind. But I must admit that after playing around with Flash Builder 4, I'm thinking I'll be using the design editor a lot more. Even when the design comes from within Flash Catalyst, you can still edit the components visually using the design editor, because either the design has been turned into images by importing a design file into Flash Catalyst, or the design is written using FXG tags, which can be understood by Flash Builder as well. I'll talk about that in one of the workflow examples in Chapter 5.

However, when roundtripping becomes enabled in later Flash Catalyst and Flash Builder releases, I believe Flash Catalyst will be used more as the design editor because of the extensive possibilities it has in that area. I will take a close look at Flash Catalyst's basic features in the next chapter. But for now, let me give you a couple of reasons why I like the new design editor more than in the previous versions of Flash Builder. Let's start by looking at a couple of panels that have been altered.

You use the Appearance panel to set global, application-wide properties and styles like the background color or the font family and font size. When you do, Flash Builder automatically generates a new CSS file with the name of the application and includes it in your application by adding the following line of code.

```
<fx:Style source="YourApplicationName.css"/>
```

This piece of code just adds a style block whose style definitions can be found in an external file. By default, Flash Builder places that external CSS file in the root of your source folder. Of course, if you want to move the style sheet to a different package you can, but you have to do it manually. It's also worth mentioning that you can name this CSS file whatever you like. It does not have to be the same as your application name, since you can also define multiple CSS files.

The Appearance panel also lets you set the theme for the application. As I've mentioned before, Flex 4 has a few themes available by default, and you can also download additional themes or create your own. The top panel section indicates the theme that is currently applied, which is the Spark theme by default for a Flex 4 application. If you click on the theme name, you get a popup dialog like the one in Figure 3-14.

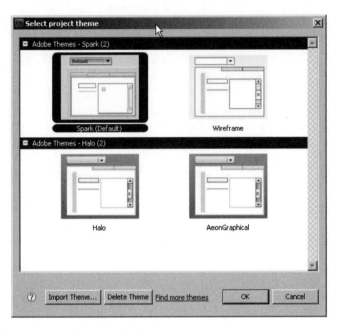

Figure 3-14. Default themes for a Flex 4 project

In this dialog, you can select another theme to apply to the application, or you can import new themes based on a CSS or SWC file. And you can remove themes from the list as well. Any theme you try to import should be Flex 4 compatible or you'll get errors on import stating that it's non-compliant.

The Properties panel has also been modified. This panel lets you change the most common properties in the standard view. However, in the category view, you can literally fill out and change all of the possible properties and styles for the component or container currently selected in the design view. The standard view is divided into 3 sub-panels:

- Common

- Style

- Layout

In the Common section of the Properties panel you can find the properties you most likely will want to change for the selected component. So, for example, if you have a button selected, you can change the label, give the button a unique id, attach a click event handler, and indicate in which states the component needs to appear. For a RadioButton you can additionally set the radiobutton group and the selected state. And for a simple container like the <mx:Application> tag, you can only set the page title.

In the Style section you can create a new skin or select an existing one for the component; or change the styling by choosing some kind of selector in the attached CSS file. Or you can change the styling by using the other styling properties and when you're satisfied with the result, use the Convert to CSS... button to add that particular styling to an external CSS file. When you click that button, you'll get a popup dialog window with some additional options as to where and how you want to add the CSS styling.

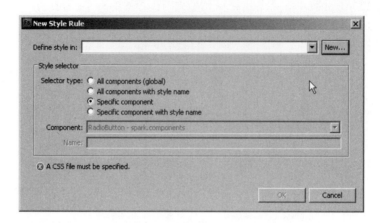

Figure 3-15. Adding a new style to an external CSS file using the design view

Figure 3-15 shows the options for adding the style attributes to a CSS file. You can either create a new CSS file or select an existing one, and you can choose the type of selector you want to use. This means you can opt for the global selector, a type selector, a class selector or a combination of these last two, depending on whether you want to reuse the style for other components or just want to apply it to this specific component.

Of course, the options in the Style section of the Properties panel depend heavily on the selected component. So, for example, when you select an application container, you can't change that many style attributes. And that brings us to the last part of this panel, namely the Layout section, where you'll find the common layout properties like x and y position, width, height, and Spark layout, to name a few. You'll also find the visual representation of the constraint-based layout (the left, top, right, bottom, horizontalCenter and verticalCenter properties) here, to facilitate setting these properties.

The handling of the DataGrid component has also been significantly improved. One of the more time-consuming tasks when creating a datagrid is defining the columns with all of their properties. In Flex Builder 3 you could use the design editor to drag and drop a datagrid component onto the stage (sometimes the application area is also referred to as a stage; the term is borrowed from Flash applications). But when you had to specify the actual columns for that grid, you still had to do it in the code, a tedious and repetitive process. A far better idea would be the ability to just specify some properties for the columns, such as width, dataField, and headerText, and have the code automatically generated. That would be a real time-saver in the development process. Well, in Flash Builder 4, you can right-click the DataGrid component and select the Configure Colums... option from the menu, as shown in Figure 3-16.

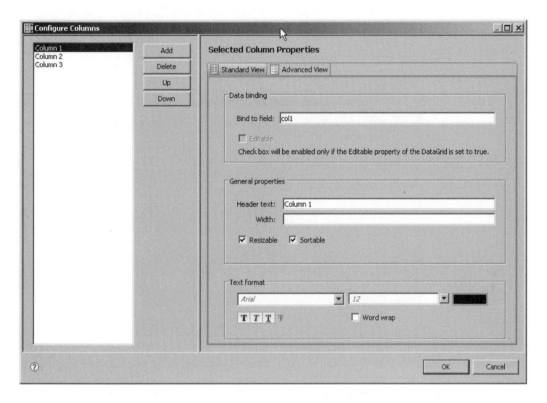

Figure 3-16. Configure datagrid columns through a popup dialog wizard.

The popup dialog that appears allows you to add, change, move, and remove columns from the `DataGrid` component that you've dragged onto the stage. When you select a specific column, you can easily use the dialog's input fields to update the property to which it is bound, change the column name that's depicted the header, or set a fixed width. You can even use checkboxes to indicate whether the column is resizable and sortable. All in all, it's a very simple and quick way to configure the columns for the datagrid in your application.

Generation of Detail Form

Now let's look at another great enhancement that's been made to the `DataGrid` component. A component like this is very often used in a design pattern called Master/Detail. This pattern handles situations where you have a list of limited data about a certain object, with a detailed form that is filled out with the proper data when an item in the list is selected. The form itself is able to update the data in the list that results from the creation, update or deletion of an object.

How does the new Flash Builder help you to tackle this? Now you can simply right-click the `DataGrid` component and select the `Generate Details Form…` option from the menu. There is a catch however: you need to have the datagrid show some data that comes back from a service call. This service call can be anything, ranging from a simple `HTTPService` to a real-time server push connection over RTMP (Real-Time Messaging Protocol) using the `DataService`. The best way to accomplish this is by using of the `Data/Services` panel and the drag-and-drop binding I'll explain later in this chapter.

Figure 3-17. Generating a form from a datagrid that is bound to the result of a service call

One of the options you can select in the popup dialog is Master-Detail, as you can see in Figure 3-17. With this option you can also choose to call an extra service when an item has been selected. You may wonder why you'd want to do that if you already have the item in the datagrid. When you have a list of hundreds of items and you're loading an entire updatable object per record, your application will take up a lot of unnecessary memory. In fact, the application may not perform at all, with the simplest tasks taking too long to be user-friendly. This is where the concept of Data Transfer Objects (DTO) kicks in. (DTOs are sometimes referred to as Value Objects (VO).

Normally in this kind of situation you'd create one DTO to fetch only the data that will actually be shown in the list and a second DTO for the full-blown object that may contain dozens of extra properties that may need to be updated. When you first load the data, you load only the limited DTOs in memory. Only when the user explicitly chooses a certain item do you fetch the extended data, with what I like to call a single fetch method. Well, this is exactly what it means when you choose to call another method when the master selection has changed.

But since we have only a very simple object to retrieve from the back end in this small example, I'll just choose to use the master record as the one to be updated in my detailed view. When you hit the Next button, another dialog appears that lets you choose which fields you actually want to display in the form and whether they are editable (see Figure 3-18).

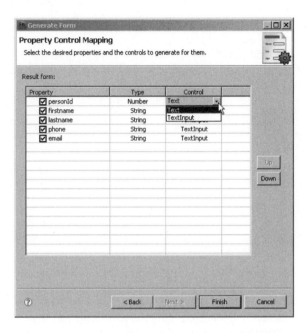

Figure 3-18. You can select which properties to show and which should be read-only

As you can see, it's very simple to change the `TextInput` field into a read-only `Text` field and to indicate which fields don't need to be shown by just clicking the appropriate checkbox. Just hit the `Finish` button and your form is created and even bound to the selected item in your `DataGrid` component. It's as simple as that. However, for the actual create, update, and delete actions you still need to do some work. This can also be accomplished quite easily using the features of the `Data/Services` panel, which I will explain in the next section.

Improved Back-End Connectivity

As I mentioned in the beginning of this chapter, Flash Builder is a tool for development. I've already explained some of the development features available, but I haven't yet talked about how to connect your Flex application to a particular back end. So let's dig into to that part of the IDE now.

Data/Services Panel

The `Data/Services` panel is new with Flash Builder 4, and it allows you to easily connect your application to an existing back end. It all starts with the definition of your Flex project. Remember that you can select different types of back-end technologies in the project's creation wizard. And in the latest version you can also change the back-end type later, as I discussed earlier in this chapter. The options in the `Data/Services` panel depend on the choice you make.

If you open the panel from the `Window` menu, you'll see the hyperlink option `Connect to Data/Service…`. Clicking on this link invokes a connection wizard that will guide you through the process of creating your back-end connection. In Figure 3-19 you can see *all* of the possibilities, because for our example `DataServices` project I didn't specify any back-end technology at all.

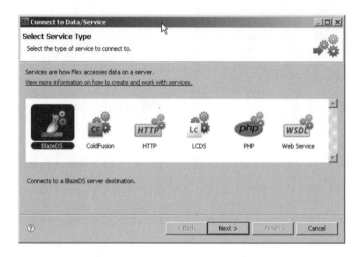

Figure 3-19. The Data/Services panel lets you connect to a whole range of back-end technologies.

The HTTP and Web Service options will always be available, no matter which technology you select. The other options normally depend on your project's properties settings. As an example, let's use the ColdFusion back end we created earlier. Select the ColdFusion option in this panel and hit Next. If you haven't yet set any specific back-end technology in the project settings, you'll get a message stating that you have to set the project's server type to ColdFusion (or whatever back-end technology you've indicated want to connect to) to be able to go any further with the wizard. If you choose to change the server type, the wizard will take you to the project's properties panel to allow you to specify the proper settings for that server type. Of course, if you've already specified the back-end technology for the project, this step will be skipped.

The next step in the wizard depends entirely on the technology you selected. For example, if you selected LCDS (LiveCycle Data Services), you'd get a list of all the destinations that have been defined in the LCDS configuration files. We're using ColdFusion, so we end up with the dialog that allows you to select a CFC (ColdFusion Component) that will act as the service API.

You can also select the name of the ActionScript service class as well as the package location for that class and the value objects that are used by this class. Those value objects in ColdFusion are also CFCs and will automatically be translated into ActionScript classes, so you get code completion and compile-time type checking. Once you've filled out the proper values on this screen, you again hit the Next button to go to the final step of the wizard and start introspection on the selected service class. For those who may never have heard about this process, this means Flash Builder will examine the class and find the public properties and methods with their types and return values. When these have been found for the entire class, they are displayed in the wizard to let you know what has been discovered and which services will be available for use in the project. In case of the PersonServices.cfc that I've selected from the ColdFusion server, the introspection will show the four remoting methods available: getAllPersons, createPerson, updatePerson and deletePerson. The remoting methods are the back-end methods that are made accessible by your application. After reviewing the methods that have been discovered, click Finish and the appropriate classes will be generated, as shown in Figure 3-20.

Figure 3-20. Using the Data/Services panel generates service and value object classes.

The classes that have been generated consist of two types: base classes and derived classes. The base classes (recognizable because their names start with an underscore) are always generated when you use the panel to reconnect to the back-end service class. You will want to perform this action whenever the service has been altered or additional services have been created. If you wish to make some local changes to the generated service class for your own convenience, you should do so in the derived class, which is just a subclass from the generated service class. But this class file is generated only when it does not exist. In many cases, this means it is generated only once. If you change your mind or don't need a service anymore for some reason, you can delete the generated classes as well by simply deleting the service in the Data/Services panel. Of course, you'll still have to delete the subclasses manually. It may be the case that you've changed them and still need them, which is why these ActionScript classes are not removed automatically.

As you can see in Figure 3-20, a folder called services is also generated. This folder contains a link to the service class on the server that has just been selected. This way, you can directly view the content of that file without having to search for it on the server. Of course, what you see here is the result of having selected a ColdFusion service class. For other types of back ends the result will differ slightly.

ZendAMF Integration

Now I've been talking about LiveCycle Data Services (and BlazeDS is quite similar) and ColdFusion, but Flash Builder 4 adds support for one more back-end technology that was disregarded in previous versions: PHP. In the past, to communicate with a simple PHP back end you often used the AMFPHP package with the gateway.php file as the link between your Flex application and the PHP service class. (See Chapter 1 for more information.) But with the new version of Flash Builder and its Data/Services panel, there is now, finally, some serious support for PHP services.

Don't get me wrong, I love LCDS for all its features. Unfortunately, the licensing costs for LCDS can be substantial, so companies demand open source products in order to cut development and deployment costs. Also, since PHP is quite common as the server technology in the cheapest hosting solutions, there is a larger market for developing Flex applications that run on PHP. Nevertheless, the most interesting and challenging projects will probably still use LCDS or ColdFusion because of their powerful features.

I discussed ZendAMF a little in the first chapter, but now I'm going to show you how easy it can be to use Flash Builder to talk to a PHP service class using the ZendAMF framework. You start out with a new project that has a PHP server type. The PHP application server needs to point to a directory, which could be, for example, the htdocs folder in a xampp installation. In the Data/Services panel, again you'll connect to a service, but this time it will be a PHP service class.

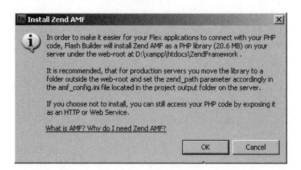

Figure 3-21. Flash Builder can automatically install the ZendAMF framework if required.

When you use a simple PHP application server package like xampp, the ZendAMF framework is not automatically present on that server. You can either choose to install it manually, as I've explained in the first chapter of this book, or you can connect to a service and let Flash Builder install the framework while going through the steps in the connection wizard (see Figure 3-21).

Bear in mind that the ZendAMF framework that is being installed on the PHP application server by Flash Builder 4 is the one that comes bundled with the install package. This is not necessarily the latest version of the framework. If it's not the latest version, a warning dialog will inform you that there is a newer version available and that you can download it from http://framework.zend.com.

Once the framework is installed, the connection wizard behaves exactly as I've explained before, with one exception. The PHP value object classes are not detected and therefore not generated. Instead, basic ActionScript Object classes are used as parameters rather than the typed remote class object. But in the Data/Services panel, you still get the services you can use to call your back-end functionality with the greatest of ease.

You can also manually configure the return type using the panel's features. You simply right-click on the proper method and choose Configure Return Type… from the menu. In the wizard that follows, you can either use a standard return type like Boolean, Date, Number, or you can choose to base the return type on the resulting value of the service call. If you choose the latter option, the method is actually called and the return value is displayed as a list of properties. From that you can opt to create a new object type or to update an existing one. If you choose to create a new return type, the ActionScript class file is placed inside the package folder that was specified for the value objects.

Drag-and-Drop Binding

Once you're connected to whatever back-end technology you've selected for your project, it becomes a lot easier to call the methods to retrieve, create, update, or delete data. Drag-and-drop binding of results from a service call is now an extension of the Data/Services panel. This means that working with the design panel gives you a lot more advantages than it did when creating projects with Flex Builder 3. There, design view was merely a tool for laying out your applications and components in a visual way, and it was useful for creating different view states. But, now, the design view has been opened up for some development features as well (see Figure 3-22).

Figure 3-22. The Data/Services panel shows the available data types and back end methods.

You can use these methods quite easily in your application by selecting one and dragging it onto a component. So, for example, you can take the getAllPersons method from the panel and drop it onto a DataGrid component. That does a couple of things to your application

- The service method is called.

- A call responder is created and configured to react to the result returned by the service.

- The result from the service is bound to the dataProvider property of the component.

And if you drop this service method onto a DataGrid component that has no columns defined, you'll see in the design view which columns will be shown, even though this concerns a runtime configuration. Well, in the past it was a runtime configuration; now when you use the connection wizard, the result type is configured automatically when the introspection detects it. Or you can specify the return type as I explained in the previous section. The resulting code will look like this:

DataServices ➤ DataServices.mxml

```
<?xml version="1.0" encoding="utf-8"?>
<s:Applicationxmlns:fx="http://ns.adobe.com/mxml/2009"
xmlns:s="library://ns.adobe.com/flex/spark"
xmlns:mx="library://ns.adobe.com/flex/halo"
xmlns:services="com.domain.project.services.*">
<fx:Script>
<![CDATA[
importmx.events.FlexEvent;
importmx.controls.Alert;

protected function dataGrid_creationCompleteHandler(event:FlexEvent):void {
getAllPersonsResult.token =personServices.getAllPersons();
    }
  ]]>
</fx:Script>

<fx:Declarations>
```

```
<s:CallResponder id="getAllPersonsResult"/>
<services:PersonServices id="personServices" showBusyCursor="true"
fault="Alert.show(event.fault.faultString + '\n' +
event.fault.faultDetail)" />
</fx:Declarations>

<mx:DataGrid x="10" y="10" id="dataGrid"
creationComplete="dataGrid_creationCompleteHandler(event)"
dataProvider="{getAllPersonsResult.lastResult}">
<mx:columns>
<mx:DataGridColumnheaderText="personId" dataField="personId"/>
<mx:DataGridColumnheaderText="firstname" dataField="firstname"/>
<mx:DataGridColumnheaderText="lastname" dataField="lastname"/>
<mx:DataGridColumnheaderText="phone" dataField="phone"/>
<mx:DataGridColumnheaderText="email" dataField="email"/>
</mx:columns>
</mx:DataGrid>
</s:Application>
```

The service method is called upon the `creationComplete` event of the `DataGrid` component, not when the application receives that event. Although this would mean that the call is triggered a little bit earlier in the application, I'm not a great fan of doing this, because in a lot of cases you have to call more than one service method upon initialization of your application. In my opinion, it's better to group them into a single method that is called when the application receives the `creationComplete` event. On the bright side, you do get default handling of the fault event and binding to the `dataProvider` property, which allows you to create a very basic application without actually writing a single line of code; just drag and drop components and services and you've got a working application.

Debugging

Now that you've created an application using all these great features of Flash Builder 4, the next part of the development process starts and you need to test your application. During these tests, it's very likely you'll encounter some kind of error. This can either be a bug in the code resulting in a runtime exception, or an error in the business logic of the application resulting in a miscalculation for example.

> *If you want to make use of breakpoints or any other form of debugging, you'll need to execute the code in debug mode, because only then are they taken into account.*

Conditional Breakpoints

The first thing you'll probably do is place a couple of breakpoints in your source code to stop the execution there, to investigate what happens in the process flow or to take a closer look at a part of the code. This kind of debugging has been around for quite some time in the previous versions of Flex Builder. Setting a breakpoint is not difficult at all. You have two options:

- Double-clicking the gray area next to the line where you want to stop the code execution.

- Right-clicking in the gray area next to the line where you want to stop the code execution and selecting `Toggle Breakpoint` from the menu.

In either case, you can see when a breakpoint has been set because there will be a blue dot next to the line number in the source code.

Now, what you are probably used to when working with Flex Builder 3 is that once the execution stops on a certain breakpoint, you can further examine the code and values for properties of variables using the Variables panel in the Flex Debug perspective. But sometimes this is not enough; sometimes you need a breakpoint only at a certain time within the execution. In Flex Builder 3 you could create a work-around by changing the code a little and adding an if statement so you'd have a specific line on which you could set the breakpoint you wanted. But when you had evaluated everything and had done enough debugging, you then needed to change the code back to what you were going to use in the release version of the application.

> *Changing code just for debugging purposes should be avoided as it can mask or introduce a bug, especially when in the face of memory problems.*

In Flash Builder 4, there is a solution specifically for this purpose. It's called **conditional breakpoints** and it allows you apply a certain condition to a specific breakpoint. Now, how exactly do you apply such a condition to a breakpoint? First of all, you set a breakpoint at a certain line of ActionScript code. This code can also be inline ActionScript code in any MXML file—as part of an event handler, for example. Next, you right-click the blue dot and select the Breakpoint Properties… option from the menu. This action opens up a properties dialog where you attach different conditions to the breakpoint (see Figure 3-23).

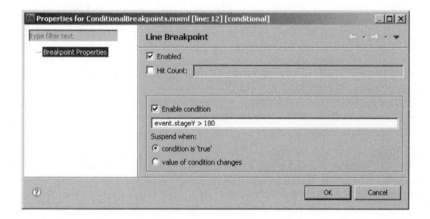

Figure 3-23. Adding conditions to breakpoints

In the example code in Flex4 ➤ ConditionalBreakpoints.mxml, there is an image of some foggy mountains. When you move the mouse over the image, the coordinates are displayed on top of the image. Now assume I want to check some values in the application when the Y position of the mouse cursor is past the 180-pixel line in the vertical (which is, in this case, more or less where the mountains become more visible). To enable a breakpoint only in that specific circumstance, the breakpoint properties panel adds the condition event.stageY> 180 to the breakpoint in the mouseMove event handler. Notice that you can also set a condition to the number of times the event has been called by setting a value in the Hit count property.

When you execute the application in debug mode and you move the mouse cursor around over the image, nothing happens until the Y position of the mouse cursor exceeds 180. At that point, execution stops and you are taken to the debug perspective where, for example, you can examine the values in other variables.

Changing Values at Runtime

Of course, debugging doesn't stop there. Once you have found what's wrong with the code, you need to alter it and debug it again. In Flex Builder 3, you had to stop the current debug session, alter the code, and start up a new debug session to see if your changes worked and the issue was resolved. Although effective, this is not a very efficient way of going through the debugging process.

In Flash Builder 4, you can now change some values during the debug process and continue debugging, without having to recompile and restart the application. And to make things even easier, changing these values has been made as simple as can be. When encountering a breakpoint, you go to the Variables panel in the Flex Debug perspective. There you select the property or variable you want to change and you click the Value column in the panel for the selected property. The value then becomes editable and you can change it to whatever you like. When you execute the next line of code, the changes are automatically applied, and the new value is applied to any assignment or calculation that is executing. It couldn't be simpler—and that's exactly what an IDE should do for you: make life easier.

Network Monitor

Nearly all Flex applications will at some point connect to some kind of back end, such as Java, ColdFusion, or PHP. But a back end can also be reached through a simple HTTP service or a web service. The way the data is transferred between the back end and your Flex application depends on the technology you use for this communication. In Flex Builder 3, you had very little insight into what actually happens during this communication. You could debug your back end by examining some log files or by integrating the back end into your Flex Builder IDE. In that case, you could start the server from within the IDE and debug the back end code with breakpoints, and watch expressions as well. On the front end, you could use the <mx:TraceTarget/> tag anywhere within your MXML code, and when you ran the application in debug mode, the Console window would show the messages sent to the back end, along with their content. In this way, you could figure out whether the channel was available and connected properly, and which content is sent to the server. But besides a confirmation that the message was sent successfully, that's basically all you knew.

Flash Builder 4 introduces the Network Monitor, a tool you can use to examine the SOAP, AMF, Remote Object, XML, and HTTP traffic that flows between your Flex application and its data services. To use this tool, you simply select Window ➤ Network Monitor from the application's menu bar. To begin monitoring your application, click the Enable Network Monitor icon on the Network Monitor toolbar, then run the debug version of the application as you would normally. As you interact with your application, the Network Monitor captures and stores all calls to remote services in chronological order. At any time, you can switch back to the Network Monitor view to see the results of each call.

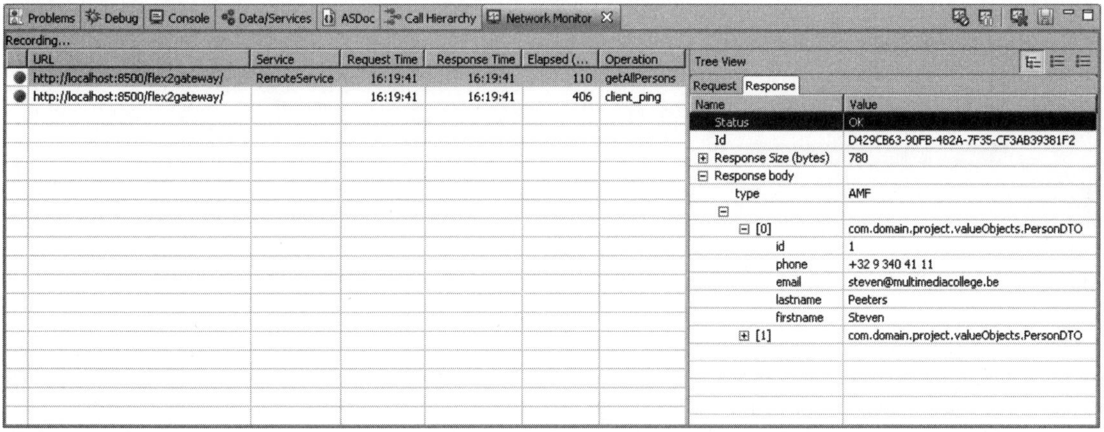

Figure 3-24. The `Network Monitor` shows the response for each back-end call made since the start of the monitoring.

When the monitoring is active, you'll find the time of the request, the requesting service, the operation and URL (only if a URL was used, of course), the time of the response and the elapsed time, as you can see in Figure 3-24. This means you can use this tool to investigate communication *bottlenecks*—situations where the execution of the code runs into certain problems that cause your application to slow down and become, therefore, less user-friendly (because you can't let the user wait too long before sending a response). Typical bottlenecks result from network latency, server memory problems, and the client computer not being robust enough for the task.

In the `Network Monitor` panel you can examine the entire back-end call, including the response and even the data that is being sent to see what exactly you're getting from the server. You can also choose whether to analyze the information while the application is running or to save the content of this panel in an XML file so you can examine it later. This is also useful for conveying information to your colleagues about what is going on or to get their help in interpreting the numbers when looking for a specific problem. All in all, it's a great tool to have in your tool box and it will help you to produce better code quality before putting your application online.

Call Hierarchy View

During your career as a developer, you have probably searched through a lot of source files looking for a certain method to find out where it is used. Usually you'd do this by either manually skimming through the files, by using the `Outline` view in Flash Builder, or by simply using the `Find in Files` dialog. The `Call Hierarchy` view gives you a tool to accomplish this task very easily. It can also help you to analyze your code and estimate the impact of code changes. It can even find out if the method you're investigating is actually *dead code* or not. For those of you who may not be familiar with the term, *dead code* means that the code is residing in the project's source files, but it is never used. Thus, it only contributes to the size of the application and it should be removed (or perhaps commented out if the code may still be needed in the future if, for example, a feature has to be disabled for a certain release).

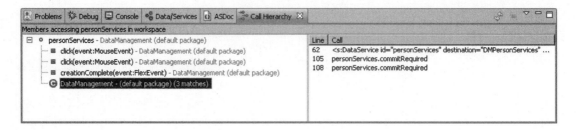

Figure 3-25. The Call Hierarchy view displays the usage of a method or variable.

To use the Call Hierarchy view, you simply select a variable or method in the code and choose Navigate ➤ Open Call Hierarchy. You can also use the keyboard shortcut Ctrl+Alt+H. The view will then be shown as in Figure 3-25, populated with the methods that use the method or property you have selected.

Within the view, you can double-click on a tree node to open and select the reference to the called method or property. In the right-hand section of the panel, you can preview the code where the reference is actually used as well. So, in the example above, the DataService instance with the name personServices is used three times in the code: once as the definition and twice in a binding statement with the commitRequired property. Double-clicking on one of these lines takes you directly to that line of code in the source file. This allows you to further investigate the use of the selected property or method in order to create a better assessment of the impact of a certain change.

The Call Hierarchy panel is not only a tool to search for dead code or for function calls that need to change because you have to add an extra parameter, for example. It is also a tool that allows you to better prepare yourself to make the change, by letting you know how many instances there are in the code, as well assess as the impact on the surrounding code, by providing you with click-through navigation on the occurrences.

Summary

In this chapter I've explained how Flash Builder 4 has evolved from Flex Builder 3 and has some new and improved tricks up its sleeve. The new features of the design editor ease the process of connecting your application to a back end, while the improved debugging capabilities and the new monitoring tools can help you create better, faster, and more reliable applications. All of the new features and tools will help you develop your applications faster, because in one way or another they make your life as a developer a lot easier.

In the next chapter I will be taking a close look at Flash Catalyst. You'll see how this product can make the life of an interaction designer much easier and, in some cases, the life of a developer as well.

Chapter 4

Flash Catalyst: bridging the gap

Maybe you've heard about this product a long time ago, as Adobe has been showing demonstration versions of this product for a couple of years now. Back then it was still code named Thermo and on every Adobe event it surfaced in one presentation or another. Even though it was only a very limited demo version, my curiosity was triggered. I had to wait a long time before any serious version was publicly available, but now it has finally arrived.

This chapter will give you an overview of the basic features in Flash Catalyst, because in the next chapter I'm going to cover the different kinds of workflows for different types of applications using Flash Catalyst in most cases. Knowing and understanding the features will help you to understand why I choose that specific type of workflow.

Because most parts of the Flash Catalyst application interface work together and act a as part of a whole, I'm going to regularly refer to later sections in this chapter to keep this chapter from becoming very confusing and to avoid having to repeat certain functionalities.

Introduction to Flash Catalyst

As a developer, have you ever been in a situation where you had a design handed to you by the designer in a file format like Photoshop or Illustrator? What was the first thing you did then? Maybe you took a deep breath? Started cursing because at first glance the design seemed like a lot of work or maybe even impossible? Or maybe you were just plain confused because you didn't know what to do with it? I'm not trying to dish on designer (myself being a developer for the main part), but sometimes they do not take the limitations of the technology into account (or maybe they are just not aware of the limitations) when designing applications. And even when they do, what should a developer do with such a file? Cut it into pieces, save them as images and use those images in the Flex application? Are you supposed to create all the CSS to try to mimic the design?

There is obviously a gap between a designer and a developer: a designer talks in pixels, while a developer speaks the language of code, which is an all togethercompletely different language. Or is it? I've already covered the basics of the new Flex 4 SDK, where there's a whole new sublanguage called Flash XML Graphics (FXG). These new tags and the new way of creating graphical representations of your components provide in part a solution to this problem. I explicitly say "in part" because it is possible to do some really crazy stuff using FXG directly in your Flex application by coding it. But it takes a whole lot of time and effort to create really wonderful designs in this way. You as a developer would try to re-create the given design to the best of your abilities and that works out pretty good. But after a while the designer comes back, looks at what you've created and says: "hmm, that label is just one pixel too far to the right" or something like that. OK, so this may be a little bit exaggerated, but it's just that they have worked out a design and expect it to look exactly as they intended it. These situations are a thing of the past now, because Flash Catalyst is exactly the product that is tackling this problem.

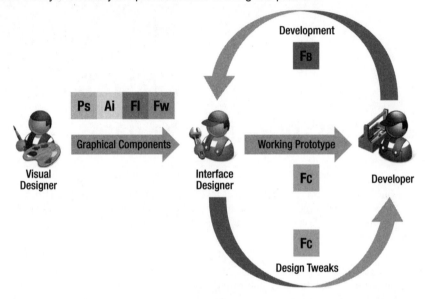

Figure 4-1: The workflow with an interaction designer between the developer and designer.

In the past there was no real interaction between a designer and an interaction designer. The designer created drawings that would kind of act as screenshots before the actual application was built. The interaction designer then defined the kind of interaction that would be necessary to make the application as user friendly as possible. But now, as you can see in Figure 4-1, Flash Catalyst is bringing a new level of interaction to the entire project workflow. So let me walk you through the basic features of this new product.

Interface overview

The first thing worth noticing about the product is the welcome screen. Here you have the option of creating a new project from scratch, using the components available in the interface. Or you can also opt for using an existing design in Adobe Illustrator, Adobe Photoshop or an FXG file. This last one can be achieved by exporting your design from within the other Adobe products in that specific file format. But I'll be covering this later on in this chapter. It is worth mentioning that the FXG format, being essentially an XML structure, can be created by any technology, so technically speaking, you could write it yourself. Or maybe we can expect other tools from other vendors to support the FXG export format at some point in the future as well.

In the interface you have some basic panels and sections available, as you can see in Figure 4-2.

- The artboard
- The Pages/States panel

- The Layers panel
- The Wireframe Components panel
- The Library Panel
- The HUD (Heads-Up Display)
- The Interactions panel
- The Properties panel

    - The Common section
    - The Component section
    - The Appearance section
    - The Filters section

- The Design-Time Data panel
- The Timelines panel

I'm only going to cover the basics for all of these panels in this chapter. Please note that this is not a specific book about using Flash Catalyst, so I'm not going to cover all the features in this product. I can recommend "Foundation Flash Catalyst" by Greg Goralski and LordAlex Leon (ISBN 978-1430228622) if you want to dig into the nitty-gritty details of Flash Catalyst.

However, you do need some understanding of how the product works and what the possibilities and limitations are in order to better understand why some workflows are the way they are.

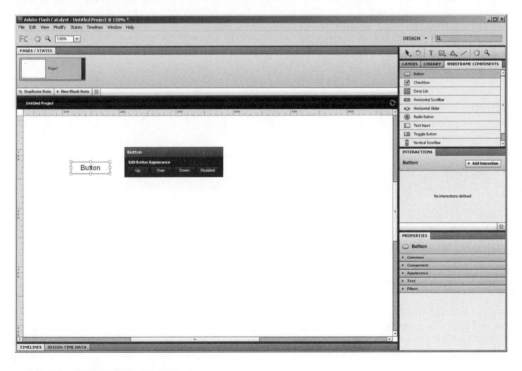

Figure 4-2: The Flash Catalyst interface.

The artboard

The biggest panel in the interface is the one where all the "magic" is going to be made visible. This panel doesn't really have a specific name, but it is referred to as the **artboard**. This is the official term that is borrowed from the terminology in Adobe Illustrator. In that tool, the artboard is the area in which you draw the design for your application. But in Flash Catalyst the meaning of this area is more similar to the stage in Flash Professional. You can place components on the artboard or outside of the application area. They are still there, but just not visible. Now why would you want to place a component in the application if it is not visible? Well, for one, in that case it is already initialized and ready for use, which could be a performance optimization, because you don't need to initialize it anymore when you actually need it. You just place it somewhere in the visible area of the application then. Another reason could be that you want the component to make an appearance from one of the sides onto the artboard using some kind of sliding animation. Then it appears to be coming out of the blue into your application.

In Flash Catalyst the artboard is exactly the same: it is your application area. So here you can also play with the concepts of letting components animate into view, just as you would in any other Flash application. Or you just use it to place your components on it to create the visual representation or layout for your application. Creating or changing layouts can be done by using the drag and drop functionality of the basic wireframe components or by importing an external structured design file. Both of these options will be covered after I've explained the interface.

The Pages/States panel

The Pages/States panel will be one of the panels you'll be using the most. This panel will provide the resulting Flex application with the necessary view states. So for example, when you select a standard button component, you will get the 4 possible states: Up, Over, Down and Disabled. In Figure 4-3 you can see how this is represented for such a button component. Each state will have its specific color to better differentiate between the states on the one hand. But on the other hand, these colors will also be used in the Timelines panel, which I will discuss later in this chapter.

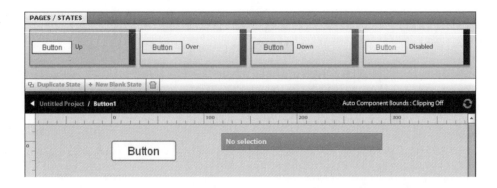

Figure 4-3: The Pages/States panel represents the states for a component or container.

Now how do you use this panel? With a standard button component, which I've conveniently dragged onto the artboard here to demonstrate my explanation, you are getting several states *out of the box.* That means that the Flex component already contains these view states in its default behavior. But what about the application or custom components? Of course you can create your own view states, just as you can do in Flex. Only now, these view states are represented visually, to make it more attractive and comprehensible. To add such a view state to your application you have a couple of options.

Remember when I talked about the view states having an inheritance structure in the Flex SDK chapter? If you want to base a certain view state on an existing one, you can select it in the panel and click on the button Duplicate State. Or you can right-click a state and select Duplicate State from the popup menu. This will **duplicate the layout completely** in the new state so you can start modifying it until you reach the desired result. The consequence of using this duplication is that when you change something in the original state, it will not automatically be reflected in the duplicated state as well. There is a solution for this. If you select the component that you have changed in the base state, then you can right-click on it and select Make Same in All Other States from the popup menu. This will share the changes with all the states that have the component already in them. So it does not automatically add the component to all states.

However, if it's a completely new component and you want it in certain other states or even in all of the other states, you can choose the option from the menu to also put it in a specific state or in all states by selecting the Share To State submenu and then choosing All States or the specific state name you want to share it on. Only the states that don't yet have that specific component will be selectable in the menu. Of course you can also remove the component from a particular state by using the Remove From State submenu in the right-click popup menu on the component. Only the states that contain this component will be selectable. The others will be grayed out.

A second option would be to create a completely different state. You can use this feature to create a so called *page*. Pages are an all together different concept than view states. You can use a view state when you are displaying the same data, but from a different perspective, with some extra fields or without certain fields. However, when you are creating a view that is basically something completely different, in Flex you would use an <mx:ViewStack> component in combination with some kind of navigation container. To actually create such a state you have again two options. The first one is to click on the New Blank State button at the bottom of the Pages/States panel. The second way of adding such a blank state is to right-click anywhere within the panel area (even on an existing state or page) and select New Blank State from the popup menu. Both options will add a new page at the end of the list of existing pages. In this new page you can then start to create the layout and content for that specific state.

Of course, since we're all just human, we all make mistakes and sometimes you have to undo stuff that you've created earlier. In code it is quite simple because you just have to delete the lines you've written. In most visual applications, you can also select an item and hit the delete key to remove it. In Flash Catalyst this works exactly the same. Well, at least for the artboard, where you can just select a component and delete it using the delete key on your keyboard. However in the Pages/States panel, you do not have the option of using your keyboard. To remove a specific state you have to right-click it and choose Delete State from the popup menu. This will immediately remove the state or page from the panel, without any confirmation message. If you select this by mistake or you have altered some other property within a certain state or page you can always use the undo option from the application menu or use the keyboard shortcut to revert the changes that you've made.

The Layers panel

If you are a designer then the Layers panel probably looks quite familiar to you if you've been working with other Adobe products like Photoshop, Illustrator or Fireworks. It is even not all that different from how the layers are depicted and created in Flash Professional. So if you're familiar with at least one of these products, you're not going to be in for a shock.

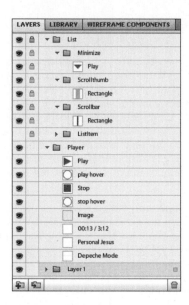

Figure 4-4: The Layers panel shows the structure of the design.

As you can see in Figure 4-4 **the layers panel basically contains the structure of your layout components**. This is exactly the same as you'd expect from an Adobe product that works with design elements. There are separate layers for the different elements and you can group one or more layers in folders. And of course a group folder can contain both layers and other group folders, so nesting of groups is supported as well. I would advise you to actually make use of these group folders as much as possible. The reason for that is that in a decent application you'll have several dozens of layers. Some of them may belong together as they are part of one component or a window that can be viewed as a separate component in the application. If you do not structure these layers, the design can become quite incomprehensive if you hand it out to another colleague to work with it, because it is not clear at all which items belong together. Structuring the layers into groups also makes it easier to get an overview of what's inside the design because at the top level of your layer structure you have fewer items.

The Layers panel also has an order in the structure. In a design components are going to be placed on top of each other. The layers that contain the items that need to be on top of other items have to be placed above the bottom items. That means that the first layer in the list will contain the top most components in the design. If you have to switch the position of one or more layers, you can just select them and drag them to the proper position. The position where they will be dropped is indicated by a thick marker between layers, above the top layer or underneath the bottom layer. You can also move layers to other group folders and even move group folders to other layer groups by using the drag and drop feature of this panel.

At the bottom of the Layers panel you have a couple of buttons to work with the layer structure. **For creating a new layer you click on the button that is completely on the left.** The layer will be placed at the top of the list, meaning it will be the top most component. The new layer will automatically be depicted as a folder. Any components that you add to that layer will be placed inside of their own layer contained in that group folder. As I've already mentioned, a group folder cannot only contain layers but also other group folders. Since creating a new layer will place the layer automatically at the top of the list and at the root level of the layer structure, creating a sublayer looks like it's going to have to have a work-around of creating that layer and then dragging it into the desired group folder. That's one way of doing things, but I wouldn't recommend it because it is just the long way around since next to the button for creating layers there's another button. This one will **create a sublayer in the selected folder**. Again, the new sublayer will be placed completely at the top, but this time it is the top of the group folder you have selected. The same rules apply to the new sublayer, so you can drag and drop it to another location as well if you've made a mistake. **The button that is located completely on the right at the bottom of the panel is to remove layers or groups from the** Layers **panel.** When you click on this button the selected layer(s) will be deleted. Again this is done without asking for a confirmation so be careful when using this feature.

Adding a layer can also be done from within the Layers panel by right-clicking anywhere in the panel (even on a certain layer) and selecting Add New Layer from the popup menu. You can also choose the Add New Sublayer from this menu and then a new sublayer will be added to the selected layer.Only when you specifically right-click on a layer you'll get the option to delete that layer in the popup menu. So either using the buttons or the right-click popup menus are valid options for working with layers.

On the left side of this panel you see **two columns with icons** in them. **The left most column contains an indication whether or not the layer is visible** in the design that is currently shown in the artboard area. You can simply click in this column next to a specific layer to make it visible or invisible depending on the current state. When you click in this visibility column next to a group folder all the layers in this group will be set visible or invisible. However, the visibility property for the individual layers is not touched so when you have a couple of sublayers that are visible and others that are not visible, the invisible ones will not automatically be turned visible when you turn on the entire group. The icons next to the sublayers will just be grayed out when the group is turned invisible.**The second column indicates whether or not the layer is locked.**Locking a layer can be done by clicking in this column next to a layer. When a layer is locked, you cannot change anything on it anymore. You cannot even move the layer from its current position in the panel. You can also lock an entire group of layers by clicking in the second column next to the group that the layers belong to. A lock icon will appear next to all of the sublayers when locking a group folder. However, if you had a locked sublayer inside the group before you locked them all, that sublayer will stay locked when you unlock the entire group.

> *I would strongly advise you to use locking on layers you consider to be finished to avoid changing any properties by accident. A wrong selection in this panel can have some undesired changes in sublayers you didn't want to alter.*

The Library panel

Next to the Layers panel you have the Library panel available. This panel contains an overview of your custom components and images that you have been using in the current project. If you are using an external library with custom components, the components in that library will also show up in this panel.

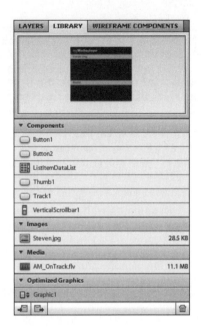

Figure 4-5: The Library panel showing the application components.

The panel is divided into 5 sections: a preview section, Optimized Graphics, Custom Components, Images and Media. The order in which these sections appear in this panel depends on the moment you're adding a section because of an asset import or creation of a custom component.The first section just displays a preview of the component or image that you have selected in the other two sections. The Custom Components section contains any custom components that you may have in your application. That means that when you select a wireframe component (which I'll discuss next) and put it onto the artboard, that component will show up in a new layer in the Layers panel, but it does not show up in the Library panel. This is because it is just a default component. But as soon as you start changing some properties on that default component, you're actually creating a custom component and that will actually be shown in the first section of this panel. When I talk about changing properties on components, that doesn't have to be something exotic. You can for instance simply change the stroke color for the outside border of a component and it will be converted into a custom component.

Another way of getting a component to show up in this panel is to manually create a custom component. How do you do that? That's quite simple. You can for example just draw a rectangle using the tools in the toolbar which you can see in Figure 4-6. When you have drawn that rectangle in the artboard area you can right-click it and select any option in the Convert Artwork To Component submenu that appears in the popup menu. You can also use the Heads-Up Display (HUD) to perform a lot of the tasks. I'll be covering the HUD and its possibilities later on in this chapter. Just remember that the names of the custom components in the Library panel are also the names of the components in the source code. That means that you will end up with the same component names when you import the Flash Catalyst project into Flash Builder.

Figure 4-6: The toolbar in Flash Catalyst.

A third way of getting a component registered in this panel is to use an external graphic like for example an Illustrator or Photoshop asset. You copy the original asset and paste it into Flash Catalyst. Since the copy/paste functionality between Adobe design tools and Flash Catalyst is fully supported, you'll end up with exactly the same graphic in Flash Catalyst, with all of its subcomponents. Now this is an ordinary graphic which is not really optimized for a Flex application. You can choose to optimize it by selecting the Optimize Vector Graphic option from the right-click menu.Optimized graphics in Flash Catalyst are basically external files that have all the MXML graphic information associated with them. So all of the vector information, all of the stroke information, all the path data, all the filters and the fill patterns will all be represented in the MXML language. All of these MXML graphics statements will then be saved into an external FXG file. The Flex compiler knows this FXG language and will optimize those types of files as a kind of external SWF assets for your application. You can check for the existence of these separate source files by taking your project into Code view, because in code view you can see the generated code and browse through the project's directory structure.Code view can be started by selected it from the combobox that is located at the top of the Flash Catalyst application. Normally this combobox is set to Design view, but you can alter it to switch to the Code view. Optimized graphics are automatically placed in an assets/graphics folder in the base src folder.

In the Media section of this panel, you'll find any video or audio files that you may have imported. You'll be using this import functionality to add movie clips (FLV or F4V) or MP3 files to your application. I'll be talking a bit more about this in the unit about the Interactions panel later on in this chapter.

Now there is also the Images section in the Library panel. This section contains any imported images you may have within your project. To import an image into your project, you have to navigate to the File menu in the applications menu bar and the select the Image... option from the Import submenu. This will enable you to import a GIF, PNG of JPG file format into the Library panel.

Once you have a component registered in the Library panel you can use this component just as if it were a standard wireframe component. That means that you can simply drag it onto the arboard to use it in your application or in of the other custom components.

Using component libraries

Once you have a complete set of library components, you will probably want to share them with other developers in your company because maybe you made these components to be the standard components in all of the business applications your company will be making. In that case I would recommend putting them in an external library. Now, how do you make such a library from within Flash Catalyst? You just have to right-click in the panel and select Export Library package... from the popup menu. This will save your components in an external FXPL file. This file type can be compared with Flash library files (SWCs) in the sense that they don't compile into an application but just hold a bunch of components. From that same popup menu you can import such a library package into the project. Or you can use the Import submenu from the applications File menu to do the same thing. Importing a library package recreates the entire library panel structure with all of its components in the proper sections. From that point on you can use those components as if they are a part of the current project.

Using an external library component in your application will result in the usage of a skin class as you can see in the code excerpt below, which is taken from the Flash Catalyst project in Code view.

Excerpt from FC_LibraryPanel.fxp

```
<fx:DesignLayerd:userLabel="Layer 1">
  <s:Button label="Button"skinClass="components.Button1"
            x="34" y="29" id="button1" includeIn="Page2"/>
  <s:List includeIn="Page1"skinClass="components.DataList1"
          x="179" y="112" id="list1">
          <s:ArrayCollection>
      <fx:String>Text 1</fx:String>
    </s:ArrayCollection>
  </s:List>
</fx:DesignLayer>
```

The usage of these skin classes is completely the same as using item renderers, for example. That means that the fully qualified class names are put as the value for the skinClass property for a certain component. When importing a library package, the library is not left as an external file which is loaded at runtime or simply compiled into the application. With the import action Flash Catalyst is actually copying all of the components into your own application's Library panel, resulting in the same project structure as if you were creating all of these components in the current project.

But the great feature about creating these library projects is the fact that you can create a whole bunch of components, put them in a library package and hand that package over to a Flex developer. He can just import that library project into Flash Builder and start using those components with the same pixel perfect positioning and all of the states and behaviors that you have created using Flash Catalyst.Importing a Flash Catalyst library project into Flash Builder can be done by selecting the Import Flex Project (FXP) from the File menu and selecting the FXPL file in the popup dialog. This action will automatically create a Flex library project. And such a library can then be used either within another Flex project or as a runtime shared library (RSL) to make use of the caching mechanism and to make the result SWF file somewhat smaller.

The Wireframe Components panel

A third panel that's on the same level as the previous two is the Wireframe Components panel. This panel contains the basic components that are shipped with Flash Catalyst by default. The usage of this panel is very simple, so I can be rather brief in my explanation of this panel.

As you can see in Figure 4-7 there are not that many basic components for you to use *out of the box*. With buttons, text input fields and a data list you can create some very basic applications from scratch or add some extra components to an already existing design. But, as I've explained in the previous section, as soon as you start altering some of the properties on those basic components, you are actually creating custom components. And these components will then again show up in the Library panel.

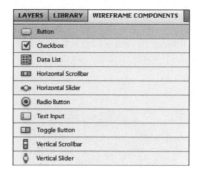

Figure 4-7: The Wireframe Components panel only contains some basic components.

Now, how do you use the components from this panel? There are two ways of doing that. The first one is the most intuitive one in my opinion: you simply **select the desired component and drag it onto the artboard**. This can be in the visible area or next to it to put it on the artboard and prepare it for some kind of appearance effect like a sliding animation for example. The second way of adding wireframe components to the application is to **select the component and choose** Insert Component **from the right-click popup menu**. This will automatically place the component in the center of the visible part of the artboard. That means that you can zoom in or out, use the artboard's horizontal and vertical scrollbars to get the component in the approximate position using this right-click menu.

When you insert the wireframe Data List component, a standard list of design-time data is automatically added for you. This helps you identify it as a list component on the one hand, but on the other hand it also allows you to specify the actual data that needs to be inside when running the resulting Flex application. Of course, if you do this in Flash Catalyst that data will always be a fixed set. Changing the data for the Data List component will be discussed later on in this chapter when I'll cover the Design-Time Data panel.

As soon as you double click on a wireframe component to edit some states or properties, that component is automatically converted into a custom component even though you haven't yet changed anything. Therefore, it will also show up in the Library *panel.*

The HUD

The Heads-Up Display or HUD is one of the most important interface components in Flash Catalyst. At the same time it is also one of the most dynamic components and therefore a little bit complex to explain, so I'll have to use a lot of examples to do so.

In its normal form, when no component is selected, the HUD is minimized, semi-transparent and contains the text No Selection to indicate you can't really do anything with it at the moment. The whole "magic" of this component starts when you select different kinds of components. So let me start with the wireframe components. If you select a simple control like a slider or a text input component the HUD will simple display in its header what type of component you have selected and it contains a small button which says Edit Parts. When you click on that button, that's basically the same as double clicking the component itself, you will be taken into the component to further drill down in its structure. Then you can select the various parts of the component to change some of the properties.

When you select a graphic like a rectangle or the thumb within a scrollbar component the HUD changes its appearance and asks you to Convert Artwork To *Component* Part, where *Component* is to be replaced with the type of the selected component. This is done using a dropdown list that indicates which parts are required for the specified component and which ones are optional. So for example, if you take a scrollbar component, the thumb (which is the thing that moves as you scroll) and the track are both required parts for the component. However, the up and down buttons are completely optional, as you can see in Figure 4-8.

Figure 4-8: The HUD displays which component parts are required and which ones are not.

Of course there are some wireframe components that are somewhat more complex in their behavior. I'm thinking about a `Radio Button`, `Checkbox` or an ordinary `Button` control, because all of these have basic view state behavior with their `up`, `over`, `down` and `disabled` states. When you double click on one of these components, you'll go into them, which means that the artboard will be blurred and disabled while you're getting to see the different view states for the selected component. Again, you can start editing the view state properties and all of the component's transitions if you like, but then you're getting a custom component again.

When you have selected vector based artwork like the shape of the button, you can also use the HUD to optimize the vector graphics. As explained before, this will create an FXG file that will be used as the skin file for the selected component. For the default wireframe button, the resulting FXG code will look like this:

```
<?xml version='1.0' encoding='UTF-8'?>
<Graphic xmlns:fc="http://ns.adobe.com/flashcatalyst/2009"
         xmlns:d="http://ns.adobe.com/fxg/2008/dt"
         xmlns="http://ns.adobe.com/fxg/2008" version="1.0">
  <Rect x="0.5" y="0.5" height="22" radiusX="2" radiusY="2" width="69">
    <fill>
      <SolidColor color="#EBF4FF"/>
    </fill>
    <stroke>
      <SolidColorStroke color="#5380D0" weight="1"/>
    </stroke>
  </Rect>
</Graphic>
```

Editing the view states for such components can be done by double clicking the component and going to the specific state you want to alter. But there's another, quicker way of accomplishing the same task and that is by selecting the component in the application and using the HUD to go directly into the component and into the specific state. You can do this just by clicking on one of the Up, Over, Down and Disabled buttons that appear in the HUD.

Figure 4-9: The HUD allows you to go directly to a specific state within a component.

Now, that all works for the wireframe components. But naturally, there are still some other component types left for me to cover. Just think about the toolbar that allows you to draw your own components from scratch. Maybe you want a triangular component to act as a certain type of array, or maybe you want a star-shaped "New" graphic in your application. For this purpose you can use the toolbar which you can find in the top right corner of the application. I've already talked a bit about it when I discussed the Library panel, so I shouldn't really have to go into much detail here. But selecting such a component gives you the option to optimize the vector graphic if you want to. But the HUD also gives you the option to convert the artwork to a component as you can see in Figure 4-10.

Figure 4-10: The HUD allows you to turn artwork into a range of components.

Of course not all possible component conversions will make sense, but you could make such a star become a Button component for example. Then you have started from a vector graphic, added some text and turned it into a usable, working Flex component. And the great part is that you're not only limited to using it in Flash Catalyst, because when you take the project into Flash Builder, the component is also at your disposal to be used in other components that you might be creating using only Flash Builder.

Since imported assets from other Adobe design products like Photoshop, Illustrator or Fireworks are basically the same as the vector graphics you drew earlier in this section, they are treated the same in Flash Catalyst.That means that imported assets can easily be converted into real working components by simply selecting them and using the HUD's conversion options. I will discuss in detail the import of external assets later on in this chapter.

The Interactions panel

What can you find in this panel? It becomes clear when you look at Figure 4-11 that in this panel you can find the event handlers for the selected component in the application. It also shows that this panel works across view states and pages to show you all the actions attached without any limitations as to when the component is shown or not.

Figure 4-11: The `Interactions` panel defines the event handlers for a component.

When you click on a certain component in a specific page or state you can add an interaction by clicking on the `Add Interaction` button in this panel. A popup dialog will appear on the panel allowing you to specify the necessary definitions for the interaction. **The first input field is a combobox containing the available events to which you want your component to react.** The items in this list depend on which component you are adding an interaction for. So for example, you have the `change`, `mouseDown`, `mouseUp`, `rollover` and `rollout` events for a `Data List` component, but you have a `click` event instead of the change event for a `Button` component. A `TextInput` component gets an additional `enter`, `focusIn` and `focusOut` events on top of the ones that are available for a `Button`.

The second input field is again a combobox, but this time it contains a list of possible actions you want to perform when the selected event occurs. Actions can range from going to another page or state, to playing a movie clip or opening another web page in an external browser window. You can even perform a series of actions upon the same event. To do so, just like in the example you can find in the FC_Interactions.fxg file in the projects that accompany this book, you can choose to repeat the `Add Interaction` action for the same event. Another option would be to select the `Play Action Sequence` item in the second input field. Action sequences are edited in the `Timelines` panel, which I'll discuss later in this chapter.

The next couple of fields depend on what action you choose in the second combobox. That means that if you choose `Go To URL`, as I've done in the example you see in Figure 4-12, the third field will be a text input field in which you can place the URL and you'll get a fourth field as well to indicate where you want the URL to load:

- In the current window
- In a new window
- In the parent window
- In the top window

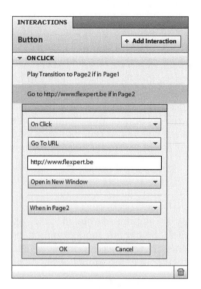

Figure 4-12: The Add Interaction dialog for a Go To URL action.

If you choose Play Transition To State, you're going to get a combobox with all the possible states. Even the current state you're on will be available, because remember I said that this panel is not state specific? That's why you see all of the states or pages here. Going to another state or page will happen instantaneously. So there is no smooth transition, let alone a nice 3D effect of some sorts. However, in Flash Catalyst you can actually add these kinds of effects, but then you're going to have to use the Timelines panel, which we'll take a closer look later in this chapter

Now, you can also use this Interactions panel to play, pause and stop a video file. But before you can actually do this, you'll need to add a video component. If you're used to working with Flash Professional, you may be looking for some kind of FLVPlayback component to add the video to your application. But if you look in the Wireframe Components panel you will not find such a component. So how exactly do you create a video component in Flash Catalyst? In this case you have to go to the File application menu and choose the Video/Sound File… option in the Import submenu. That will let you browse for an MP3, FLV or F4V file to import. Once the file is imported, it is put in the artboard area and you'll also find another layer has been added to the Layers panel. In the Library panel there's also a change because now a subsection Media has been added as well. This section contains the video component you've just imported. Now, if you would like this video to play as soon as the application is shown, you just have to click on the artboard area, go to the Interactions panel and add an interaction for the On Application Start event. The action for the event will be Play Video and then you'll get a third combobox with a list of the available video components. Just select one and the video will automatically start to play when the application is run. Of course, you can attach this action to the click on a button or another component as well.

On the video component itself you can also add some interactions. So for example you could undertake some action when the video has finished playing by reacting to the On Video Play Complete event. Or you just wait for the video to have loaded completely before you start playing it. The choice is yours…

The last input component you have in the popup dialog when adding an interaction is the conditional statement in case of the fact that the interaction needs to be played in a specific state or page. Again this is a combobox containing the values Any State and Application. The latter one contains several states, which are actually the available states or pages in the application. So, when you choose Any State, the interaction will always be executed, no matter what state you're in or what page you're on. Of course, this only works when the component you're adding the interaction to is visible in more than one state or page. However, when you select one of the states, you'll see the condition appearing in the Interactions panel for that specific component. An example would be Play Transition to State if in Page 1. Now, I'm taking the example of transitions because that is definitely going to be a situation where you are going to make use of these state specific interactions, because you can use these to create what is called *transitions* between states in your application. Transitions are basically a group of effects (or behaviors as they are called in Flex) that are played on one or more components that change, appear or disappear between different view states. You can define transitions for every kind of view state change. But again, I'll be covering this in detail in the section about the Timelines panel, because that's where you are going to define the effects.

The Properties panel

The Properties panel will also play an important role in your application development using Flash Catalyst. This is because this panel will contain the most common properties you might want to change. For the samples I'm about to use in this section I've imported the library package I created earlier in this chapter. So I already have a couple of custom components at my disposal.

This panel I again divided into several sections such as Common, Component, Appearance, Text and Filters. The sections that will be shown and the exact content for each and every one of these sectionsdepends entirely on the component you have selected. So for example, only on a Data List component, you'll have the Allow Multiple Selection checkbox in the Common section. Or a Media component, such as a video component will not have the Text section, because there is no text to set. But let's take a closer look at what these sections have to offer us in terms of facilitating the creation of Flex applications.

Common

First up is the Common **section**. This one is fairly stable in the sense that it contains, as the name indicates, the most common properties you may want to change for the selected component. These properties could be x and y positions or width and height properties for a certain component. That means that you can use the artboard area to drag your components to a certain location or to resize them by clicking one of the borders and dragging it. But for pixel perfect positioning this is not always the most convenient way. So, in this section of the Properties panel, you can position a component on the exact pixel you want it to be. As you can see in Figure 4-13 there are two ways of changing the values for positioning properties: either you click on the number and a text input component will be shown and you can enter a specific value straight away. Or you can hold the left mouse button down over the number and start dragging in all directions. Dragging to the left will decrease the number, while dragging in the other direction will increase it. This works just like the way you may be using it in the CS4 design tools. Other properties that can be found in this section are Opacity, Rotation, Label, Enabled, Source (in case of an image or media component), Video Controls ... As I said before, it all depends on which component you have selected on the artboard.

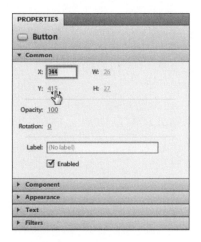

Figure 4-13: Changing the properties can be done in two ways.

Component

A second section in the Properties **panel is the** Component **section.** This section contains component specific settings concerning the interaction with the user. You can find the tab index here, or the indication whether or not the component accepts mouse events, or even the tooltips you get with the fly-over hint on the component at runtime. You can also find the default volume for a media component in this section. The section doesn't show for images and optimized graphics. Should you want to capture mouse events on images for example, you're going to have to turn the image component into a button component by using the right-click popup menu and selecting a component from the Convert Artwork to Component submenu.

Appearance

Next, there is an Appearance section, which contains some more component specific settings like the blend mode, the color for the focus rectangle and a couple of other settings. For those of you that are not familiar with design applications like Photoshop or Illustrator, a blend mode indicates the way the component is displayed in combination with the background; it is basically the way that layers will interact with each other. As you can clearly see in Figure 4-14 there are a lot of possible blend modes available in Flash Catalyst.

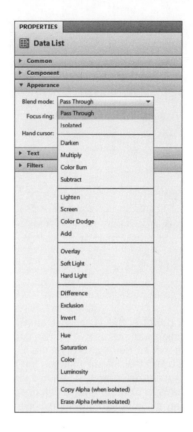

Figure 4-14: Flash Ctalyst has a lot of blend modes available.

Now, since there are so many to choose from and since as a developer you might not be familiar with the concept of blend modes, let me explain a couple of them:

- Normal: This is the default. The layers will not interact in any way and so the top layer will be completely opaque, hiding the layers that are underneath the component.
- Multiply: Multiply darkens the lower layer based on the darkness of the upper layer. No part of the image will get lighter. Any applied tone darker than white darkens the lower layer and white becomes transparent.
- Screen: This is kind of the reverse of Multiply, because with this blend mode you lighten the lower layers based on the lightness of this component. The result will always be lighter.
- Overlay: This is actually a combination of the previous two. This blend mode multiplies the light colors and screens the dark colors.
- Darken: Darken compares each pixel value of the component you set the blend mode for to its counterpart's pixel value of the layer underneath and chooses the darker of the two to display.
- Lighten: This is the exact opposite of Darken, so the lightest pixel is chosen to be displayed.

These are only a few possible blend modes to use when designing your application using Flash Catalyst. There are a lot of good resources to be found on the Internet regarding the other blend modes. Often you will find some examples demonstrating the effects as well. So, if you want to dig into this design technique, I gladly refer to Google as the start point for your quest.

Text properties

The Text section will only be available when the selected component actually has some text on it. Now, when you have selected a custom component from the Library panel this section will display a message:

> *To edit a custom component's text styles, edit the text in the component's content.*

This means that you'd have to double click the component to go into the component's layers and select a text part in there to style. For wireframe components, you can edit the text properties directly. You could do this for example with a TextInput component.

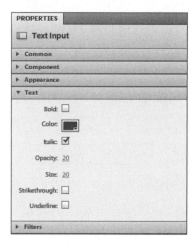

Figure 4-15: The Text properties section for a TextInput component.

All of the properties that are depicted in Figure 4-15 are editable and apply for a TextInput component. So for example, you can change the font color, the font weight and font style. The Opacity and Size fields are again editable by either dragging left and right on the value to respectively decrease and increase the value, or by clicking on the value and typing some values directly in the text input field that appears.

Filters

The final section in the Properties panel is the Filters section. In this part of the panel you're able to apply some basic filters on the selected components by clicking on the plus button after the Add Filter label. Available filters are:

- Blur
- Drop Shadow
- Inner Shadow
- Bevel
- Glow

- Inner Glow
- Inner Glow

Selecting any of these filters will add it and enables some extra filter specific properties. For example, you have the `Low`, `Normal` and `High` setting for the amount of blur you want to apply to the selected component. The `Drop Shadow` filter has some more properties available like the angle for the shadow, the distance (meaning how far the shadow needs to go from the component) and blur and color properties for the actual shadow.

Figure 4-16: Components can have multiple filters aplied using the `Properties` panel.

As you can see in Figure 4-16, you can also apply multiple filters on the same component. The result will be a combination of the specified filters and their properties. All of the options in the Properties panel combined will enable you to create some very nice looking components by only using the wireframe components in Flash Catalyst.

Of course, setting thes properties, appearances and filters cannot only be done in Flash Catalyst. As we've seen in Chapter 2, you can still create all of this directly in Flash Builder as well. Therefore, you can also modify these properties, appearances and filters after having imported the project. So you as a developer can still contribute to the design in your own familiar way.

The Design-Time Data panel

When you have a `Data List` component in your application you can add some data to it using only the Flash Catalyst application interface. I've already covered the creation of such a component when I talked about the `Library` panel. This creation of a `Data List` component has the requirement to indicate the repeating item in the component. This is the part that will be repeated for every item in the list's `dataProvider`. Now, when you create such a component Flash Catalyst will automatically create a design-time data list to simulate the data that would eventually be placed in this component. This way you can design the subtleties needed to display the data exactly as you want to and you can already see the result when executing the SWF file generated by Flash Catalyst. Or you don't even need to run the applicationat all since the data is also visible while you are designing the interface.

Now, Flash Catalyst will create a couple of dummy items when you create a Data List component and point out the repeating item. However, the generated data is merely a number of copies of the original data you assigned to the repeating item. This may very well be enough for allowing you to design the way the item is depicted in the resulting application, but sometimes you need to vary your data to see if the result is still looking like what you had in mind.

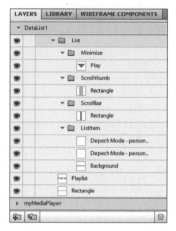

Figure 4-17: The structured layers for the example in the FC_DesignTimeData.fxp project.

The example in Figure 4-17 is the basic layer structure for creating this example Data List component. After doing some conversions on the graphics, you have your custom component. By selecting all the layers in the Item group folder and setting it as the repeating item for the list component, Flash Catalyst automatically created 5 records as design-time data. You can find this data in the Design-Time Data panel. As I mentioned before, at this time all of the data is exactly the same. But don't worry, you can simply change this by selecting the cell you want to change and typing a new value for that cell. This allows you to simply create basic design-time lists that still represent a realistic view.

Of course, now you still have only 5 items in your list. Maybe you are using this design-time data to create a dynamic prototype which you need to demo. Well, in that case, you can add as many rows as you like by clicking on the Add Row button at the bottom left of this panel. This action will create a copy of the selected item in the list and place it directly underneath that selected record. So, you cannot only use this button to add data at the end of the list, but you can also use it to insert items at any position within the list. After adding a couple of items, the Design-Time Data panel could look like what you see in Figure 4-18.

TIMELINES	DESIGN-TIME DATA	
	Text 1	Text 2
1	Steven	Peeters
2	Mieke	Allaert
3	Ilyan	Peeters
4	Rhune	Peeters
5	Andrew	Shorten
6	Ryan	Stewart
+ Add Row		

Figure 4-18: You can add and delete desing-time data for the selected list component.

Of course, when you're able to add records to the Data List component, you should also be able to remove them again. And the Design-Time Data panel is no exception. You just select the item you wish to delete from the list of records and click the delete button, which is located next to the Add Row button. You just have to keep in mind that again there is no confirmation dialog, which means that pressing this button immediately deletes the selected item.

Unfortunately, this panel is not really useful to create large fixed data sets to use in your application, because you need to create and edit each and every item individually. That makes it very time consuming for larger data sets.

This design time data will remain visible in the source code when you take your Flash Catalyst project into Flash Builder. It's even hard coded as the dataProvider property of the Data List component. There, you need to change this into the actual back end data and most likely you will also place the data in a separate ArrayCollection for convenience.

The Timelines panel

I've already discussed the Interactions panel in this chapter. In that section I talked about adding custom actions and going to different states. Attaching these interactions was quite easy, but going from one state to another was just instantaneous, without any fluency to it. The way the application transitions from one state to another is exactly what you are going to use the Timelines panel for.

If you are a developer and you're already used to working with Flex 3 applications, you've definitely used view states before. Now, these Flex 3 view states are exactly the same as what we simply call states in Flash Catalyst. Well, at least in one form, because the Pages/States panel can also be used for creating separate pages, as I've also explained before. The concept of Flex 3 states goes on in the sense that you had ways of animating the changes between two different states. This kind of animation was specifically called **transitions**. These transitions could be general or for a specific state change, depending on what you wanted to accomplish. That's where there's a difference between working with view states in Flex Builder/Flash Builder and creating view states using Flash Catalyst: in the latter one you need to specify the transition for each combination separately. That's the downside. But on the upside, another difference is that now you can use a visual representation of your animations and transitions, which makes it easier to understand what exactly happens when you switch from one view to another.

In this section I'm going to work with the FC_Timelines.fxp file to illustrate certain points. You can find the file in the projects that accompany this book. The situation I'm facing in this example is a data list in which you can search for a certain individual. This could be a Twitter search application, like we're going to make in the next chapter. Or it could be an Active Directory listing or maybe even a product selector. The choice is yours. But the essence remains the same since we have the application in a normal state and in the search state. Both states are depicted in Figure 4-19.

 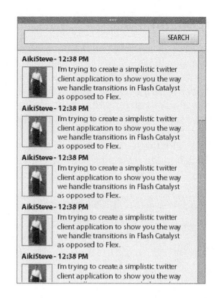

Figure 4-19: The two states for the application.

Now, if you would create only these two states, add an interaction on the dark gray bar to open and close the search part of the application, you would get the effect that it just jumps from one state to the other and back again. I'm quite sure you all agree that this is not really user friendly. Therefore you should add some kind of transition between the states to make the change more smoothe. In this example I've made the button and the input field invisible in the base state. At the same time I've repositioned the background rectangle for the search part and the dark gray bar (which will act as the trigger). So, by default, if you look in the Timelines panel you'll see a couple of effects already on different parts of the application.

Now, if you look at this panel, you'll notice **two major sections**. On the left side you have a subpanel in which you can find all the State Transitions available for the current component, or in our case for the application: Page1 ➤ Page2 and Page2 ➤ Page1. There is also another section called Action Sequences, which contains all the custom animations. I'll address these custom animations shortly later on. At the top of this left subpanel you'll find a search box that allows you to search within the list of transitions and custom action sequences in case you have an extensive list for either one of them of maybe even for both of them. **On the right side of the panel you'll find the timeline.** This timeline can somewhat be compared with the timeline in Flash Professional, but there is at least one major difference: in Flash Catalyst you don't work with key frames. Instead, the animations in this tool are expressed in actual time based frames. An animation doesn't last 31 frames, but just 1 second. You don't have to set the framerate for a Flex application explicitly, although you could do this of course.

Sometimes reducing the framerate for an application when it is sent to the background can help you to increase the performance and/or the decrease the impact on system resources when they are not needed. Lee Brimelow has an excellent video tutorial about this on his website. The tutorial is more oriented towards general Flash applications, but you can apply the same tricks to a Flex application as well. You can find this tutorial at http://theflashblog.com/?p=1138.

Working with the timeline

Now you know you are going to work with a timeline, but how do you make use of it in Flash Catalyst? There are two main ways of working with the timeline: using the smoothing function or setting the animation manually. The first option will automatically create a certain length for the animations. But all of the animations occur at the same time. Chances are you do not want this to happen all at once. That means that after the smoothing you're probably going to do some manual changes anyway. To use this smoothing functionality, you need to click the Smooth Transition button at the bottom of the timeline subpanel. On the same button you also have a little arrow. If you click that one a dialog will popup. This dialog, as shown in Figure 4-20, allows you to change some default settings for the smoothing. You could change the duration of the effects or you could choose to not let all of the effects at the same time.

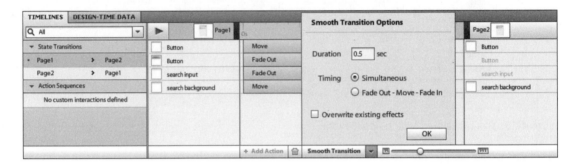

Figure 4-20: The default settings for the smoothing function on transitions.

As you can see in Figure 4-20, all effects happen at the same time and are instantaneous. But when you use these default settings and you click the button, all effects will be expanded to last half a second. This is also the standard duration when you use effects directly in Flash Builder. If you want to spread the effects a little more to get an even smoother transition, you just have to drag and drop an effect on the timeline. Sometimes that will even be necessary, like in the example I'm using here. The intention is that the search part slides up and only then the button and text input component will fade in. Of course, the reverse action will occur when the search part needs to be hidden again. So I'm going to have to make the effects kind of sequential to get the proper result. Otherwise the input component and the search button will appear in thin air and then the background rectangle will slide behind it. Not quite what I was hoping for. You could solve this by sliding the components with the background, but I've chosen a different effect here.

Now, what I've done in this example is move the Fade In effect to the end of the Move effect, but not entirely sequential. I just created a very small overlap, so the fade effect starts just before the move ends. This technique helps to create a more fluent transition instead of being chopped up into mere sequential pieces. The reverse transition has the Fade Out effect first and the Move starts just before the fade ends. The result looks like what you see in Figure 4-21.

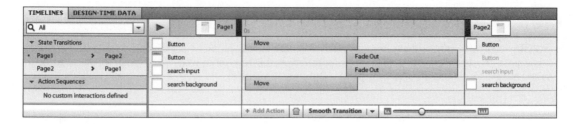

Figure 4-21: The visual representation of the transition to show the search part.

Not only can you drag these transitions to another location on the timeline, but you can also stretch the length of the transition effect by selecting the effect and dragging the end to the appropriate length. This way you can make the effect last as long as you want. By default you only see about 2 or 3 seconds on the timeline. For most actions this will be enough, but sometimes when you have an elaborate transition (e.g. fade out, move, fade in, move other component, glow...) you can't see the entire effect anymore. But the people at Adobe have thought about this as well and **at the bottom of the right subpanel you can find a slider component that allows you to control how much time you want to see in the Timelines panel**. The more you drag the indicator to the right, the more you zoom in and therefore you will see a lesser amount of time. Dragging it to the left will zoom out and allows you to see a bigger timeframe.

Adding effects manually

All of the actions that you see in this example have been automatically created by Flash Catalyst because I made some changes to the application in the second state. Based on what I changed, certain transition effects are placed on the timeline. Remember that I talked about creating interactions that will play actions sequences? Well, here you can define them as well. Or you can add you custom interactions to the ones that have already been created by Flash Catalyst. The button next to the slider allows you to delete the selected effect from the timeline. The `Add Action` button allows you to add a custom effect to the already existing transition. Let's assume that instead of a fade in effect on the button, I want to make a 3D rotation on it. I simply resize the fade in effect to basically zero length and at the same time I'm adding a `Rotate 3D` effect on that button component and make it spin a full circle in all 3 directions. And with a couple of clicks I get a completely different kind of effect on that button.

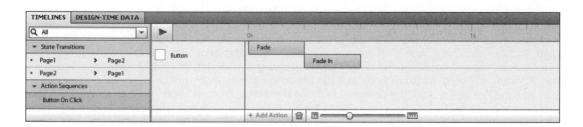

Figure 4-22: The visual representation of a custom action sequence.

What I've done in the example project is to create a `Blur` effect on the button when it is clicked. It's actually a sequence to impose the blur and then revert it back to normal. Still, I didn't write a single line of code. That's how powerful this tool is for creating view state transitions.

Building applications using Flash Catalyst

Now that you know what the tools are within Flash Catalyst, you know what you can do with it. But how do you integrate the tools in your project development. In the next chapter I will explain in detail what the possibilities are for different kinds of projects. But here I would like to give you the basic options that you have.

Building applications from scratch

First of all, you can build entire applications from scratch using Flash Catalyst. For doing so, you make use of the wireframe components. Of course you can use the Import Library function in the Library panel to import custom components that you have created earlier or that someone else has created for you. As I mentioned before, exporting libraries is an excellent way of sharing components between developers. Unfortunately, changing the library does not mean that existing Catalyst projects are going to be affected automatically when recompiling them, since importing a library actually creates a copy of the library objects in the Library panel.

But anyway, what can you do with an application that is built using only Flash Catalyst? Well, you certainly can rule out applications that use some form of back end communications. That's because you can't code anything in this tool. You can't even load an XML file at runtime. So what kind of applications can you make using only Flash Catalyst? Basically, any application that doesn't require some form of server connection or data retrieval.

Now, you may think that there are not a lot of Flex applications that only contain fixed data and you're probably right. But what about simple fixed value listings, master-detail compositions or just pure informational sites that don't need a complex graphical representation? You can use basic wireframe components and style and tweak them to look very nice instead of the basic look. A lot of text components on a static website that requires some fancy transitions between components. This is an ideal target for just using Flash Catalyst as your website development tool. But you probably know there is not a very big market for these kinds of websites or applications. So, is Flash Catalyst a product you can use stand-alone, without any other tool involved? I'm not convinced it is going to be used that often just by itself.

Integration with Creative Suite 5

Although building applications from scratch using only Flash Catalyst can be done, the real power of the tool lies in the fact that **it integrates perfectly with the Adobe design tools like Photoshop, Illustrator and Fireworks**. This allows you to create some very complex and nifty designs, using vector graphics, images, custom scrollbars, logos... In case of Photoshop and Illustrator, you can just create a new Flash Catalyst project based on a PSD or AI file. When you create your design using Fireworks, it is not that straightforward anymore, because you can't just import a Fireworks file. In this case you're going to use the Export to FXG feature from the Commands menu in Fireworks. This will export the design in FXG format, so you can import it in Flash Catalyst by clicking the From FXG File… option in the welcome screen.

Figure 4-23: You can import a design from other Adobe design tools.

When you import a design that was structured in layers in the original design tool, that structure will still be available in the Layers panel. Even the names of all the layers are preserved after the import. From that point on you can move the layers around, make certain layers visible or invisible depending on the view state or page you are working on. You can also select the components on one or more layers and convert them into custom Flex components. This way you can make a nice looking component into a button for example. From that point on, this component will act and behave just like a standard button. It will have up, over, selected and disabled states, just like any other button.

Creating mindblowing graphical components

In the past you could do a lot of things by writing a lot of custom code or by using third party library components like for example the *FlexLib* library (http://code.google.com/p/flexlib/). This library contains a lot of custom components like an enhanced button, a horizontal accordion and even a component that simulates fire. And the good thing is that it is opensource, so you can use it freely in your projects. Another great library that I've used in my Flex 3 projects is called *Degrafa* (http://www.degrafa.org/). Degrafa is a declarative graphics framework that is compatible with Flex 2 and Flex 3. And it is also opensource licensed. You can use this framework for example to create those WEB 2.0 buttons with a glossy gradient background with a minimal amount of effort. It also has components for charting, classes for fills and strokes, fonts, skins and programmatic drawing. But the essence of using these kinds of libraries was always that you had to re-create the original design to the best of your abilities. That's a thing of the past with Flash Catalyst, because now you just convert artwork into fully functional components.

But now with Flash Catalyst the really interesting stuff starts when you need to create components that were otherwise nigh-on impossible to create or that would take days to get them right. I don't know if any of you have ever tried their hands on creating a completely custom scrollbar in a Flex application? If you do, you're sure going appreciate this new product. It used to take a lot of time to get the custom scrollbar to work because you had to do a lot of coding for drawing the component and getting it to synchronize with the data list it belonged to. But now, it literally takes just a few minutes to create a fully functional custom scrollbar with any design you can imagine. I'm not kidding here. I've done this in a couple of my presentations where I create a data list with a custom scrollbar in maybe just over a minute. That's how powerful a tool Flash Catalyst is to help you create visually attractive Rich Internet Applications.

Editing your Flash Catalyst graphics in Illustrator

And it doesn't just stop there either. When I talk about integration with the CS5 design products, so far I've only covered one direction. I've just covered the import functionality where you can take an existing design and use it "as is" in Flash Catalyst (except for Fireworks designs which need to be exported as FXG first). Flash Catalyst is also capable of turning this workflow around and letting you edit the design again in Illustrator. It doesn't really matter if you've already converted the artwork into a component, you can still edit it directly in Illustrator. This is done by selecting the desired component and selecting Edit in Adobe Illustrator CS5 from the right-click popup menu.

Selecting the option to edit the component in Illustrator will automatically open Adobe Illustrator and show you the component, so you can alter its properties. What is striking in this option is the fact that you don't only see the selected component, but you're seeing the entire page as shown in Flash Catalyst. It is just the selected component that will be editable. But having the surrounding components visible as well helps you a great deal in scaling components or changing color gradients to match the other colors in the page or view state. Additional advantages are shown in Figure 4-24, where it becomes clear that you do not only get the surrounding area with the editable component. If you take a closer look at the Layers panel, you'll notice that the editable part has a couple of layers. And if you look even closer you might recognize the layer names being the names of the states of a button component. That's right, I've converted the artwork into a Button component and now I'm editing it again and automatically I'm getting the view states in Illustrator as well. This allows me to edit all of the graphical parts for a certain component at once instead of having to do this over and over again for every state of that component.

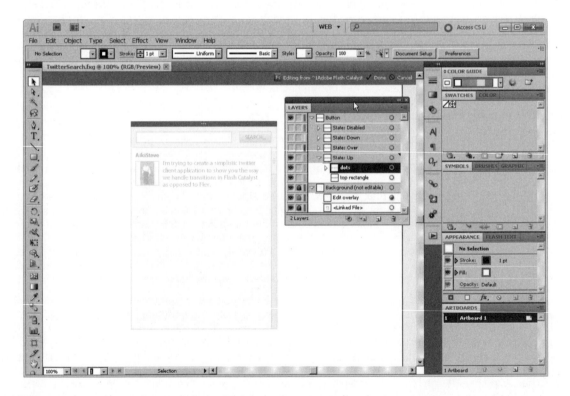

Figure 4-24: Editing a Flash Catalyst component in Illustrator CS5.

Once you're done editing the component, you only have to click the Done or Cancel button at the top of the art board. When you save the changes you will be presented with an options dialog that allows you to set some FXG options before returning to Flash Catalyst. The changes are integrated in the Flash Catalyst project as the edited components are automatically updated with the new design. It's a great asset to be able to use Illustrator as the tool to adjust the design for more complex operations than what you can do in Flash Catalyst alone.

When you edit a Flash Catalyst component in Illustrator, you do not modify the original Illustrator file that you imported when starting on the project. Illustrator is just temporarily used as the design editor to make some adjustments. The original design file remains untouched during this process.

If you select one or more bitmaps from the artboard, you can also choose the Edit in Adobe Photoshop CS5 option from the right-click popup menu. This will have a similar effect as when you are using Illustrator. That means that you get to keep the entire surrounding environment as a read-only background, so you can better adjust your design to suit the circumstances where the component is used. The difference with using Illustrator CS5 is that you just have to save and close the edited component to actually integrate the changes back in Flash Catalyst.

Round tripping between Flash Builder and Flash Catalyst

I've already mentioned this concept a few times in the previous chapters, but let me refresh your memory on this one. Round tripping in this view is actually being able to use both Flash Builder and Flash Catalyst to make changes to the same project at any given time in the project workflow without breaking anything. You know now that it is possible to import a Flash Catalyst project into Flash Builder and add some ActionScript code to it or change some layout features by writing some lines of FXG code. But can you do it the other way around?

Unfortunately, the answer is "no". Although people at Adobe have assured me this is high on the priorities list, round tripping is not part of the first release of Flash Catalyst. That means that when you have a design update you need to do, you can perform the changes in Flash Catalyst, but you cannot automatically merge the changes in the Flash Builder project. In the previous chapter I've talked about the comparison tool in Flash Builder to accomplish this task, but in essence, it still remains a manual task.

A tool for the "devigner"

I've been guiding you through the different aspects of the Flash Catalyst interface and I've also provided you with the possible options to start creating your Rich Internet Applications using this tool. But a question that remains open at this point is: who is going to use this tool? The designer? The developer? Is there a need for some kind of new job description? Well, to put it quite simple: all of them. Until some time ago people were always put into a category: either you were a developer or you were a designer. There were some developers that tried their best at being a designer as well. And some of those were actually quite good at it. And of course you had the other way around as well: there are some good designers out there who can manage themselves in writing code. But it is very hard to combine and be good at both because the areas of expertise require a different mindset. To put it to the extreme: designers think in pixels, developers in code.

But lately there's been a change. With the surge of RIAs and the increasing request for developers and designers who specify in this area, more and more developers start developing an interest in design. And more and more designers are digging into code. This is creating a new breed of professional people out there, which are often referred to as *devigners*. Though the term sounds quite fancy and rolls well off the tongue, in fact it is nothing more than a combination of both roles to create a new job title.

But as I mentioned before, not only devigners are going to use Flash Catalyst, but also developers and designers can use it. **Pure developers can make simple mock-ups and wireframes** which show how the application should work. And then they can give that project file to a designer and let them make it look nice and user friendly. The designer gives it back to the developer and he can then again start with attaching the back end of the application in Flash Builder. **Pure designers can create some very nifty designs and import them in Flash Catalyst.** Because they know what part of the design should be visible in what circumstance, they can use the tool to create a working application without writing any code. Once the application runs according to the design, they hand over the project to the developer. The code behind it to attach it to a database for example can then be written by that developer to complete the functionality of the application. The last category of people who are going to use this tool can be found in Figure 4-1. There I placed an Interaction designer in the middle of the process. With this I'm trying to indicate that working with a product like Flash Catalyst can become a job on its own. I can imagine there are some companies doing loads of RIA projects that have some employees who are very good at defining the way people are interacting with your application. **An interface designer takes a design and turns it into a user friendly working application.**This is not the same as designing the application, because although a design may look good, the way the user navigates from one screen to another, the amount of effects and their impact on what the user sees on screen are also very important.

> *All of these profiles will be able to use the tool, but it will be more suited for some and less for others. But isn't that the case with any program?*

Building AIR applications with Flash Catalyst?

All this time I've been talking about creating Flex applications from scratch or using an external design file from Illustrator, Photoshop or Fireworks to import into Flash Catalyst and start adding interactions to the design components. But Flex is only part of the Rich Internet Application solutions. There's also the AIR technology, which allows for some extra features such as full system access, USB storage detection, microphone access… I've already talked about these extra features a bit at the end of the first chapter, so I'm not going to go into any details here.

But the question now is: can you create AIR applications with Flash Catalyst? And the answer is: YES! And it's quite simple as well. Since every Flex application can be turned into an AIR application, it shouldn't be that difficult to use Flash Catalyst to generate an AIR application. OK, this conversion is not always straightforward as it might be necessary to add some more runtime configuration for connecting to a back end, but that's done in Flash Builder anyway.

How is it done? Well, you can't just say that you're going to create an AIR application when you create a project. The conversion into AIR lies in the way you publish the application. To publish your application you have to go to the `File` menu and choose the `Publish to SWF…` option.

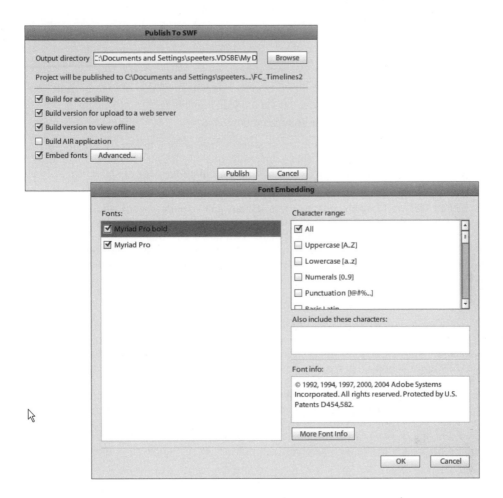

Figure 4-25: The options dialog when publishing a Flash Catalyst application.

The dialog that shows up when selecting that option can be seen in Figure 4-25. At the mouse cursor on the image you can find the option Build AIR Application. This option will compile your Flash Catalyst application into an AIR application instead of a Flex web application. You could also opt to include the fonts that you've used in your design. Check this feature when you have used a custom font or a font that you're not sure of the user has available by default. Fonts like Verdana and Tahoma are quite common, but for example Helvetica is not available by default. So to make your application design look exactly like you want it to (because font types can cause some serious issues with your layout), you should embed the font into the application.

However, when you embed fonts in a Flex project, you have to keep in mind that the file size is going to increase drastically. But you don't need all of the characters in a font (at least most of the time), so as you can see in Figure 4-25, you an also opt to include only a certain subset of the font from within the Publish To SWF dialog.

What you end up with when publishing an AIR application from within Flash Catalyst is three different directories:

- `AIR`: which contains the AIR install file to distribute
- `deploy-to-web`: which is basically the Flex web application version of your project. This one also contains the externalized SDK, RPC and text layout frameworks.
- `run-local`: which can be used for debugging purposes

You just take the AIR install file and distribute it or create a badge for it to place it on the web. Creating a badge has the advantage that the AIR runtime is also automatically installed when the user doesn't have it already. Otherwise he would get some error stating that the computer doesn't know how to treat this type of file. That's how simple it is to convert your interactive design into an AIR application.

However, building AIR applications has more to it than just exporting your application using the AIR technology. There is also the problem that Flash Catalyst doesn't support the usage of digitally signed certificates for your applications. That means that you can never distribute it with an authorized indication to help users understand that this is a program from a certain company and that that company has been thoroughly checked by an independent agency, like *VeriSign* (http://www.verisign.com) or *Thawte* (http://www.thawte.com) for instance. This means you can probably trust what is being installed. Is this mandatory? Not really, but it will help you to gain trust from the user in this day and age of malicious software lurking around on every corner of the Internet.

Now, you're probably going to distribute an AIR application using an install badge anyway. That means that you're not going to be able to publish your application using only Flash Catalyst. You'll have to go into Flash Builder and create a badge to put on some website. And while you're at it, why not attach a digital certificate for AIR applications when making a release build. If this means you're always going to use Flash Builder to make your actual AIR application, then why would Adobe allow you to create such applications from within Flash Catalyst? You have to remember that Flash Catalyst is not just a tool to create Flex applications. You an also use it to create your initial mockups, or intermediate versions that you send off to the client for inspection. They don't need to have this install badge and/or a digital singed certificate. The client knows it where it comes from and should trust the contents. If not, he would probable not be working with you, right? So, this is the reason why you can publish an AIR application directly from within Flash Catalyst.

Summary

Flash Catalyst is a tool a lot of developers have been waiting for for a very long time. It simplifies the integration of complex design elements. It is especially useful when having to collaborate with designers, integrating their creativity. But it's not a tool that can be used by only developers. Designers can help out in the Rich Internet Application workflow by making their designs come to life. For this, they need to add view states and interactions, but they do not have to code anything. Or maybe it's time for a new kind of job on your team: the interaction designer. In that case, he will be the bridge between the designer and the developer.

Having this new tool available for all these different kinds of profiles is definitely changing the way RIAs are being build. In the next chapter I'll take you through the different kinds of workflows for different applications and show you how much Flash Catalyst can help you achieve a much better result with less effort than without it.

Chapter 5

Choosing the Best Workflow

Now that you are familiar with the new features of Flex 4 and Flash Builder 4 and the basics of Flash Catalyst, I'm going provide an overview of where and when each of these applications are used in the development process of a Rich Internet Application (RIA). In this chapter, I will use small examples for each workflow situation to illustrate my points and to help you understand why I've chosen that particular way of interacting with other colleagues.

In the past couple of years, the way people develop applications has changed significantly. Developers come from a line of products that use client-server technology. Designers have occupied themselves more in the web technologies. I'm not saying designers don't work on client-server applications, because well designed usability is very important in that arena as well. But I think that in the world of business applications there is more work cut out for interaction designers than for pure artwork designers. RIAs have combined both worlds into web applications. That means that now it is becoming increasingly important for designers and developers to work together. As mentioned in the previous chapter, Flash Catalyst is making an attempt to bridge the gap between those worlds. So, how do you use this product in the real world?

In this book, I consider a workflow to be a combination of the concept of iterations in creating the project and the interaction between the designer and the developer. Before we dig into the different application types and their workflows, look at Figure 5-1 for a diagram of a typical designer-developer workflow looks like for a RIA. As you can see, there are some tasks that are sequential and some that can be performed at the same time. For example, a developer can start working with an initial design as soon as it is more or less stable. In other words, the design can still change, but there should only be minor changes or additions at best. If more radical design changes are required, the design will have to be re-imported, which could have some serious consequences such as major code rewrites.

Figure 5-1: Adobe WorkFlowLab showing the typical workflow for a RIA project.

In this workflow, which is an elaborate version of the workflow depicted in Figure 4-1 in the chapter on Flash Catalyst, you'll find some very different aspects from design to release. Note that I didn't include the requirements and business analysis as well as the technical analysis; those steps all precede this workflow. However, in the chapter about project management, I'll dig a little deeper into all of the steps and how they work in an interactive or agile development process when creating RIAs.

> *The workflow depicted here is only an example workflow to give you an idea of the steps involved in developing RIAs. The actual detailed workflow will differ from project to project and even depends on the team composition.*

The largest block in this workflow is the actual development process because here all of the parts come together, from implementing the design to developing back end services and using them in Flash Builder 4. As soon as the prototype is approved and the first parts of the design are ready, you can start developing the back end services. In some cases, you will be able to start directly from the analysis documents. For example, when you have use cases available, you can start somewhat earlier on the back end development. Since design updates can occur during development when the previous design is already implemented, I've also extended the development process to exceed the design updates to allow for some extra time to implement the changes.

In the chapter on Flash Catalyst, I talked about who is going to use this product, but let me give you some examples of feasible applications. Although these examples are quite small, they all represent certain kinds of applications you could encounter on a larger scale when working on RIAs.

Since there are many Flex applications out there with more every day, it is nearly impossible to provide a workflow for every detailed type of application. So I'm not going to split them up into simulators, websites, widgets, etc. For convenience sake, I've split up the workflows into different general types of applications:

- Simple design

  - Simple functionality
  - Complex functionality
  - Connected to a back end

- Complex design

  - Simple functionality
  - Complex functionality
  - Connected to a back end

> *When I talk about a simple design, I'm not only covering very basic layouts using only wireframe components. Although it is possible to create a Flex application in Flash Catalyst using only the wireframe components, in reality, there will almost always be some back end functionality involved and/or some design elements that are difficult to create without importing them from Illustrator, Photoshop or Fireworks.*

Simple Design, Simple Functionality

Let's start with the easiest one in concept, but maybe the most difficult one to find a useful application for: A simple design with some static text that has the need for some nice looking page changes or visually attractive indications. What application adheres to these ingredients?

I was thinking about a manual that comes with an application. The design doesn't have to be complex; just some windows with links on the left side and the actual content on the right side of the application will do the trick. And since the content of the manual is not very likely to change much once the application is released, you could consider this to be rather static content. You could even turn this into an AIR application, but for now I'm just going to assume the manual can be found online in the form of a Flex web application. An obvious advantage: after any changes to content or layout, you just upload the it to the server and the next visitor automatically gets the changed version.

A Product Manual Application

Let's take a look at how such an application could be built and which products are involved in its creation. There is not one right answer, as a lot depends on the experience of the staff involved in building this application. How many people are going on be working on this? **This is a typical application that can easily be built by one person.** Now, what profile is needed for such an application? This can be both a developer and a designer/interaction designer. But since this kind of application has little visually impact, it will probably fall to a developer. However, both profiles are most likely going to use the same product: Flash Catalyst.

The designer/interaction designer perspective

The designer/interaction designer has two options from which to start: He could create the application's design using a design tool such as Photoshop, Illustrator or Fireworks, or he could use Flash Catalyst directly and start using the wireframe components. Since Flash Catalyst closely resembles those design products, and because the design requirements are so minimal, I think a designer should start directly with this product. Otherwise, he has to create the design and import it into Flash Catalyst to just re-use the same components.

So, to start working on this application, open Flash Catalyst. You are going to create an application from scratch, so when you get the welcome screen, select the `Adobe Flash Catalyst Project` option in the `Create New Project` section. This will show a popup dialog (see Figure 5-2) where you can set the project name, the width and height of the application, and the background color. Name the application Workflow_Manual, leave the width and height to the default values of 800 by 600 pixels, but change the background color to the hexadecimal RGB color `#2b4381`.

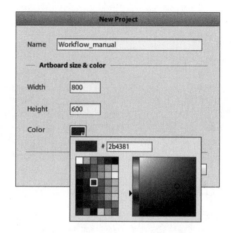

Figure 5-2: The options dialog for creating a new project from within Flash Catalyst

Clicking the `OK` button on this dialog will take you into the program. The first thing you should notice is the fact that your art board now has the selected background color. If you run the application (although there's nothing in it yet), you'll notice that the entire browser area is filled with the selected color. You actually specified the background color for the wrapper that will contain your Flex application as well. **The first thing you're going to do is set the background color** for the actual application. If you click on the art board, you'll notice that you cannot change anything using the panels. However, you can always access the `Modify ➤ Artboard Settings` … option from the application menu, which allows you to change these settings once the project has been created.

Creating the application layout

Because I want this application to look a little slick even though it's just a very basic design, you're going to **draw a rounded rectangle the same size as the application**. This creates a new layer in the `Layers` panel. Why you would need to draw a rectangle of the same size as the entire application, since one will be covering the other? Well, our top rectangle has rounded corners, so it doesn't actually cover the other rectangle entirely. And you're going to **set these corners to a radius of 20** in the `Common` section of the `Properties` panel. Once you deselect the rectangle, you'll see the background color coming through in the corners. That's why it needs to be there.

As mentioned, the application will have two main sections: the navigation pane on the left side and the actual content on the right side. These two sections will be ordinary rectangles with white backgrounds. The left one will be quite small, having a width of 200 pixels; the right one will occupy the remainder of the available width, taking into account that there has to be some spacing around the rectangles as well as some room for an application title, as shown in Figure 5-3.

- Left rectangle settings:

  - width: 200
  - height: 530
  - x: 20
  - y: 50

- Right rectangle settings:

  - width: 550
  - height: 530
  - x: 230
  - y: 50

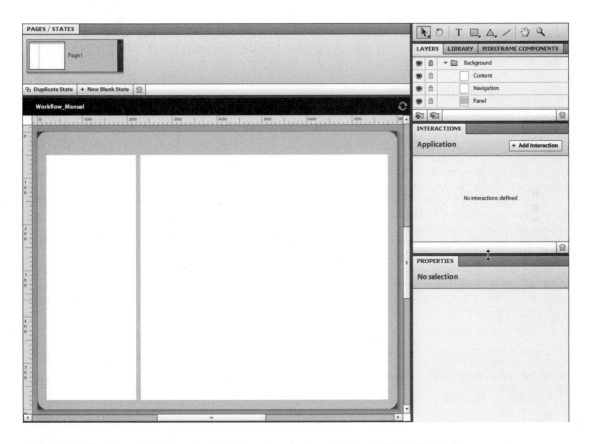

Figure 5-3: The layout is defined by drawing a bunch of rectangles in Flash Catalyst.

That's it for the background items in the application. With these actions, you have defined the layout completely. Lock all of the background layers individually or click in the second column of the Layers panel next to the sublayer. Now, we are ready to add some content to the application. **Let's start with adding a title for the application at the top** of the layout. Create a Text component roughly at the top of the application and insert the following text: Flash Builder and Flash Catalyst: the new workflow. You'll see that it is rather small for a title, so you're going to adjust the font. Select the text and go to the Common section of the Properties panel (it is the only section available this time) and **change the font to Verdana, set the font weight to bold, and change the size to 26, leaving the color at #2b4381**. You cannot change the coordinates or the text component, because now you're only editing the text properties and not the component properties. You need to select the actual component and **set the x position to 20** so that it aligns with the left rectangle and **set the y position to 15** so that it is nicely positioned in the header area.

You will see the new layer for the text component being added to the Layer1 sublayer, which you should change into "Background" to give a proper indication as to what the layer represents. This is not what I had in mind, so create a new sublayer in the Layers panel and name it "Content." Drag the text component into the new sublayer and rename the item layer to "Title." In the same sublayer create two additional sublayers called "Navigation" and "Explanation." The first one will hold the items from the left rectangular pane and the second one will contain the actual content for the selected item in the left pane. For the next step, you're going to add the navigational items, so select the "Navigation" sublayer in the Layers panel before adding the components. This will assure you that the new item layers will be created in the "Navigation" sublayer.

Creating the navigation

Create a text component and insert the following text: Ch. 1 – Flex Overview. Change the font to Verdana, size 14. Change the (x, y) position of the component to (25, 57).It is the intention that you can click on the text component to go to the proper page. That means that the text component should be turned into a button component. But before you perform the conversion, you're going to **create the over and selected state for the button by drawing some rectangles**. For the over state, you draw a rectangle of 200 by 30 pixels and set both the Stroke and Fill colors to #5380d0. Make sure that it fits perfectly in the pane area by placing it at the coordinates (20, 50) and name the selected layer "Over state." Then copy the rectangle layer, leave it at the same position, change the colors to #2b4381, and rename the copied layer to "Down state." Make sure that the rectangles are placed after the text or the text will be completely covered by them. Don't worry about the text not being very readable at this point; you'll fix that in the created button component. For making the actual button component, you need to select both rectangle layers and the text layer. Either use the Heads-Up Display (HUD) or right-click the selected layers in the Layers panel and select the Toggle Button option from the Convert Artwork to Component submenu. You need to choose this type of component because you are going to indicate to the user which chapter they're reading.

> Note that you always have several options in the Flash Catalyst interface to perform a certain task: you can use the right-click menu in the Layers panel or you can use the HUD, and vice versa. You can even opt for the right-click menu on the components or the menubar at the top of the interface.

You now have a button component, but you still need to define the different button states for it. That's where the rectangles come into play. Double click the component to go into the component. In the Pages/States panel, select the Up state. In this state, you need to make sure that both rectangles are hidden, so you'll just get the text on the pane's background color. For the Over state, make the Over state rectangle visible while the Down state layer remains invisible. Of course, you do exactly the opposite for the Down state of the new button component. For the text settings in the button, change the text color in both the Over and Down states to #cccccc. However, set the label font weight to bold only for the Down state. Then you select the text for the button and convert it to the Label part by using the HUD options. Since we're working with a toggle button, there are four additional states, namely the Selected Up, Selected Over, Selected Down and Selected Disabled states. These states represent the button states when the button is selected. To adjust these states, copy the normal states to the respective selected states and change the Selected Up state to match the normal Over state. This way, the user will know which part of the content he's looking at.

Now that you have a working button component for the first chapter, you just **copy the button component you've just created in the application and paste it a couple more times** to have a couple of chapters, each with its own title in the navigation pane. Each one of these labels will now be a button instance with the rollover color and selected color that you've just created. **Change the layer names** to "Chapter 1," "Chapter 2," etc. Don't forget to change the Label in the Properties panel for each button. Finally, make sure to reposition them so they all line up underneath each other. Then lock the Navigation sublayer to avoid accidentally changing something to the layers in that sublayer. The application structure should now look as like that in Figure 5-4.

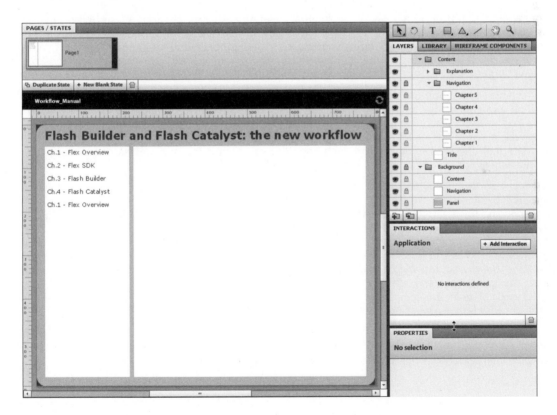

Figure 5-4: The layout after defining the buttons for navigating through the application.

Creating the content

Once you've done this, you can go on with the right side panel of the application. Here, you will define the actual content for the different chapters by creating text components for each chapter and adding them to the Explanation sublayer. To add the text component, you select the Text tool from the toolbar at the top right of the Flash Catalyst interface. When the application starts, it will show **a startup screen with the default text "This application acts as the manual for the project. Please select a chapter to view more information about it."** When you've created this new item layer with text, rename it as "Welcome screen" and make sure it is located in the Content sublayer. To position it properly, you need to select it and go to the Common section of the Properties panel to change the (x, y) position to (240, 60). Make sure the type of the text in the combobox is set to Area Text. Then you can click on the width and the height to set those values to 530 and 30, respectively. Finally, change the font family to Verdana.

After you've created this component, copy and paste it into the "Explanation" sublayer by selecting that folder before pasting the copied layer. This will automatically add the copied item to the sublayer instead of the current level. Rename the copied item layer to "Explanation 1" and change the height property for the text to 510 pixels, so it occupies the entire area. Because I want a decent amount of text in here, I'm going to use a small cheat and copy some text from a Lorem Ipsum generator (http://www.lipsum.org). This web site allows you to generate a given amount of text, divided into paragraphs. The text is in Latin and it doesn't really mean anything; it just serves as a representation of real text in typical paragraph length, word lengths and overall density. Go to the web site and request for a text that is two paragraphs long. Copy and paste it into the current text component. Make sure you also repeat the selected item from the menu in the header and set some additional subheaders in the text, as shown in Figure 5-5. This should fill up the component quite nicely.

The next step is to **copy the current layer four more times and rename them appropriately, so you have an explanation for each item in the left panel of the application**. However, you now have the same text for every component, so you need to **alter some text**. The easiest way for this example would be to delete some text or let the generator create a new paragraph. Whatever option you chose, it's important that the text be different on each page, so you'll know that the buttons actually take you to different pages.

Now that you have the content ready to go, you need to create the actual pages for the application. Each page will be linked to a selected item in the left panel. Clicking on such an item will show the corresponding page. Go to the Pages/States panel, rename the current page "Welcome," and **duplicate that page five more times** so that you have a page for each selected item plus the first welcome screen. The next step is to configure each page individually. Select the Page1 page, and make the Explanation 1 content visible while you hide the other content. You also need to indicate that the user is actually viewing that page, so you set the Toggle Button component for Page1 to its Down state. For that, you'll need to select the component and check the Selected property in the Properties panel. This will show the Selected Up state for the component even when you're not clicking on it. The indication you made earlier in this project will then always be visible.

When you're done with the first page, you repeat the process for the other pages, making the appropriate content visible and changing the proper button to indicate where the user is within the application. At this point, the interface should look like the one shown in Figure 5-5.

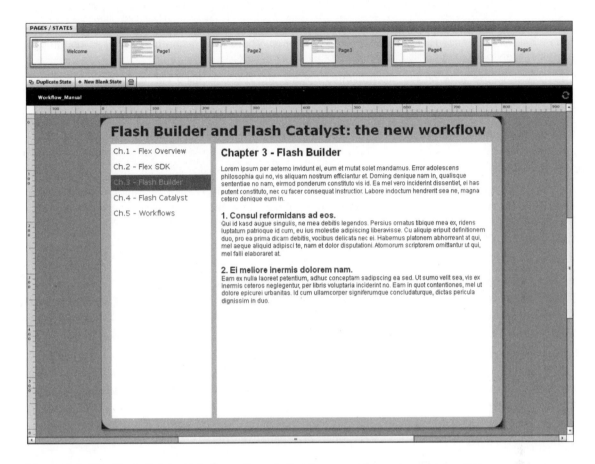

Figure 5-5: The Flash Catalyst interface after creating the pages for each navigation item.

Adding the Interactions

The final step is to define the actions on the buttons to display the proper page associated with that button. Select the first button and create a new interaction in the `Interactions` panel. Choose the action `Play transition to State` and select `Page1` in the combobox as the state to select when the button is clicked. Leave the interaction filtering to `When in Any State` to make sure that this action is played wherever you are in the application. Select the second button and perform the same actions, but set the state to show to `Page2`. Perform these tasks for the other three buttons. Now, we have a working application, but the states just jump from one screen to the other. It would be nicer to have a little fade in and fade out effect to make the transition look smoother. One way to do this is to go to the `Timelines` panel and drag and drop each transition to its appropriate place, extending it for a certain amount of time. However, there's another way, and it's faster!

In the `Timelines` panel, you can automatically smooth your transitions between two states by just clicking on the `Smooth Transition` button. First, go to the options by clicking on the arrow shape next to that button. In the options dialog, select the radio button for `Smart Smoothing`, instead of the default `Simultaneous` option. This option will put the different actions in sequence instead of having them play simultaneous. Then, select the first transition in the list, scroll down to the end of the list, and click the last transition while holding the <SHIFT> key down. This will select all the transitions at once and will make the actual timeline appear empty. When you have selected all the transitions, hit the Smooth Transition button, and all of the transitions will be smoothed at once. That's a lot faster than having to go through each and every one of them, hitting the button for every transition.

This concludes the work on the small manual application. The only thing left to do is to publish the application. To do so, go to the File menu and select Publish to SWF… In the options dialog, select the desired location where the application should be compiled to and leave the default options. After clicking the Publish button, Flash Catalyst will compile the application into a working Flex application that you can then deploy to your web server.

Conclusion

An application such as this one could be created either in Flash Catalyst or in Flash Builder. However, I've chosen the Flash Catalyst approach because there is no need to write any code, since the view states and their interactions are created and implemented a lot faster this way. And since this chapter is all about using the most efficient workflow for each type of applications, Flash Catalyst is the way to go here.

> Often, you will need to provide an application like this in several languages. Don't worry! You just load the content dynamically, either from a database or from an external translation file, depending on the language settings for the user. This concept is called localization and requires some additional ActionScript code, so you cannot create a localized application using only Flash Catalyst.

The next application creation process will add some complex functionality but without a back end connection for retrieving data. You'll just stay on the client side and make use of one of the improved Flash Player 10 features: the local file access.

Simple Design, Complex Functionality

The next type of application is one with a rather simple design, but more complex functionality. You're still not using a back end technology, but you could require some file access for example. Or maybe you need to perform some conversions on user input data and just display it on screen. What kind of application fits this bill?

I've already given the answer away by suggesting file access. So, for this example, I would like to create a very basic photo resize application. This application allows you to select a photograph from your local hard drive and create a thumbnail image from it based on a percentage provided by the user. In this case, it would be more useful to have this application on the desktop, so I suggest we turn it into an AIR application.

A Photo Resizer

Who is going to work on such an application? There are two paths you can go on. The first one involves a designer and a developer. The designer could use Flash Catalyst to create the working mockup application and the developer attaches the code to it. But since this specific application requires much more code than design, and since the design is very simple (as you can see in Figure 5-6) I would prefer the second path of **having the developer do the design as well**. This means that the developer needs to know a little about how to work with FXG, the new Flex graphics syntax. The developer will be working in Flash Builder.

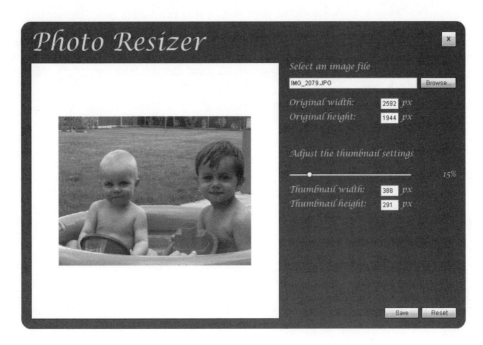

Figure 5-6: This is what the Photo Resizer application will eventually look like.

The Developer Perspective

First, create the project. **Open Flash Builder 4 and create a new Flex project**. Make sure you set the application type to Desktop to create an AIR project. Name the project "Workflow_Resizer" and don't set any server type. When requested, name the **main application file   PhotoResizer.mxml** and hit the Finish button. You have just created an AIR project with a main application file and an XML configuration file. Let's **set the proper values in that configuration file before actually starting to program the application**.

Set the application id in the XML file to be.flexpert.FCFB.projects.PhotoResizer. This name has to be unique for the application. As long as you're running this locally, there shouldn't be any problem but maybe there is already a PhotoResizer application somewhere on the internet as an AIR application. If the application id is the same, this could pose some problems, because this application is used by the AIR runtime to create your Encrypted Local Store (ELS) directory to store some application specific data. If your application id is not unique, two totally different AIR applications could be writing in the same ELS. **In the initial window section, set the** systemChrome **to none and the transparent property to true. This is necessary because we are going to use rounded corners on a custom chrome. Set the application** width **to 900 pixels and the** height **to 600 pixels.** Since you're going to use a custom chrome that has no handles for resizing or buttons for minimizing and maximizing, you can't resize from within the application, you might think that you don't have to worry about these settings. However, in Windows you can right-click on the application in the taskbar and choose those options. In order to avoid this, you need to set the minimizable, maximizable and resizable properties to false.

Creating the Application Layout

Now that you have the application properties set up, you can start with creating the layout. Remember that you are using Flex 4 now, so you can make use of the advanced graphics tags in the code editor. Keep in mind that the application layout is set to absolute by default, so the first component that you define in the code will be placed on the bottom layer and other components will be placed on top of it. **Let's start with the application background**. This is a rounded rectangle with a purple gradient fill color. For this, you make use of the `<s:Rect>` tag. On top of the background color, define a white rectangle of 500 pixels by 500 pixels to contain the image:

Excerpt from Workflow_Resizer ➤ *PhotoResizer.mxml*

```
<s:Rect x="0" y="0" width="900" height="600" radiusX="20">
  <s:fill>
    <s:LinearGradient rotation="90">
      <s:entries>
        <s:GradientEntry color="#2e064c"/>
        <s:GradientEntry color="#480c56"/>
      </s:entries>
    </s:LinearGradient>
  </s:fill>
</s:Rect>
<s:Rect x="20" y="80" width="500" height="500">
  <s:fill>
    <s:SolidColor color="#ffffff"/>
  </s:fill>
</s:Rect>
```

If you run the application now, you will notice that the application doesn't show just the custom chrome, because there are still some minor issues. First of all, notice that there is a status bar at the bottom of the application. To remove that status bar, set **the** `showStatusBar` **property to false in the** `<s:WindowedApplication>` **tag**. You will also notice that the rounded corners have a straight corner behind them. To remove this straight corner, **set the** `backgroundAlpha` **property to zero**. Because you are going to do some more styling, it is best that you **create a separate CSS file in a folder called "css"**. You need to manually create this folder in the root of your project. If you create this CSS file through the file creation wizard of Flash Builder 4, you will automatically get the Halo and Spark namespaces set up for you. In the CSS file, add the `backgroundAlpha` property for the `WindowedApplication` tag. For adding the CSS file to the application, you need to include the following line of code in your application:

```
<fx:Style source="../css/styles.css"/>
```

At this point, you can show the application, but there is no way to close it. For that, you will **add a** `Button` **component to create a close button**. Set the label to a simple "X" to resemble the Windows style close buttons. Make the `width` and `height` equal to 30 pixels and attach a generated event handler for the `click` event. The click handler will automatically be placed in an `<mx:Script>` block. Just add the statement `nativeWindow.close()` to the method to close the application. But for readability reasons, we are going to place the ActionScript code in a separate file inside of a package called "controllers." Create an ActionScript file in that package (not a class), copy the generated ActionScript code into that file, and include the file in your application by adding this line of code:

```
<fx:Script source="controllers/PhotoResizer.as"/>
```

Add a label with the application title "Photo Resizer" at (x, y) position (20, 15) and add the `styleName` "titleLabel." Of course you need to add this class selector in the CSS file. Because I used the Lucida Calligraphy font in this application I want to make sure that it is visible on all platforms, so embed the font in your application. This can also be done in the external CSS file by adding the following styles (but don't forget to copy the font to an assets directory in the root folder of your project):

Excerpt from Workflow_Resizer ➤ css ➤ styles.css

```
@font-face {
  src: url("../assets/LCALLIG.TTF");
  font-family: myFont;
}

.titleLabel {
  font-family: myFont;
  color: #E7D0D0;
  font-size: 36;
}
```

Creating the Content

You still need to **add an** `<mx:Image>` **control to contain the selected picture on top of the white rectangle you created earlier on**. To place the image in the center of this square, you have to create an `<s:Group>` component with the same size as the rectangle and at the same location. Since an image can be either in landscape or portrait, you need to set not just the size for that image, because that would distort the image, but also the `maxWidth` and `maxHeight` property to 500 pixels and the `maintainAspectRatio` property to `true`. The image itself should be placed in the center of this white rectangle, so you also have to set the `horizontalCenter` and `verticalCenter` properties to zero.

The layout of the components on the right side of the application is pretty straightforward. There are a couple of options to create that layout. The first one would be to give all the separate components their proper x and y positions. This is exactly what would happen when you use Flash Catalyst to create your application design. But in this case, I've chosen the option of using several groups of components with specific layout settings like `<s:HorizontalLayout/>`. This helps in spacing the components all at the same distance instead of having to calculate every position with a pixel perfect positioning:

Excerpt from Workflow_Resizer ➤ PhotoResizer.mxml

```
<s:Group right="20" top="80" bottom="20" width="340">
  <s:Label text="Select an image file" styleName="textLabel"/>

  <s:Group left="0" right="0" top="30">
    <s:layout>
      <s:HorizontalLayout/>
    </s:layout>
    <s:TextInput width="262" id="fileInput" editable="false"/>
    <s:Button label="Browse..." id="btnBrowse"
            click="btnBrowse_clickHandler(event)"/>
  </s:Group>

  <s:Group right="0" top="320">
    <s:layout>
      <s:HorizontalLayout/>
    </s:layout>
    <s:Button label="Save" id="btnSave"
            click="btnSave_clickHandler(event)"/>
    <s:Button label="Reset" id="btnReset"
```

```
                    click="btnReset_clickHandler(event)"/>
    </s:Group>

    <s:Group left="0" top="70">
      <s:layout>
        <s:HorizontalLayout/>
      </s:layout>
      <s:Label width="180" text="Original width:"
               styleName="textLabel"/>
      <s:TextInput id="origWidth" maxChars="4" width="37"
                   editable="false"/>
      <s:Label text="px" styleName="textLabel"/>
    </s:Group>
    <s:Group left="0" top="98">
      <s:layout>
        <s:HorizontalLayout/>
      </s:layout>
      <s:Label width="180" text="Original height:"
               styleName="textLabel"/>
      <s:TextInput id="origHeight" maxChars="4" width="37"
                   editable="false"/>
      <s:Label text="px" styleName="textLabel"/>
    </s:Group>

    <s:Label y="170" text="Adjust the thumbnail settings"
             styleName="textLabel"/>

    <s:Group left="0" right="0" top="210">
      <s:layout>
        <s:HorizontalLayout verticalAlign="middle"/>
      </s:layout>
      <s:HSlider id="slider" left="20" width="250" value="100"
                 maximum="100" showDataTip="false"
                 click="slider_changeHandler(event)"
                 thumbRelease="slider_changeHandler(event)"/>
      <s:Label text="{slider.value}%" textAlign="right"
               styleName="textLabel" width="100%"/>
    </s:Group>

    <s:Group left="0" top="240">
      <s:layout>
        <s:HorizontalLayout/>
      </s:layout>
      <s:Label width="180" text="Thumbnail width:"
               styleName="textLabel"/>
      <s:TextInput id="currentWidth" maxChars="4" width="37"
                   editable="false"/>
      <s:Label text="px" styleName="textLabel"/>
    </s:Group>
```

```
<s:Group left="0" top="268">
  <s:layout>
    <s:HorizontalLayout/>
  </s:layout>
  <s:Label width="180" text="Thumbnail height:"
           styleName="textLabel"/>
  <s:TextInput id="currentHeight" maxChars="4" width="37"
               editable="false"/>
  <s:Label text="px" styleName="textLabel"/>
</s:Group>
</s:Group>
```

Except for the `slider_changeHandler` method, all of the event handlers have been automatically generated. **You also need to copy those generated methods to the external ActionScript file.** I'll cover the ActionScript code in just a bit. But before you can start on the actual code, there is still some styling to do. So open the external CSS file again and add the following code for the `Label` and `Button` components:

Excerpt from Workflow_Resizer ➤ css ➤ styles.css

```
s|Label {
  color: #333333;
}

s|Button {
  corner-radius: 0;
}

s|Button#btnClose {
  font-weight: bold;
  corner-radius: 5;
}
```

Adding the Interactions

At this point, you have completed the layout of the `Photo Resizer` application, but the hard work still needs to be done in ActionScript. Let's start with the initialization of the application. Go to the external ActionScript file and **create a simple private function `initApp`**. (Don't forget to call this function in the `creationComplete` event for the application.) In this method, you are going to **make sure that the application is always placed in the center of the screen** by using the `Screen.mainScreen.bounds.width` and `Screen.mainScreen.bounds.height` properties to calculate the x and y position of the application. **You are also going to initialize the file filters** to only allow images of the types JPG and PNG to be loaded in the application. For that purpose, you have to create a `fileFilters` array in the application and add a `FileFilter` instance for each file type, specifying how the type is shown in the system dialog and what extension the file type has.

The next step is actually loading the file. This particular process flow starts with the user clicking on the `Browse…` button. In the click handler for this button, add an event listener to the `File` instance called "image" that you define at the application level. Then, open the system's browser dialog to open a file by using the `browseForOpen` method on that `File` instance, providing the file filters as a parameter. The next step is executed when the user selects a certain image on his computer. In that selection event handler, remove the event listener for the file selection again (this is mainly to aid garbage collection). Then, set the text property for the fileInput field on screen to the name of the selected file to show in the application which file has been selected. Add an event listener for the Event.COMPLETE event to be notified when the file has been loaded in memory and call the load method on the File instance. When the image has been loaded, you need to copy the content of that image to a [Bindable] ByteArray variable which is bound to the source property of the <mx:Image> control on screen to actually show the image in the application. You reset the slider and load the image data in a Loader object to determine the width and height of the original image. This is not done instantaneously, so before commencing the loadBytes method on the Loader object you need to attach an event listener to be notified when the load has been completed. In this last event handler, remove the event listener again and assign the width and height properties to the proper TextInput fields on screen. The code should look like this:

Excerpt from Workflow_Resizer ➤ *controllers* ➤ *PhotoResizer.mxml*

```
private var image:File = new File();
[Bindable]
private var newImageData:ByteArray;
private var fileFilters:Array;
private var loader:Loader;

private function initApp():void {
  // Center the application on the screen
  var centerX:Number = Screen.mainScreen.bounds.width / 2;
  var centerY:Number = Screen.mainScreen.bounds.height / 2;
  nativeWindow.x = centerX - (nativeWindow.width / 2);
  nativeWindow.y = centerY - (nativeWindow.height / 2);

  fileFilters = new Array();
  fileFilters.push(new FileFilter("JPEG file (*.jpg)", "*.jpg", "*.jpg"));
  fileFilters.push(new FileFilter("PNG file (*.png)", "*.png", "*.png"));
}

protected function btnBrowse_clickHandler(event:MouseEvent):void {
  image.addEventListener(Event.SELECT, fileSelected);
  image.browseForOpen("Select a file", fileFilters);
}

private function fileSelected(event:Event):void {
  image.removeEventListener(Event.SELECT, fileSelected);
  fileInput.text = image.name;
  image.addEventListener(Event.COMPLETE, imageLoaded);
  image.load();
}

private function imageLoaded(event:Event):void {
  image.removeEventListener(Event.COMPLETE, imageLoaded);
  newImageData = image.data;
  slider.value = 100;
  loader = new Loader();
  loader.contentLoaderInfo.addEventListener(Event.COMPLETE, loadComplete);
```

```
  loader.loadBytes(newImageData);
}

private function loadComplete(event:Event):void {
  loader.contentLoaderInfo.removeEventListener(Event.COMPLETE, loadComplete);
  origWidth.text = currentWidth.text = String(loader.width);
  origHeight.text = currentHeight.text = String(loader.height);
}
```

Saving the resized image is not hard work at all. This is mainly because the `newImageData` variable contains already the resized image. So you can use this variable directly in the `save` method of the `File` instance. And that's all you need to do in the click handler for the Save button. **The** `Reset` **button will rest the current resized image to the original again.** This means that you have to reset the `newImageData` to the `data` property of the `File` instance. But it also means that you have to reset the slider to 100% and adjust the `width` and `height` values of the resized image on screen.

The final piece of code to write is the actual resizing and the event handler on the slider component that will trigger this resizing. Let's start with the latter. When the slider value has changed, either by clicking on the slider bar or by releasing the thumb after the user dragged it to another position, you need to **calculate the size of the thumbnail image** by applying the percentage value to the original `width` and `height`. To make sure that you don't end up with some decimal pixel values, use the `Math.floor` method for the calculation. Once you have calculated the new image size, you call the `resizeImage` method, providing it with the new width and height parameters.

In this `resizeImage` function, you are going to perform the actual resizing. Start by creating a non-transparent `BitmapData` object the size of the thumbnail. Read the transformation matrix from the `Loader` instance for the original image, and use the `scale` method on it to determine how the image should be scaled down. Then place the scaled down version in the `BitmapData` object you've just created by using the `draw` method. This is all you need to do for resizing the image. Of course, now you're stuck with `BitmapData` instead of a JPG or PNG image, so you still have to convert it to the same encoding as the original file. Check for the original file type by examining the `extension` property of the `File` instance. If it's a JPG, you use a `JPEGEncoder` to convert the data into an encoded image you use again on the `<mx:Image>` component. Otherwise, you have to use a `PNGEncoder`. In either case, call the `encode` method and assign the result to the `newImageData` variable. Because of the binding metadata tag, this will trigger an update on the image on screen and will show you the shrunken version of the image:

Excerpt from Workflow_Resizer ➤ controllers ➤ PhotoResizer.mxml

```
protected function slider_changeHandler(event:Event):void {
  var w:Number = Math.floor(loader.width / 100 * slider.value);
  var h: Number = Math.floor(loader.height / 100 * slider.value);
  currentWidth.text = String(w);
  currentHeight.text = String(h);
  resizeImage(w, h);
}

private function resizeImage(w:Number, h:Number):void {
  var bmp:BitmapData = new BitmapData(w,h, false);
  var mt:Matrix = loader.transform.matrix;
  mt.scale(w / loader.width, h / loader.height);
  bmp.draw(loader, mt);
```

```
if(image.extension.toUpperCase() == "JPG") {
  var jpgEnc:JPEGEncoder = new JPEGEncoder(100);
  newImageData = jpgEnc.encode(bmp);
} else {
  var pngEnc:PNGEncoder = new PNGEncoder();
  newImageData = pngEnc.encode(bmp);
}
}
```

When you run the application now, you can load an image on the screen, select a percentage to resize to, and save it again to your local hard drive. The image format will always stay the same; if you start out with a PNG file, the saved thumbnail will also be a PNG file. You will notice some serious lag in the resizing. This is mostly due to the encode method, especially for the JPEGEncoder, which is a standard Flex codec class.

> *The algorithm used in this example is just a basic resizing algorithm that uses a transformation matrix to get the job done. For better results, you should look into bilinear and bicubic resizing algorithms. A bicubic algorithm is more appropriate for creating thumbnails; bilinear resizing is more suited to enlarging photographs.*

Conclusion

Although there are some design elements present, it's more efficient to create the entire application from within Flash Builder, since you really don't need the services of a designer for this simple project. Managing your resources is an important factor when figuring out the most efficient workflow for a certain project.

In the next workflow, you'll keep the design rather simple, but this time you're going to connect to a back end technology to retrieve data at runtime. Again, you will need to use Flash Builder to do some additional coding.

Simple Design, Connected to a Back End

As you know, Flex is a framework that is based on the Flash technology, but it is a completely different set of tools. In the past, many business applications have been developed in some version of Flex. Quite frankly, these business applications almost always looked like, well, business applications. No fancy graphics, no complicated designs. This is exactly the type of application I'm talking about here: this next type of application is one with a simple layout design and a need to **connect the application to an existing back end technology**. This type of application is more common than the previous two types.

Again, this would be a nice application to have on the desktop, so you will turn it into an AIR application. This will also give you the opportunity to see how to create an AIR application that is not compiled from within Flash Catalyst. This provides three advantages:

- You can attach complex functionality and connect to a backend, which is not possible in Flash Catalyst.
- You can use a digitally signed certificate to identify yourself as the publisher of the application.

- You can create a badge installer that will automatically install the AIR runtime when the user doesn't already have it.

A Twitter Search Client

Now, **these are applications for which you are typically going to call upon different profiles**. There will be a designer, and he will create the application design using tools such as Photoshop, Illustrator of Fireworks. The application flow (or mockup) will then be created by the interaction designer (a role that could be performed by the designer as well). He will then create a working version of the application in Flash Catalyst, minus the actual data. Once this mockup application is working, the interaction designer will pass it to the developer, who will import the created project and edit the code to attach the back end to it. As you will see, there is a bit more involved than calling a back end method and catching the result. Some things are going to require changes to actually get the application to work properly.

I'm assuming that the design is fully released before the developer starts working on it. This indicated that there is a straightforward workflow with only one action happening at a time. Figure 5-7 shows the final application.

Figure 5-7: The Twitter search application

Note that the results you see in your application will not match what you see in Figure 5-7 because this application captures a real-time snapshot of the latest tweets on Flash Catalyst (the search string).

The Designer Perspective

When the application is first conceived, all you know is what it should do. That's it. If you're lucky, there might be some rough sketches on paper.

Since this book is not about the Adobe Illustrator product, I'm not going to take you step by step though the entire design process. You can find the completed design in the `Workflow_TwitterSearch` *folder that accompany this book.*

Time to start the thinking process! Open your preferred design tool, which, in this case, is Illustrator. The concept is quite simple, so the layout should be simple and straightforward as well. Therefore, it should not take you very long to come up with the design for this application. However, you do have some liberty and you decide that the section with **the search fields should disappear** when the user is just reading the tweets in the application. You don't have to explicitly create a separate layer so that it is shown, because you can specify this in the project's design documents. The interaction designer will devise some kind of transition for hiding and showing that part. You do, however, **provide a handle to act as the trigger for these transitions at the top of the application** in the form of a fully colored bar with three dots on it to indicate that the user can interact with that part of the application.

You also **specify a custom scrollbar component**, because you feel that the standard Windows- or Mac-like scrollbars don't really go well with the rest of the design. So, instead of using the standard look and feel of a scrollbar, you leave out the up and down buttons at the top and bottom of the scrollbar and just use the thumb and track to give it more of a slick look.

Of course, some content needs to be shown, and your job is to design the look of that content. Since you don't have access to real-time data in a design tool, you **create one mockup data item that will have to be extrapolated to a list of the retrieved results**. In this list, you are going to show a header which contains the name of the person who posted the tweet, the avatar image of the author and of course, the actual tweet itself.

For convenience, it is best that you **split up your design into several layers and sublayers and give the layers a proper name**. Strictly speaking, this is not necessary, but I would advise you to do it anyway. It will make life easier for the interaction designer, because otherwise he could become confused about the purpose of a button generically named <path>. Next, create several groups to contain the layers that belong together. If you're quite happy with the design, your job as a designer is finished, and you can pass on the Illustrator file to the interaction designer.

The Interaction Designer Perspective

As I mentioned before, the interaction designer could also be the designer, but for the sake of the workflow, let's assume that this is a different person. This should be someone who has a lot of experience with the way people interact with a certain program. It is not only important to identify the transitions and make them pretty; it is even more important to identify the user group to know what you need to do with the interactions. IT people, administrative personnel, and children will interact with the applications in very different ways.

Creating the Application Layout

As an interaction designer, you receive the design created by one of your colleagues and now you have to turn it into an application. Which tool are you going to use for that? That's obvious: Flash Catalyst. Open the program, and on the welcome screen, choose the option of creating a project `From Adobe Illustrator AI File…` A dialog box will allow you to select the design file that was handed to you by the designer. In the import options dialog, keep everything editable, but change the application size to match the size of the actual maximum size of the application, which is 305 by 417 pixels. (The design is actually 416.25 pixels, but we'll fix that in Flash Catalyst.) You'll notice that the art board doesn't match the content of the design, so you have to select all the design elements and drag them to the proper position on the art board. **You will also notice a minor issue in the scrollbar thumb with the alignment of the small lines.** Just select the bottom one and correct the position. Now you should be all set to start working on creating the applications interactions and component definitions.

The first thing you should do before working on view states is create all of the necessary components. It's just easier if you define them first, rather than having to distribute them to other states afterwards. Start by selecting the "top rectangle" and "dots" layers from the Layers panel. Right-click on the selection on the art board, and select Convert Artwork to Component ➤ Button. This will turn it into a Button component. As shown in Figure 5-8, you will see that the layers have been merged together into one layer called "Button."

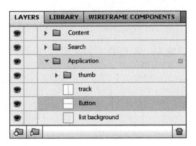

Figure 5-8: The "dots" sublayer and the "top retangle" layers have been merged into one single component.

The next few components are the ones that are located in the search box. **There are actually two components that need to be created: a text input and a button.** Creating the text input field is fairly simple. You just have to click on that component on the art board and use the right-click popup menu again to convert it into a Text Input component. The part where you can type the text is automatically created by Flash Catalyst, and it even takes a certain amount of padding into account. That is all you need to do for this component. **For the button, you have to select both the Search... label and the rectangular component behind it** and convert the selection to a Button component. Naturally, a button has different view states for hovering and selecting it (we don't use the disabled state in this application), but at this point, all of those states appear exactly the same. So, to change this you have to **double click the component** and Flash Catalyst will take you into the component states for the button.

Once inside the Button component, you'll see the four button states at the top of the application: Up, Over, Down and Disabled. Just leave the Up state as is and select the Over state in the Pages/States panel. In that state, select the button background and rotate it so that the gradient is turned upside down. This will be the indication that the mouse pointer is hovering over the button. For the Down state, do the same thing and add an Inner Glow filter in the Filters section of the Properties panel. For the filter, you set the following properties:

- Color: #666666
- Blur: 5
- Strength: 2

Leave all the others as they were. This will give the user an impression that the button is actually being clicked.

Creating the Data List with a Custom Scrollbar

The final component you have to create is the actual content. For that, you are going to **create a** Data List **component**. To create such a component, you need to select the remaining layers: Content, thumb, track and list background. Again, right-click the selection and use the Convert artwork to Component ▶ Data List option to start the conversion. Now you have merged all of these layers into a single component. But don't worry; just as with the Button component, you still have the separate layers inside of the component itself. And you are going to need those layers, because at the moment your component is still incomplete. You still have to define the repeating item for the list. So, double click the component to see all of the layers again. Select the Content layer in the Layers panel to select all of the content subitems. Right-click that selection and choose the Repeated Item option from the Convert Artwork to Data List Part submenu. This action will automatically generate five items in the Design-Time Data panel and they will also be placed underneath each other in the list. Add a couple more items in this panel by clicking the Add Row button a couple of times. This way you can actually test the applications scrollbar in just a minute. Position the Data List Part and resize it to fit the entire Data List area.

To create that scrollbar, first **select the** thumb **and** track **layers, right-click the selection and convert the artwork to a** Vertical Scrollbar **component**. Next, double click the scrollbar component to assign its parts. First, select the thumb sublayer and convert the selection to the Thumb part of the scrollbar by using the right-click popup menu. Then, select the track layer in the Layers panel and convert that selection to the Track part of the scrollbar. Those two parts are the only ones that are required and that's all you need to do to have a working scrollbar on the Data List component. If you test the application now, you should be able to use the scrollbar to scroll through the list that is still filled with design-time data.

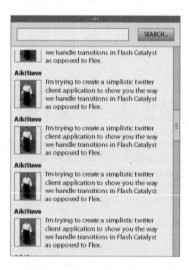

Figure 5-9: The scrollbar is working with design-time data without having to write any code.

For a final touch on the look and feel of the Data List component, you are going to **add some view states to the repeated item** so the user can select one and knows which item he's hovering over with the mouse pointer. Go back up one level and double click the repeated item. This will take you into that part of the component and it will show you a single instance, which you can now modify. If you look at the Pages/States panel at the top of the application, you'll notice that the Over and Selected states are defined for you. Moving on, you need to determine the size of one item. You can do this by **creating a white rectangle, measuring 290 by 84 pixels, as the bottom layer of the component**. I've chosen the color white because that also the background color for the data list, which means that in the Normal state you won't see any background color on an item. You are going to **reuse that same rectangle in the other states**, but with different colors. At the moment, only the Normal state will contain that rectangle. The easiest way of getting the rectangle in the other states at the same position and with exactly the same size is to select it and then select the option Share to State ➤ All States from the right-click popup menu. Once you've done that, the rectangle is available in all the states. Then you select the white rectangle in the Over state and change its fill color to #CCCCCC in the Common section of the Properties panel. Go to the Selected state and change the fill color of the background rectangle to #999999. This is all you need to do, because as Figure 5-10 shows, you now have an indication of selected and hovered items in your list. This also concludes the creation of the components for the application.

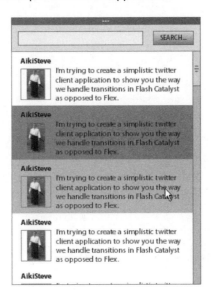

Figure 5-10: The repeated item now has visible Over and Selected states.

Adding the Interactions

The last thing you need to do in Flash Catalyst is define the interactions/transitions that will show and hide the search box at the top of the application. But before you can start on that, you still need to define the two application states, so you need to **duplicate the** Page1 **state** in the Pages/States panel. **In the first page, hide the text input field and the button components** by clicking in the first column for those layers in the Layers panel. This will make them invisible in the initial state. However, you're still left with an empty box. To solve that issue, **select both the box and the top button component (that will toggle the other state) and move them down until eventually only that top button component is visible**. The search box background will slide behind the rest of the application.

Next, trigger the view state change by selecting the top button component and adding an interaction to it with the following properties:

- Event: On Click
- Action: Play Transition to State
- State: Page2
- Condition: When in Page1

Add another interaction to return to Page1, but only when the application is already in Page2. This will allow you to toggle between the two states using the small button bar at the top of the application. Don't worry about the white background coming through now at the top of the application. You will fix this in Flash Builder when you make the application transparent.

At this point, the transitions are working properly, but the application just jumps from one state to the other. To make it more user friendly, you are going to create a nice little animation which will make the transition between two states a little smoother. Happily, Flash Catalyst has automatically created the basic effects for you, depending on the property changes that you have made in the first view state. Thus, there is a Fade In and Fade Out effect for both the text input field and the Search… button. The top button and the search box background color will get a Move effect. But all of these effects happen simultaneous and instantaneous. **You need to select each transition in the** Timelines **panel, hit the** Smooth Transition **button and organize the effects on the timeline to get a smoother transition.** For the transition from Page1 to Page2, you first move the components into place, and just before that effect is finished, you start the fade in of the text input component and the button. For the transition back to the initial state, you first do the fade out of these components, and just before that effect has finished, you start the move effect on the background and the top button component. This will render your transition very smoothly.

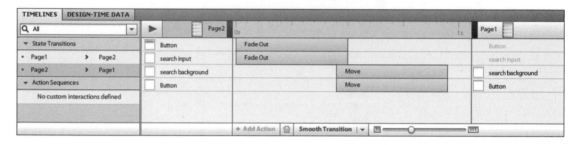

Figure 5-11: The repeated item now has visible Over and Selected states.

At this point, you've completed your job as interaction designer. You've taken a static design which was structured into several layers and converted it into a working application with some nice transitions as an added value. Flash Catalyst has created an FXG file for this project, which you can now transfer to the developer in your team for attaching the back end service call to the application and putting the results in the data list instead of the static data that's in there now.

The Developer Perspective

As a developer, you receive an FXG file, created by Flash Catalyst, from your interaction designer, and you import it into Flash Builder using the Import Flex Project (FXP)… from the File menu. Name the project 'Workflow_TwitterSearch" and locate it next to the FXG file of the project. Take a look at the project structure; you'll notice that Flash Catalyst has created several custom Flex 4 components for you. Those components come from the conversions that the interaction designer has done on the original Illustrator file, and they are located in a separate package within your project.

If you open the Main.mxml file, which contains your main application and is the starting point for your application, you'll notice there are a couple of new namespaces you might not recognize from working with basic Flex 4 projects. You'll also notice that there are a lot of <fx:DesignLayer> tags in your code. Each of these tags represents a layer in the Layers panel inside of Flash Catalyst. (When round tripping between Flash Builder and Flash Catalyst is enabled, these extra namespaces will allow you to take your modified project back into Flash Catalyst for design adjustments. This is planned for the future; in the current version, it is still not possible.)

Retrieving the Data at Runtime

You'll also notice that the <s:List> component has a dataProvider set to a fixed ArrayCollection. This data is actually the dummy data that the interaction designer used in Flash Catalyst to verify the workings of the custom scrollbar component. This is also exactly what you need to change, because you are going to replace that fixed data with the data that is returned from the Twitter search call. So, the first thing you need to do is **remove that fixed dataProvider and replace it with a** [Bindable] ArrayCollection that you define in the <fx:Script> block; call this variable "searchResults."

The next step is to actually call the Twitter search API. This is done by using an <mx:HTTPService>. Defining that service in your code is slightly different from what you may be used to in previous versions of Flex, because now you have to place it inside of an <fx:Declarations> block. Basically, everything that concerns services and call responders or items that are not directly shown on screen has to be placed inside such a code block. **Create an** <fx:Declarations> **block underneath the** <fx:Script> **block and place the** HTTPService **definition inside of it**. Give the service an id of 'service", but don't define a URL for it, because you are going to set it dynamically when the user hits the search button. **In that same block of declarations, you also define a** <s:CallResponder> **tag, named** serviceResponder, that defines the result and fault handlers for the service call. When you define both handlers, let Flash Builder generate the methods that will be executed when these events are fired. At this point, your <fx:Declarations> block will look like this:

Excerpt from Workflow_TwitterSearch ➤ *Main.mxml*

```
<fx:Declarations>
  <s:HTTPService id="service" />
  <s:CallResponder id="serviceResponder"
                   result="callresponder1_resultHandler(event)"
                   fault="serviceResponder_faultHandler(event)"/>
</fx:Declarations>
```

Note that the responder is not yet attached to that service; you'll do that in the next step. But first, you need to **fill in the generated event handlers.** In the serviceResponder_faultHandler, display an Alert message that shows the faultString property that is returned from the service. You can find this property in the fault property of the event parameter. In the callresponder1_resultHandler, set the bindable ArrayCollection variable to the result.feed.entry property of the event parameter. You can find this out by looking at the result XML object that is returned from the service API. That's all you need to do, because due to the binding, when the results return from the service call, the data in the list will be updated automatically.

The final steps of the application lie in the actual calling of the Twitter search API. **Search for the button component with the** Search… **label on it and attach a click handler** to it. Again, let Flash Builder generate the event handler because it's a time saver. In this button1_clickHandler, which you can now find in the <fx:Script> block as well, you have to dynamically generate the URL to which the HTTPService needs to connect. This is done by concatenating the base search API string with the search string that can be found in the TextInput field. Now that the URL is all set, you simply call the send method on the HTTPService. But you still need to attach the responder to this service, and you do that by setting the token property of the responder object equal to the token that is returned by the send method. The event handler will look like this:

Excerpt from Workflow_TwitterSearch ➤ *Main.mxml*

```
protected function button1_clickHandler(event:MouseEvent):void {
  service.url = "http://search.twitter.com/search.atom?q=" + textinput1.text;
```

```
    serviceResponder.token = service.send();
}
```

Adjusting the Item Renderer to Display the Runtime Data

The application is working properly, but you still need to **change the item renderer** for the `<s:List>` component, because at this point, that renderer is working with the fixed data that came from `Flash Catalyst`. If you were to run the application now, you would get the results as shown in Figure 5-12.

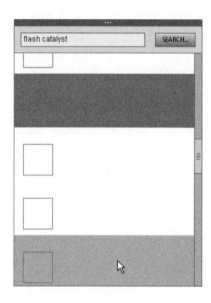

Figure 5-12: The search API is working but the item renderer still needs to be adjusted.

As you can see, the search results are displayed nicely, but the application didn't fill in the information in the item renderer. To fix this, go to the RepeatedItem1.mxml component, which you can find in the components package in your project structure. In that file, make the following adjustments. First, you'll see the `<mx:Image>` control which has its `source` property bound to `data.image1`. This data property is actually holding the entire feed entry object, so you can examine this feed structure to determine that the `source` property needs to be changed into `data.link[1].href` to get the link to the avatar of the author. In the `<s:RichText>` components you'll see that the design-time data is also still present in the `d:userLabel` properties. That was used inside of Flash Catalyst. But you can find the text property that already contains some binding expression to `data.text1` for the tweet content and `data.text2` for the author's name. The first one needs to be changed into `data.title`, because it is the `title` property in the XML that actually holds the content of the tweet. For the second `<s:RichText>` component, you need to change this to `data.author.name`, because that is the property that contains the author's name. And now you're set to test the application again.

There is only one thing left to do. The application has been imported from a Flash Catalyst project file. That means that it is still just a Flex application. I said that you were going to create an AIR application. Well, that's the final step. Go to the `Package Explorer`, select the project, and right-click on it. This will show a popup menu where you can **choose the** `Convert to Flex Desktop Project…` **option from the**

Add/Change Project Type **submenu**. You are then asked if it is alright to convert the <s:Application> tag into an <s:WindowedApplication> tag. Click the OK button and save the changes in the Main.mxml file. Now you have a working AIR application, but **there are still some minor changes to be made because you are going to create a transparent application** so the white background is not visible when the search box is hidden.

Go to the XML application configuration file and change the following settings:

- systemChrome: none
- transparent: true

In the main application file, adjust the <s:WindowedApplication> tag to remove the backgroundColor and preloaderBaseColor and then add the following properties:

- backgroundAlpha: 0
- showStatusBar: false

And now you're done and ready to test your Twitter Search application one final time. You'll see that the background is now completely transparent, giving the impression that the search box is really sliding out of the application. That's how easy it is to convert your Flex application into an AIR application using Flash Builder 4.

Oops, the Design is Missing Something!

Notice that there is no close button for this application. Adding a close button could be done in the top button component, for example. When round tripping is enabled between Flash Catalyst and Flash Builder, this task will be very easy: as developer, you will give your code back to the interaction designer so that he can add such a button, and the FXG file would be returned to the developer to add the actual code to close the window.

But for now, you're left with two options: create a close button yourself or ask the designer to adjust the design so it contains a close button. In this exercise, I'm going to show you how to incorporate this small design change.

The Interaction Designer Changes

Take back the FXG file that Flash Catalyst created earlier; it is the same file that the developer used to create the project. **Create a white cross on the right side of that component** simply by drawing two intersecting lines. Set the width and the height of the lines to 7 pixels and position them so they are more or less aligned with the center of the scrollbar in the application. Select the two layers that have been created by this action and **convert them into a** Button **component by** selecting the Convert Artwork to Component ➤ Button option for the right-click popup menu.

Now you have a button that will act as the close button. However, at this point, the button only exists when the component is in the Page1 state. So, to make the button appear in the other states, select the Share to State ➤ All States option from the right-click popup menu for the application. Save the project using a new filename and hand it over to the developer.

The Developer Changes

As a developer, you cannot just re-import the Flash Catalyst file and merge it automatically with the changes that you've already made to the existing project. You are going to have to do this manually. Create a new project by choosing Import Flex project (FXP)... from the File menu in Flash Builder 4.

When you select the same file as with the first project, you will get the option to overwrite the existing project or create a new copy in a separate project. Choosing the first one will overwrite everything in your project; that's not something you want to do right now, since you've already done the code for the back end connection. Instead, give this new project a separate name.

The easiest way of comparing these projects to see what has been changed is to select the Workflow_TwitterSearch project and choose Compare Project with Version… ➤ Workflow_TwitterSearch_close, which is the name I gave the copy project. This will give you an overview if the changes between the projects. This is not unlike a versioning tool such as SVN or CVS. If you look at what's different in the project structure, you'll notice in the components package that there is now a Button3 component. Less noticeable is the fact that this new component is now used in the main application file. What you need to do now is copy the new component into the components package of the existing application. Then **copy the line of code that puts the new component in the application from the Main.mxml file in the new project to the existing application, like so:**

Excerpt from Workflow_TwitterSearch ➤ Main.mxml

```
<s:Button skinClass="components.Button3" x="294" y="43" id="button3" y.Page2="1"/>
```

If you use the comparison view in Flash Builder, you can just copy the changes from one file to the other without having to go into the files themselves. Since the close button is located at the application level, it will have to move together with the search box component. As a result, you also need to copy **the transitions between the two view states for the new button component into the existing application:**

Excerpt from Workflow_TwitterSearch ➤ Main.mxml

```
<s:transitions>
  <s:Transition autoReverse="true" fromState="Page2" toState="Page1">
    <s:Parallel>
      ...
      <s:Parallel target="{button3}">
        <s:Move duration="500" autoCenterTransform="true" startDelay="450"/>
      </s:Parallel>
    </s:Parallel>
  </s:Transition>
  <s:Transition autoReverse="true" fromState="Page1" toState="Page2">
    <s:Parallel>
      ...
      <s:Parallel target="{button3}">
        <s:Move duration="500" autoCenterTransform="true"/>
      </s:Parallel>
    </s:Parallel>
  </s:Transition>
</s:transitions>
```

Then you need to go into the main application file and **add an event handler** to the click event on the Button3 component. Again, to save some time, let Flash Builder 4 generate the event handler. This will automatically create the <fx:Script> block and place the generated event handler inside of the code block. Now, the only statement you need to write in this event handler is nativeWindow.close(). That's all it takes to close your AIR application from within the application itself.

Figure 5-13: The finished AIR application also has a close button.

Although it will be wonderful to have this round tripping between Flash Builder and Flash Catalyst in future versions of the products, it does not mean that there cannot be an iterative development cycle involving both development and design. This is proven by the project you've created just now.

Conclusion

Even though this is still a rather simple design for an application, the fact that it contains some custom elements such as the scrollbar makes it more adequate to involve Flash Catalyst in the creation process. As mentioned before, if you've ever tried to create a custom scrollbar, you'll definitely appreciate the possibility to create one in Flash Catalyst with just a few clicks. Adding the runtime data cannot be done in Flash Catalyst, so you have to involve a developer to implement that feature in Flash Builder.

Naturally, you could argue that you don't really need a designer for this workflow, since the interaction designer could have created every part of this application from within Flash Catalyst. This would have been a viable solution.

In the next application, you'll turn down the functional complexity. On the other hand, you're going to step up on the ladder of design complexity. This will increase the necessity of using a product such as Flash Catalyst.

Complex Design, Simple Functionality

In this next workflow, I'm going to talk about the basic functionality again. Only this time, it's going to be combined with a complex design. Now, when I talk about complex design, it doesn't necessarily mean many complex graphical components, nor does it indicate a huge number of different pages or view states. Rather, it means that there will be some elements that are pretty hard to create with the basic components (even though you can do quite a lot with styling); it might be more convenient to use elements from a design tool instead of trying to create them from scratch.

A Static Website

For this type of workflow, I've chosen to create a static website with some complex elements. The design for this website will be created in Photoshop and then taken into Flash Catalyst to convert the design elements into working Flex 4 components. **This project would require two profiles: the designer and the interaction designer.** Of course, as with the previous workflow types, both profiles could be the same person. It all depends on the availability of such distinct roles in your company.

Now, let me give you a rough situation sketch of the project specifics. The website is created for a tour operator, offering information about the tours, including pictures and a popup with a world map to indicate where these tours will take you.

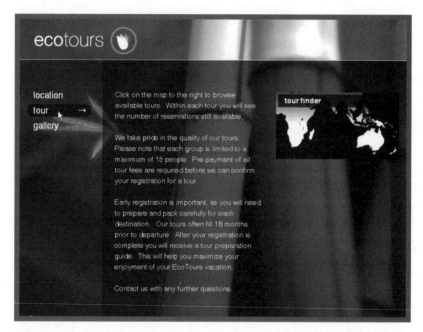

Figure 5-14: The finished website will have some static text and a `tour finder` component that will trigger a world map popup.

The Designer Perspective

In this project, everything starts with the design of the website. In the first steps of the process, it doesn't really matter whether or not the website is going to be attached to a database or not. The designer doesn't really care about this. If you know up front that there is actually going to be some kind of back end technology involved, you can take this into account and maybe incorporate some fetch, search, or refresh buttons in your design. In this example, however, you know the website will be contain only static content, so you don't have to worry about a database.

As a designer, you can make life easier on the interaction designer by splitting up your design into several layers and layer groups for components that logically belong together. Also, give the layers some meaningful names to identify their purpose. Finally, although you don't *have* to create all of the items that will be shown on the screen, it will be more convenient if you at least create the more complex graphical parts. As I mentioned before, styling in Flash Catalyst can get the interaction designer quite far in making some nice looking components. But either it will take up more time to do so, as it is not intended to be a pure design product, or it will be nigh on impossible to create some components starting from the basic wireframe components.

For this application, **create a separate design composed of two main columns**: the navigation on the left and the information on the right side of the application. Make sure that you create the Over state for the navigation buttons, since it contains a small custom arrow shape. **For the** Location **page, add some text with general information about the locations of the tours and a bit of explanation about the company does.** This content is very basic and straightforward. **The** Tours **page has some basic information in its content, but there is also a button that will take you to the** Tour Finder **popup.** However, this button is not just an ordinary button. Instead, it is a small image of a world map with the title on top of it in a gray but partly transparent box. When the user clicks on this in the finished website, a popup will be pop up. So, this **popup is also something you need to create**. Draw a rectangle over both the content and the navigation, so that it covers the text in the application. However, do leave some spacing around the edges as shown in Figure 5-15 to make it look like it's a popup window. Otherwise, it will look more like another page. In the right top corner of the popup rectangle, create a close button to allow the user to remove the popup. Within this component, **you need to show a large world map and indicate the tour locations** by drawing some rectangular shapes over it. **The last page of this website contains a gallery of pictures** that have been taken on site, so the user gets an impression as to what to expect from these tours. Place the pictures inside of a white square to give the impression of an actual slide. Underneath the photo, set a title for that particular slide.

Figure 5-15: The popup does not cover the entire website area.

Finally, look closely at the EcoTours company logo, which looks like a flower in a circle. **You need to draw inside of a design product like Photoshop**, because it is made out of several droplets rotated around the same point and with slightly different fill color opacities, letting the underlying droplets shine through to create the desired effect. This shape would be impossible to draw inside of Flash Catalyst.

At this point, your job as the designer is done and you can pass on your Photoshop file to the interaction designer to turn the static design elements into working components.

The Interaction Designer Perspective

As the interaction designer, you are going to receive the completed design file. In this example, I'm using a PSD file, but you could be receiving an Illustrator file or an FXG file that has been saved from within Fireworks. The first thing you need to do is open Flash Catalyst and create a project based on the provided Photoshop design file. In the wizard, leave all the image and text layers editable, flatten the shape layers, and keep the dimensions of 800 by 600 pixels. These should all match the suggested settings.

Creating the Components

Let's start with the tour map popup window. There are actually two ways to create the proper components for this window. In the first one, first create a separate view state for this popup page, and then create the necessary components for that state. These components would only be available in that particular state. In the application you're going to make, this is all very well possible since those components are only going to be available in that state alone. You can share certain components with other states if this is required, but it's optional. The second option would be to create all of the required components in one state and then duplicate that state, so the components exist in all states. I personally prefer the latter, because it can save you some time and headaches trying to figure out why a certain component doesn't work in a particular view state.

Make sure that the layer with the popup window is visible. In the PSD file that comes with this example, that layer is called "tour finder popup map." In the Layers panel, **select the close button and convert it to a** `Button` **component** by selecting the `Convert Artwork to Component ➤ Button` option from the right-click popup menu. That's all you need to do for the popup window. I will come back to the close button later when you need to implement the view state transitions. So for now, just hide the popup layer again.

Since the rest of the content is quite static, focus on the navigation buttons first. If you look at the `Layers` panel and open the `navigation` sublayer, you will see two item layers for each button component: the label for the button and the `Over` state, which is marked by a rounded rectangle with an additional arrow on the right side of the label.

Figure 5-16: The design shows two distinct layers for each navigation button.

Select both the location **and** location over **layers and convert them to one single Button component** in the same way as before. Once the conversion is done, double click the component to dive into it. **In the** Up **state, make sure the** location over **layer is not visible** by clicking in the first column of that layer in the Layers panel. This will ensure that only the text part is visible in this state. Another option would have been to delete the selected graphic, since that would have resulted in the removal of the graphic in that particular state only. The rectangle graphic would still remain visible in the other button states. **Leave the** Over **state as it is and change the color of the label for the** Down **state.** Select the Down state and click on the button label. In the Properties panel, set the text color in the Common section to #485a10 to give it the same dark green color as the bounding rectangle of the application itself. Then return to the application level and test the results by hitting <CTRL>+<ENTER> or by choosing Run Project from the File menu.

When you test your button component now, you'll notice that the Over state is only set when you're actually over the text part of the button. Personally, I find such a thing very annoying because the area that reacts is way too small. So let's change this. Go back into Flash Catalyst and double click the button component again. **In the** Up **state, instead of removing the button background completely, just make it visible again.** However, that's not what you want, because now it seems like the Over state is always shown. Select the background graphic and go to the Properties panel. In the Common section again, you'll find a property called Opacity. This actually indicates the inverse transparency level, which means that if you have an opacity level of 100, the graphic is completely visible. **Turn the opacity level down to zero** to make the layer completely transparent. The layer seems to be invisible, but it will still be there. If you test the button component again, you will see that the area that reacts to the mouse pointer is much bigger now.

Once you're satisfied with the results of these actions, **perform the same actions to create the other two buttons**. Again, select both layers for the button and adjust the Up state so that the reaction area is big enough. Then adjust the Down state to change the text color of the button label. Once you've done this for the remaining buttons, test the application again to see the results of your actions.

Figure 5-17: The graphical elements are now converted into buttons with a different appearances for each state.

At this point, there is one more component to create: the trigger to call the popup tour finder map window. First, **go to the** tour **page layer and make it visible**, hiding the other content layers to avoid confusion. On the right side of the page, you'll see a small image of a world map with a title on top of it. These are not two separate layers, but actually one layer that has fused together the two component parts. This is not something that Flash Catalyst has done, because if you look at the original PSD file, you'll see that it's one component event there. **Select that image and convert it into a generic component** by selecting the Custom/Generic Component option from the Convert Artwork to Component submenu. Because you are not going to need any view states whatsoever on this component, there's no reason to turn it into a button.

Creating the Pages

All of the components are set up. Now it's time to create the different pages in the website. To do so, duplicate the first page and make certain part of the design visible/invisible depending on what information should be shown on that particular page. In this website, you have three pages and a popup window, for a total of four different pages that have to be constructed. **Go to the** Pages/States **panel and duplicate the first page three times. Rename the pages** so that their names match the names of the actual menu items or the popup name. The result should match those shown in Figure 5-18.

Figure 5-18: The graphical elements are now converted into buttons with a different appearance for each state.

Adjust the visibility of the different content layers in the Layers **panel so that only the appropriate data is actually visible for each page.** In the first page, the Location page, make sure that only the location page layer is visible in the content section; for the second page, it would be the tour page layer. For the third page, the gallery page layer should be set to visible in the Layers panel. The fourth page, the one with the tour finder map on it, is somewhat different. Since this map will cover the entire content area, it shouldn't really matter what else is visible, because this layer will be on top, hiding everything that underneath it. But I prefer to think about the process flow and make the pages seem natural, similar to when you create such a website using Flash Professional. So the TourFinder page will have the tour page layer visible as well as the popup layer.

Adding the Interactions

With the pages set up, you can now add the actual navigation. Select the first button component in the navigation bar on the left side of the application. In the Interactions panel, **add a new interaction** by clicking on the Add Interaction button. In the interaction settings, apply the following properties:

- Event: On Click
- Action: Play Transition to State
- State: Location
- Condition: When in Any State

For the Tour button, add a similar interaction, but refer to the Tour state. For the third button, do the same thing again, but set the state to Gallery. **Adding these interactions can be done in any state;** you can have any page selected in the Pages/States panel, since the interaction is placed on the component and not for a particular state. However, you still need to call the TourFinder page, and for that you need to be in the Tour state. (Well, that not entirely true, because you can also select the little world map that you've converted into a generic component from the layers panel. But I find it more convenient to select the appropriate page so the component that will trigger the view state change is actually visible.) But anyway, you have to **select that little map and add an interaction that will show the** TourFinder **page**. But this time, things are a little bit different. Since this popup should only be shown when the user is already within the Tour page, you need to adjust the interaction properties slightly to this:

- Event: On Click
- Action: Play Transition to State
- State: Location
- Condition: When in Tour

And of course, you need to be able to close the popup and return to the Tour page in the final website. Go to the fourth page and **select the little close button. Add an interaction to this component that goes back to the** Tour **page**, but only when the website is already on the TourFinder page. If you run the application/website now, you'll see a working website.

But when you change pages in the website as it is constructed now, the site just jumps from one page to another. I think you should **add some animation to give it a dynamic boost**. Let's start with the **popup tour finder map**. In Flash Catalyst, in the Timelines panel, you'll see that there are interactions defined for going from every page to every other page. in this case, you're only interested in two of them, namely for going from Tour to TourFinder and vice versa. Keep it simple by just letting the popup window **fade in when it needs to be shown and fade out when it needs to be hidden**. These animations have already been created for you by Flash Catalyst when you made the popup layer visible/invisible in all the pages. All you have to do is drag the animation length to make it last 0.5 seconds. If you test this, you'll see that this is a good duration for such an animation.

For the other page transitions, you are going to make it easy on yourself. Before smoothing the transitions between the pages, click on the arrow symbol next to the Smooth Transition button in the left bottom corner of the Timelines panel. This will pop up a settings dialog. Select the Smart Smoothing option for the Timing property. That way, you don't have to manually drag the effects to the proper location for each transition. Once you've done that, go over the transitions between the pages one by one, hitting the Smooth Transition button every time.

The final step in producing this website is to actually publish the SWF file. You can do that by choosing the Publish to SWF… option in the File menu. Select the location where the published application should be placed and leave the default settings. At the selected location you will then get a deploy-to-web directory, which you can copy to your web server so everyone can access that website. That's all you need to do to get this website working.

Conclusion

Since this type of application relies heavily on the design and doesn't require any complex calculations or runtime data retrieval, it is obvious that you start out with the design file and take advantage of the fact that Flash Catalyst can import that file directly. Since you have the proper layer structure, creating the custom components and pages is a piece of cake since that is exactly what Flash Catalyst does best.

In the next workflow, I'll take you through the process of creating an application with a complex design that uses some complex functionality but does not connect to a back end technology.

Complex Design, Complex Functionality

In this particular workflow, I'm going to use a complex design with some advanced gradients and shapes, which would be pretty hard to do with just Flash Builder. So yes, you are going to use Photoshop for the design of this application. But you're also going to apply some complex functionality without connecting to a back end technology. The reason why I make a distinction between complex functionality and connecting to a back end is because a back end connection isn't necessarily very complex. However, both types require some custom ActionScript coding, so they cannot be made using Flash Catalyst alone because you can't really code in that tool.

A Simulator

For this specific example, I've chosen a simulator type of application, specifically a mortgage simulator that works in both directions. You can enter the amount you wish to borrow and calculate the down payment for a given interest over a certain amount of years, or you can enter the down payment amount and see how much you can get you can borrow at a certain interest rate.

The complex functionality lies in two parts for this application. First, there is the calculation that needs to happen in order to get the output results. Second, there is also a graph in the application showing you how much you have actually paid after the mortgage has been paid off completely. I've always found this figure to be quite depressing because it's usually a lot higher than you'd expect.

This application will only give you the result as an indication. In the real world, you may want to keep these calculations in a database and ask the user for his email address in order to follow up and try to close the deal or make an appointment with a local office. The finished application will look something like what you see in Figure 5-19.

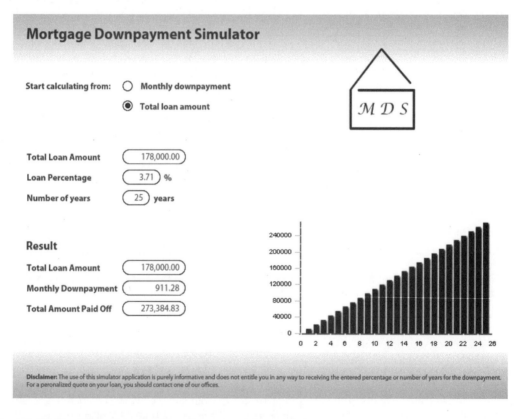

Figure 5-19: The finished application with an example request.

Who is going to work on this application? Since it is a complex design with some custom built components, **there has to be a designer on the team**. To get that complex design converted into a working application, you are going to use Flash Catalyst to make it easier on yourself. But that also means that **the team will include an interaction designer**. Now, as I've mentioned before, the role of the interaction designer doesn't necessarily have to be fulfilled by a different person. It could be the designer, or even the developer in some cases, but as Flash Catalyst becomes more accepted as a valuable tool in the development workflow for RIAs, this role will become a separate job on the development team. And of course, since there are calculations to be made and a graph to be added, you also **need a developer in this application**.

The designer perspective

As usual, you start with the design for the application. This time you're using Photoshop and you'll **start with an 800 by 600 pixel white canvas** that will act as the background for the rest of the application. To freshen up the background and make it look somewhat modern, **select a rectangular area of 150 pixels high** at the top of the application and make it as wide as the entire application canvas. Then **apply a gradient fill** with a color range from #177904 to #ffffff. Set the opacity for the gradient to 30% to get the proper effect of a soft color. Then, **duplicate that layer**, move it to the bottom of the application canvas, and rotate it 180 degrees to get the opposite effect at the bottom. That's all you need to do for the background.

In the green top section, add the title "Mortgage Downpayment Simulator" in the same green color as you used for the gradient. **In the bottom section, add a disclaimer message** stating the fact that using the simulator does not entitle the user to obtain that mortgage percentage and so on. All the text in this application will be in the same green color, #177904.

The first future interactive part of the application is **giving the user the choice to start calculating from a total amount to borrow or from a down payment amount**. Since it will never be possible to have both at the same time, it's obvious that you use a radio button for this. You could use a default radio button in Flash Catalyst, but let's make the selection dot green as well as the radio button's border. You create such a custom radio button by **drawing two concentric circles** on separate layers with the biggest one being the outer circle and filling up the second one with the green color you've used before. Then you duplicate the layers to create the second radio button.

About one third down from the top, you start the user input questions. The first input question is also the one that depends on the selection that has been made with the radio buttons. That means that at this position there will have to be two different questions: one for the total loan amount and one for the monthly down payment. **The text input field itself will again be a custom component.** For that, you need to draw a rounded rectangle that is big enough to contain the number 9,999,999.99 in a 14 point regular font. Actually, you need to add this text manually on a separate layer as this layer. And for those two questions, you place both the labels and the text input components at the same location, since only one will be visible at a time.

Repeat the process again for getting the mortgage percentage and the number of years the user want to pay off the mortgage. Of course, you need to size the input fields according to the possible values for those fields. After all, it's quite illogical to size the input field to get the number of years exactly the same as the input field for the loan amount. At this point, you're done with the user input and your design should look something like Figure 5-20.

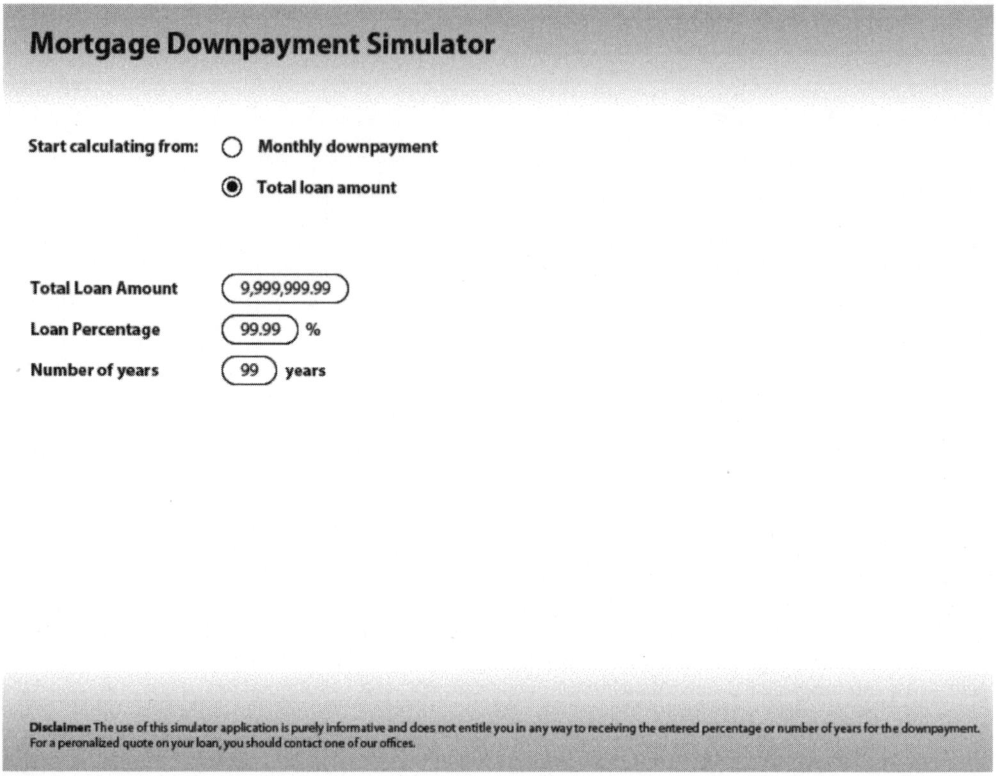

Mortgage Downpayment Simulator

Start calculating from: ○ Monthly downpayment

◉ Total loan amount

Total Loan Amount   (9,999,999.99)

Loan Percentage   (99.99) %

Number of years   (99) years

Disclaimer: The use of this simulator application is purely informative and does not entitle you in any way to receiving the entered percentage or number of years for the downpayment. For a peronalized quote on your loan, you should contact one of our offices.

Figure 5-20: The input part of the application is done. Notice the radio button can be selected and deselected because it consists of two layers that can be made (in)visible separately.

For the output variables, you're going to have three values. They're all possibly huge numbers: the total loan amount, the down payment amount, and the total amount paid off after the number of years from the input field. **Duplicate the layer that holds the total loan amount three more times and move those down to the last third section**, preceded by a subtitle "Result."

On the right side, at the top of the application, place the company logo, which in this case is the acronym for the simulator title. You create this by typing "M D S", with a space in between the characters. To make it look a little less dull, let's put it in a different font called Lucida Calligraphy and make it a 24 points size. Surround the acronym with a house contour which seems to be drawn with a single pencil stroke, like you see in Figure 5-21.

Figure 5-21: The logo for the simulator application has the shape of a house.

The final part in this design is to insert a placeholder for a dynamic graph that will represent the paid off amount for the duration of the mortgage. Since this will be a basic Flex column chart, it is not necessary to completely draw it because you won't be able to reuse the graphics anyway. You only need to draw a rectangle as a placeholder to indicate the size the graph should eventually get and provide the necessary design comments inside of it, stating what the graph should represent and which color to use.

At this point, the design phase is done and you're ready to pass the Photoshop file on to the interaction designer who will make it come to life.

The Interaction Designer Perspective

For this design, the interaction designer will have a very important task to do, because he can now make or break a well structured application. That is because the design is working with several custom components and you don't always have to convert each design element into a component. In Flash Catalyst, you can also reuse custom components, just like you would in Flash Builder. In fact, you *should* reuse components in Flash Catalyst.

When you import the Photoshop design file into Flash Catalyst, make sure that you opt to flatten the shape layers (although this should be the default setting in the options dialog). This will optimize the resulting file size a little. Now, let's start with creating the custom components.

Creating the Components

The first one is a radio button. Go into the Layers panel and **select both the outer and inner circle layers for a radio button**. Use the Heads-Up Display (HUD) or right-click popup menu to convert it into a Radio Button. **Inside of the component, make the inner circle invisible for the** Up **and** Over **state.** All the other component states have the inner circle visible as this will indicate that the radio has been selected. In the Library panel, rename the custom component to "MyRadioButton." You could do the same thing for the second radio button, but that would mean that you are creating two components that look and behave exactly the same. That would be overkill, and it would make your code less clean. Instead, **drag the new custom component onto the art board and place it in exactly the same location as the designed radio button**. After the positioning is done, make the designed radio button invisible by clicking on the first column of the two circle layers in the Layers panel.

The next component you create is the text input component. **Select one of the biggest text input components outline and text content and convert it to a custom text Input component.** You can do this by either using the HUD again or by choosing Convert Artwork to Component ➤ Text Input from the right-click popup menu. Strictly speaking, it is not necessary to edit the component parts, because in this case the label is automatically assigned as the Text Display part. But you will notice that in this particular design, the text is not positioned correctly, so you'll need to adjust it by double-clicking the component to edit the parts. **Resize the** Text Display **part so it fills the entire rectangular area** of the component as shown in Figure 5-22 and, since we're dealing with a numerical display, make it **align to the right**. You can set the alignment using the Common section of the Properties panel or again by using the right-click popup menu and choosing the Align ➤ Right option.

Figure 5-22: The Text Display part needs to be stretched and right aligned.

Once you've created that custom text input component, go into the Library panel and **rename the component** to "MyLargeTextInput". Just like with the radio button, you can now reuse that newly created component. **Drag that component from the Library panel onto the art board and place it at the exact same position as the first output field**. Once the positions match, you can **make the existing output field from the design invisible** because you won't need it anymore. Then you need to **repeat this process two more times** for the other two output fields. And since the output fields are only used to display the results from the calculations, the user doesn't need to be able to fill in a value in those fields. So, in the Properties panel, set the Enabled property to false by unchecking the checkbox in the Common section.

Making the design layers invisible has the advantage of being able to use them in other states or pages. And you can also revert to them to create another custom component type. But remember that they will remain within the generated Flex code. This means that they will be compiled into the resulting SWF file, resulting in an unnecessary larger file size. Removing the layers would be a good idea when you want to optimize the SWF file size.

You may assume that you can now use that same text input component for the other two input fields as well. Unfortunately, you cannot resize a component instance in Flash Catalyst. There is no *9-slice scaling* available, which means that the tool does not know how to resize a custom component. 9-slice scaling means that you divide your component into 9 virtual sections. The outer sections will remain untouched while the middle section is scaled. The best example can be found in a button with rounded corners. The 9 slices for this kind of component are:

- Left, top corner
- Top horizontal border
- Right, top corner
- Left vertical border
- Middle section
- Right vertical border
- Left, bottom corner
- Bottom horizontal border
- Right, bottom corner

When you resize a button component, the rounded corners are not going to be resized at all. Only the middle row (meaning the vertical borders and the middle section) is going to be resized.

Since you can't use this scaling principle in Flash Catalyst from a design file, you're going to have to **make separate components for the other two input fields**. Repeat that creation process for these two fields, and name the custom components aptly "mySmallTextInput" and "MyMediumTextInput." By the time you're done with creating the custom components, your Library panel should like that in Figure 5-23.

Figure 5-23: The library panel components should be reused in this application.

Creating the Pages

Remember that you still have to define the view states because the first input field is going to change depending on the choice the user has made with the radio buttons. **The first step is to duplicate the entire page**. Name the first page "Monthly" and the second one "Total." **The first one will naturally display the input when the user starts calculating from the monthly down payment, while the second page will start the calculations from the total mortgage amount.** In the first page, make sure that the Monthly Downpayment radio button is selected, the down payment input field is visible, and the total loan amount input field is turned invisible. For the second page, do it the other way around. These are the only two states that you need for this application. Everything else will remain visible whether or not there are some values filled out in the input fields.

Of course you need to specify how the user is going to navigate from one state to the other. This will be done by clicking on one of the radio buttons. **Select the first radio button and add an interaction to it**. In this interaction, specify that when the radio button is clicked, the application should navigate to the second page. **Apply the same logic to the second button.** Test your application by running it from within Flash Catalyst. Normally, you would still have to do something in the Timelines panel to make a smooth transition between the two application states, but in this case you can **just leave the view state transitions as they are**, so the state change is instantaneous.

Don't forget that you have to leave the placeholder for the graph visible for the developer in the next step. He will then have to physically replace that placeholder with an actual charting component using Flash Builder 4.

You may have noticed that you didn't create a button component to trigger the calculation. The is because in this application you are going to check the input field values and start the calculation as soon as there is a valid value. This is something that the developer will have to address.

The Developer Perspective

As the developer, you get the Flash Catalyst project from the interaction designer. There is still a lot to be done, so let's dive straight into it. First, **import an FXP project**, which is the project that has been created using Flash Catalyst.

In the code, you have to seek out the input and output values and use bindings expressions on every one of them. You will even want to restrict the user input to only numerical characters, so they can only provide correct data. But first things first; in order to use binding expressions, you'll need to create certain variables to bind to. **At the top of the** `<fx:Script>` **block, define five new variables and declare them** `[Bindable]`, so you can use them in the binding expressions later on. Let's make them all of the `Number` type and name them as follows:

- `amount`: for the total loan amount input and output field
- `downpayment`: for the monthly downpayment input and output field
- `percent`: for the percentage input field
- `years`: for the number of years input field
- `paidOff`: for the output field to show the amount you've paid off at the end of the mortgage

To show the values in the input and output fields properly, you're going to need to **use some** `<mx:NumberFormatter>` **instances**. To declare these formatter class instances, you'll need to wrap them inside of an `<fx:Declarations>` code block, like so:

Excerpt from Workflow_Simulator ➤ *Main.mxml*

```
<fx:Declarations>
  <mx:NumberFormatter id="cf" precision="2"
                      decimalSeparatorTo="." decimalSeparatorFrom="."
                      thousandsSeparatorTo=","/>
  <mx:NumberFormatter id="pf" precision="2"
                      decimalSeparatorFrom="." decimalSeparatorTo="."/>
</fx:Declarations>
```

> In this example, I've used two different *NumberFormatter* instances for the currency values and the percentage value. You could use one and the same, but I've chosen this option to make sure I can easily modify the percentage format later if I need to.

Of course, now that you have the variables defined as well as the `<mx:NumberFormatter>` instances, you need to **initialize those variables**. For that, you need to **define a** `creationComplete` **event handler at application level**. For convenience, you are going to let Flash Builder generate the event handler. And in that event handler, you set all the variables that you have just defined to zero. Once those variables have been initialized, you can now start writing the binding expressions. The `TextInput` field for the number of years is directly bound to the _years variable. The input field for the percentage value is bound to the expression `pf.format(_percent)`. All the other input and output fields are bound to the similar expression, but this time with `cf` as the id of the formatter to use and each field bound to their respective variables. If you run the application now, it should look like Figure 5-24.

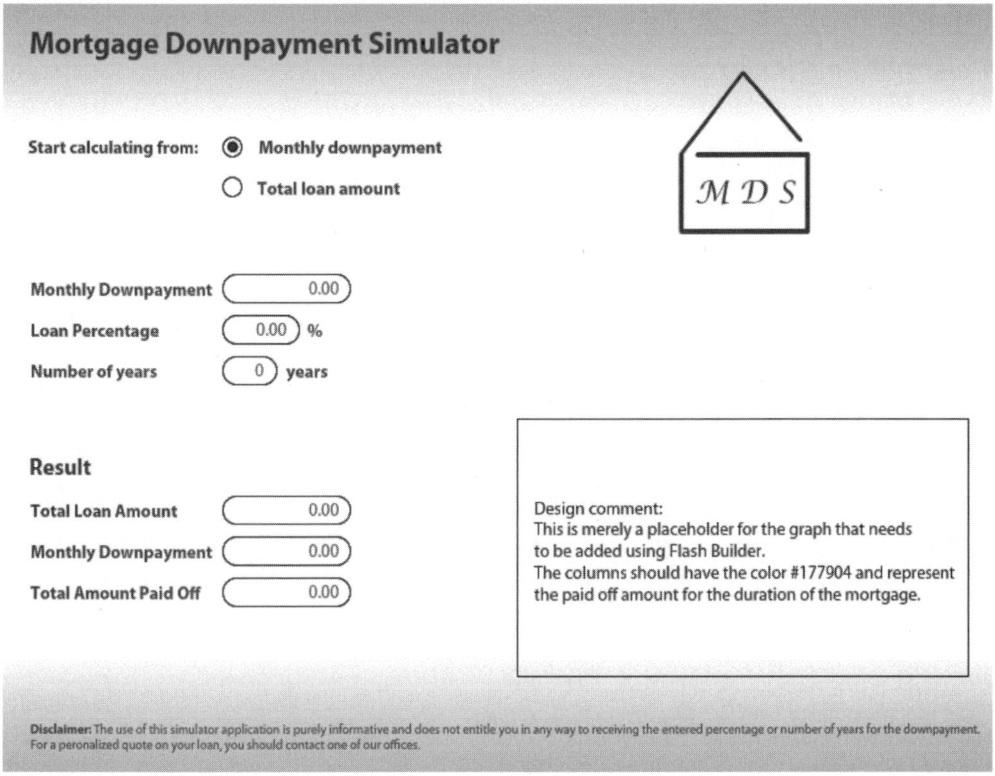

Mortgage Downpayment Simulator

Start calculating from: ● **Monthly downpayment**

○ **Total loan amount**

M D S

Monthly Downpayment (0.00)

Loan Percentage (0.00) %

Number of years (0) years

Result

Total Loan Amount (0.00)

Monthly Downpayment (0.00)

Total Amount Paid Off (0.00)

Design comment:
This is merely a placeholder for the graph that needs
to be added using Flash Builder.
The columns should have the color #177904 and represent
the paid off amount for the duration of the mortgage.

Disclaimer: The use of this simulator application is purely informative and does not entitle you in any way to receiving the entered percentage or number of years for the downpayment.
For a peronalized quote on your loan, you should contact one of our offices.

Figure 5-24: The input and output variables are now initialized.

Adding the Calculation

Since the application doesn't have a button to trigger the calculation, you'll need to do it another way. As mentioned previously, you are going to check whether or not all three input fields have been filled out. There are two options on when you trigger the calculation. The first one is when the user tabs out of a field. You have to remember that a user does not necessarily fill out the fields in the proper order. So, **you have to capture the** change **event on all four input fields to call the** calculate **method.** Yes, I really said *four* input fields, because the first field is dynamically switched when another option is chosen. So, even though only three fields are visible at a time, there are four in total. Now, **for those same input fields you are also going to capture the** enter **event**, which is triggered when the user hits the <ENTER> key when editing one of those input fields.

The next step is to perform the calculations. There are two parts in the calculation, because either the user has inputted the total amount and you have to calculate the monthly down payment, or he has provided the monthly down payment and you have to calculate the total loan amount. The calculation itself is rather complicated, as you would expect with financial calculations. **The formula to compute the monthly downpayment is as follows**:

$$M = P \left[i(1 + i)^n \right] / \left[(1 + i)^n - 1 \right]$$

With:

- M = monthly downpayment
- P = total mortgage amount
- i = annual percentage / 12
- n = number of downpayment months

But this is only the calculation in one direction. When the user has inputted the monthly down payment amount, you'll need to compute the total mortgage amount by applying the adjusted formula:

$$P = M \; [(1 + i)^n - 1] \; / \; [i(1 + i)^n]$$

Calculating the total amount needed to pay off the mortgage is then simply done by taking the monthly downpayment and multiplying it by the number of months the user has provided (in the form of years, though). Of course, you only need to perform this calculation when the input fields have been filled out correctly and the user hits either the \<ENTER\> key or he tabs out of the input field:

Do not forget to remove the "," from the value before converting the text *property of the first input field to a numerical value. Otherwise, you will end up with the input field being blanked out for apparently no reason.*

Excerpt from Workflow_Simulator ➤ Main.mxml

```
private function calculate():void {
  var pattern:RegExp = new RegExp(",", "g");

  _percent = Number(percentInput.text);
  _years = Number(yearInput.text);

  var pct:Number = _percent / 1200;
  var months:Number = _years * 12;

  if(currentState == "Total") {
    _amount = Number(amountInput.text.replace(pattern, ""));

    if((_amount > 0) && (_percent > 0) && (_years > 0)) {
      // Formula is M = P [i(1+i)n]/[(1+i)n - 1]
      _downpayment = _amount * (pct * Math.pow((1 + pct), (months)))
                              / (Math.pow((1 + pct), months) - 1);
      _paidOff = _downpayment * months;
    }
  } else {
    _downpayment = Number(downpaymentInput.text.replace(pattern, ""));

    if((_downpayment > 0) && (_percent > 0) && (_years > 0)) {
      // Formula is P = M [(1+i)n - 1] / [i(1+i)n]
      _amount = _downpayment * (Math.pow((1 + pct), months) - 1)
```

```
                    / (pct * Math.pow((1 + pct), (months)));
        _paidOff = _downpayment * months;
      }
    }
}
```

If you run the application at this point, you will see that the calculation happens when all three input fields have been filled out or when one of them has changed. That means that the basic functionality is complete. But **don't forget that you still have to create the graph** that appears on the right side of the application. What is this graph supposed to show? It shows the paid-off amount for as long as the user is paying off the mortgage. In other words, if you have a 25-year mortgage, it will show 25 columns with the increasing values of the total amount the user will have paid off by the end of those years. This requires an `ArrayCollection` that will hold the data for all those years. **You do this by looping over the years**, calculating the paid off amount every time, and putting the result in the next item in the `ArrayCollection`. However, to be able to use the item in the charting component, you need to convert it into an object before adding it to the collection. So, for each looped item, you have to define an untyped object with two properties. The first one is called "year" and holds the index plus one, while the second property is called "paidOff" and contains the calculated value.

> Before you can add the actual charting component, you might have to add the charting library components to the project. You can do this by going to the project's properties and adding the `datavisualization.swc` file to the `Build Path`. You can find this library in the SDK folder of your Flash Builder installation.

Adding the Graph

For the final part, you still need to **create the graph component** that will show a column chart. Naturally, you're going to make use of the `<mx:ColumnChart>` tag, since there is no Flex 4 equivalent available yet. Position the chart at exactly the same location as the placeholder, adjust the size to 370 pixels by 200, and be sure to remove that placeholder, since it has no use anymore. For the chart itself, **set the** `dataProvider` **property to the** `_graphData` **property you've just filled out in the** `calculate` **method.** Define the two axes to be linear and set the `year` property of the `dataProvider` as the `xField` property of the `<mx:ColumnSeries>` tag. Also, set the color for the series to the same value as the green color for the text in the application:

Excerpt from Workflow_Simulator ➤ Main.mxml

```
<mx:ColumnChart id="chart" x="414" y="324" width="370" height="200" visible="false"
                showDataTips="true" dataProvider="{_graphData}" enabled="false">
  <mx:verticalAxis>
    <mx:LinearAxis id="va" minimum="0" maximum="{_paidOff}"/>
  </mx:verticalAxis>
  <mx:horizontalAxis>
    <mx:LinearAxis id="ha" minimum="0" maximum="{_years + 1}"/>
  </mx:horizontalAxis>

  <mx:verticalAxisRenderers>
    <mx:AxisRenderer axis="{va}">
      <mx:axisStroke>
        <s:SolidColorStroke color="#177904" weight="2" caps="square" alpha=".75"/>
```

```
        </mx:axisStroke>
      </mx:AxisRenderer>
    </mx:verticalAxisRenderers>
    <mx:horizontalAxisRenderers>
      <mx:AxisRenderer axis="{ha}">
        <mx:axisStroke>
          <s:SolidColorStroke color="#177904" weight="2" caps="square" alpha=".75"/>
        </mx:axisStroke>
      </mx:AxisRenderer>
    </mx:horizontalAxisRenderers>

    <mx:series>
      <mx:ColumnSeries xField="year" yField="paidOff">
        <mx:fill>
          <s:SolidColor color="#177904"/>
        </mx:fill>
      </mx:ColumnSeries>
    </mx:series>
  </mx:ColumnChart>
```

In this chart, you will also notice that I've included an `AxisRenderer` to change the default look and feel of both the horizontal and vertical axis. This way, you don't get the ugly thick blue-ish color for the axes, but rather a thinner axis with a green color that matches the rest of the application.

When you run the application now, you'll see that when the calculation is performed, the graph is also shown because the visibility has been set to `false` upon initialization. Otherwise, there would be a graph without no values displayed. The application is fully functional at this point.

Conclusion

Although this application doesn't seem to have many design elements, you mustn't forget the fact that there are some custom components here, such as the text input fields and the radio buttons. These components can be created in Flash Builder by working with the Flash XML Graphics (FXG) syntax. In fact, everything you create in Flash Catalyst can be done in Flash Builder. It's just a choice of deciding which tool is best suited for the job. In this case, it's easier to work with the design file and convert it into custom elements rather than writing a lot of FXG code.

Naturally, this particular application does require the involvement of the developer, because he needs to create the graph and work out the calculations. However, these calculations do not depend on external values or indexes that get adjusted every year, so there's no need for a back end solution.

In the next and final workflow, I'll show you how to create a complex application that is also connected to a back end.

Complex Design, Connected to a Back End

In this final workflow, I will talk about how best to integrate an application that consists of a complex design and is connected to some form of back end. It doesn't require a huge number of complex graphical components; having just one complex design item is more than enough to fall into this category. The connection to a back end could be almost anything ranging from an `HTTPService` to a `RemoteObject` or even a `DataService` with data push technology via an RTMP connection. This is also the category you will encounter the most since Flex is often used in business applications because it's easy to integrate different types of back end technology. On the other hand, design is becoming increasingly more important, even for business applications. And as the design phase in the project workflow grows, the design will become more complex and end up in a state where a product like Flash Catalyst becomes crucial in getting the application finished on time. Maybe you can create the design with Flash Builder alone, but it will certainly take up more time than when you use Flash Catalyst to start from an existing design format. It might even be impossible to recreate the design manually in Flash Builder.

A Solar Panel Monitor

I've recently installed solar panels on the roof of my house. Being a developer by nature, I naturally installed a logging system attached to the inverter, so I can monitor how much power the panels deliver at any given time. The standard behavior of this logging device is to put the data on a certain website so that a standard graph can be accessed from any place in the world. But I want to create my own custom graph so I can use it on my personal website. A graph is only one component, so you may think it does not really belong here in this workflow category. However, the graph I envisioned was going to be a bit too complex to draw in Flash Builder. Figure 5-25 shows the design for my graph.

Figure 5-25: The solar panel's current output will be displayed as a gauge.

> *This is only the start for the application. You will be adjusting some components later on in this section without the need for a designer intervention.*

Again, who is going to work on this application? **In this particular case, most of the work will fall to the designer and the developer.** The designer will have to construct many layers to create a three-dimensional kind of shadow effect on the edge of the gauge. He will also have to make sure that the numbers are evenly spaced because the developer will need exact measurements in order to calculate the rotation of the red indicator. **There is also a requirement for an interaction designer, but he will play a minor part in this application**, because there are not a lot of moving components. The developer is the person that will collect the necessary data from the remote server, convert it into useful information, and perform the calculations that will determine the rotation angle for the indicator.

The Designer Perspective

This project is conceived from the developer's point of view, but it's the design that will place it in this workflow category. So, the designer will actually play a big part in the workflow for this application. I created the design in Illustrator again, but you could also do it in Photoshop.

First, draw the outer edge of the gauge, since the entire design will be created from the outside in. **Draw a circle and apply a light-gray-to-dark-gray linear gradient.** Then, tilt the gradient slightly to an angle of minus 70 degrees. This will be the outer edge of the gauge. Next, **draw another circle on top of the first one**, but this time make it a little smaller. Apply the same color gradient, but in a radial gradient. Instead of keeping the large gradient flow as the default, change the gradient entry points so that they lie very close to each other towards the outside of the circle. This will be the semi three dimensional look of the gauge's edge. **Add yet another slightly smaller circle**, but this time the radial gradient should go from black to a very light gray color, again placing the entry points close together toward the edge of the circle. This layer will form a hard line for the inner edge and add some reflection effect to the gauge. **The final circle you need to draw is again slightly smaller than the previous one.** This time, fill it entirely with the gray color #B3B3B3 to make up the inner color of the gauge. This layer forms the background color for the rest of the gauge. You should now have something like what you see in Figure 5-26.

Figure 5-26: At this point, the basic setup for the gauge is complete.

Adding the Indicators

Now that the basic setup is complete, you can start on the most difficult part of this design. You need to indicate the value of what the arrow is pointing to. In other words, there has to a scale on the gauge showing the intervals. **This scale is drawn by a bunch of lines in a circular fashion, labeled at 200W intervals. The hardest part here is to make sure that all the intervals are exactly the same.** This is mandatory if you want your indication to be calculable. I did this is by drawing two lines at the proper rotation angle to establish the interval. Then I copied those two lines and pasted them over and over again rotating them every time so one of the lines would overlap one of the previous ones, gradually completing the circle. Since my solar panel installation is quite small, you only need to do this until you reach the 3200W marker.

I'm not saying this is the best way of doing this, since I'm not using Illustrator on a daily basis and I do not consider myself to be a designer. But it certainly did the job perfectly for me in a small amount of time. Note that once you have completed the circular references, you have a bunch of duplicate lines in the same location. Remove the duplicates to optimize the Illustrator file for future use in Flash Catalyst.

After you have drawn those lines and added the numbers to match the intervals, you are also going to add **four text fields to indicate the current power output and the total output for the day**. I specifically said *four* text fields, because you are going to have to align the text labels on the right side while aligning the actual values on the left side. This results in the same layout as you would get when using <mx:FormItem> tags in Flash Builder. Splitting them up also has the advantage that you will have only part of the text as a dynamic component, and therefore you need to do less formatting to construct the value shown on screen.

The final part of the design is **the arrow**. Draw a triangular shape and set its base point exactly on the center point of the circles you drew earlier. This center point will act as the rotation point in Flash Catalyst later on. Now, **to make it more realistic you need to hide the base of the arrow behind a knob**. To have this knob with the proper shading, copy the first circle you drew (the one with the linear gradient) and resize it to a 25 pixel diameter while keeping the same rotation angle for the gradient. This layer will be on top of the arrow, hiding its base as was intended.

At this point, the design part of the application is finished and you can hand over your Illustrator file to the interaction designer to create the necessary dynamic components.

The Interaction Designer Perspective

As the interaction designer in this team, it is your job to take the design and create the proper components so that the developer can set them to the proper value or location depending on the values retrieved from the server. As with any other complex design, start by opening Flash Catalyst and importing the design file to create a new project. In this specific application, there is not that much work cut out for you. Nevertheless, your role in the workflow is crucial.

After importing the Illustrator design file, you need to create a custom component from the arrow indicator. **Select the arrow image path from the** Arrow **layer in the** Layers **panel**. If you just convert that layer to a component, you're going to have some problems with rotating the component. When you rotate the shape using the rotation tool in Flash Catalyst (or when you'll rotate the component using Flash Builder later on), you use its center point. In this application, however, you should rotate it around the middle point of the base line of the triangular shape. The easiest way to fix this is to make sure that the intended rotation point is also the exact center point of the component. **Create a rectangle measuring twice the height of the arrow** but with the same width. Place it on the same (x, y) position as the arrow itself. **Select both the rectangle and the arrow shape and convert them to a custom generic component** by selecting the Convert Artwork to Component ➤ Custom/Generic Component from the right-click popup menu.

Figure 5-27: The arrow shape needs to be extended to rotate around the proper baseline point.

But now the custom component still has a colored rectangle showing. To hide it, just **double click the custom component** to dig into it. In the only state for that component, **set the rectangle layer to invisible** by clicking on the first column in the Layers panel for that particular layer. Setting this item layer to invisible does not alter the size of the custom component, so the center point will still be the middle of the base line of the triangular shape.

After you've created this custom component, rotate it so that the arrow points directly to the marker that indicates zero output, as shown in Figure 5-27. If you use the Properties panel to manually set the rotation angle, you will rotate the component around its left top corner, but that's not what you want. You can use it, but then you will have to adjust the (x, y) position of the component in order to place it again in the proper location in the gauge. It's easier if you just **select the rotation tool and rotate the component**

until the red arrow indicates the first power output indicator. This will then be the base position for the arrow in the application.

As I mentioned in the beginning of this section, your part as an interaction designer is not that big, since you only needed to create the arrow component. Now you're done and ready to hand over the Flash Catalyst project to the developer.

The Developer Perspective

As the developer of this project, you receive the Flash Catalyst project in the form of an FXP file. The first thing you need to do is create a new project in Flash Builder, based on the file you received from the interaction designer. But instead of keeping the standard main application file name, use "SolarLogger.mxml". This will also become the application name when it's published. You can do this by renaming the Main.mxml file in the `Package Explorer` panel.

Retrieving the Data at Runtime

Your first task is to get the data from the server. Since the logging device is putting data on the server every 10 minutes, you're going to retrieve it at the same interval. That means that, in theory, the values in the application would incorrect for just under 10 minutes. The values to retrieve are actually generated from the custom data format using a JavaScript file. In my case, this file is located at `http://www.solarlog-home2.eu/pv-peeters/min_day.js`. **You'll be retrieving this dynamic server page using an** `<s:HTTPService>` **tag in a** `<fx:Declarations>` **code block**. Name the service "loader" and set the `url` property to the URL I've just mentioned. Set the `result` handler to call the `convertData` method and let Flash builder generate the `fault` handler for you. In this fault handler, just display a standard alert box with the error message that is sent back by the service. The MXML object should look like this:

Excerpt from Workflow_SolarPanels ➤ *SolarLogger.mxml*

```
<fx:Declarations>

  <s:HTTPService id="loader"

                 url="http://www.solarlog-home2.eu/pv-peeters/min_day.js"

                 result="convertData(event)"

                 fault="loader_faultHandler(event)"

                 showBusyCursor="true"/>

<fx:Declarations>
```

At this point you've only defined the `HTTPService` object; the dynamic server page isn't called yet. As I mentioned before, you'll need to do this every 10 minutes. You'll have to create some kind of timer to trigger the calling of the service at the given interval. In the `<fx:Script>` block, **define a** `Timer` **instance**. Instantiate this variable in the `application_creationComplete` event handler and **set the** `delay` **parameter in the constructor to 600,000**. Although this may seem like a large number, since this parameter is specified in milliseconds, it specifies the 10 minute interval. To react to the timer interval you need to **add an event listener that will trigger the** `fetchData` **method**. In that method, call the dynamic server page to actually retrieve the data. Then start the timer and call the `fetchData` method manually, because otherwise the method will be called for the first time after the first 10 minute interval has passed. Be sure to pass `null` as the parameter for the `fetchData` method, because it has a required parameter due to the fact it is also set as an event handler. This is what it should look like:

Excerpt from Workflow_SolarPanels ➤ *SolarLogger.mxml*

```
protected function application_creationCompleteHandler():void {
  timer = new Timer(600000);
  timer.addEventListener(TimerEvent.TIMER, fetchData);
  timer.start();
  fetchData(null);
}

private function fetchData(event:TimerEvent):void {
  loader.send();
}
```

If you test the application now from within Flash Builder, in either normal or debug mode, you'll see that it works just fine. But if you were to put this on the server, you'll see an error. This is a classic issue with the cross domain security policy of the Flash Player, as you can see in Figure 5-28. A cross domain issue is basically a problem with the Flash Player security not allowing you to connect to a server other than the one the SWF file originated from.

Figure 5-28: The cross domain error only shows when the application is started from a server.

Solving the Cross Domain Issue

There are two ways to solve this cross domain issue. The first one is to add a crossdomain.xml file or to alter an existing one. What does such a file look like? It used to be quite simple, but the rules for this file have changed a little bit with Flash Player 10. It is not enough anymore to just set the allowed domains; you also have to set the `site-control` property to actually allow the `crossdomain` file to be used. However, using this method to get around the security issue is not always possible, because there's a catch. You actually need to place such a crossdomain.xml file in the root folder of the remote web server from which you want to retrieve a data file. Very often you will not have access rights to do so, because remote servers are often hosted by a different company and you will not have the sufficient access rights to create or alter that file.

That's why there's a second option, which you are going to use in this project. You are going to create what is called a `ProxyService` using LiveCycle Data Services, BlazeDS, ColdFusion or almost any other back end type. In this particular case, you are going to use a PHP file to accomplish this goal. The technique is simple, since you are calling a server file on your own server, and that file will actually get the data from the remote server. Thus, you're no longer bound by the security restrictions of the Flash Player, so you won't be getting that error anymore. **Create a new PHP file**, called "getSolarData" in a separate folder in the project. In this file, take the "url" parameter from the HTTP request and get the contents of that URL using PHP methods, resulting in the following file content:

Workflow_SolarPanels ➤ *php* ➤ *getSolarData.php*

```php
<?php
  echo file_get_contents($_POST["url"]);
?>
```

To use this PHP file, you also need to make some changes to the Flex code. The url parameter of the HTTPService class will now point to the PHP file instead of pointing directly to the remote data file. But now, you also need to adjust the service class to make sure that it's working with the POST request method. This also means that **you have to provide the previous URL as a parameter to the service call**. You do this by creating an untyped object with a "url" key that contains that remote URL as value, and you provide this object as a parameter for the send method of the HTTPService. If you were to test this version of the application, you would see that there are no more errors.

Interpreting the Retrieved Data

Now that you have retrieved the data from the remote server, you need to see what exactly is coming back and extrapolate the proper data from it in the convertData method. What you're getting back is actually one big string of comma separated values (CSV), split into multiple lines, as you can see in Figure 5-29. So you have some conversion work to do. First, you need to convert the string into an array of CSV lines. Therefore, **split the string on the newline character** and place the results in an Array instance called "csvData". Make sure you define this in the application scope, because you're going to need it outside of this conversion method as well. Then, loop over the array that you've just created to further split up the CSV data and turn it into an array of objects. Because you are going to sort the list of objects, it is going to be easier if you use an ArrayCollection instead of just an Array.

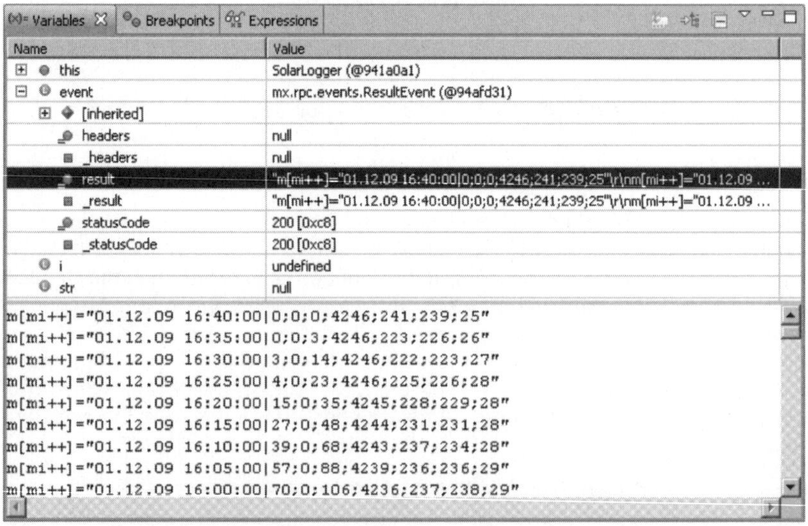

Figure 5-29: An example of the data that is being returned from the dynamic server page.

The first thing to split from each record is the date and time information. To do so, use the split function again, but this time you need to split on the pipe symbol. This creates an array with two elements: the first one being the date and time information while the second one contains the actual data for that given time. Then you convert **that date and time information into an actual date field**, because you'll need it to sort on later on in this conversion method.

The second array element contains the actual data, but it is split up into different values. **Split the CSV data based on the semicolon character, create an Object instance, and add the following values to it:**

Excerpt from Workflow_SolarPanels ➤ *SolarLogger.mxml*

```
var contentArr:Array = arr[1].split(";");
obj.P_MomentTotal = contentArr[0];
obj.P_MomentString1 = contentArr[1];
obj.P_MomentString2 = contentArr[2];
obj.P_TotalDay = contentArr[3];
obj.P_DC_String1 = contentArr[4];
obj.P_DC_String2 = contentArr[5];
obj.param6 = contentArr[6];
```

The installation on my roof consists of 2 strings. That's why there's a P_MomentString1 and P_MomentString2 indication the power output of each string at the time this data record was written. There are a couple of another data fields in the record as well, but the ones I'm interested in for this particular application are the P_MomentTotal and P_TotalDay values. The first one provides the total generated power output at that particular time (this obviously varies depending on the amount of sunlight shining on the panels) and the latter is the total amount that has been produced throughout the entire day. After setting all of these values to the object, add it to the ArrayCollection instance called "solarData". After this loop, you have the entire result string split up into the values you need. **Apply a descending sort on the** ArrayCollection **by using the** SortField **class on the date field.** This will place the most recent information at the top. And as a final statement in this conversion method, **call the** updateScreen **method**, which you obviously need to create as well.

Adjusting the Labels and Arrow Rotation

In order to be able to update the text labels and indicator position, you need to give them a proper id. Locate the CustomComponent1 component, which is the arrow indicator, and change the id to "arrow". To make sure the component will always remain centered in the application, remove the x and y properties and set both horizontalCenter and verticalCenter properties equal to zero. Then, locate the text labels that hold the values that have to be set dynamically. For the label that contains the text "2400W", set the id to "current" because this field will hold the current power output. The field that holds the total amount of generated kilowatts during the day gets the id set to "total". For both of these fields, you can remove the <s:content> tag completely, since it is only necessary for displaying the text inside of Flash Catalyst.

In the updateScreen method, **set the text property of the** current **label to the** P_MomentTotal **property** of the first item in the ArrayCollection. Don't forget to append the "W" character as the indication that the value is expressed in Watts. **For the total label, set the text to the** P_TotalDay **value.** But you have to divide it by 1,000 first because the value is expressed in Watts and you are going to show it in kilowatts. Of course, you also need to attach the unit indicator "kWh" at the end of the value. To rotate the arrow from its current base position to the position that points to the value on the scale, the calculation becomes more complex. And to make the rotation look smoother you are also going to **use a** <s:Sine> **easing function**. Since this easing function is not actually a component that is displayed on screen, you need to define it inside the <fx:Declarations> code block. All you have to do is define it and give it the instance name of "easer".

To apply this easing function, you first need to have an effect (or behavior, as it is sometimes called in Flex). **Define a** `Rotate` **effect in ActionScript and provide the** `arrow` **id as a parameter to the constructor.** Then set the following properties on the effect:

- `duration`: 2000
- `easer`: easer
- `angleFrom`: arrow.rotation
- `angleTo`: 151 + (0.0871 * solarData.getItemAt(0).P_MomentTotal)

The calculation for the angleTo property is somewhat mystical, but it is really quite simple. The value of 151 is the rotation angle when the arrow hasn't moved yet; this is the start position for the arrow indicator. The end point of the rotation should be where the arrow points towards the proper value on the scale in the gauge.

> *This is why it was so important in the design phase to have the indicators all at the same interval. Otherwise, this would become very complex to calculate (although a logarithmic or exponential scale would also have been possible).*

This means you have to divide the scale into tiny bits that represent 1W per angle unit. After some trial and error, I came up with the value of 0.0871; so each Watt in output is represented by rotating the arrow indicator over an angle of 0.0871 degrees. Of course, you still need to actually perform the animation for this effect, so as a final line of code in this method, add `rotate.play()`. If you place this application on a web server now, you should see that it works just fine and that the arrow is rotated as soon as the values have been read. And since you're working with a 10-minute timer interval, it should automatically update itself every 10 minutes.

There's just one more thing to do. When you run this application you'll notice that the dynamic text fields are covered for quite a bit and when the arrow indicates a rather low power output level. This makes readability difficult. So, move those text field a little bit to the right to make them more visible. The easiest way to do that is to go to the main application file again, and **for the four text components involved, set the** `fontSize` **to 10.** However, sizing the text components like this puts them a little bit too close to each other, so you'll have to adjust the y positions as well. The first row of text remains at the same location, but **for the other two text components you set the** y **coordinate to 132. The two static labels need to get a** `right` **constraint value of 85 pixels, while the two dynamic text components get an** x **coordinate of 125.** This will ensure that the arrow doesn't cover too much of the values and make them unreadable when the power output is rather low.

> *You can also find the working solar panel monitor in the sidebar of my personal website on* `http://www.flexpert.be`. *You can right-click on the component and chose the* View Source *option to look at the source code; however, it's the same code as you've just created here.*

Conclusion

This final application type will require all of the workflow profiles: the designer, the interaction designer, and the developer. The role of the interaction designer is rather small and could be skipped in favor of freeing up a resource for another project. That does not mean that the workflow described is not the best one, however, because you also need to take into account the fact that it would cost more time for the developer to complete that particular task. And since we're talking about efficiency here, you should take advantage of the possibilities of Flash Catalyst to make life easier on everyone.

Summary

It's clear that different kinds of applications require different approaches. There are applications that can be created using only Flash Catalyst or only Flash Builder. But with the coming of Flash Catalyst, the interaction between the developer and the designer team has become a lot tighter. They can now collaborate on different levels: The designer can create the basic Flex application and developers can better understand the design elements and are more capable of working with the provided design files. No more re-creating the Flex application from scratch!

I must admit that it helps a lot when you understand the way designs are created and how they should work. That is why there is also a third audience for this tool, the interaction designer. He will form the bridge between the developer and the designer. But for this to work, he has to have an understanding of both worlds to get the most out of Flash Catalyst.

In the next chapter, I will take you through a complete e-commerce site, from design to working application. This will help you better understand the value of the tools and how the interaction between the designer and the developer has improved. One of the benefits of this new workflow interaction is that it will shorten the development time, because you can reuse the existing design instead of having to recreate it all over again.

Chapter 6

Case Study: An E-Commerce Site

In the previous chapter we looked at workflows for various kinds of applications. The examples were purposely rather small, so we could cover them in a reasonable amount of time. In this chapter, we'll walk through a bigger, more complex application in which we'll encounter different kinds of problems. Here' you'll come across real-world situations and learn how to solve them in Flash Catalyst.

Understanding the Project

You'll be creating a commercial web site where visitors can buy photos. Development tasks include making items display in a list that lets viewers take a closer look at specific photographs. But the site should be more than just a web shop, so you'll also need to create a page with background information about the photographer, another with contact information in case potential buyers wants to ask questions, and of course, a general home page. On the design side, because the pictures will be of nature scenes, the entire site should have elements that create a nature theme.

This application may seem no bigger or more complex than the previous examples, but don't be fooled—some elements will become headaches if you're not careful. And most often, developers make their biggest mistake before they've even started the project—they start thinking in code straightaway. Take special care to avoid doing so. You need to maintain a "helicopter view" of the project. You have to detach yourself from what think you'll need to do to make it work and just look at the functionality required.

If you were the site designer, early on you might be thinking about design elements—nice screen transitions, a cool new logo, a certain font to use, or a blend mode to employ. Likewise, as a developer, right off the bat you're probably thinking about the implementation—data grids, combo boxes, and input fields. But the problem isn't entirely clear yet, so it may turn out that your ideas aren't the best solution.

I know this because I've been there myself and I've worked with lots of other developers who fall into the same trap. There's no shame in that, because you tend to solve problems from what you've learned in the past. But sometimes you need to change the way you work to find a better solution. This will also lead to you being a better developer and learning new things you can use in later projects.

Analyzing the Project

When you start examining the project to determine its needs, most likely you immediately try to get a high-level technical overview. But your analysis should include another part that should impacts the design and implementation—the target audience. An application that will be used day in day out by professionals is certainly going to look completely different from one that has a wide range of visitor profiles. Our application fits the latter category, so it must be accessible to people that fit a variety of profiles. So, **it needs to be easy to navigate, visitors must immediately understand what the application is for, and the functionality should be limited to just what's necessary.**

Once the concept of the application is clear, you can start thinking in somewhat more detail. We're still talking about implementation at a high level, though, not how we're going to realize our goals in code. And even with design elements, discussions should stay at a high overview level—the actual design will emerge from what we determine at this stage.

By now you may be asking, "How do I force myself to take a helicopter view of the project?" The simplest approach is to employ pen and paper—just write down what functionality you think you need to include. If what you're writing concerns technical issues, eliminate it from the functional analysis and move it to the technical analysis. Another helpful approach is to place yourself in the position of the site user and ask, "What do I, the user, want?" Customers don't usually care about how features are implemented under the hood; they just want the functionality.

A mind map can also help. This is basically a graphic that shows the links among concepts. Again, write down everything concerning functionality that comes to mind, but do so in a tree-like structure that shows how thoughts link to one another. The result may contain technical specifications and implications, but that's okay. You just extract them when making your functional analysis. Mind mapping is becoming quite popular, though the maps can become complex and hard to interpret later. There are other techniques as well, but delving into all of them would just take us too far off topic.

Functional Analysis

On a general level, you need to create a site that consists of two columns. The left one will hold the navigational and optional components relevant to the page being shown. The right side will hold the actual content. Only one page will be visible at a time.

Since the home page is the first page visitors see, it should give a clear overview of what the site's about. There needs to be a section on what visitors can find and another on where to go next. The page should also be visually attractive, so it requires more that text alone, which would be boring. Visitors should also see a direct link to the page containing the photos for sale. The second page will have a short bio of the photographer, including his status as an instructor, but no picture is necessary.

The third page will contain the crux of the site—the photo gallery. Pictures must come from a database to make for easy extensibility when more are added. Each picture should be accompanied by a price tag that's always visible, as well as a details button. When clicked, it will produce a bigger version of the photo plus some information about where the shot was taken. As a design constraint, this has to be done in a pop-up window that overlays the gallery. After visitors log in, they'll be able to directly add a photograph to their shopping carts.

On the left side of the page there has to be a way to select certain kinds of pictures based on categories. The site operator should be able to extend the category list as the picture database grows. Of course, only the categories that are available should be selectable, and category should show all pictures.

Users should be able to log in from any part of the site. Once at the log-in screen, the user will need to provide a username and password. The application will attempt to validate the credentials, and if it fails, show an error message. Of course, a user can't log in without registering for an account, so this page requires a link to a registration page. To help prevent spam bots from misusing the registration process, we'll need a CAPTCHA (Completely Automated Public Turing test to tell Computers and Humans Apart) component.

CAPTCHA components display a machine-generated image containing a few symbols (such as letters and numbers) in a graphic format that's been made difficult for computer programs to read but that humans can still make out. When the code the potential registrant enters differs from what the CAPTCHA displays, the registration doesn't continue.

Once logged in, visitors must be able to add photographs to their shopping carts, so gallery pages need to adjust to provide this functionality in an easy-to-use, intuitive fashion. Once visitors log in, they can see the number of items they put in their shopping carts (these are cleared every time the application is started again). After visitors complete their shopping, they need a checkout procedure.

> Since this book deals with the workflow between designers and developers, the checkout procedure isn't implemented in this example. There are various ways of creating such procedure as well as online-payments facilities, but they all depend on the technology you use and the payment-handling partner you choose. Delving into all of this would take us too far off topic.

As a final page, we have a contact form that lets users pose questions or post remarks concerning the site. This requires us to get users names, e-mail address, and of course, their messages. The information will be sent to us via e-mail. Once the e-mail has been sent, the site will display a confirmation message. Of course, we want to prevent spam mail from here as well, so this page needs a CAPTCHA component as well. If the CAPTCHA validation fails, the mail isn't sent.

That's all we need to create for this application. Figure 6-1 shows what the application flow will look like. Notice that there's one link directly between two pages. All the other navigation is done through the navigation bar on the left side of the web site.

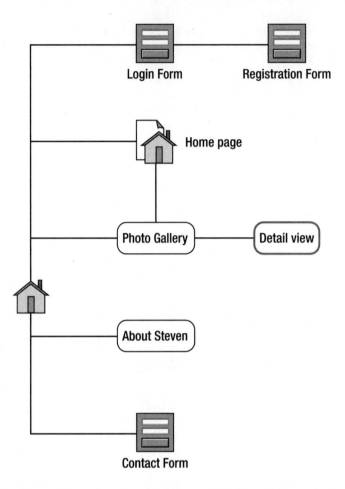

Figure 6-1. The application workflow shows how visitors navigate through the web site.

Team Composition

For this application, you're going to be part of a project team that will consist of multiple developers and designers. The question you need to ask is whether or not it's possible to perform certain design or development tasks simultaneously. For that you need to make a list of the general tasks at hand:

- Designing the application
- Creating the database
- Developing the back-end functionality to connect to the database
- Developing the back-end API to which the Flex application will connect
- Developing the front-end Flex application

It's obvious that in this case you can start working on the database while designing the application. There'll have to be some interaction, of course, between the developer and the designer as to which fields will be available to show or fill out. Otherwise the designer could be creating some nifty designs with fields that don't even exist in the database. And then the debate follows about which should be adjusted. Are those fields really necessary? Then the database should be adjusted. Or maybe they're just nice-to-have items and you don't want them in the first version of the application. Most of the time, this will already have been discussed in the technical analysis of the project.

But I think you'll agree with me that working on rich Internet applications isn't always that straightforward. In the next chapter I'll also discuss the iterative approach to collaboration, which businesses have widely adopted as the method to go with when developing such applications.

At any rate, when we take the tasks you need to do to complete the application and put them in a time-based schema together with the non-development tasks (such as analysis and testing), you'll end up with something like Figure 6-2.

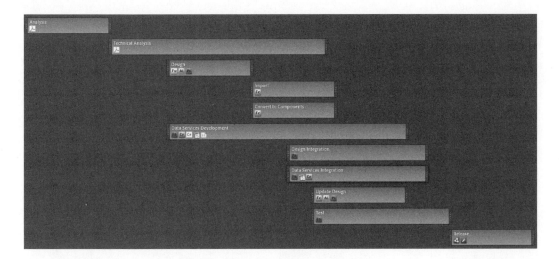

Figure 6-2. The time-based schema for the project-creation process

There may be a couple of facts about this project process flow that strike you. For instance, I've deliberately made the `Technical Analysis` phase quite large and have it overlapping part of the `Data Services Development` and `Design Integration` phases. This is because I'm assuming an iterative development process where you start developing one part of the application while you're still working on the detailed analysis of another.

You might also find it peculiar that this workflow takes into account the possibility of the design changing after you've begun connecting the design to the back-end API. As you've seen in the chapter on Flash Builder, we might merge a new design with an already existing one that has been changed in Flash Builder. Once round-tripping between Flash Builder and Flash Catalyst is enabled, this will become much easier to do, but you can already do it with the current version of the products.

Finally, notice that back-end development and design phases can start at the same time, since they don't interfere with each other except when some points need to be clarified, as I explained earlier in this section.

Designing the Application

Now that we have the details sorted out we can start working on the design. There are a lot of tools that let you create a design for a web application, but since we're going to turn the result into a Flex application, choices are rather limited: Photoshop, Illustrator, or Fireworks. The last is very good if you want to make a quick working prototype of your application before getting the final go-ahead to actually start developing. But you can't directly import a Fireworks file into Flash Catalyst. That's a small drawback, since you can do the import if you first save your work as an FXG file.

But for this application, let's assume you're going to use Photoshop to create the design. This lets you simply start working on that file in Flash Catalyst, and you can still directly edit the file in Photoshop CS5 once you've done some conversions. So, let's get cracking!

I'll be explaining how the design is created and why I've chosen to carry out some procedures in certain ways. But since this isn't a Photoshop book, I'm not going to cover all the steps in detail, which would take us too far afield.

What's important to remember is that structuring your design well and giving decent names to layers—not just layer 65*, for instance—will help the interaction designer create the proper interactions and identify the right components and states.*

Before we go into the design, let's take a look at what the application will become by the end of this chapter (Figure 6-3).

Figure 6-3. The home page of the completed application

Creating the Application's Layout Structure

Let's assume we're allowed to start working with a rather high screen resolution. If we're going to display enough pictures simultaneously and still have them be decently visible, we'll have to put a lot of information on-screen, so we'll work at a resolution of 1,280 by 800.

This is quite high, so site visitors will need big displays capable of handling that resolution. Though businesses tend to have smaller monitors with more constrained capabilities, this application is targeted more at consumers, and many of them own big screens that display even higher resolutions than we need, so I think we can get away with our choice.

Now we need to work on the background for the application. First, let's set the background color for the design to pitch-black. And, as noted earlier, since we're displaying nature scenes, it would be great to have a nature-oriented theme throughout the site. Toward that end, I've chosen a wooden board as the entire background for the website.

But the problem with the picture you choose for a web site's background is that it has to fit all kinds of resolutions and still look pretty. That's why we'll make certain our choice will blend in with the black background, which will show when the application appears on a high-resolution screen. To make sure the background blends in, we need to create an overlay that makes the wooden background fade to black on all four sides, as you can see in Figure 6-4.

Figure 6-4. The background image occupies the entire design and fades to black on all four sides.

The next thing to do is to create the actual container for the web site information. This isn't just going to be a rectangular component—we're going to make it a little more complex. Start out, though, with a nice, white rectangle measuring 940 by 585 pixels. Create rounded corners at the top of the container by cutting away the two corners, then replacing them with white circles that will blend in perfectly with the existing rectangle.

Now we'll make a kind of bulge on top of the container, near the left corner. To do so, create another layer and draw an ellipse. Size it to be 300 pixels wide and 127 high, then position it so the leftmost part of the ellipse is in the same as the leftmost part of the rectangular shape. You can merge those layers into a single one or keep them separate, as I've done in the example. If you don't merge them, I'd suggest placing the container layers you've just created into a group called "container," which you can easily lock and make visible or invisible.

Before locking this layer group, though, you still need to position the entire container dead center. The easiest way is to select both the group and the background image and use the toolbar to center them. Once you've done so and are pleased with the result, you can lock this group layer and start working on the next piece of artwork.

Creating the Tabs to Log In

When we went through the analysis of the web site, we noted that there had to be a way for users to log in from every part of the site. For that purpose, create two tabs at the top of the container. The easiest way is to duplicate the entire layer group you just created except for the bulge, producing a nice rectangle with rounded top corners. Merge that into a single layer, then resize the layer to make it just 87 pixels wide, keeping the aspect ratio intact. Make a duplicate of the layer to use as the second tab.

You need to place the layers for the two tabs underneath the layer group so the tabs are slightly hidden and show only the top 22 pixels. Label the left tab "Web site" and the right one "Log in" using the greenish color #a4bf89.

To give the tabs a button look, on each draw a gradient color on top of the white background. The colors should range from white to the same shade of green (#a4bf89) you just used for the text component. To represent the selected state for the tabs, you need to create another layer with a colored gradient overlay. In this case, the colors will range from #e4ff9c to #edffba, and the text color will be a lighter shade of green, #5fbb14. Apply a little drop shadow on the leftmost tab, and make it overlap the right tab a bit, so the left tab appears to be placed on top of the right. The result should look like Figure 6-5.

Figure 6-5. The web-site container holds two tabs, one of which allows users to log in from anywhere in the site.

Adding Design Elements

In the next part of the design, you'll be working with some very complex elements. As part of the nature theme, we'll use a leafy vine, as shown in Figure 6-6. You'll have to warp and fill the leaves with a green gradient. Make the vines start at the bottom left of the container and grow to the very top of it. Make use of the bulge's curvature to ensure that the vines aren't straight, giving them a more realistic flair. Do this a couple of times until you're happy with the result and don't feel constrained by the white web-site container. If you'd like, you can use the surrounding wooden texture for the same purpose.

Naturally, to accomplish this you'll need multiple layers, so you can place items on top of each other. Another reason for using more than one layer is so the vines won't be fixed to one another, letting you change their positions later if you want. One layer will hold the thicker vine that runs from the bottom left of the container to the top left. To make this vine blend better with the rest of the container, you need to create a layer mask for it, so the vine becomes gradually visible from the bottom to the top.

If you were to import this design into Flash Catalyst at this point, you'd notice that the gradient visibility wouldn't show. Masking isn't supported at this time, so it's completely ignored. This is one of the design constraints you have to take into account when creating a design for a Flex application. You can solve the issue by applying the layer mask so it's blended with the layer instead of just being a mask.

Figure 6-6. *The vines on the left side of the application give the interface a more dynamic look.*

Finally, put the name of the site, "NATURE PHOTOGRAPHY" in the top right corner of the white container.

Adding the Navigation Bar

To start building the navigation bar, create a column about 270 pixels wide on the left side of the container. Give it the underlined title "NAVIGATION" and set the font size to 20. In the navigation menu, we'll provide these four navigation items:

- Home
- About Steven
- Photo Gallery
- Contact me

Separate the menu items from each other by drawing a small line between them. Each item needs to indicate when it's in a selected state, so users know which page they're viewing at any given time. To create the indicator, pick a menu item and draw a rounded rectangle shape with a gradient fill color behind it. Make the colors range from #d6ef8e to #eeffaa, then back to the first color at the bottom of the rectangle. This will indicate that the menu item has been selected and also act as the hover state.

Normally you'd have to do the same for every menu item, but since you're going to work with Flash Catalyst to create the menu items as buttons, you'll be able to reuse the same component. That means that you only have to create this selected state once. The other menu items will have the same state available, since they'll just be different instances of the same component.

The Shopping Cart

In the middle of the navigation column you need to add a section labeled "MY SHOPPING CART" containing just one sentence, which for now will say "There are currently 12 items in your shopping cart." The number will actually be replaced dynamically by the exact number of items in the user's shopping cart. Place a button labeled "CHECKOUT" underneath this sentence. Clicking on the button will, of course, take the user through the checkout procedure.

As with the four navigation-menu items, this button will need to indicate when it's in the pressed state. This section will appear only when a user has logged in. But since it's in the navigation sidebar, add it to the same layer group. Flash Catalyst and Flash Builder will have to make sure these layers are visible only in contexts in which they apply.

The Search Box

At the bottom of the navigation sidebar, add another section. This will contain a drop-down combo box that will display the names of the photo gallery's picture categories. While we could get the list of categories from the database, we have only four, so we might as well hard-code them. Give the combo-box drop-down section a light-gray background color and the following selections:

- All
- Waterfalls
- Reflections
- Lakes
- Mountains

I've deliberately chosen not to place the items in alphabetical order, assuming that the top items will be the ones users will be most likely to look for. You can, of course, choose alphabetical order if you find it more suitable.

The combo box itself needs a color gradient that will indicate when the box has the input focus. Use the same greenish colors as before for this and all gradients in the application. Next to the combo-box rectangle, draw a small square with a downward-pointing arrow in it. When pressed, this will trigger the opening of the combo-box drop-down list. As soon as a user makes a selection, it will appear in the combo box, and the drop-down list will vanish.

Below the combo-box, place a button that, when pressed, will actually carry out the selection the user made for filtering the photos to view inside the photo gallery. Note that this button will be hidden when the drop-down list is showing.

This last section in the sidebar will show only when the user is looking at the photo gallery. With all other pages, this section has no use and should be hidden.

Now that you've finished the sidebar section of the site, your design should look like that shown in Figure 6-7.

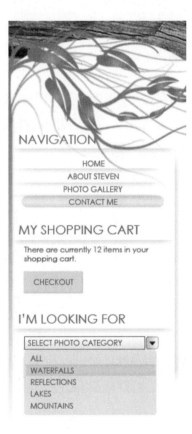

Figure 6-7. This shows the completed sidebar for the web site. Notice that the button in the I'M LOOKING FOR section is hidden by the drop-down list.

Adding the Content

Now we can start working on the right side of the web site design, where the actual content appears. Let's start with the home page.

The Home Page

In the top left corner, place a vertical image. Use one of the pictures that will also appear in the gallery. Be aware that it's best to copy the image into the design rather than linking to an external file because when you import the design file in Flash Catalyst, the linked image may not display correctly. Next to your image, write a `Welcome` title and some information about what visitors can expect from the site.

Do the same thing in the bottom right corner of the content area, this time using another image from the pictures directory. To the left of the image, write the title "`Where to go from here?`" along with some text describing where visitors can find the pictures. That's fairly straightforward, right? But wait, let's make that bottom image a bit more special. Let's add some overlay effects to draw the attention to that image, as it will also be a kind of button component that will take the visitor directly to the photo gallery in the final application. The home page should now look like the one in Figure 6-8.

Figure 6-8. *The finished home page already has some images on it to give the visitor an idea of what to expect from the site.*

Keep in mind that not every feature of the design tools, such as Photoshop or Illustrator, is available in Flash Catalyst. As a result, some things are not possible and others have to be done differently. In Flash Catalyst, for example, you can't use paths to place text on, so if you import the design as is, you'll see that the text warping won't work properly. To solve this issue, you have to turn that text into a bitmap by rasterizing the layer. That way, it will display correctly.

The About Page

The next page we'll tackle is the About Steven page, which will contain a small bio about the photographer. That would be me, since I'm the one who took all of the pictures in this application. On the right side of the content there is a picture of me, with the ACI logo (Adobe Certified Instructor) underneath. Again, copy the picture into the design file instead of linking to the external image to avoid problems later on in Flash Catalyst. That's all there is to this page (see Figure 6-9). That was easy, wasn't it?

Figure 6-9. The About page is quite simple in its design

The Photo Gallery Page

The next page will be a bit more complicated because it's the one that's really the whole point of the web site. This is the Photo Gallery page, and its purpose is to display a list of small photographs and allow a visitor to get a larger view of a selected photograph or add it directly to the shopping cart. However, this last capability should be available only when the user is logged in, so we'll have to create some components:

- A list of photographs
- A detail view
- A way to interact with a list item to show the detail view
- A way to interact with a list item to add it to the shopping cart

The List of Photographs

Let's start with the list, and let's use the concept of slides for presenting the photographs. With this, you can use the white surroundings to place additional data or buttons, which will help visitors reach the detail view, for example. Start by drawing a square with a size equal to one-third of the content container's width.

Make sure you leave enough space to accommodate a scrollbar later on. Add an inner bevel effect to the square to give it a kind of 3D look. In the bottom left corner, set the price to a fixed number. Don't worry about this, because the actual price will be retrieved from the database when the application is finished. In the bottom right corner, create two buttons: one with a shopping cart icon to let users add an item directly to the shopping cart, and one with an eye to go to the detail view for that particular list item. In the center of the square, place a sample image measuring no more than 120 pixels wide or high.

Once you have created that first item, copy it so you have nine of them—three items in three rows. You'll see that the last item won't fit, but don't worry; just leave it partly outside of the content area. This is something that will have to be fixed in Flash Catalyst later on, but the interaction designer needs to know how the list is supposed to look.

As an additional feature, let's add a fade out effect at the bottom of the list. In Photoshop you'd normally do this by adding a layer mask to the entire list component's group layer. But as I noted earlier, Flash Catalyst doesn't support masking, so how can we achieve this goal? Well, you have to do it the old way and create a new layer on top of the component, and on that layer you draw a gradient opacity fill going from white to transparent. This method will have the same effect and it's Flash Catalyst-proof as well.

Since we're working with a list component that is going to be filled out by retrieving data from the database, we don't know how many items will actually be in the list. Thus, you have to take into account that there are probably more items in the list than there is room to display, so you'll have to **create a scrollbar for the list component** as well. Since the entire web site is built around a nature theme, let's create a custom scrollbar by drawing a curved vine on the right side of the list component. At the top, draw a couple of leaves pointing upward; these leaves will act as the up-button for the scrollbar. Do the same at the bottom of the scrollbar to create a down-button. Finally, add a small rounded rectangle that will act as the thumb. Now your scrollbar component is complete and the design for this page should look like the one in Figure 6-10.

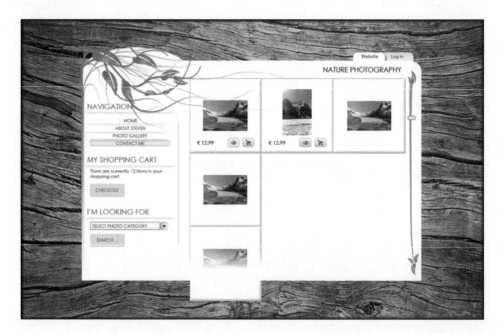

Figure 6-10. The design for the photo gallery fade out the list at the bottom and has a custom scrollbar.

The Detail Pop-up

But that's not the end of this page, because we still need a design for the pop-up screen (which was a design constraint, remember?) for the detail view. This view will lie on top of the photo gallery, so start with a white square measuring 550 by 480 pixels and add a drop-shadow effect to it. Put a picture inside the square measuring a maximum of 400 pixels wide or high, and enter the location where the picture was taken underneath. Lastly, add a close button—a simple circle with an x inside. And now you're really done with the photo gallery page.

The Contact Page

The last page of the navigation menu is the Contact me page, which is pretty straightforward and contains only a few input fields and a button. But we want to avoid getting lots of spam from automated processes, so we'll **add a CAPTCHA image** to it. I've used a CAPTCHA image generator I created a while ago. I'll explain its workings a little when we reach the coding part in Flash Builder, but if you want to read about it now, take a look at my blog post at http://www.multimediacollege.be/2008/10/a-decent-flex-captcha-component-using-only-actionscript/.

You need to create four input fields:

- Name
- E-mail
- Message
- CAPTCHA validation

The first two fields and the validation field are merely single-line text input fields. To create them, you can reuse the selected item rectangle from the combo box component created earlier in the sidebar for the filter criterion. And you can apply the same gradient color for the focus color for those text input fields. The Message input field, however, will be a multiline field, so it should be made a little bigger than the ordinary text input fields. The same gradient applies for the focus color, so that will remain the same, only a little bit more stretched.

The Login Page

Now we've taken care of the normal web site flow, but we still need to allow users to log in or to register to obtain a login. Let's start with the Login page, which has **text input fields** for the username and the password, **and a button** to start the login procedure. Again, you can copy this button from the shopping cart section in the sidebar. Underneath the button, place the text "Not yet registered? Register here." This text should be underlined to make it look like the hyperlinks you see in regular HTML-based web sites.

Of course, when you provide a login procedure for a user, you have to keep in mind that the procedure won't always be successful. A user can make a typo, or someone who is not registered might try to access the secure section of the web site. This means you have to **provide an error message** for when the procedure fails. Let's put the error message all the way at the bottom of the form and make the text color red to indicate that it's really a fault and not just an informative message. The error message won't be shown at the first login attempt, and it will be hidden as part of the initialization process every time the user returns to this page from anywhere within the site.

The Registration Page

The final page of the design will let users register to create a valid account for ordering photographs from the site. This is the Registration page (see Figure 6-11), and it's where you'll collect more data about the user, including the following fields:

- First name
- Last name
- E-mail
- Password
- Retype password
- CAPTCHA validation field

Again, we'll use the CAPTCHA image generator to avoid getting wrong data in the database because of automated attempts to get a valid account.

Now **place two buttons next to each other u**nderneath the input fields. The first button will start the registration procedure, which will validate the data that has been provided and check to see if the requested user name is still available. When this is not the case or when the passwords do not match or some fields haven't been filled out, **an error message will be shown at the bottom of the form**. The second button allows the user to cancel the registration procedure and return to the login page.

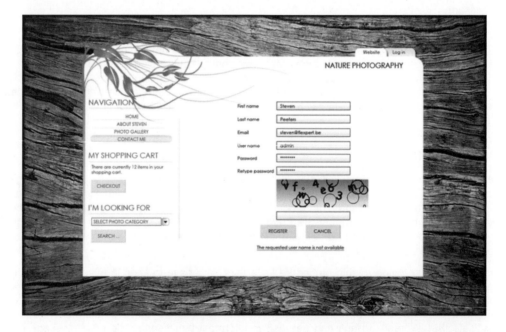

Figure 6-11. The Registration *page contains a CAPTCHA validation to keep invalid users out of the database.*

At this point we're done with the application's design, so we're ready to hand it over to the interaction designer who will convert the static design into working Flex 4 components that can be completed further using Flash Builder 4 to connect to the database.

Bringing the Application to Life

As the interaction designer on the team, it is now your job to take the design and turn it into working Flex components that can be completed with live data in Flash Builder later on.

> *Although it's not necessary, it is always a good idea to reuse as many components as possible. In this design, doing so means there will a lot of layers from the design file that will have to be made invisible, because those layers are in essence copies of the same component. It's probably better to just delete the original layers, because invisible components still reside in the code and will be compiled into the application, even though they are never used. Removing those layers will decrease the resulting application size drastically.*

The first step is to import the Photoshop design file into Flash Catalyst. When you have selected the file, you are presented with an Import Options dialog box (see Figure 6-12). The important settings are Color, Shape layers, and Import non-visible layers. Remember that in the design, you faded the wooden texture to black on all sides, so in this options dialog you need to set the color to black as well, because this will also be the background color for the HTML wrapper that holds the Flex application. The Shape layers setting should be set to Crop, because otherwise some shapes will be flattened with surrounding colors included, and that's not what you want.

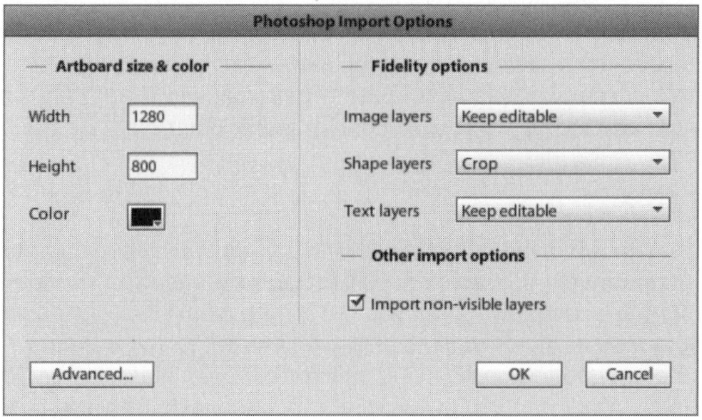

Figure 6-12. The Import Options dialog

When you import this design file, you'll get a warning saying Skewed items are not supported in Flash Catalyst and may look incorrect. But don't worry, there aren't any skewed items in this Photoshop design file. However, should you ever need to use them, you can always rasterize the layer into a bitmap to solve the issue.

The Components

Before you can start working on all the different pages, **you need to create the custom components**. Just as with the design, we'll start with the sidebar. First, however, it's best to lock all the layers except for the navigation layer group, to avoid making unwanted changes to other layers or components.

The Navigation Items

In the Navigation sublayer group, select the CONTACT ME and hover menu item layers. Use the HUD (Heads-Up Display) or the right-click pop-up menu to convert the selected layers into a Toggle Button component. We're using a Toggle Button instead of an ordinary Button component so the button will stay selected to indicate which page the user is viewing. Make the hover layer invisible in the following component states:

- Up
- Disabled
- Selected, Disabled

In the Over state, leave the selection color enabled, but set its Opacity property to 50 in the Common section of the Properties panel. Next, select the text layer in one of the component states and set it as the Label part using the HUD again. Center-align the text and make it fit the entire width of the component. This allows the button to be reused for other menu items as well. At the moment, the properties are only for the state you're currently working on, so you need to make the component look exactly the same in all other states by right-clicking the text part and selecting Make Same in All Other States from the pop-up menu or the HUD.

When you go back to the main design page and select the Library panel, you'll see the newly created component. Change the generated name to MenuButton by double-clicking on the component name in that panel. Now drag that custom component and place it over the other menu items, providing the proper label, of course. When you're done, delete the original menu-item layers to optimize the resulting SWF file by selecting them in the Layers panel and clicking the garbage can icon in the bottom right corner. For safety reasons, you should lock the Navigation sublayer at this point.

The Shopping Cart Box

In the Shopping cart box group layer, select the Checkout button group layer to select all the parts for the button component, then **convert this artwork collection into a Button component**. Now double-click the component and perform the same action as you did for the MenuItem component—set the Label part and make it wide enough for other labels to fit as well. Don't forget to share the new label width with all the other states, and keep the gray button background only for the Down state. When you're done, change the component's name in the Library panel to MyCustomButton to make it more recognizable in the list.

When you're done, you can take that component and replace the Search button design layer group in the Search box sublayer with it. Again, to optimize the eventual file size, delete the original design layer in the Layers panel. But that's not all there is to do for this section of the sidebar.

Creating the Combo Box

You also need to create a combo box. Now, at the time or writing Flash Catalyst doesn't really support directly creating a combo box component from a group of design elements. That's a pity, but we have to deal with it. I've partly based my method on InsideRIA's blog post at http://www.insideria.com/2009/

`10/flash-catalyst-beta-2-combobox.html`, which describes how they solved this problem. In essence, you have to break down the combo box into basic parts, and what I've come up with is the idea that a combo box is really nothing more than a `Toggle Button` with an extra `Data List` component in the toggled state. But that still doesn't make it an easy component to create from scratch. Furthermore, the fact that the selected item must be displayed in the collapsed combo-box state means we'll have to do some custom programming in Flash Builder later to dynamically fill that value, depending on the selected item in the `Data List` part of the component.

Let's start working on this component by selecting the `Drop-down` and `Drop-down values` layer groups in the `Layers` panel and converting them to a `Custom/Generic Component`. Rename that component to `SearchComboBox`. Double-click the newly created component, select the combo-box rectangle, the selected value, and the arrow button, and convert them into a `Toggle Button`. Double-click the component again and assign the label for the button, making it as wide as possible to fit the entire component and sharing this change with the other states as well. Render the `Focus color` layer invisible for the `Up` and `Disabled` states. Before continuing with the other states, you have to convert the `Drop-down values` layer group into a `Data List` component. So, select that group and choose `Convert Artwork to Component` ➤ `Data List` from the right-click pop-up menu.

In the component, **you still have to indicate the list items and their states**. Double-click the new component and choose the selected item in the design to create the `Repeated Item` part. Space the items 2 pixels from each other, fill out the `Design-Time Data` panel to contain the five possible selection items, and remove the other values in the design layer. Double-click the `Repeated Item,` then remove the background color for the `Up` state. For the `Over` state, select the background layer and set the `Opacity` level to 50 in the `Common` section of the `Properties` panel. This will show a difference between a selected item and one the user is hovering over. That's it for the `Data List` component, so go back up one level using the bread crumbs at the top of the artboard. Rename the list component to `SearchValuesList` in the `Library` panel.

Again, go up one level to the `SearchComboBox` level again. In this component, you still need to make the list component visible in the proper state. In fact, you still need to define the proper states in the component. So, go ahead and duplicate the state in the `Pages/States` panel three times and name the states appropriately

- Up
- Over
- Down
- Disabled

In the `Up` and `Disabled` states, make the data list invisible because this will be the normal state. In the `Over` state, set the toggle button's `Selected` property to true by marking the check box in the `Common` section of the `Properties` panel. This will show the selection color for the combo box. Do the same for the `Down` state. You also have to make the `SerchValuesList` component visible. In the `Disabled` state, set the button component to disabled by unchecking the `Enabled` checkbox in the `Common` section of the `Properties` panel.

Now you've defined the states for the component, but **you still have to define how the application will go from one state to another**. Let's start with the `Data List` since this is the easy one. Select the `SearchValuesList` component in the Layers panel and add the following interaction:

- Event: `On Select`
- Action: `Play Transition to State`

- State: Over
- When: When any item is selected

Going back to the Over state keeps the focus rectangle displayed after a selection has been made in the list component.

You could choose to use the Mouse Down event as well, but then you can't cancel the event by dragging outside of the component. On Select is the list equivalent of the click event, so that's the one to go for in this example.

For the combo box itself, things are slightly more complicated and you have to define a few interactions (see Figure 6-13). Let's handle them in the same order as the chain of events that take place when a visitor uses this component. The first event that happens is the user hovering over the component. So, add the following interaction for the combo box component:

- Event: On Roll Over
- Action: Play Transition to State
- State: Over
- When: When in Up

The next event is the user clicking on the combo box to open it. This means the component has to go from the Over state (not the Up state) to the Down state, so add the interaction:

- Event: On Click
- Action: Play Transition to State
- State: Down
- When: When in Over

The user can then go in two directions. Either he selects an item in the list, which you've already covered by capturing the event on the SearchValuesList component, or he cancels the selection. In this last case, the user actually clicks on the combo box component again, which is why you needed to add a condition to the view state change before. Now you need to add a similar interaction, but the other way around:

- Event: On Click
- Action: Play Transition to State
- State: Over
- When: When in Down

Now the combo box is closed again, but the hover color is still visible. There is only one more possible event and that is the user moving the mouse cursor away from the combo box. So, the combo box component needs one last interaction to go back to the normal state:

- Event: On Roll Out
- Action: Play Transition to State
- State: Up
- When: When in Over

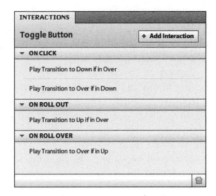

Figure 6-13. *The transitions for the* `MyCustomComboBox` *component*

Adding all of these events to the component turns your generic component into a working combo box. If you like, you can add more transitions to the view state changes to make the (dis)appearing of the data list a little smoother, but it is not strictly necessary for our user experience.

I know it's been a bit of work to get this far, but we're done with the component for now, so go back to the main design level and rename the component to `SearchCombobox`. We'll pick this component back up when we reach the Flash Builder integration section.

The Navigation Tabs

Now let's make the custom tab at the top of the content area in the application. Three layers are available for each tab: the label, the white container, and the gradient selection overlay. Select the layers for one of the tabs and convert the artwork into a `Toggle Button`. Again, you need to dive into the component's states, so double-click it. First, assign the label part for the component. Make sure the label is as wide as possible and apply the changes to all other states by choosing `Make Same in All Other States` from either the HUD (this becomes available when something in the current state is different from the other states) or from the right-click pop-up menu.

Regarding the hover and selection colors, there's still some work to do in the button component. In the Up state, make the `hover` layer in the `Layers` panel invisible by clicking in the first column on that layer. This displays just the white background for the tab in its normal state. The `Over` state will have the hover layer visible, but you have to select that layer and turn its `Opacity` property in the `Properties` panel down to 50. You can do the same for the `Selected, Over` state. All of the other states have this selection layer set to visible.

Now go back to the main design level. Before using this component again, you should rename it in the `Library` panel to `MyCustomTab`. This will help you identify the component later if you need it. Moreover, this is the name for the custom component in the source code as well. It's always better to have meaningful names for components instead of some generated generic name. Drag the newly created component onto the artboard and position it directly over the second tab in the design. Change the label to the proper text and completely remove the design group layer that contains the tab from within Photoshop. Just make sure that the second tab is on the proper layer level, so it displays exactly as before—a little bit behind the first tab.

The Home Page Photo Button

We just covered the components that are directly visible at all times. But there are some components that need to be created from specific web site pages, such as the home page. If you make the home page visible in the `Layers` panel, you can see that the image in the bottom right corner should actually be a trigger to go directly to the photo gallery. In the `Layers` panel, select the `image button` layer group so all of its subcomponents are selected. Now you need to convert the artwork to some kind of component, but which one? Well, in this case you want to react to a click event, so you might think you should convert it into a `Button` component. But you don't really need the different button states for this component, so that wouldn't be the best choice. For this example, let's convert the artwork into a generic component, using either the HUD or the `Convert Artwork to Component` ➤ `Custom/Generic Component` from the right-click pop-up menu. We'll be coming back to this component later when declaring the pages and the interactions to move between them.

The Custom Text Input Fields

Next we need a `TextInput` component. Remember you created a couple of these for the `Login` and `Register` pages? At the moment, they're still only drawings so you have to convert them. Go to the `Login` page, select the first text input field and its content and convert it to a generic component. Why not convert it immediately to a `Text Input` component? Well, it's basically because **you want a special focus color on the input field and you can't set it directly on a Text Input component**. But in the custom component, you select the bounding box and the text and convert it into a `Text Input` component. Then you double-click the component to dive into it. Assign the text content to the `Label` part of the component and size it as large as possible to still fit in the component. Now go back up one level to reach the custom component again. Create a second view state in which you show the focus-color layer, while hiding it in the first state. Of course, you still need to create the interactions to go from one state to the other. The first state is the `Normal` state and will be shown by default. So when the user gets the focus on that field, it needs to change to the second state, which you call `Focus`. So the first interaction is:

- Event: `On Focus In`
- Action: `Play Transition to State`
- State: `Focus`
- When: `When in Normal`

The second action is simply the other way around. And there you have your custom focus color for the Text Input component. Just rename it to MyCustomTextInput and you're ready to reuse it. Replace the second input field with the newly created component and remove the original design layers. If you run the application now, you'll see a blue focus color appearing on top of the custom component—and it looks kind of hideous. Well, in the Flash Builder coding part of this exercise, we'll adjust the custom component a bit to fix this. You also don't have to worry about the password not being displayed as a password field, because we'll fix it as well in that stage of development.

Reusing Existing Components

You now need a button component for the login page, and you've already created such a button. You can drag the `MyCustomButton` component from the `Library` panel on the `Login` page and place it directly over the existing one. Don't forget to change the label for the button to LOGIN and remove the original design layers. The final component for this page is the hyperlink to the Registration page. At the moment, this is just fixed text, but you need to be able to capture the click event on it. But since you don't need the button states here, you can just turn the text into a generic component again.

That's it for the Login page, but you have to perform similar tasks for the Registration page. Make that page visible and replace all the text input design components with MyCustomTextInput component instances that you drag onto the artboard from the Library panel. The two buttons at the bottom of the form should be replaced with instances of the MyCustomButton component from the Library panel. **For each button, you have to specifically set the label to match the existing design buttons' label.** When you're done adding the fields, remove the original design layers. Be careful not to remove the label for the text input field that indicates what kind of information is expected. See Figure 6-14.

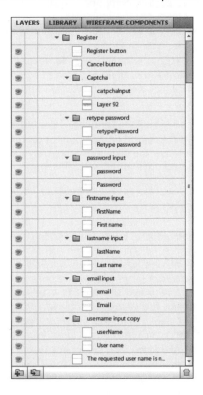

Figure 6-14. *The* Registration *page's layer layout should look something like this.*

On the Contact page you also need to replace the text input items with the existing MyCustomTextInput component. Again, just as with the previous pages, you need to remove the original design when reusing the custom component to keep the resulting SWF file size as small as possible. However, on this page you have not only ordinary text input components, but a text area as well. This is a new component to create, but **there's a slight issue with this component—there is no separate layer for the focus color**. But don't worry, you can create the necessary layers right here in Flash Catalyst. All you need to do is create an extra layer with a white rectangle and place it underneath the existing rectangle with the gradient focus color. Make sure that the stroke color is set to #666666 and set the Opacity property in the Common section of the Properties panel to 50. Disable the fill color for the new rectangle so the gradient still shines through at this point.

Creating this Text Area component is much like what you've done already for the custom Text Input component. Select the text content layer, the focus-color rectangle layer, and the white rectangle layer you just created and convert them into a custom component using either the HUD or the Convert Artwork to `Component` ➤ `Custom/Generic Component` option from the right-click pop-up menu. Double-click the new component, select the white rectangle and text from the `Layers` panel and convert that selection to a `Text Input` component. Rename that new component to `MyTextArea` in the `Library` panel. Assign the existing text to the `Label` part of the component and resize it to fit the entire component area. Don't forget to push this change to the other component states as well using the HUD or right-click pop-up menu.

Now go back up one level to reach the custom component again and create a second view state in which you show the focus-color layer while hiding it in the first state. You still need to create the interactions to go from one state to the other. The first state is the `Normal` state and will be shown by default. So when the user gets the focus on that field, it needs to change to the second state, which we'll call `Focus`. You've already done this for the `MyCustomTextInput` component, so you can take a look at the interactions you created there to do the same here. When you're done, rename the component to `MyCustomTextArea`. And that's it for this component, though we'll pick it up again later in Flash Builder to do a little more so we can use it appropriately.

There's one more component you need to replace, and that's the button at the bottom of the form. Just as with the previous pages, drag the `MyCustomButton` component on the artboard and place it directly over the existing button. After that, just remove the existing design layers for that button, since it is now an instance of that component. And now you're done with this page and you can lock it to avoid any unwanted changes to the layers.

The Photo Gallery Component

There's one last page—the actual photo gallery. Here you need to create a few new components to get the list working. Let's start with the custom scrollbar. If you are a Flex developer, how many times have you created a custom scrollbar? Probably not that often, because it was generally a pain to do so. Getting the custom scrollbar to work properly required a lot of low-level programming, and that takes a long time. But now, **in Flash Catalyst, it takes just a very few minutes to create such a custom scrollbar.** Open the `Photo Gallery` layer group and select the scrollbar sublayer group, which selects all the necessary components for our custom scrollbar. Next, use the HUD or right-click the components and choose `Convert Artwork to Component` ➤ `Vertical Scrollbar` from the pop-up menu. Click on the `Edit Parts` button in the HUD to dive into the component, select the `Thumb` layer and assign it to the `Thumb` part of the component. Of course, you need do the same with the `Track` layer and the `Up` button and `Down` button layer groups. You'll see that the layer groups are going to be converted into a single custom component again. And that's it! Now you have a fully functional scrollbar you can use in the application. But before you move on, rename the custom scrollbar component to `MyCustomScrollbar`.

The Repeated Photo Item

The next piece of the puzzle is the repeated item in the data list. This will be a single component, but with several different parts on it, like a price tag and buttons. Open the `Photos` sublayer group and select all the layers, except for the photo copies and the mask layer, then convert those layers into a `Custom/Generic Component`. Inside that component, you'll see a few different components, including two buttons that still need to be created as Flex buttons.

> *If you open, for instance, the `info button` layer in the `Layers` panel, you'll notice something has gone wrong with the import of the Photoshop design file: the hover color has gone missing. And you'll see the same problem with the normal button gradient color that was there in the design file. The layer is still there, but the gradient fill color is not. This is because Flash Catalyst can't display all of the effects you can create in Photoshop.*

How do you fix this issue? Do you need to go back into Photoshop to flatten the shape layer and re-import the design file and start all over again? For some issues, you might have to do that, but not in this case. Here we can solve the problem using Flash Catalyst's capabilities. So, draw a rounded rectangle that fits inside of the existing outer stroke for the button. Set the `Corners` property in the `Common` section of the `Properties` panel to 3 and move the new layer all the way down to the last line of the layer structure. This will place the outer stroke on top of the rectangle you've just created and the border will always be visible, no matter what. Now, remove the border from that rectangle and fill it with a gradient that ranges from #ffffff to #acacac. This will be the fill color for the button in its `Up` state.

Create the same rounded rectangle and move it down the structure again, but this time fill it with a gradient ranging from #ffffff to #edffba. This will be the fill color for the `Down` state. Remove the empty layers from the `Layers` panel for this component. Select the `info button` layer so all parts of the button are selected and convert it to a `Button` component. In the `Up` and `Disabled` states, make the gradient hover layer invisible by clicking in the first column of the `Layers` panel next to that specific layer. In the `Over` and `Down` states, make the gradient hover layer visible and the normal gradient layer invisible. For the `Over` state, you also need to select that gradient hover layer and set the `Opacity` property in the `Common` section of the `Properties` panel to 50 to make a distinction between hovering and pressing on a button. Finally, rename the component to `MyInfoButton`.

> *Unfortunately, you can't reuse this button because it's not actually a label that changes, but rather the image on the button. So, for the shopping cart button, you'll have to perform the same actions.*

Once you've created the second button, rename it to `MyShoppingCartButton` in the `Library` panel. And you're done with the repeating item for now. Don't worry about the fact that all of the images are going to be the same. The developer will adjust this dynamically, depending on the data that is being returned from the database later on in Flash Builder. The last thing you need to do, before continuing with the rest of the components, is to rename the component you've just created to `MyListItem`.

Creating the Tiled List Component

Now, what you still need to do is to create the actual list component, so **select the** `MyListItem` **component on the artboard, as well as the custom scrollbar, and convert them into a Data List component** using either the HUD or the right-click pop-up menu. When doing this, it's best to hide the other copied photo elements in order to keep your design view clean and consistent. Once you double-click the component and assign the `MyListItem` instance as the `Repeated Item` part of the component, Flash Catalyst automatically creates five instances of that item in the Design-time Data panel. Since the design requires a `Tile` list three items wide, you should add several more items to the `Design-Time Data` to reach an item count of 12. This will eventually result in 4 rows, which means you'll be able to test the scrollbar as well. But at this point, you don't have a `Tile`. You are stuck with an ordinary list. To fix this, select the list component and go to the `Layout` section of the `Properties` panel. There you'll find a button bar at the top of that section, which gives you the choice of three different layouts:

- Vertical
- Horizontal
- Tile

Select the last one to create that Tile component. In the same section, set the vertical and horizontal spacing to zero. This will ensure that the items are placed directly next to and underneath each other, as in Figure 6-15. You may have to adjust the position of the list items slightly to the left to make sure they don't interfere with the scrollbar. But now you also see that the component is a lot bigger than the white website container, so resize the list to fit within the white page container.

Figure 6-15. *The* Data List *component can be converted into a Tile using the* Properties *panel.*

When you double-click the list items, you will see the repeated item separately and you'll also see that the item has Over and Selected states. In both states you should disable the highlight overlay layer because you don't need it for this application. This way, the item will be displayed exactly the same in all circumstances.

After that, go back to the main design level using the bread crumbs at the top of the artboard, and rename the component you just created to MyCustomPhotoList. Don't forget to remove all the copied photo items in the layers panel, because at this point they are excess baggage and only increase the file size of the resulting SWF file.

Calling the Detail Pop-Up

The final component to create is the detail pop-up window that will be triggered when the user clicks on the info button for a particular list item. **You could create a separate component from the pop-up design layers but it isn't necessary**, and not doing it makes your life a little easier in going from the gallery to displaying the pop-up and back again. So just make the pop-up component visible by clicking in the first column of the Layers panel on the pop-up layer group. Select the two layers that are used to create the close button. Again, you don't need any specific button states here, so converting it to a Custom/Generic component will do, because you can capture the On Click event on this type of component as well. Rename the newly created component to MyCustomCloseButton. We'll pick this up in the next section when you create all the different pages.

The Pages

Now that you've created all the necessary components and have reused them as much as possible, let's create the necessary pages. For this application, you need six different pages in addition to the home page. But rather than create these pages individually, you are better off setting this tab in its selected state by checking the `Selected` property in the `Common` section of the `Properties` tab. After that, duplicate the first state six more times, naming the states as follows:

- Homepage
- About
- PhotoGallery
- PhotoPopup
- Contact
- Login
- Register

The Home Page

To set everything correctly for the `Homepage` you need to make some adjustments in the Layers panel to make certain items visible or invisible. First, make sure that the `Homepage` state is selected in the `Pages/States` panel. Let's start with the menu items in the navigation sidebar. Here, select the `Home` menu item and set it in the selected state using the `Selected` property in the `Common` section of the `Properties` panel. Next you need to set the appropriate content to visible, so make the `Home` sublayer group under the `pages` layer group visible by clicking in the first column of the `Layers` panel on that specific layer. Make the other pages invisible since only one page should be shown at a time. The shopping cart box in the sidebar should also be invisible at this point. It will be made visible dynamically later on in Flash Builder when the user is logged in. The search box should be removed as well, since it has no meaning on this page.

Now you can add the interactions to go to this page or to go from here to the photo gallery. Select the `Home` button in the navigation sidebar and add the following interaction to the component:

- Event: `On Click`
- Action: `Play Transition to State`
- State: `Homepage`
- When: `Any State`

This action assures that the user, wherever he might be in the web site, can always go directly to the home page. Similarly, you need to add an interaction to the image at the bottom right of the home page. You turned this image into a custom component to be able to capture a click event on the entire image area. Now, add the following interaction to that image:

- Event: `On Click`
- Action: `Play Transition to State`
- State: `PhotoGallery`
- When: `When in Homepage`

The About Page

That's it for the `Homepage` state. Now let's move on to the `About` page. Select the `About` page in the `Pages/States` panel at the top of the Flash Catalyst user interface. For this page, you naturally have to alter the navigation menu items in the navigation sidebar to display the `About Steven` item in the selected state. Adding the interaction to get to this page is similar to the interaction you just created for the `Home` menu item. And, of course, you also have to set the About Steven page to be visible in the Layers panel and make sure it is the only layer that is visible for the pages layer group. Again, be sure to make the shopping cart and search boxes invisible. This page doesn't require anything else right now.

The Photo Gallery Page

In the PhotoGallery page, things are a little different, though here, too, the shopping cart box should be invisible. It will be made visible later on by the developer. However, **the search box is of vital importance for this particular page, so you must leave it visible**. Visitors have to be able to go from this page to the PhotoPopup page to view a particular photo in detail. Since this will require some extra coding for capturing the click event in the proper place, the developer will have to make sure that the view state transition will actually take place. And, of course, you mustn't forget to set the proper menu item in its selected state to indicate that this page has been selected.

Although calling the pop-up page will be done in the code, going back from the pop-up window to the gallery page can be done using Flash Catalyst. Select the PhotoPopup view state in the Pages/States panel. The left sidebar should look exactly the same as with the PhotoGallery page, because that page will be underlying this one. However, even though these components may look the same, in this page they should not be accessible, since the pop-up window needs to be modal. Modal windows are windows that block the rest of the application until they are closed. To make them inaccessible, you can select each component in the sidebar and set its Enabled property to false by unchecking the check box in the Common section of the Properties panel. The items to be set disabled are:

- All menu items
- The filter combo box
- The Search button

Disabling the filter combo box is a little bit different, since this is a custom component and is not disabled by just unchecking a check box. For this component, you just have to set it in the Disabled view state to disable the button part. To set this state, use the State combo box in the Common section of the Properties panel, as shown in Figure 6-16.

Figure 6-16. Disabling the filter combo box is done by setting the component in its Disabled state.

To close the pop-up window, select the `Close` button and add an interaction to it using the `Interactions` panel. This interaction should return the application to the `PhotoGallery` page:

- Event: `On Click`
- Action: `Play Transition to State`
- State: `PhotoGallery`
- When: `When in PhotoPopup`

The Contact Page

For the `Contact` page, things are quite simple. Again, the sidebar components need to be changed so they appear the same as in, for example, the `Home` page. Of course, the proper menu item has to be set to it `Selected` state to indicate that the user is actually viewing this page. The other items in the navigation sidebar have to be set to their normal state, since only one menu item can be selected at the same time.

The Login Page

For the `Login` page, we'll alter the original design a bit, because it will make the application more user-friendly and less confusing. The first thing to do after selecting the `Login` page in the `Pages/States` panel is to display the proper page by setting the `visibility` property to the proper value for the pages in the `Layers` panel. Instead of showing the navigation sidebar, we'll hide it completely. But that leaves the `Login` page design in a somewhat awkward position, so you have to adjust that as well. The easiest way to adjust this page is by selecting the `Login` page in the `Layers` panel. (Make sure it is unlocked because you are going to change it). This will select all items in that layer group. Now add the white rectangular container to the selection by holding the <CTRL> key down when clicking on that specific layer. Choose `Align` ➤ `Horizontal Center` from the right-click pop-up menu on the artboard. This ensures that the components are all centered in the container. However, you do have to make some manual adjustments to the input fields, since the label and input parts will be both centered as well. So, you have to pull them apart again and reposition the labels in view of the accompanying input field.

For the registration link, you still have to add the interaction that will take the user to the `Registration` page. Select that component and add the following action in the `Interactions` panel:

- Event: `On Click`
- Action: `Play Transition to State`
- State: `Register`
- When: `When in Login`

Now you have to do just one more thing for this page—set the proper tab in the heading of the white content container. For this page, **the Website tab should be deselected and the Login tab selected instead**. You can do this using the `Properties` panel as we've seen before. Remove the error message at the bottom of the form by making it invisible in the `Layers` panel. The rest of this page will be handled in Flash Builder while coding.

The Registration Page

The `Registration` page needs the same sort of design changes as the `Login` page. Start by removing the entire sidebar because it has no real use here, and center the rest of the page on the white container. Because we used a very simple technique to create the `Login` page, we had to redo some things by hand. Now, for two input fields it wasn't that much work, but the `Registration` page has more input fields. Also, there's another way of quickly repositioning the page content to the exact center of the container. What you need to do is select the entire `Register` layer group and convert it to a custom component. Then you select both that component and the white content container and align them on their center points. Now, because the CAPTCHA is a little bit bigger than the input fields, the component doesn't look quite right visually. Fix this by sliding the component 20 pixels to the right. As you can see, the labels for the input fields have remained at their relative positions, so that's the manual work you don't have to do anymore. The `Registration` page should now look as shown in Figure 6-17.

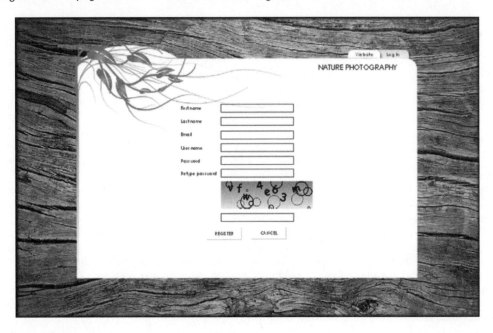

Figure 6-17. *The* `Registration` *page does not show the sidebar and requires some adjustments to the design.*

The next step is to turn the custom component back into separate components, because it is in essence an unnecessary component. Select the custom component and revert it back to artwork by selecting the option `Revert Component to Artwork` from the right-click pop-up menu. However, this doesn't remove the custom component from the `Library` panel, so go to that panel and remove the `RegisterCustomComponent` from the list of library items by selecting it and clicking on the little garbage bin icon at the bottom right corner of the panel.

Be careful not to delete the wrong library item, because Flash Catalyst doesn't have a confirmation dialog when you delete items from the Library panel. If you accidentally remove the wrong item, however, you can always use <CTRL>+Z on Windows and <CMD>+Z on MacOS to undo the removal.

There are two final adjustments to make to this page to complete it in Flash Catalyst. First, remove the error message by clicking in the first column of the Layers panel on the appropriate layer. This will not really remove the layer, but the action renders it invisible. Next, notice that the `Website` tab at the top of the white container is selected; deselect it and select the `Login` tab, just as you did before in the `Login` page.

Navigating the Tabs

Before you can hand over the living design, **you still have to get the tabs at the top of the white content container working**. Even though the tabs don't switch layer positions upon selection, we'll still treat them as a kind of toggle button bar or radio button group. By this I mean that when one tab is selected, clicking on that tab should have no effect at all. The easiest way to do this in Flash Catalyst is by setting the component to disabled after selection, and setting the other tabs to enabled at the same time. For this, you don't really have to do much at all. You just set the `Website` tab to disabled for all the actual web site pages. It should only be enabled in the `Login` and `Register` pages. And for the `Login` tab, you just do it the other way around. The actions that change the pages will then automatically enable or disable the proper tabs.

And speaking of these actions, you still need to add them. So, select the `Website` tab button and add the following interactions to go to the Homepage when the tab button is clicked:

- Event: `On Click`
- Action: `Play Transition to State`
- State: `Homepage`
- When: `When in Login`
- Event: `On Click`
- Action: `Play Transition to State`
- State: `Homepage`
- When: `When in Register`

> You could also use the `When in Any State` condition, but I've chosen to implement only the events in which the tab should actually react. This helps to prevent faulty behavior when the application needs to be changed and someone else forgets to set the tab button to disabled, for example.

For the `Log In` button, you implement the same interactions, but only for each page that actually contains web-site content, so you end up with the interactions panel shown in Figure 6-18.

Figure 6-18. *The Interactions panel contains 5 separate actions with the same effect for the same button.*

At this point we're done with the project in Flash Catalyst and we're ready to hand it over to the development team, who will connect this application to a ColdFusion back end to retrieve the photo gallery data at runtime. The team will also use that data to modify the item renderers in the photo gallery page to display dynamic data, instead of the static photographs you used to create the tiled photo list.

Hooking Up the Application to the Back End

Remember that the project development cycle illustrated in Figure 6-2 shows `Data Services Development` as a simultaneous task with `Design` and `Design Integration`. This means that you can write part of the back-end functionality before the design is converted into a working application. For instance, you can create the database way before building any interaction requirements. You know what data is necessary for the application. It is only later that you can define the necessary access methods, when the interaction functionality is created in Flash Catalyst. Only then do you know the necessary access methods—that is, the API. And even then, you still might have to add, change, or remove certain API methods, depending on the implementation in Flash Builder as you're attaching the application to the back-end API.

Creating the Database

As I've mentioned, you can create the database during the early stages of development, though you may well have to alter some aspects of it during the development cycle. Because our example doesn't deal with the check-out procedure, the database is really simple and requires only two tables, `User` and `Photo` (see Figure 6-19):

- `User`: this table contains the data for the registered user and will be used for the login procedure.

    - `user_id INTEGER`: the primary key
    - `firstname VARCHAR(50)`: the first name of the user
    - `lastname VARCHAR(50)`: the last name of the user
    - `email VARCHAR(100)`: the email address with which the user registered
    - `login VARCHAR(20)`: the username to log in to the application
    - `password VARCHAR(50)`: the encrypted version of the user's password

> **Security warning:** *You should never store passwords as plain text in a database. Encryption is absolutely mandatory and should be at least a 256-bit encryption to keep your data safe. A system of encryption/decryption such as the BlowFish method can be used, but I'm more a fan of hashing methods. This is a way of encrypting the data so that decryption is impossible. If you forget your password, the only solution is resetting it!*

- `Photo`: this table contains all the necessary data for each photograph in the gallery. Photos are divided into categories by means of fixed strings.

    - `photo_id INTEGER`: the primary key
    - `photo_name VARCHAR(100)`: the description of the photograph
    - `price DECIMAL(4;2)`: the price of the photograph
    - `thumbnail VARCHAR(100)`: the location of the thumbnail relative to the application's location

- `location VARCHAR(100)`: the location of the large version of the photograph, relative to the application's location
- `category VARCHAR(50)`: the category to which the photograph belongs

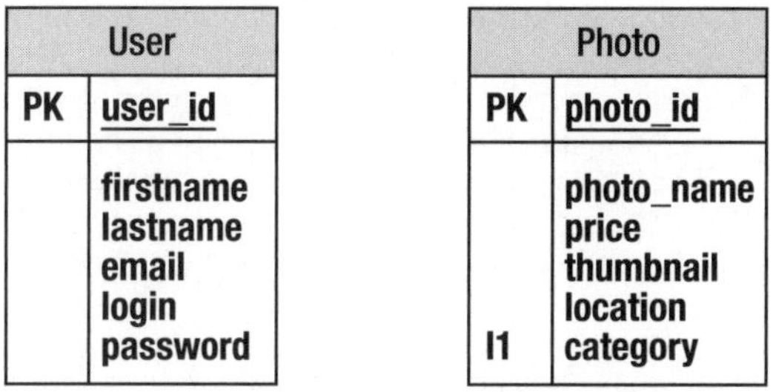

User	
PK	user_id
	firstname
	lastname
	email
	login
	password

Photo	
PK	photo_id
	photo_name
	price
	thumbnail
	location
I1	category

Figure 6-19. *The database is very simple because there's no check-out procedure.*

The tables in the database are completely self-sufficient, which means they don't have any relations with other tables. Of course, you could extend this Entity Relationship Model by taking the categories apart and creating a one-to-many relationship between the tables `Category` and `Photo`, since one category will be used for several photographs.

Should you want to extend this application, perhaps by retaining the chosen items of a previous session, for example, or with a complete check-out procedure, the additional database tables would render the Entity Relationship Diagram (ERD), which is a graphical representation of the database structure, a bit more complex, but still fairly simple. You'd need to add tables such as `Order` and `OrderItem`, where `Order` would contain the total amount for the order, the invoice and shipping address, and a collection of `OrderItem` objects, which in turn would contain a photograph and quantity.

Writing the Back-End API

Now that the database is set up, you can start working on the back-end functionality. For this application I've chosen to use a MySQL database to store the data. To access the data I've chosen ColdFusion, mainly because it is a very quick way of creating the back-end functionality for this application. The reason it's quick is you can use the ORM (Object Relational Mapping) feature of ColdFusion 9, which lets you connect to the database without having to write any SQL statements at all.

A good starting point for any back-end implementation is to decide whether you need to use some kind of design pattern or application framework. I'll be talking about this in detail in the next chapters of this book. Since this application is rather limited in its functionality, I've decided that a real framework is not necessary here; instead we'll implement a couple of basic design patterns that I've borrowed from my days as a Java developer.

Before getting started, I'd like to issue a little warning. This section becomes technically quite heavy and it may prove difficult to understand if you're not used to ColdFusion or if you're not a developer. Nevertheless, it contains valuable information about creating services that need to be accessible from within a Flex or AIR application. However, you don't have fully understand the inner workings of the ColdFusion back end to be able to use the services presented later in this chapter, when we reach the "Adding Dynamic Data to the Application" section.

Enabling Object Relational Mapping (ORM)

Before starting to code the Hibernate (ORM) features in ColdFusion, you have to define the database connection in the server's admin console. To do this, go to the `Data Sources` section of the ColdFusion Administrator, create a new data source called `webshop`, and connect it to the MySQL database. This is another great feature of ColdFusion: you only define the data source once, and any number of applications can connect to it using only that data-source name. If you change the database afterward and leave the data-source name unchanged, you shouldn't have to do anything at all to your ColdFusion code, especially if you're using the ORM feature, because you don't have any database-specific SQL statements. Well, you might have written some custom SQL statements for performance reasons, and those might have to be altered to apply to the new database. But I can guarantee you still won't have to change much code.

Security tip: Using Object Relational Mapping (ORM) instead of coding all of your SQL statements also diminishes the risk of SQL injection attacks on your site. What is a SQL injection attack? Well, many SQL statements have parameters that come from the web site's URL. Putting them directly in your SQL statement allows users to guess the parameters. If they are wrong, the web site usually displays a nice message with more information about the database name, table names, user credentials or even server connections than you'd really like to share. That leaves your application vulnerable to malicious attacks. ORM prevents SQL injection, thus adding an extra level of security to your application.

You need to manually enable this ORM feature in order to use it. When creating a ColdFusion-only application, you do this in the `Application.cfc` file where you initialize your application. But we haven't written an entire application in ColdFusion; this will be just the back end. How do we initialize remote method calls so we can use Hibernate? Well, when you call a ColdFusion component from Flex, the server also looks for that `Application.cfc` file somewhere in your application structure. Since the search goes from the CFC level to the root of your application, I suggest placing that file in the root of your application structure. Suppose you use the structure shown in Figure 6-20 for your back end ColdFusion code.

Figure 6-20. The project structure for the ColdFusion back end code

As you can see, the `Application.cfc` file is located in the top folder of the structure. The folder `webshop_backend` is the project name in ColdFusion Builder, which I've used because it can help generate code and has support for code completion and code hinting for ColdFusion 9. If you're using the Flash Builder Premium version to develop your Flex applications, ColdFusion Builder is automatically included (though not in the Standard version, unfortunately), so you can use the same product for both back-end and front-end development.

As I noted, you need to manually enable the ORM feature. Here's the code to add to the Application.cfc file:

be ➤ *Application.cfc*

```
<cfcomponent output="false">
  <cfset this.ormenabled=true/>
  <cfset this.ormsettings={datasource="webshop", dialect="MySQLwithInnoDB"}/>
</cfcomponent>
```

The datasource property refers to the name of the data source you created in the server's admin console earlier in this section. The dialect property should be filled out with a value that is actually database-dependent.

Creating the Data Transfer Objects (DTOs)

When you look at the project's structure in Figure 6-20, you can see two subfolders that will contain the code you're about to write. The first one is called dtos, an acronym for *Data Transfer Objects*, which is a design pattern also known as *Value Objects* (http://java.sun.com/blueprints/corej2eepatterns/Patterns/TransferObject.html). This pattern takes data from possibly several database tables and sends it to the front-end client as a single object. Normally, you'd attach an extra *Data Access Object* (DAO; http://java.sun.com/blueprints/corej2eepatterns/Patterns/DataAccessObject.html) to the DTO to actually perform all the fetch statements, but since we're using Hibernate to perform the fetch statements on the one hand, and the DTO holds the same data the DAO should have on the other hand, I've skipped using a DAO all together. Now, let's take a closer look at how the User DTO is created in ColdFusion with the help of ORM.

be ➤ *flexpert* ➤ *webshop* ➤ *dtos* ➤ *User.cfc*

```
<cfcomponent output="false" persistent="true" accessors="true">
  <cfproperty name="user_id" ormtype="integer" fieldtype="id" generator="native"/>
  <cfproperty name="firstname" ormtype="string"/>
  <cfproperty name="lastname" ormtype="string"/>
  <cfproperty name="email" ormtype="string"/>
  <cfproperty name="login" ormtype="string" getter="false"/>
  <cfproperty name="password" ormtype="string" getter="false"/>
</cfcomponent>
```

You start by defining the component. Because this component will not generate output to the screen on its own, you have to declare output="false". The component's properties will have to be written to the database or fetched from it, so the component has to be set to be persistent. A very nice feature of ColdFusion 9 is that you don't have to create the getter and setter methods anymore as in Java. True, in tools such as Eclipse, you can have these methods generated, so it's not a whole lot of work. But not having to write them at all is even better! The reason you don't have to write these accessor methods is that you can let ColdFusion generate them by just adding the accessors="true" statement to the component tag.

Each <cfproperty> tag specifies a field that corresponds to a field in the database table. You have to make sure that the name attribute is exactly the same as the name of the field in the table. The ormtype attribute corresponds to the field type in the database. For properties such as the login and certainly the password, you don't want to actually fetch them and display them on screen, so you have to set the `getter` attribute to false. This renders the property write-only, so you can set it for a new user but it won't be accessible for display.

The second Data Transfer Object is called `Photo` and is located in the same subfolder as the `User` DTO. This object matches the database table with the same name and provides accessor methods to create, update, and delete photographs. As with the `User` DTO, you create the `Photo` DTO as a separate ColdFusion component using the same syntax, so you are still profiting from using Hibernate to handle the queries.

be ➤ flexpert ➤ webshop ➤ dtos ➤ Photo.cfc

```
<cfcomponent output="false" persistent="true" accessors="true">
  <cfproperty name="photo_id" ormtype="integer" fieldtype="id" generator="native"/>
  <cfproperty name="photo_name" ormtype="string"/>
  <cfproperty name="price" ormtype="float"/>
  <cfproperty name="thumbnail" ormtype="string"/>
  <cfproperty name="location" ormtype="string"/>
  <cfproperty name="category" ormtype="string"/>
</cfcomponent>
```

So far, nothing is really functionally defined yet, so next you'll create the API to which the Flex application will connect. In other words, the components and methods you are about to create are actually the ones you'll use in Flash Builder to perform basic *CRUD* operations: Create, Read, Update and Delete.

To do this, however, you need more insight into how the application will gather data, and that means you have to wait for certain parts of the interaction design to be completed before you can start working on these methods. You *can* start earlier, of course, but chances are you'd have to alter them, which means doing the job all over again. I know this is a worst case scenario, but I've encountered such situations in the past and I can say with certainty that it can create frustration for both developers and designers when endless discussions start about how much work it takes for either profile to alter the functionality. So good workflow planning is essential to be as productive as possible without having to redo things or wait for another to complete certain parts. This is not easy, especially when you're new to the development environment. I will talk a bit more about this in the next chapter when I look at managing RIA projects.

Creating the Assembler Classes

So, just as with the DTOs, we'll start working on the `UserAssembler` class first. We'll call this component `UserAssembler.cfc` because it fits in a design pattern called *Transfer Object Assembler*. This design pattern is very often used in conjunction with the DTO pattern. If you'd like to know more about how this pattern relates to the DTO pattern, you can read more about it at http://java.sun.com/blueprints/corej2eepatterns/Patterns/TransferObjectAssembler.html.

Again, you create a new CFC component and place it in a separate folder called `assemblers`, which is located next to the `dtos` folder. In that component, you start off again with a `<component>` tag, and since this component will not put anything on screen, you again set the `output` attribute to `false`. An assembler class should never execute queries on the database. Instead, it just assembles the data into DTOs and sends them back to the front end. The queries are normally handled by the Data Access Object (DAO), but since we are using the ORM feature in ColdFusion, this functionality is also situated in the DTO classes. In any case the assembler class is not going to be persisted, so set the `persistent` attribute in the `<component>` root tag to `false`.

Now, if you look at the design and the Flash Catalyst mock-up application, you may notice that there are a few methods that must be implemented:

- findUser(login): this method checks for the existence of a user with the same login. You use this method when trying to create a new user, to avoid duplicate login names. The method returns a true or false value depending on whether the login was found.
- createUser(user): this method actually creates a user. The second parameter in the EntitySave method forces an insert statement.
- getUser(id): this method retrieves a unique instance of the user based on its unique identifier.
- loginUser(login, password): this method searches for a user with a login and password equal to the ones provided in the arguments list.

Here's the code resulting from adding these methods:

be ➤ *flexpert* ➤ *webshop* ➤ *assemblers* ➤ *UserAssembler.cfc*

```
<cfcomponent output="false" persistent="false">
  <cffunction name="getUser" returntype="be.flexpert.webshop.dtos.User"
              access="remote">
    <cfargument name="login" type="string" required="true" />

    <cfreturn EntityLoad("User", {login=#login#}, true)/>
  </cffunction>

  <cffunction name="findUser" returntype="boolean" access="remote">
    <cfargument name="login" type="string" required="true" />

    <cfset user = EntityLoad("User", {login=#login#}, true)/>
    <cfreturn isDefined("user")/>
  </cffunction>

  <cffunction name="loginUser" returntype="any" access="remote">
    <cfargument name="login" type="string" required="true" />
    <cfargument name="password" type="string" required="true" />

    <cfreturn EntityLoad("User", {login=#login#, password=#password#}, true)/>
  </cffunction>

  <cffunction name="createUser" returntype="be.flexpert.webshop.dtos.User"
              access="remote">
    <cfargument name="user" type="be.flexpert.webshop.dtos.User" required="true" />

    <cfset EntitySave(user, true)/>
  </cffunction>
</cfcomponent>
```

> Notice that in this component, you never use any query at all. You just call the *EntityLoad* and *EntitySave* methods and let ORM handle the queries for you. This makes it very easy to write a simple back-end API in virtually no time.

This assembler class is now ready to be used. But there is one more class you have to create before you can start working on your project in Flash Builder. Well, you don't really have to wait for it to be completed, because right now you or another developer can start working on the user-related functionality in the application, such as the login, the conditional showing of the shopping cart, or the registration process. But since moving back and forth between ColdFusion and Flash Builder would only cause confusion, we'll stick to de back-end code for now and complete that first.

Next to `UserAssembler.cfc`, create a new component and name it `PhotoAssembler.cfc`. This assembler class will perform exactly the same tasks as the `UserAssembler`, but this time the data that is gathered is a bunch of photographs. The methods required by this API class depend again on the functionality that is defined in the design and interaction for the application:

- `getAllPhotos()`: this method simply retrieves all the photographs from the database without any constraint. It is used when the filtering combo box in the application's sidebar is set to `ALL`.
- `findPhotosByCategory(category)`: this method searches for all photographs for which the `category` field matches the category that is provided as the method argument.

The search for the `category` field is deliberately made case-insensitive to achieve better results. This is something that should be done in the front end as well, but since in many projects front-end and back-end developers are completely different people or even different teams, you can't rely on anyone else to perform all the checks. Moreover, at some point the front end or back end may be replaced by a completely new technology, and who knows if the developers will remember certain constraints, such as the category being in uppercase in the database. All of a sudden, your application isn't working anymore, just because of one line of code.

Thus, the code for the `PhotoAssembler` should look like this:

be ➤ *flexpert* ➤ *webshop* ➤ *assemblers* ➤ *PhotoAssembler.cfc*

```
<cfcomponent output="false" persistent="false">
  <cffunction name="getAllPhotos" returntype="Array" access="remote">
    <cfreturn EntityLoad("Photo")/>
  </cffunction>

  <cffunction name="findPhotosByCategory" returntype="Array" access="remote">
    <cfargument name="category" type="string" required="true">

    <cfreturn EntityLoad("Photo", {category="#UCase(category)#"})/>
  </cffunction>
</cfcomponent>
```

With the completion of the second assembler API class, we're now done with the back-end code. Well, at least for now, because once you start implementing this in Flash Builder, you may find you still have to make small adjustments to the methods. Or you may even need to create some extra methods because you've overlooked some functionality. Taking this into account, plus the fact that another developer could have already started working on the user functionality in the project, it's clear that the development process requires constant interaction between front-end and back-end developers.

Adding Dynamic Data to the Application

Now you've reached the point where you can begin working in Flash Builder. To start, import the Flash Catalyst project using the `Import Flex Project (FXP)` option from the `File` menu in Flash Builder, and name the project `webshop`. This creates a project folder with the same name in the selected directory. Once you've imported the project, you'll see a couple of packages or subdirectories as shown in Figure 6-21.

Figure 6-21. *The project structure after importing the Flash Catalyst project*

You'll notice in the project's structure that there are a lot of bitmap assets in the `assets.images.webshop` package. These bitmaps are necessary to create certain effects and are also used in the custom scrollbar, for example. The `components` package contains all of the custom components you created in Flash Catalyst. It is filled with custom buttons, the combo box component, text input fields, and so forth.

Adjusting the Flash Catalyst Components

If you run the application right now, you'll see that the menu works and all the pages display correctly, and even the custom scrollbar works, although it is still only static data that is being displayed. But when you go to the contact page, for example, you'll see a big, ugly focus rectangle around the text input fields.

Setting the Custom Focus State on the Text Input Components

Remember that in Flash Catalyst you set an inner gradient color to be the focus color? Well, now you have to get rid of that blue focus rectangle. The easiest way to remove it is by setting the `focusAlpha` on the `<s:TextInput>` tag in both the `MyCustomTextInput` and `MyCustomTextArea` components to zero.

We also want to be able to treat the custom input fields just like a normal `TextInput` component. To do this, we need to add some getter and setter methods to the component in order to set the `text` property to the actual input part of the custom component. And, of course, you need to do the same to set the input field to display as a password when using this component in the registration or login page. In the `<fx:Script>` block, add the following code:

Excerpt from components ➤ MyCustomtextInput.mxml

```
public function get text():String {
  return input.text;
}

public function set text(value:String):void {
  input.text = value;
}

public function get displayAsPassword():Boolean {
```

```
    return input.displayAsPassword;
}

public function set displayAsPassword(value:Boolean):void {
  input.displayAsPassword = value;
}
```

Of course, you need to perform the same task on the `MyCustomTextArea` component as well, to make sure that the custom component can be used as if it were a Flex framework `TextArea` component. That's it for the text input components, but there are other components that require attention before we start adding the back end to the project.

Wiring Up the Combo Box Component

Let's focus our attention on the combo box component now. You'll find it in the `components` package as `SearchComboBox.mxml`. One aspect of the component that isn't working yet is that when you select a certain value in the drop-down list, the label in the button part is not automatically updated. By default, all items should be visible in the photo gallery, so you have to initialize the component to have that item selected. On the `<s:List>` component in the source, you simply set the `selectedIndex` property to zero. This initializes the component when it's first created. For the `<s:ToggleButton>` tag, you simply change the value of the `label` property to `ALL`. Run the application now and you'll see the component properly initialized this time.

Next, let's set the label correctly when an item has been selected in the drop-own list. On the `<s:List>` component, you can see that an event handler for the `change` event has already been declared for returning to the `Over` state. This handler will react to both a mouse click and a selection made using the arrow keys. Now, locate that event handler and set the label of the button component to the selected item in the list component. You may need to add some identifiers for the components before you can refer to them in your ActionScript code. Don't forget that you are dealing with a complex data structure as list items, so you should reference only the text part of the item to assign it to the `label` property of the `<s:ToggleButton>` component.

Excerpt from components ➤ SearchComboBox.mxml

```
protected function list_changeHandler():void {
  currentState='Over';
  button.label = list.selectedItem.text1;
}
```

Making Properties Publicly Available

If you test the application again at this point, you'll see you have a working combo box. However, you'll be using the component in conjunction with other components and it would be nice if you could just treat it as if it were a regular Flex combo box. This means you're going to have to add a couple of getter and setter methods to make it more developer-friendly.

Excerpt from components ➤ SearchComboBox.mxml

```
public function get selectedItem():Object {
  return list.selectedItem;
}
```

```
public function set selectedItem(value:Object):void {
  list.selectedItem = value;
  button.label = list.selectedItem.text1;
}

public function get selectedIndex():int {
  return list.selectedIndex;
}

public function set selectedIndex(value:int):void {
  list.selectedIndex = value;
  button.label = list.selectedItem.text1;
}

public function get text():String {
  return button.label;
}
```

> *Don't forget to set the label for the button component when setting a `selectedItem` or `selectedIndex` property, because setting those property doesn't automatically trigger the `change` event. A `change` event is triggered only by some kind of user interaction. To have automatic triggering when a value has been set programmatically, you need to capture the `valueCommit` event instead.*

The CAPTCHA Component

Now we'll create the CAPTCHA component from scratch. To do so, we'll use a component that is completely written in ActionScript and that handles the validation for the entered code as well. I know it's probably not the most secure implementation, although there are several ways to prevent getting around this component. I'm not going to explain the component in detail here because you can find a good explanation at `http://www.multimediacollege.be/2008/10/a-decent-flex-captcha-component-using-only-actionscript/`. All you have to do is download the `CaptchaImage.as` class, which you'll find at the bottom of that post, and make some minor adjustments because this component was written for Flex 3 projects. Here's what you have to do:

- Replace the `mx.controls.Label` import statement with `spark.components.Label`.
- Remove the import statement for the `mx.controls.TextInput` component and replace all `TextInput` declarations with `MyCustomTextInput`

Now, in the main application file, search for both instances of that CAPTCHA component and replace the existing image and accompanying input field with this component. You can find a `<s:BitmapImage>` tag in the `Captcha` design layer. Make sure to add the `noise="[0xacacac, 0xedffba]"` attribute to the tag to get the same gradient background colors as in the image. And don't forget to position it on exactly the same coordinates as the original `<s:BitmapImage>` component. Of course, the component needs to be refreshed and to generate new CAPTCHA code every time it is displayed, so in the `<fx:Script>` tag, locate the `registerLink_clickHandler` method and add a call to the `refreshCaptcha` method of the `CaptchaImage` component.

Embedding the Font

If you compile the application, you'll get an error that says you can't use local font embedding when `embedAsCFF` is used. This property is used in the CSS file you'll find in the default package of the application. And this message concerns the font embedding you're doing in the `CaptchaImage` class, so you have to change that `Embed` metadata tag a little, to the following:

Excerpt from components ➤ CaptchaImage.as

```
[Embed(source="C:\\WINDOWS\\fonts\\Comicbd.TTF",
       fontName="boldFont",
       fontWeight="bold",
       advancedAntiAliasing="true",
       mimeType="application/x-font")]
```

> *Obviously, this will work only on Windows machines, so if you're working on a Mac, you'll have to adjust the path to your own fonts directory. In fact, you'll have to alter the font embedding sources that are located in the main CSS file as well to make them refer to your own file paths.*

Making Properties Publicly Available

After saving the file, you'll get a whole bunch of other compilation errors concerning the `MyCustomTextInput` component. Since there are other getters and setters relating to the maximum number of characters and which characters are allowed that are being used in this source, you have to add them to the component as well. So, go back to the `MyCustomTextInput` component and add the following methods in the `<fx:Script>` block:

Excerpt from components ➤ MyCustomTextInput.mxml

```
public function get maxChars():Number {
  return input.maxChars;
}

public function set maxChars(value:Number):void {
  input.maxChars = value;
}

public function get restrict():String {
  return input.restrict;
}

public function set restrict(value:String):void {
  input.restrict = value;
}
```

This should solve all of your compilation problems. Now you're ready to test-drive the application with this new component. The result should be the same as in the Flash Catalyst project, but now the code is generated dynamically each time you visit the registration page. When you're satisfied with the result, replace the CAPTCHA bitmap image one more time in the `Contact` design layer.

At this point, we're almost half way there, but there is still one big component that isn't working yet: the photo gallery with its buttons and the photo pop-up window. But don't worry, we'll take care of that when we work on that page in the next section.

Connecting the Application to the Back-End API

Now that we have the basic components all set up, let's look at how some of the pages still require additional work. Let's start with the Homepage. In this page, everything seems peachy but you can still find a small usability flaw in the workings, which is that a first-time user doesn't have a clue that you can click on the bottom right image on that page unless he thoroughly reads the text. And even then, when he hovers over the image, there's no indication if it will react to something. With a button, it's slightly different because buttons have several states indicating some form of interaction is possible. And buttons are well-known to everyone, which also helps. To solve this usability issue, we'll add a hand cursor that appears when someone hovers over that image (see Figure 6-22). This is a really simple trick that immediately improves the usability, because people are used to seeing a hand cursor when hovering a hyperlink in HTML-based web sites. To add this cursor, go to the ImageButton component and on the <s:Group> root tag inside of that component, add the following properties:

- useHandCursor="true"
- buttonMode="true"

The first one ensures that the hand cursor is shown when a user hovers over the item, while the second one is necessary to actually show that cursor. If you don't provide it, the first property is ignored all together.

Figure 6-22. When hovering the image, a hand cursor is shown.

That final touch makes the first page in our site complete. There is no dynamic data to be shown here, so you can go to the second page, which is called About Steven. Here, everything seems to work just fine—mainly because there is also no dynamic data and no user interaction attached to this page. So let's move on to the third page of the web site. This is the Photo Gallery page and it requires a lot of work to get it up and running with the dynamic data. So, let's start coding!

The Photo Gallery

The first thing you need to do is initialize the page when it is shown, except when returning to this page from the pop-up window, which we'll handle in a few moments. The easiest way to trigger that initialization is by using the event handler that triggers the application to go to this view state. At this point, you should start a database fetch operation to retrieve all of the photographs, and also reset the search combo box to the first item in the list, ALL. The latter task is quite easy, because you have created a method to easily set the selected item or index for this custom combo box component. Use the selectedIndex property to reset the selection to that first item. The component itself will take care of the proper setting of the label and selection in the list part. The second action to take is to connect to the database. In Flex 3 projects, you'd probably create an `<mx:RemoteObject>` tag that would have some configuration in either LiveCycle Data Services or BlazeDS, depending on the ColdFusion version you were using (remember we're using the ColdFusion 9 server as a back-end technology). Then you'd have to create that server DTO on the front end in ActionScript as well.

Using the Data/Services Panel

Luckily, in Flash Builder 4, the `Data/Services` panel makes connecting your application to a back end child's play. So, go ahead and click on the `Connect to Data/Service` link in the `Data/Services` panel.

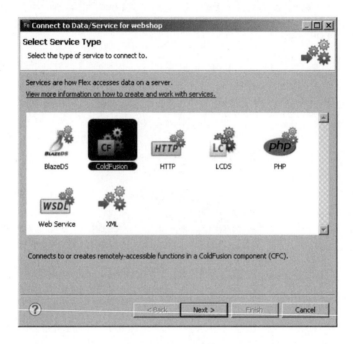

Figure 6-23. *The application is not yet configured for a specific back-end technology, so all the possibilities are still available.*

As you can see in Figure 6-23, many options are available for connecting to the back end. This is because the project is imported from a Flash Catalyst project and we haven't yet configured which back-end technology to use. Since you are working with ColdFusion, choose that option in this dialog and click `Next`. A confirmation dialog will pop up, asking if you are sure you want to configure the project this way. Next, fill in the details about your ColdFusion installation. Make sure to choose `ColdFusion Remoting` as the `remote object access service` for the application. Validate the configuration and click `OK`. Now browse to the `PhotoAssembler` class you created earlier and adjust the package settings so that it only creates a `be.flexpert.webshop.services` package, because later on you are going to add the `UserAssembler` to this package as well. Press `Finish` to complete the operation.

Dynamically Filtering the Photos

In order to use this new service, you have to declare it first. So, after making a new namespace for this services package, create an <fx:Declarations> block inside the main application file. In that block, define the service you want to use as well as an <s:Callresponder> class that will determine the result handler for the remote method call. Use one general fault handler for the service class, since in this application we only show an error message and nothing more. To actually call the method, create a new private method called findPhotos with no arguments. In this method, check the selected value of the searchCombo component to determine whether you need to fetch all photographs or just a small selection. When calling the remote methods, you also need to attach the CallResponder class to it. Otherwise, the result handler will never be called.

Excerpt from Main.mxml

```
<fx:Declarations>
  <services:PhotoAssembler id="photoService"
                           fault="faultHandler(event)" />
  <s:CallResponder id="photoHandler"
                   result="photoResultHandler(event)" />
</fx:Declarations>

<fx:Script>
  ...
  private function faultHandler(event:FaultEvent):void {
    Alert.show(event.fault.faultString, event.fault.faultCode);
  }

  private function photoResultHandler(event:ResultEvent):void {
  }

  private function findPhotos():void {
    if(searchCombo.text == "ALL") {
      photoHandler.token = photoService.getAllPhotos();
    } else {
      photoHandler.token = ➥
photoService.findPhotosByCategory(searchCombo.text.toUpperCase());
    }
  }
  ...
</fx:Script>
```

> *Normally, in an application like this, I would be using some kind of application framework when calling remote services. I'll discuss a number of frameworks later on in Chapter 8 and I'll provide an example that is implemented in all those frameworks, so you can clearly see the differences and similarities and choose the one that suits you the most.*

Configuring the Returned Data Type

When you place a breakpoint on the result handler and run the application in debug mode, you'll see that the call is already being made and that initially all items in the database are being returned by the remote service as an `ArrayCollection`.

Name	Value
⊞ ◉ this	Main (@110880a1)
⊟ ◉ event	mx.rpc.events.ResultEvent (@defc5e1)
⊞ ◆ [inherited]	
◢ headers	null
▪ _headers	null
⊟ ◆ result	mx.collections.ArrayCollection (@161dd781)
⊞ ◆ [inherited]	
⊟ ◉ [0]	Object (@15ce4ad9)
◢ category	"MOUNTAINS"
◢ location	"images/AthabascaGlacier1_popup.jpg"
◢ photo_id	1
◢ photo_name	"Athabasca glacier from a distance, Canadian Rocky Mountains"
◢ price	7.949999809265137
◢ thumbnail	"images/AthabascaGlacier1_gallery.jpg"
⊞ ◉ [1]	Object (@16eece99)
⊞ ◉ [2]	Object (@16eecb51)
⊞ ◉ [3]	Object (@16eece71)

Figure 6-24. *The returned value from the remote service is an* `ArrayCollection` *of photographs.*

You can see in Figure 6-24 that each item in the collection is completely filled out, but the item itself is still only of the `Object` type. That's something we need to fix next. To do so, we have to configure the return type for the remote method calls. Go to the `Data/Services` panel and select the `getAllPhotos` method, then right-click on it and select `Configure Return Type…` from the pop-up menu. Leave the default option on the first dialog selected, as this will create a class for the return type based on the properties in the object that is being returned. On the next screen, the wizard even suggests the name `Photo` be used for the DTO class. This name is also determined from the name of the ColdFusion component DTO you created earlier. The property types are automatically converted into ActionScript types as well and you'll see that the `price` property is of type `Number`, because it contains a decimal value. Just accept the defaults and hit the Finish button. This will create the `Photo` class in the `valueObjects` package you specified earlier when creating the `services` package in the back-end connection wizard. Run the application again in debug mode and, at the breakpoint, you'll see that the `Object` classes in the `ArrayCollection` return value for the remote method call have changed into instances of `be.flexpert.webshop.valueObjects.Photo` classes, which is exactly what we wanted to achieve.

However, we've only defined the return type for the `getAllPhotos` method, and we're calling the `findPhotosByCategory` method as well. Select this method and choose the `Configure Return Type…` again from the right-click pop-up menu. But this time we're not creating the return type again, because we've already done that. Instead, choose the other option in the dialog and select the `Photo[]` data type in the combo box. And that's all you need to do to configure the return type for this method.

The next step is actually calling the proper remote method when the selection in the combo box has changed. To do this, you have to call the `findPhotos` method in the `change` event handler. But that event handler can't yet be defined, because the `change` event is not thrown by the `SearchComboBox` component. You have to make sure that the custom component broadcasts that specific event at the proper time. So, open that component file and start by declaring the event that will be thrown, using a `<fx:MetaData>` block.

Excerpt from components ➤ *SearchComboBox.mxml*

```
<fx:Metadata>
  [Event(name="selectionChanged", type="flash.events.Event")]
</fx:Metadata>
```

> As you may know, defining this [Event] metadata tag is not strictly necessary. You can still capture the event being thrown by the component and your application will still work. In that case, though, you'd have to capture the event using the addEventListener method in ActionScript. So, I would advise you to always define this metadata because it also allows you to capture the events in the MXML tags, which can be quite convenient.

Now you need to change the actual throwing of the event. In the change event handler for the list component, you need to dispatch the event using the dispatchEvent ActionScript method. Don't forget that the name of the event you're dispatching needs to be exactly the same as the name you specified in the [Event] metadata tag or the system won't work.

Back in the main application file, you need to add the appropriate event listener on the SearchComboBox instance for the event you just dispatched. All you have to do when this event is dispatched is call the remote method again. So, instead of letting Flash Builder's code hinting generate a separate event listener method, just call the findPhotos method in the MXML attribute value directly to save some unnecessary coding.

Using the Returned Data in the Item Renderer

We still need to set the retrieved ArrayCollection as the dataProvider for the custom Tile component, so add a [Bindable] ArrayCollection to the application and fill it up with the retrieved values from the remote service. For the <s:List> tag in the Photo Gallery page, remove the fixed dataProvider and replace it with a binding reference to the property you just created. If you test the application now, you'll still see that the same photograph is always shown, but the number of items in the gallery varies depending on the selection in the searchCombo component instance. So, the next step in getting this page to work is adjusting the itemRenderer so it displays the photographs dynamically. If you look at the <s:List> tag in the main application file, you'll notice the skinClass attribute that defines which skin is used for this list component. Go to that skin class and search for the <s:DataGroup> tag. This will tell you the itemRenderer that is used for displaying each individual item in the list. Now go into that specified RepeatedItem component; we need to adjust the MyListItem component to pass on the data property to that custom component. It is the MyListItem component that requires the most work right now, so let's dig into it.

First, let's create a [Bindable] private property called _photo, which is of type Photo. This is the property you are going to set from within the RepeatedItem class using a public setter method. This allows you to write a binding expression on the visual components that represent part of the data contained in this property. Currently the photograph that is being shown is represented using a <s:BitmapImage> tag. However, this tag does not support dynamic setting of the source property. So replace that tag with an <mx:Image> tag, setting the source property to the location of the photograph's thumbnail. Also replace the x and y coordinates with constraints, placing it dead center for the horizontal position and 10 pixels above the middle in the vertical direction. Otherwise, the photos taken in portrait mode will be placed over the buttons at the bottom of the component. Next, add a CurrencyFormatter instance that formats the price tag with a Euro symbol and keeps the decimal places limited to 2 digits. And use that CurrencyFormatter to display the price tag for the photograph. The code for this component should now look like this:

Components ➤ *MyListItem.mxml*

```xml
<?xml version="1.0" encoding="utf-8"?>
<s:Group xmlns:s="library://ns.adobe.com/flex/spark"
              xmlns:fx="http://ns.adobe.com/mxml/2009"
              xmlns:d="http://ns.adobe.com/fxg/2008/dt"
              xmlns:fc="http://ns.adobe.com/flashcatalyst/2009"
              xmlns:mx="library://ns.adobe.com/flex/mx">
  <fx:Script>
    <![CDATA[
      import be.flexpert.webshop.valueObjects.Photo;

      [Bindable]
      private var _photo:Photo;

      public function set photo(value:Photo):void {
        _photo = value;
      }

      public function get photo():Photo {
        return _photo;
      }
    ]]>
  </fx:Script>

  <fx:Declarations>
    <mx:CurrencyFormatter id="cf" currencySymbol=" € " precision="2"/>
  </fx:Declarations>

  <s:states>
    <s:State name="Normal" fc:color="0xcc0000"/>
  </s:states>
  <s:BitmapImage source="@Embed('/assets/images/webshop/edge1_s Outer Stroke.png')"
              d:userLabel="edge1's Outer Stroke" x="0" y="0"/>
  <s:BitmapImage source="@Embed('/assets/images/webshop/edge1.png')"
              d:userLabel="edge1" x="1" y="1"/>
  <mx:Image source="assets/{_photo.thumbnail}"
          d:userLabel="photo1" horizontalCenter="0" verticalCenter="-10"/>
  <s:RichText color="#666666" fontFamily="Century Gothic" fontSize="14"
          d:userLabel=" 12.99" whiteSpaceCollapse="preserve"
          x="21" y="166"
          text="{cf.format(Math.round(_photo.price * 100)/100)}"/>
  <s:Button skinClass="components.MyShoppingCartButton" x="105" y="159"/>
  <s:Button skinClass="components.MyInfoButton" x="146" y="159"/>
</s:Group>
```

We could have used a public *accessor for the* _photo *property as well, but keeping properties* private *and accessing them using getters and setters is part of the best practices in object-oriented programming.*

I will talk about the best practices later on in this book.

Using Custom Events to Trigger the Detail Pop-Up

If you copy the pictures to a `photos` subdirectory in the `assets` package, you now have a working photo gallery application, with the filtering working as well. Next up is triggering the pop-up that shows the larger version of the photograph, plus the description. We'll do this by adding a click handler to the appropriate button in this component. However, the pop-up window has been created as a separate view state on the application level in Flash Catalyst, so you can't just set the `currentState` property to that state. You could choose to set the `currentState` property directly on the application, but then your custom component relies heavily on the current application setup, and reusability becomes virtually impossible. In this exercise, we'll create a custom event that will bubble all the way up to the main application level. This event will also contain the necessary data to set the photograph image and text dynamically in the pop-up window. The custom event class is called `PhotoEvent` and is situated in the `be.flexpert.webshop.events` package. The class inherits from the basic `flash.events.Event` class and has one additional property that holds a reference to the photograph data. You should also not forget to override the `clone` method; this is important when bubbling events to higher levels. From within the `MyListItem` class, dispatch an instance of that custom event type and add the photo data to that event.

Using the Runtime Data in the Detail Pop-Up

In the main application file, we need to add an event listener for the `PhotoEvent.DETAIL` event, because this is where we'll switch the current application state to show the pop-up window. Here we also change the `currentState` property and set the data aside in a `[Bindable]` property, so we can refer to it in a few moments when using binding expressions. Now search for the design layer that holds the pop-up window. There are actually two design layers that hold a pop-up window: one for landscape pictures and the other for portrait pictures. You can remove the design layer for the vertical pop-up completely; we constructed it in the original Photoshop file merely to indicate how the pictures should be shown in this pop-up window. In the other design layer, we'll change a few things to get it working dynamically. For instance, you need to add an `<s:Group>` tag to apply a vertical layout policy, so the picture and its name are always displayed in the same fashion and centered in the pop-up dialog, whether the photograph is in portrait or landscape. So, alter the `<fx:DesignLayer>` code block to the following:

Excerpt from Main.mxml

```
<fx:DesignLayer d:userLabel="popup" visible.PhotoGallery="false">
  <s:BitmapImage blendMode="multiply"
                 source="@Embed('/assets/images/webshop/background_s Drop Shadow.png')"
                 d:userLabel="background's Drop Shadow" x="488" y="169"/>
  <s:BitmapImage source="@Embed('/assets/images/webshop/background_s Outer ➡
Stroke.png')" d:userLabel="background's Outer Stroke" x="490" y="170"/>
  <s:BitmapImage source="@Embed('/assets/images/webshop/background1.png')"
                 d:userLabel="background" x="492" y="172">
    <s:mask>
      <s:Group x="0" y="0">
        <s:Path data="M 0 0.75 L 549.95 0.75 L 549.95 480.15 L 0 480.15 L 0 0.75"
                winding="evenOdd">
          <s:fill>
            <s:SolidColor color="#ff0000"/>
          </s:fill>
```

```
        </s:Path>
      </s:Group>
    </s:mask>
  </s:BitmapImage>
  <components:MyCustomCloseButton x="995" y="182" d:userLabel="Close button"
                                  click="closebutton_clickHandler()"/>
  <s:Group width="505" verticalCenter="10" horizontalCenter="125">
    <s:layout>
      <s:VerticalLayout horizontalAlign="center" gap="20" />
    </s:layout>
    <mx:Image source="assets/{_selectedPhoto.location}"/>
    <s:RichText color="#666666" fontFamily="Century Gothic"
                fontSize="16" kerning="off"
                d:userLabel="Athabasca Glacier, Glacier National Park, Canada"
                whiteSpaceCollapse="preserve" width="100%"
                text="{_selectedPhoto.photo_name}" textAlign="center"/>
  </s:Group>
</fx:DesignLayer>
```

Now we're finished with the photo pop-up window, leaving just one more thing to do for the Photo Gallery page: adding the photo to the shopping cart. The shopping cart in this application is only virtual and doesn't have a database equivalent, which means it can be represented by a simple ArrayCollection that is initialized every time the application starts up. In the <fx:Script> block of the main application file, add another [Bindable] property called _shoppingCart. Items are added to this shopping cart by clicking the appropriate button in the photo gallery, and we'll use the same system of event handling to notify the application that the user wants to add a certain photograph to the shopping cart. The only difference is that you have to create a second event name for this event. In the event handler, just add the photo object from the event to the shoppingCart property. Then set the number of items in the shopping cart box equal to the number of items in the shopping cart.

Now you have completed the Photo Gallery page and you can continue working on the other features of this website.

The Contact Page

The Contact me page is very simple, with just a few input fields. The only really specific item in this page is the CAPTCHA component, which needs to be validated before the e-mail message is sent. So, when the user hits the Send button, the CAPTCHA must be validated first in the event handler. To validate the component, call the verifyCode method. If the code is valid, the method returns true so you can use it in a conditional statement to control the process flow that follows. If the validation fails, the component automatically refreshes the CAPTCHA code to prevent any automated processes from guessing the code over and over again.

> Normally, upon successful checking of the code, you'd then call a remote back-end method to actually send the e-mail message to the address specified as the recipient. However, this would take us too far off topic for the purpose of this book, so it is not implemented in this exercise.

The Login Procedure

Next, let's look at the `Login` page. This page has two input fields, and a button that triggers the validation. That validation button needs an event handler to react to the `click` event. Let Flash Builder generate the event handler method to save some time. In that handler method ,you need to call the remote method on the ColdFusion server. But at this point, there's no service defined that can help you with this. So, before launching a back-end call, go into the `Data/Services` panel again and connect to another service. Obviously, this is a ColdFusion service again, but this time you are going to connect to the `UserAssembler` class, which you can find in the same location as the `PhotoAssembler` you connected to earlier. Just make sure that both the `services` and `valueObjects` packages refer to the same `be.flexpert.webshop.services` and `be.flexpert.webshop.valueObjects` respectively, so the ActionScript classes are placed in the same packages as the classes for the `PhotoAssembler` service.

Once the ActionScript service classes are generated, add the `UserAssembler` and accompanying `CallResponder` classes to the `<fx:Declarations>` code block. Remember that you either get a `User` object or `NULL` returned from the service. So in that result handler, you have to make a distinction between a failed and a successful call to set the error message's visibility property on the `Login` page. Change the `id` attribute value for the `<s:RichText>` component to `loginError` and set the `visibility` property to `true` in case the login procedure has failed and a `NULL` value has been returned. On the other hand, when the user has successfully logged in to the web site, you have to:

- set the user object apart for future reference.
- reset the error message.
- keep an indication that the user has logged on successfully.
- reset the shopping cart.
- go directly to the Photo Gallery page, because that's the only reason the user needs to log in.

The result handler method should now look like this:

Excerpt from Main.mxml

```
private function loginResultHandler(event:ResultEvent):void {
  _user = event.result as User;
  _shoppingCart.removeAll();
  if(event.result == null) {
    loginError.visible = true;
    _userLoggedIn = false;
  } else {
    loginError.visible = false;
    _userLoggedIn = true;
    currentState = "PhotoGallery";
  }
}
```

Once this event handler is all set up, you can also bind the visible property of the shopping cart box to the `_userLoggedIn` property. This makes the shopping cart box is visible only when the user has logged in successfully.

The final task for this page is adjusting the "hyperlink" text on the page to display a hand cursor. Remember how you did that for the bottom right image on the homepage? Well the system behind this is exactly the same, so you need to add the following attributes to the `<components:RegisterLink >` tag:

- userHandCursor="true"
- buttonMode="true"

And we're done with the Login page, as you can now log in and go to the registration page if you don't yet have an account.

The Registration Procedure

The final step in completing this exercise is making sure a user can register on the web site, so let's take a look at the `Register` page. This page is quite similar to the `Contact` page in that it has input fields and a `CAPTCHA` validation component. When the user hits the Register button, the validation needs to take place and then the user can be registered, but only if the login doesn't already exist.

So, our first task is to add an event listener to the `Register` button to capture the event when the user clicks on it. In that event handler method, we validate the `CAPTCHA` code by calling the `verifyCode` method on the component. When this method returns true, it means that the code was correct and you can move on with the normal process flow for creating a new user. But you still have to verify whether the login that was provided already exists. For that, you need a remote method call, because you have to check this in the database. Luckily, we created a method to do exactly this. So go ahead and rename that custom text input field's `id` to `username` and call the `findUser` method with the given input from that field as a parameter. To capture the return value from this remote method, create another `<s:CallResponder>` instance in the `<fx:Declarations>` code block. In the result handler for this responder, you have to check the return value from the remote method call. If the result is `true`, the login has been found and you have to display the error message by setting its visible property to true. However, if the result is `false`, you can create the user by calling another remote method from the `UserAssembler` service. Again you have to define yet another `<s:CallResponder>` instance to capture the result for that specific back-end call. In that responder, you can assume that the user account has been created. The user still has to log in manually, but you can direct him to the Login page automatically, so he can do that.

Notice that in this example we are storing the password directly in the database as a plain text field. In real world applications, this is simply not done, because databases are popular targets when attacking an application. The password data must be encrypted, preferably with at least a 256-bit encryption method. I usually use hashing systems to prevent decryption algorithms from cracking the password. But because this is not part of the workflow itself, I've left this out in order to focus on the tasks at hand.

And this step concludes this exercise. When you run the application, you'll see the photos being loaded from the database, depending on the filter criterion you selected in the search box. The custom scrollbar is also working perfectly and registered users can log in to gain access to the shopping cart.

Summary

In this elaborate exercise, I've taken you through the entire workflow of a small e-commerce web site. Although this web site is not yet complete and parts are still missing, you can see that some parts can be done simultaneously and some need to be sequential. This may be the case because you need information from another process before you can start working on a certain part. Or it may be that working sequentially reduces the time you'll need to spend on reworking existing code when other parts are very likely to be change during the development process.

In the next chapter I'll take you deeper into the realm of managing these kinds of projects. I'll provide some tips and tricks to make sure the quality of your code is taken to a next level. I'll also take you through some very interesting ideas and techniques to manage rich Internet application development processes, and I'll discuss the project team setup and how choosing the right people for the right job can mean the difference between a successful project and a failure.

Chapter 7

Managing RIA Projects

In the previous chapters, I've looked at how different kinds of applications require different approaches. They also require different skill sets and a collaboration of different profiles to bring the project to a good end. In this chapter, I'm going to take a step back and try to explain things form a helicopter viewpoint. In other words, I am going to take a closer look at the consequences of these new products on team compositions and development lifecycles. I'll also take a closer look at several tools that can help you increase the quality of the code you produce.

Mind you, this is not going to be a chapter about project management strategies or tools such as SCRUM, PMI/PMBOK, PRINCE2, etc. This will be a chapter about managing RIA projects and how the arrival of Flash Catalyst has changed the way you should look at these projects.

Projects and Complexity

In the previous chapters, I've taken you through a couple of examples to illustrate some points regarding the workflow on different kinds of application. However, all of these applications were rather small. Do the same suggestions apply on larger projects? Your initial reaction might be, "No, larger projects require a different approach, because they are more complex, involving many more people and numerous project files."

However, upon closer consideration, are these projects really all that different? There is still a design phase alongside the development phase. The differences have to be found in the size of the project and its consequences. What does that mean in reality? First of all, chances are you will have a lot more formal documentation on the project in the form of an official requirements analysis, a lot more meetings to attend, and a lot less contribution in the project phase you are not assigned to.

The first difference is not so bad. More documentation means that the project is strictly defined, including a fixed procedure for filing bugs and change requests. This allows you to calculate the consequences for a change request and its effect on the deadlines. Documenting the project and setting boundaries also forces the client, either external or internal, to think about what he really wants. Maybe the client says he wants A but, in fact, he needs B. Defining A clearly on paper and having the client sign it usually triggers some questions and thoughts about what they really want to see built. From my experience, this often leads to another round of discussing the content and starting all over again with the requirements phase. However, once the requirements are fixed and signed, the rest of the project lifecycle is easier to manage.

So, elaborate project documentation is something you should not view as a hassle, but rather as a blessing. I've done my share of large and well-documented projects as well as smaller and undocumented ones, and I've found that the ones that are formally documented are a lot easier to manage because of the strict boundaries. The undocumented ones were just plain awful because you get trapped in an endless discussion loop about what is a bug and what is a feature. In some cases, this messes up your initial planning completely.

The second item on the consequences list is that all of these details need to be discussed formally in meetings. This does not mean that you cannot or should not discuss things casually in the hallway—the best ideas are born from casual conversations, so by all means, don't *just* do meetings. However, meetings are necessary, and there are some basic rules you should apply when organizing meetings:

- **Only invite the people who are really necessary.** When people are at your meeting, they cannot be developing or designing on your project.
- **Send the agenda via email up front.** This allows the participants to better prepare themselves and to decide whether or not they should attend (unless they are required by you, of course).
- **Try to keep the meetings as short as possible.** A good rule of thumb is a maximum of 2 hours. Try to match the agenda to this length; if that's not possible, organize several shorter meetings. People only have a limited concentration span, which means that they will retain less information the longer the meeting takes.
- **Make formal decisions.** There is nothing as frustrating as going to a meeting where nothing is decided. It is a waste of everyone's valuable time
- **Share the meeting notes.** Make sure that everyone who was invited (even those who could not make it for some reason) gets the notes from the meeting. This way, everyone is up to speed on the decisions that have been made, the tasks everybody has to perform, etc.
- **Follow up on decisions.** If certain decisions have been made, make sure they are actually carried out. This should be the task of either the lead developer or the project manager, depending on the level of technical complexity. Does this require a follow-up meeting? Not really. Follow-up meetings are great for formally closing the topics or tasks that needed to be done. But following up on the assigned tasks can be done individually or through a bug and issue tracking tools such as JIRA (http://www.atlassian.com/software/jira/) or Bugzilla (http://www.bugzilla.org/).

As a third consequence, I noted that you will probably not contribute much to the other project phases. In other words, as a developer on a large project, you will be further away from the design than when you would be working on a small project. On the other hand, designers will also be less involved in the actual implementation. This is because you're working in larger teams and the collaboration is going to be different due to the nature of the project team.

Project Team

Let's talk about the project team for a moment. Some projects will require large teams while others can be done by a single person. In the examples I provided in chapter 5, you already experienced the differences in profile requirements for these small applications. But what if you take this up to a higher level?

Team Compositions

In every kind of project you always have to stop and think about a couple of things before starting on it. The first is composing the project team: how many people are going to work on the project and what profiles do you need? The first part of that question depends on a couple of factors:

- How many people do you have available?
- What's the timeframe in which the project needs to be completed?
- How many people can actually work on it together without interfering with each other?
- How many different profiles does it take to complete the project?

When you're a small company with ten employees, you might find yourself in a situation where you have to place everyone on the same project. But in a larger company, this will rarely be the case; teams are more likely to be formed dynamically depending on the type of project and its size rather than always having to work with the same four or five people.

One important thing to keep in mind when deciding on the team composition is the fact that one and one don't always make two. In other words, working with more people generates a certain overhead because you also need to manage them. Obvious scenarios include when one designer or developer has to wait for the other one, or when the front-end developer has to wait for the designer to complete (part of) the application design before he can get started. Thus, simply doubling the number of developers or designers on the team isn't going to cut your design or development time in half. So, **let's compare the different project team sizes and the consequences**.

Let's start with a small project team that works on a Rich Internet Application (RIA). What exactly do you need to create a small team that can complete an entire application? Well, you at least need a designer and a developer. (Yes, you can argue that projects can be made by a single person, but since we're talking about team compositions and the workflow between the team members, two people is the minimum requirement to be able to use the term "team.") I would also add an interaction designer, but for the moment, this task will lie with the designer. However, I've called out this specific role in the workflow depicted in Figure 7-1; I will explain why later on in this chapter.

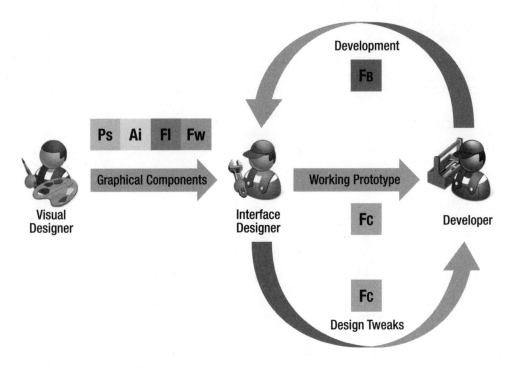

Figure 7-1: The basic workflow when creating a RIA project with a small team.

This workflow is pretty straightforward. It begins with one Photoshop, Illustrator, Fireworks or Flash file as the design. The interaction designer starts to work on that file when the design is finished, because he needs the entire file to import in Flash Catalyst. Once the interactions and custom components have all been created, the resulting project is then transferred to the developer, who will attach it to the back end and add live data to it.

What are the advantages of having such a small project team? Well, for starters, you don't have to manage that many people, so the project planning is quite simple. Another advantage is that the communication between the team members can be direct and fast. It's not a matter of sending dozens of emails to everyone to keep them all current on what's going on, since the team members will be working closely together. **The disadvantages** of having such a small team are also quite obvious. Because there is only a small team and every person only has one brain and two hands, the timeframe in which the project is developed is going to be long. Likewise, decisions will often not be formalized, which can lead to confusion and missed deadlines. This can, in turn, lead to a frustrated team as well as a frustrated client.

Let's take a look at the consequences for larger project teams. What is the definition of a larger project team? Possible scenarios range from multiple designers over multiple interaction designers to multiple developers or any combination thereof. Every scenario requires a different approach to managing the project: more things can happen simultaneously but some things will always have to be handled in sequence. Let's assume the worst case scenario where you have multiple developers, multiple interaction designers, and multiple visual designers at your disposal for a certain project, as shown in Figure 7-2.

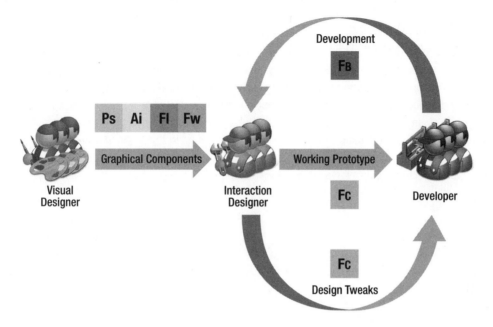

Figure 7-2: A scenario with multiple people working on each area of the project lifecycle.

How you do manage several designers and interaction designers working on the same file if your design is structured into one file? Well, you don't! Instead, you **split up the design into several parts** and you have each designer work on a separate part. At the end of the design process you then have two options:

- Keep the design file as a separate part to continue the development process.
- Integrate all of the design files into one large file which then becomes the final design.

The latter one has its advantages because from that point on, the project workflow remains exactly the same as with the smaller project team: an interaction designer takes the file and converts it into custom components and view states before sending it off to the developer team. But the workflow I'm talking about here does not have just one interaction designer. Instead, it has multiple interaction designers that need to work together on the same project, so the first option is the better one. **Keeping the design files separated enables multiple interaction designers to work on different parts of the project at the same time.** (Remember to use versioning or check-in/check-out tools!)

Senior developers are usually aware of this, but in this case designers and interaction designers will also have to agree to use some form of design and naming convention in the project parts. By design conventions, I mean that there has to be a certain way of creating design elements. When do you create a separate layer or layer group? Do you rasterize an effect or do you leave it as a separate layer mask? Naming conventions are more obvious since you have to agree upon a common way of giving your design layers appropriate names.

Otherwise, you will end up with inconsistencies in your design layers or Flash Catalyst components. Even worse, these inconsistencies will affect the way the application works. And that is certainly not user friendly! A user expects the same behavior in all parts of the application.

And even when you choose that option, you still have two choices:

- Keep the Flash Catalyst files separate, export them as Flex library projects (as discussed in chapter 4 on Flash Catalyst), and integrate them using Flash Builder by importing those projects and attaching them to another Flex project in which you use all of the created components.
- Create a separate Flash Catalyst project where you first import the library projects and then create the integrated design, which you can then pass on to the developer team as one project.

Even though the first option is viable in a situation where you have several components that will also be used in other projects as well, I would opt for the second option because it is easier to create the integrated project in Flash Catalyst than in Flash Builder. And using the right tools for the job is what efficient project development is all about. You should end up with a situation similar to the one in Figure 7-3.

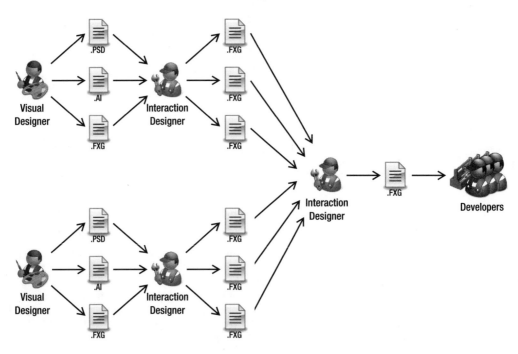

Figure 7-3: A conceptual schema of the workflow process in larger project teams.

Now that the possible workflow for this larger project team has been made clear, let's take a look at the **advantages and disadvantages for using larger project teams** to complete a certain Rich Internet Application. Let's start with the positive note. The first advantage is that more people can do more in the same amount of time, resulting in a smaller project timeframe. (Note that project timings are calculated in man days and not actual calendar days). Another advantage is that part of the team can be a separate group located in another facility or outsourced to another company that specializes in a specific aspect of the project lifecycle. The final advantage is actually the large scope of the project, which requires that decisions be well documented, deadlines formalized, etc., making it easier to keep the project on track.

Of course, there is also a downside to this way of working and the main disadvantage lies in the fact that decisions are formally made. This means you cannot just have a casual one-on-one conversation for solving things because many people have to be in the know when a certain decision has been made. Often this will result in having to wait for a day or two before you can get everyone together to discuss certain issues and how they should be resolved. Luckily, not every designer or developer has to be present at these meetings, but in case of a critical issue, this approach can set you back on your timing and deadlines. However, this does not mean that one-on-one follow-up and casual guidance cannot be performed in this situation. As I said, not everyone has to be involved in the decision making process, but they do have to be notified of these decisions.

Naturally, having a very small team or having multiple designers, interaction designers and developers are not the only possible options when putting together a project team. Any composition that falls in between these extremes is going to have an adjusted workflow that will also fall in between the two examples that I've given. It is nearly impossible to describe each and every possible workflow situation, because there are so many possibilities.

Collaboration has Changed

Now that you have your teams, how do they collaborate? Until now, you had collaboration between designers and developers on a very high level. Designers were creating some nifty designs and the developers tried their best to recreate that design in Flex code. For the most part, that was doable; sometimes, however, it was just plain impossible or it took an incredible amount of time to recreate parts of a design. As I mentioned in the Flash Catalyst chapter, have you ever tried to create a custom scrollbar in Flex? It is really hard to do. Thanks to Flash Catalyst, it now takes a few minutes. So recreating designs has become a lot easier than it used to be.

But this new product also brings a new role in the project team: the interaction designer. I'm saying it's a new role when, in fact, it has been around for quite some time, but I think it has never been more clearly defined as a separate role than it is now. Sometimes a designer, or even the developer, will take up that role in smaller projects or smaller project teams. But it is definitely a separate area of expertise which can be fulfilled by a separate person—someone who knows a lot about usability and user expectations. You can have an awesome design, and the developer may have been able to recreate it completely and get it working just the way you want it to, but if the application doesn't feel natural to the user, he won't be happy with the application.

We've all seen those lovely Flash website designs that leave the user wondering, "What am I supposed to do now? Where can I click something and where is the information hidden?" This way of designing and developing can be good as a design showcase, but it is inappropriate for RIA because you will lose many of your potential customers or visitors. In other words, a beautiful design without intuitive interaction is nothing more than a TV with only one channel: it's great to look at, but you get bored quickly and turn it off.

The interaction designer is the one that will make sure that the design is also functional. He will be the link between the designers and the developers. In this specific workflow, he brings the design to life and prepares the application for the developer, so the developer doesn't have to worry about the design. But another part of the interaction designer job is going back and forth between the designer and developer, keeping them in check with the preordained target. If a developer can't attach data too certain design element, perhaps the design has to be altered. On the other hand, maybe the developer needs to find another approach to get the data into that design element. Or maybe the way the component works has to be altered. It all depends on how much time each alteration will take and how much stress has been put on a certain part of the project.

Considerations include if the design is fixed because all applications for a certain company have long been the same. If so, you are probably not allowed to change the look and feel of that component. Another scenario might be that you're stuck with a database that already exists and you can't alter any tables and have to do with the data you get. In that case, you might have to change the design a little bit so it can cooperate better with the data at hand.

So, this "new" role in the project team is a very important one. It is not only Flash Catalyst that will form the bridge between the designer and the developer. The interaction designer has the same task to perform, and he too can make or break an application by constructing the wrong custom components, making too many unnecessary components, creating the wrong view states or creating view states on the wrong component level, etc. The responsibility that comes with this role should not be underestimated.

Agile Development

When people talk about a methodology for developing projects, they often refer to "agile development". But what exactly does that mean?

> *Agile software development refers to a group of software development methodologies based on iterative development, where requirements and solutions evolve through collaboration between self-organizing cross-functional teams. The term was coined in the year 2001 when the Agile Manifesto was formulated.*
>
> *Agile methods generally promote a disciplined project management process that encourages frequent inspection and adaptation, a leadership philosophy that encourages teamwork, self-organization and accountability, a set of engineering best practices intended to allow for rapid delivery of high-quality software, and a business approach that aligns development with customer needs and company goals.*
>
> Wikipedia

Now, this quote doesn't really say much more than the fact that it is not one methodology but rather a whole bunch of them. It also reveals that iterative development is involved, and that it is more of a project management term than it is a development term. But let's take a closer look at these two subtopics.

Methodologies

When you talk about agile development, you need to understand that it is not so much a separate methodology but rather a combination of proven techniques to better manage, maintain, and deliver your project. Some examples of early agile methodologies were:

- *Scrum*: `http://en.wikipedia.org/wiki/Scrum_(development)`
- *Extreme Programming*: `http://en.wikipedia.org/wiki/Extreme_Programming`

■ *Feature Driven Development*:
`http://en.wikipedia.org/wiki/Feature_Driven_Development`

All of these methodologies put a heavy stress on iterative and incremental development. In 2001, the **Manifesto for Agile Software Development** (`http://agilemanifesto.org`) was published. This short document states that some characteristics of a project should be valued more than others in favor of finishing the project on time:

■ **Individuals and interactions** over processes and tools

■ **Working software** over comprehensive documentation

■ **Customer collaboration** over contract negotiation

■ **Responding to change** over following a plan

The first bullet stresses that when developing software, you are still working with human beings. The people behind the process are more important that the process itself. If you don't interact properly with your project team members, your project is doomed. For example, if the developer who was assigned a task hasn't done it—because he wasn't aware of that he was assigned this task—you have a problem. This is quite obvious.

The second bullet says that it is better to have software that is working and is delivered on time than a whole bunch of documents with very well written specs but no working software. Don't be mistaken here: this statement doesn't say that you shouldn't document your project. You should always do that. But often documenting the project takes more time than actually developing it. Remember that documentation for the project is not only the analysis, but also includes code commenting and test reports. So, documentation: Yes! But just don't overdo it.

The third bullet talks about putting the customer first. Of course you have to negotiate the contract with the customer. After all, you have a business to run and people need to get paid. However, once those negotiations are over, the client is now someone you work with. You need to consult them regularly and involve them in your entire project lifecycle instead of treating them as a customer buying a product off the shelf. Customers rarely know exactly what they want when they first contact you. Changes happen during the course of the project. Keep in touch.

In my entire career as a developer, I've never worked on a project that didn't deviate from the specs over the course of the development process. Sometimes the specs were even written during this process. This is not really the way to go, but sometimes you just don't have the choice when you're working on something that is designed to be working in a volatile environment.

And that is exactly what this last bullet is about: accepting changes. Again, thinks links everything together. You need to treat the customer as a partner. When you have a problem, don't start guessing for the solution. Involve the customer, because they will better understand the causes and the best solutions. You might have to make changes to already written code; sometimes you need to take these changes into account straight away and sometimes they need to be treated as an extension because they endanger making the deadline. In such a case, the contract might have to be altered—or maybe not, depending on the relationship you've already built up with the client. It can be quite troublesome when the changes are extensive, but eventually the client will get what he asked for, and that is how you get a happy customer.

How does the agile development differ from other methodologies such as iterative development, waterfall modeling, or cowboy coding?

In case of iterative development, agile development also promotes the use of iterations to produce software on a timely basis. But instead of going through iterations than can last months, agile development favors iterations in terms of weeks or even days for smaller features.

Even though the waterfall model is still in use, it has little in common with agile development. In the waterfall model, there is a strict set of rules and phases that you need to adhere to. Projects are first documented and refined. Only then can the development process start. This approach has a drawback, however; it does not allow for changes to be applied while you're still working on the project. Changes will often be treated as change request from the start and will have to be documented in detail first before implementation. Agile development promotes handling changes while you're still coding, and it stresses collaboration versus relying heavily on the project documentation.

Cowboy coding is a term to indicate that no methodology whatsoever has been used. You just see a problem and fix it without even considering the consequences for other developers or programs that the project needs to collaborate with. In this way of working, much time is lost in bug fixing, because bugs are introduced by fixing another problem. Testing these applications in an iterative development process can be quite the hassle, because everything has to be tested and retested from the beginning which each deliverable.

Iterative Development

The basic idea behind iterative development is to develop a software system incrementally. This allows developers to gain deeper insight into the specific problems with the project and benefit from the way problems have been solved in the earlier iterations. The development process starts with initial requirements (which tend to change as the project progresses). Then the project is cut into pieces, and each piece becomes an iteration. Each iteration is incremental, which means that it is built on top of the previous iteration releases to get to the final product at the end of the day.

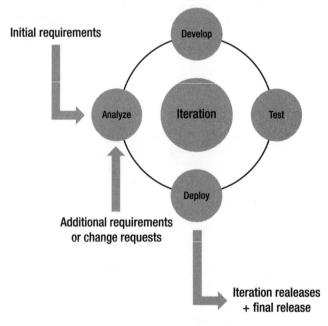

Figure 7-4: The iteration lifecycle of a project in agile development.

I've already named one advantage of using the iteration approach: making use of what you have learned along the way. But of course there are other advantages too. One advantage is that because you're working with small iterations, you can easily adapt to changing circumstances. When the client starts testing an iteration release and he sees something he does not like or some malfunction, the amount of code that you potentially have to rewrite is going to be rather small. Even when something has to be rewritten completely, it is not the end of the world. Imagine, instead, if you weren't using the iterative process, and the client didn't approve the end result: it would mean a massive setback in your budget to have to start all over again. Agile development counters this because usually a client has to formally approve each iteration release, thus that part of the application can be considered finished.

> *Even though iterations are approved and considered finished, that does not mean you shouldn't test them in the next iteration. Bugs can be introduced with the next feature or by changing a component that was already in use in previous iterations. Testing should be very thorough. Too many developers test their code only the way it should work. They should spend a lot more time testing what shouldn't be working to see if something weird happens with the application in such a scenario.*

FlexPMD: A Useful Tool

When developing projects for a client, it is important to get the finished product delivered on time and within budget. However, it is also very important that the code you deliver is of a high quality. That means that you need to be mindful of how you are coding and writing comment in the code. . I will cover this further in the chapters about using frameworks and the best practices later on in this book.

But how are you going to check the code for weird constructions, uncommented classes and methods, etc.? You need to perform code reviews. Obviously, code reviews should not be done by the developer who wrote the code in question. An independent reviewer (an external auditor or another developer from your team) should review the code, verify its structure, etc. This procedure can be very time consuming.

Happily, there are a couple of tools that can help you perform code reviews. One is FlexPMD; it's an Eclipse plug-in that you can add to your existing Eclipse IDE or Flash Builder (since the latter is built on top of Eclipse). You can download this plug-in on the open source website of Adobe at `http://opensource.adobe.com/wiki/display/flexpmd/FlexPMD+Eclipse+plugin`, where you also find the instructions on how to install it.

Let me show you how this tool can help you create better code. The tool focuses on improving code quality by detecting violations against some best practices such as:

- **Dead code**: This is a phenomenon where some of the code (methods, variables, constants, etc.) is never going to be executed. Since it is useless, it's a bad practice to leave that code in the project; it just adds to the file size.
- **Inefficient code**: Some code can be written in a more efficient way. Efficient doesn't always mean less code, but it does mean that the code will execute faster or require less memory usage.
- **Overly complex code**: Sometimes you have situations where you find yourself nesting loops into other loops or creating conditional statements that seem endless. You should review these situations as they can be the cause for latency in your application.
- **Lengthy code**: Classes and methods of thousands of lines should be revised as they might be overly complex. Classes like this are very often hard to maintain, even though they can be documented extensively.

- **Incorrect use of the Flex component lifecycle**: Flex components have a lifecycle to which your code should adhere as well. For example, you should only add certain components to Flex containers in the `createChildren` method.

To see this in action, **duplicate the `Workflow_Resizer` project** you created in the workflow chapter and rename it ResizerPMD. Then open Flash Builder (if you haven't already done so) **and import the project** using the `Import…` option from the `File` menu. Choose the option `Existing Projects into WorkSpace` in the popup dialog and point to the workspace directory to see which projects you can import. Right-click on the project to choose the `FlexPMD ➤ Add FlexPMD Nature` option from the popup menu, as shown in Figure 7-5.

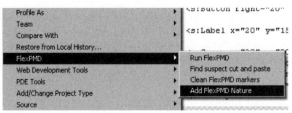

Figure 7-5: The FlexPMD plug-in installs a new option in the Eclipse menus.

Selecting this option will make sure that the FlexPMD plug-in is run every time a file in the project is saved. However, the plug-in is also run automatically at this point. You can also manually start this checking. To do that, you have to choose `FlexPMD ➤ Run FlexPMD` from the right-click popup menu. Once the check has been performed, you can look at either the `Problems` view or the `FlexPMD View` at the bottom of the IDE interface. It may well be that the latter one doesn't show up automatically. If so, you can display it by going to the `Window` menu and choosing the `Show View ➤ Other…` option. In the popup dialog that follows, you will find a new category called `Flex Quality`. Within that category, you'll find the views that are related to the Flex PMD plug-in. Figure 7-6 shows the results for this check.

Rule	Message
☐ ⚠ PackageCase	1 violation
📄 src.controllers.PhotoResizer.as	A package name should be lower case (flash.display.BitmapData). Detects when a package definition contains upper case characters
☐ ⓘ CodeBehindInMxml	1 violation
📄 src.PhotoResizer.mxml	Avoid using code behind files. Code behind files are tightly coupled with the view, not unit-testable, not easy to navigate the code c…
☐ ⓘ CopyrightMissing	2 violations
📄 src.controllers.PhotoResizer.as	The copyright header is missing in this file
📄 src.PhotoResizer.mxml	The copyright header is missing in this file
☐ ⓘ TooShortVariable	2 violations
📄 src.controllers.PhotoResizer.as	This variable name is too short (3 characters minimum, but 1 actually). Detects when a field, local, or parameter has a very short name
📄 src.controllers.PhotoResizer.as	This variable name is too short (3 characters minimum, but 1 actually). Detects when a field, local, or parameter has a very short name

Figure 7-6: The FlexPMD check reveals several warnings about code not being written according to the best practices.

As you can see, the plug-in generates several warnings about violations against the best practices that have been commonly accepted in the Flex world. However, these warnings to not mean that your code is incorrect; you created and tested this application before so obviously it is running perfectly. The warnings act as a tool to help you make your code conform to other people's code, so that everyone can find their way in each other's code. This can be very important if the project will be maintained by multiple developers; it can save you a tremendous amount of time trying to figure out where to insert a certain change request, because you already know where to look.

> *It is important to remember that this check is based on a basic set of rules created by Adobe. These rules are configuring automatically with the default settings. However, you may not agree with these rules all the time. Happily, there is an option of creating your own set of rules. Thus, you can use this tool to verify your code against your own coding and naming conventions.*

Let's take a closer look at some of the warnings. The first one states that you shouldn't have used any uppercase characters in your package names. Now, if you double click on the warning in the **FlexPMD View** panel, it will take you to the appropriate source file and even directly to the line that generated this warning. In this case, you'll see that it generates a package warning where there is no package defined, because you've just used the code behind principle when creating this file. So, this error has been generated incorrectly. But the next warning gives a clue as to why this first one was generated. It recommends that code behind shouldn't be used because:

- The files are tightly coupled.
- The component is not unit-testable.
- The code is not easy to navigate.
- The code behind file is not reusable.

Although the tool has a point, it does not mention that it is always a good thing to separate your design layer from the code. This is called the Model-View-Controller principle, which is applied here on a smaller scale. The fact that the code behind file is simply included using an `<fx:Script>` tag does indeed mean that it is probably not reusable. There are other ways of making your code behind reusable, but I'm not going to dig into them here as that would take us too far off topic right now. But suffice it to say that in this case I don't agree with the standard set of rules in the tool.

The next couple of warnings tell you about code commenting issues. Commenting your code is always necessary as it is part of the project documentation, even more so when you use the ASDoc styled notation (which is essentially the same as JavaDoc). This allows you to automatically generate your own *livedocs* for the code, similar to the Adobe *livedocs* that allow other developers to browse through the class functionality and gain better insight into its usage and possibilities. These particular warnings are about the copyright notice. According to the standard coding guidelines, every source file should have a copyright notice at the top. So, to remove these two errors, you have to double click them one by one and adjust the code. For the **PhotoResizer.as** ActionScript file you just add the following line of code:

```
// Copyright Steven Peeters (c), 2010
```

Include this line of code completely at the top of the file. When you save it and you have the **Monitorize** toggle button selected in the **FlexPMD Outline** panel, you should see the warning disappear. It is slightly different for the MXML file because you can't use ActionScript style comments, so you have to add the copyright notice like this:

Excerpt from Main.mxml

```
<?xml version="1.0" encoding="utf-8"?>
<!-- Copyright Steven Peeters (c), 2010 -->
<s:WindowedApplication xmlns:fx="http://ns.adobe.com/mxml/2009"
```

```
xmlns:s="library://ns.adobe.com/flex/spark"
xmlns:mx="library://ns.adobe.com/flex/halo"
showStatusBar="false"
creationComplete="initApp()">
```

You have to include the notice after the XML definition to be able to use the XML based comment notation. Saving the MXML file also gets rid of the warning. If it doesn't happen automatically, you can always start the FlexPMD plug-in manually by selecting `FlexPMD ➤ Run FlexPMD` from the right-click popup menu on the project.

The last two violations are indicating that some variables are too short. This warning is generated because of the best practice rule that says you should give all of your variables meaningful names. Of course you're going to use x and y within `for` loops. But using s to store a dynamically generated string doesn't say anything about what that string should contain. What does it mean? What is it supposed to contain? Giving meaningful names such as `query`, for example, makes it much clearer as to what this variable is expected to contain. When you double click on those errors, it takes you to the calculations where the width and the height are plainly indicated with a w and h. Change these variables into `calcWidth` and `calcHeight,` respectively, to avoid naming conflicts with the actual `width` and `height` of the application, and adjust the rest of the code to work with the new variable names. Note that saving this file does not automatically trigger the FlexPMD checking again, unless you have set the **Monitorize** option by toggling the button in the **FlexPMD Outline** panel, which you can show in the same way as you did with the **FlexPMD View** panel. Run the plug-in again and you'll see the warnings have disappeared. That's how easy it is to improve the quality of your code.

Now, let's take a look at a larger project that contains a whole bunch of files and components and see how that affects the behavior of the FlexPMD tool. Duplicate the **Webshop** project and name it WebshopPMD. Add the FlexPMD project nature to the new project and run the check procedure. You'll notice that you now get many more warnings, as shown in Figure 7-7.

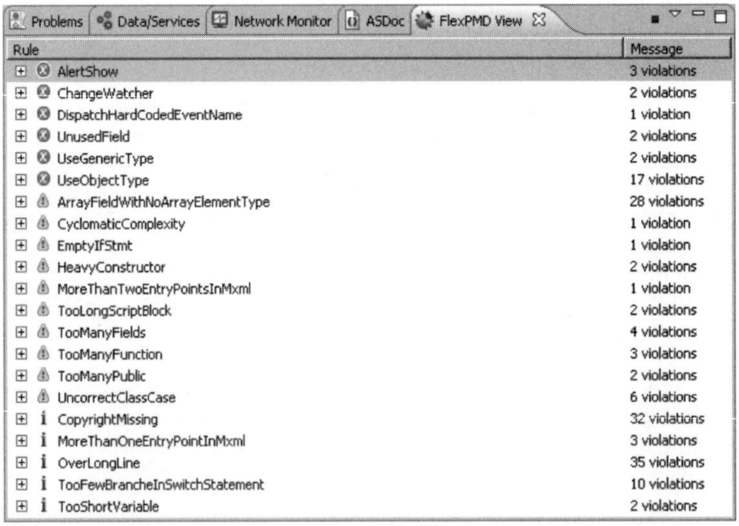

Figure 7-7: The `WebshopPMD` project generates many more warnings.

When you open up the details for each violation, you'll notice that a lot of them come from the code in the components that were generated by Flash Catalyst. Even though the FlexPMD plug-in is released by Adobe, the code generated by Flash Catalyst is still in need of some improvements. Is this a bad thing? Not really; coding and conventions are only a set of rules that some people agree upon as a way of implementing code. Most of the time, these conventions are not going to have any effect on whether or not the application is working. They just make to code easier to maintain by developers other than you.

Let's take a look at some of the warnings that have been generated and see which rules we are violating. The first one is quite obvious, but I do not necessarily agree with it. It states that you should not use the static method `Alert.show` to handle errors but rather a more general error manager. The reason for this is to have a general and uniform way of handling errors in your application. When you use `Alert` boxes scattered all over the application, it's going to be harder to revise them all when the error handling changes, for example. However, since all of the violations are within the same main application file, I don't think this poses such a problem in this particular application. So, you can just leave it like that. It's going to be a whole different story when you start to use application frameworks, which I will cover in the next chapter.

In the **SearchComboBox.mxml** file, the `selectionChanged` event is being thrown by dispatching the hardcoded string. This should not be done, as it would mean revising the entire code when the name of the event changes. To fix this error, you would have to create a custom event class to dispatch your custom data using a custom event name. In this case, you would also define the event name as a static constant in that event class. But because you are only dispatching a notification without any additional data, I find it to be overkill to create a custom class for that, since it would also contribute to the resulting SWF file size. However, when you have a lot of custom notification events in your application, you could opt to create one single class that just defines all the event names you require. An alternate option would be to define the static constants in the main application file. This file is also always accessible from every location in the project. Since you only have one custom notification event in this application, let's choose the latter option. **You first have to define a static constant in the main application file before altering the code in for the combobox, as shown:**

Excerpt from components ➤ SearchComboBox.mxml

```
<fx:Script>
  ...
  protected function list_changeHandler():void {
    currentState='Over';

    button.label = list.selectedItem.text1;
    dispatchEvent(new Event(FlexGlobals.topLevelApplication.SELECTION_CHANGED));
  }
  ...
</fx:Script>
```

Another thing to remember is that when you define the [Event] metadata tag, you cannot use these constants to declare the event name you are dispatching. When the event name changes, you will have to review your custom components and MXML code that captures those events anyway. Strictly speaking, it is not necessary to define that metadata tag to get your application to capture the event. But in this case, you cannot capture the event using MXML code. You have to capture it using the `addEventListener` method in ActionScript. That's a big drawback; it means that even though you are dispatching the event through a constant reference now, you still have to write it out in the metadata tag.

The next violation is the one that is defined as **UseObjectType** in the list. There are a lot of them and most are inside the generated classes, but two are located in the **SearchComboBox.mxml** source file. This time, the errors are regarding the parameter in the setter method and return value in the getter method for the `selectedItem` property. At the moment, the object type is just the plain generic `Object` class. Since this class is the basic class for every object type, you can provide anything as a parameter to that setter method. It would be better to have strict typing to avoid the chance of having runtime errors when this component is going to be used by other developers who are not quite sure exactly what is expected as a parameter type. So, let's adjust this as well.

The first thing to do is **create a custom class that represents the item in the combobox**. You can create that class in the `be.flexpert.webshop.valueObjects` package as well, since this is the package that contains all the data objects that are used in the application:

be ➤ *flexpert* ➤ *webshop* ➤ *valueObjects* ➤ *SearchItem.mxml*

```
// Copyright Steven Peeters (c), 2010
package be.flexpert.webshop.valueObjects {
    public class SearchItem {
      private var _image:Class;
      private var _text:String;

      public function SearchItem() {
      }

      public function get image():Class {
        return _image;
      }

      public function set image(value:Class):void {
        _image = value;
      }

      public function get text():String {
        return _text;
      }

      public function set text(value:String):void {
        _text = value;
      }
    }
}
```

Creating this class with its custom properties will also have an effect on the way the items are defined for the custom combobox component, especially since the names of the properties are different now. Therefore, you have to **alter the code in the combobox component** to this:

Excerpt from components ➤ *SearchComboBox.mxml*

```
<fx:Script>
  ...
  protected function list_changeHandler():void {
    currentState='Over';
```

```
    button.label = list.selectedItem.text;
    dispatchEvent(new Event(FlexGlobals.topLevelApplication.SELECTION_CHANGED));
  }

  public function get selectedItem():SearchItem {
    return list.selectedItem;
  }

  public function set selectedItem(value:SearchItem):void {
    list.selectedItem = value;
    button.label = list.selectedItem.text;
  }
  ...
</fx:Script>
...
<s:List selectedIndex="0" skinClass="components.SearchValuesList"
        x="0" y="22" visible.Up="false" id="list"
        change="list_changeHandler()" visible.Over="false"
        visible.Disabled="false">
  <s:ArrayCollection>
    <vo:SearchItem image="@Embed('/assets/images/webshop/ ➥
hover item.png')" text="ALL"/>
    <vo:SearchItem image="@Embed('/assets/images/webshop/ ➥
hover item.png')" text="WATERFALLS"/>
    <vo:SearchItem image="@Embed('/assets/images/webshop/ ➥
hover item.png')" text="REFLECTIONS"/>
    <vo:SearchItem image="@Embed('/assets/images/webshop/ ➥
hover item.png')" text="LAKES"/>
    <vo:SearchItem image="@Embed('/assets/images/webshop/ ➥
hover item.png')" text="MOUNTAINS"/>
  </s:ArrayCollection>
</s:List>
```

Of course, the changes don't end there, because the custom skin class is also making use of those properties to display the data properly. So you'll have to adjust those as well to work with the new SearchItem class. When all the changes have been made, you'll notice that the violations in the **FlexPMD View** panel have disappeared.

The last violation I want to take a closer look is also the last one in the list. It states that a certain variable name is too short. When you double click the violation, you are taken to the MyListItem component that acts as the item renderer for the photo gallery. When you click on one of the buttons, an event is dispatched to the outside world. This event is declared as the variable e in the event handlers. Although this is only a small method and the purpose of this variable is quite clear, coding conventions state that you should give all of your variables descriptive names to clarify their purpose. Therefore you should **change the event variable name to something like photoEvent**. This does not change anything outside of those methods, so changing the variable name is all you need to do to get rid of these violations:

Excerpt from components ➤ *MyListItem.mxml*

```
protected function button1_clickHandler(event:MouseEvent):void {
```

```
        var photoEvent:PhotoEvent = new PhotoEvent(PhotoEvent.DETAIL, _photo, true);
        dispatchEvent(photoEvent);
}


protected function button2_clickHandler(event:MouseEvent):void {
        var photoEvent:PhotoEvent =
                        new PhotoEvent(PhotoEvent.ADD_TO_SHOPPINGCART, _photo,
true);
        dispatchEvent(photoEvent);
}
```

Of course, there are many more violations that can be adjusted to help clean up your code and keep it in check with the standard coding conventions. But when you're working on internal projects, you'll probably have your own set of rules for your own coding conventions. That's no problem because you can declare your own rule set for the FlexPMD plug-in. I'm not going to cover this in detail; you can find information on how to create your own rule set on the open source site of Adobe at http://opensource. adobe.com/wiki/display/flexpmd/How+to+add+your+own+rule.

Summary

Managing RIA projects is the same as it used to be for client-server projects. The rules and calculations, however, are different when working on larger applications and/or with larger project teams. Also, working as a team will affect the way you write your code. It is very important that you write code that other developers can easily understand. To that end, I've shown you how you can use FlexPMD as a tool to help you and the other developers conform to coding conventions and keep the code structured.

Another helpful tool is the application framework; it allows developers to structure the code in such a way that even developers from other companies can find their way when necessary. In the next chapter, I will take a closer look at some of the most frequently used application frameworks and discuss the similarities and differences.

Chapter 8

Frameworks

In the previous chapter, I mentioned the use of application frameworks as being a best practice when developing applications with larger teams. Such a framework can be a well-known one developed by other people or companies, but it can also be a custom framework that has been developed by your company. In this chapter, I'm going to focus on the official ones and more particularly on the ones that are most commonly used when developing Flex applications.

Let me start by briefly explaining what an application framework is and what it can do for you. A framework is actually a group of design patterns that work together to structure your project code. Frameworks do not only apply to Flex code; they can also apply to plain ActionScript, Java, PHP or even ColdFusion code. All of these programming languages and environments have their own set of commonly used design patterns that are considered best practices. Most of these frameworks have specific class definitions or basic classes which you can inherit from to facilitate the process of implementing the framework. Strictly speaking, this is not even necessary, as a design pattern is simply a generic way of solving a specific problem that many developers before you have encountered. Some people have decided on formalizing a solution as a design pattern; others have taken combinations of design patterns they need most of the time when developing applications and molded them into a framework.

So how do these application frameworks improve the collaboration in your development process? Actually, the collaboration is only going to affect the developers, since frameworks only relate to the way you structure the code. Thus, designers or interaction designers will gain nothing from using frameworks. For developers, however, using a framework will formalize the way the back end services, view interactions, and data management is conducted in the application. As a result, when you're working with multiple developers, each one will know exactly where to look in the application files to make some changes or even just to find out what's going on in the application. This will speed up the development process, although you have to take into account the time it requires to implement the application framework. However, from my extensive development experience, I can guarantee that you will reap the benefits from this extra effort in the long run.

Even though there are many good frameworks such as Cairngorm, Prana (Spring-ActionScript), Parsley, Robot Legs and others, covering all of them in detail would just take too long. So in this chapter, I will cover Mate, PureMVC, and Swiz.

> *Before we get started on the details of each framework, it is worth noting that each framework isn't necessarily completely independent. In fact, you can combine different parts of different frameworks. In the past, I successfully used the `ModelLocator` and `ServiceLocator` principles of the Cairngorm 2 framework together with the `Notifications` principle of the PureMVC framework. Keep this interoperability in mind; you're not stuck using everything from a single framework!*

I will explain how each works and then provide the same example code for each framework in order to demonstrate the similarities and differences between them in a practical way. However, before I get started, there are a few things to note.

First of all, if you're new to these frameworks, **you don't have to use them**. They are not going to make your application work better. They are just an aid to help you keep your code structured in a certain way. If you're not feeling quite comfortable with the basic code, don't rush it. Instead, familiarize yourself first before heading down the road of complex frameworks.

Secondly, **there is no such thing as** *the* **framework**. There is no miracle worker that solves all of your problems. Every framework does its job well. It is just a matter of taste and what you're used to from your past development experience that will help you decide which framework is right for you.

You also don't have to use every aspect of a certain framework if you feel that it doesn't bring you any benefits. You can easily implement only certain parts of a framework. In these situations, however, you're most likely talking about a custom framework and no longer about the actual framework you started out with.

Know when not to use a framework! Implementing an application framework can be time consuming, especially when you're new to them. One of the best practices is to keep your resulting application as small as possible. Adding several files to a small project just because you absolutely want to use a certain framework can result in a SWF file that is a lot bigger than it would be without a framework. Don't get me wrong here; I'm all for using application frameworks, but for some small applications, you're better off not using any framework in terms of development time and application size.

> *It is also important to remember that the choice of framework on the front end side does not affect the back end technology at all. You are not bound to using a certain back end technology, nor to using some framework on the back end side. Those two technologies should be completely separate, so you can always change, for example, the front end technology without having to rewrite the back end functionality.*

The Example Application

Until now, I've deliberately avoided using any frameworks in the front end code to keep things as simple as possible. But now you are going to create and modify an application to work with the different frameworks that I will cover in this chapter. The application is an extension to the LiveCycle Data Services introduction example that I provided in Chapter 1. The start project is called **ContactsNoFramework** and can be found in the projects that accompany this book. It's a basic management console that can perform the basic CRUD operations (**C**reate, **R**ead, **U**pdate and **D**elete) on a database table. Inside that table, you will find records of people with their first name, last name, phone and email address. The application uses the `RemoteObject` class to connect to the Java back end code.

ID	First name	Last name	Phone	Email
1	Steven	Peeters	+32 9 340 41 11	steven@multimediacollege.be
2	Frederik	Van Hecke	+32 9 340 41 11	frederik@multimediacollege.be

First name | Steven
Last name | Peeters
Phone | +32 9 340 41 11
Email | steven@multimediacollege.be

[New] [Delete] [Save] [Cancel]

Figure 8-1: The application only has a basic look.

As you can see in Figure 8-1, the application only has a basic look and feel to it. I don't want the visual code to get in the way of demonstrating how the frameworks are actually implemented in the code. I've tried to keep things as simple as possible for a real world example, so you can focus on the important things for this chapter.

In the `PersonDTO` class file in the Flex project, you will notice an additional `clone` method when comparing it to the project in Chapter 1. This method is necessary to avoid the data in the grid being updated on screen before the user has saved the changes. It is also used in order to implement a cancel button that reverts the changes in the form data to the original version when updating a record.

The back end code for this project is quite simple and can be found in the **Contacts_backend** project in the projects that accompany this book. You have one access point, which is the `PersonAssembler` class. This class holds four methods, one for each CRUD operation, and routes the service calls to the Data Access Object (DAO), which will effectively execute the database operations. Just as before, there are some helper classes to connect to the database and to provide custom exceptions to the front end in case of an anomaly.

Mate

Mate (pronounced 'mah-tay') is a tag-based, event-driven Flex framework that is relatively new. Since Flex applications are also event-driven, the framework builds on top of that mechanism to add some rules and features such as dependency injection. With dependency injection you decouple high-level modules from low-level services by not having to worry about the service's lifecycle in that high-level module. These rules or design patterns will help you structure your code and facilitate all parts of your application to get the data and objects they need. Figure 8-2 shows you how the framework operates.

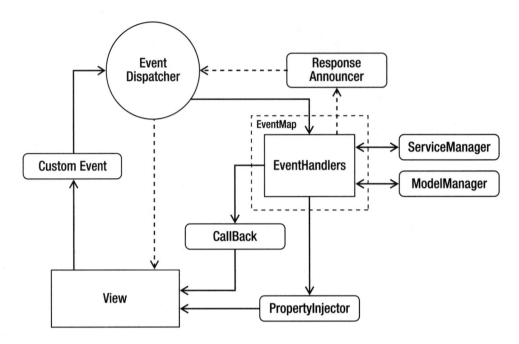

Figure 8-2: The Mate framework diagram

This diagram represents only one of the possible routes to follow when using the Mate framework. Not all of the possibilities have been used in the example code that follows. If you want to know more about the different possible flows in Mate, read the documentation on the Mate framework website (http://mate. asfusion.com) and take a closer look at the different diagrams (http://mate.asfusion.com/page/ documentation/diagrams).

Now, let me briefly explain the process flow for this particular framework so you'll get a basic understanding of how the framework works. The starting point is the view. Within this view, you throw a *custom event*. A custom event is an event class you create yourself that extends the basic event class `flash.events.Event`. An advantage of using custom events is that you can create whatever property you like on that event class to send along some additional data together with your event notification. It is imperative that this event bubbles so it reaches the event handlers in one or more event maps via the basic Flex event dispatching mechanism. The event handlers are then going to call one or more back end service methods. When the result comes back, you will have three options:

- Save the data in the model and use the principle of *property injection* to get the data back to the view. This property injection is part of the dependency injection feature and actually takes care of the property getting from where its lifecycle is managed to where the property is used in high-level components.
- Use a `ResponseAnnouncer` to send the result directly back to a result handler in the view.
- Call a method on the view directly using a `CallBack` tag.

In all cases, the view will update itself because of the binding expressions that bind the data to one or more visual components.

Since the entire framework is event-based, you get the advantage of the black box principle where a certain component can request for data but doesn't have to care how the data is fetched. On the other hand, the service class that fetches the data just needs to provide that data to the component and doesn't care what exactly the component wants to do with it. Maybe it wants to display the data in a list, or maybe it just needs the data to start another process.

How exactly does the Mate framework work? Before you can start using this particular framework, you have to duplicate the project without the framework and rename it ContactsMate. Then you **download the library and attach it to the project**. Download the SWC file at `http://mate.asfusion.com/ page/downloads`, making sure you choose the Flex 4 version. Attaching it to the project couldn't be simpler: you just have to copy the downloaded file in the `libs` folder, since every library in that folder is automatically linked to the project.

The Code

The first change you have to make to the project is to **create a custom event** that inherits from the basic `flash.events.Event` class. However, you have ensure that the event bubbles because the entire framework system relies on this. So, go ahead and create a new package called `be.flexpert. contact.events` in which you create the `PersonEvent` custom event class. **Modify the constructor so that the event will always bubble** by passing it as a fixed value to the constructor of the super class. However, you cannot remove it from the parameter list, as it is necessary later on in the framework structure. Also, create a private variable (with public accessor methods) that holds an instance of the `PersonDTO` class, as this will contain the data that is necessary to perform the service calls you are going to make in a few minutes.

Within the Mate framework, each service operation will be triggered by a different event type. The Flex best practices say that an event type should be declared using a constant string definition. This means you have to define four different string constants in this class: one for each service call of the CRUD operations. The finished event class should look like the following code:

be ➤ *flexpert* ➤ *contact* ➤ *events* ➤ *PersonEvent.as*

```
public class PersonEvent extends Event {
  public static const READ:String = "fetchPersons";
  public static const CREATE:String = "createPerson";
  public static const UPDATE:String = "updatePerson";
  public static const DELETE:String = "deletePerson";

  private var _person:PersonDTO;

  public function PersonEvent(type:String, bubbles:Boolean=true, ➡
cancelable:Boolean=false) {
    super(type, true, cancelable);
  }

  public function get person():PersonDTO {
    return _person;
  }
```

```
  public function set person(value:PersonDTO):void {
    _person = value;
  }
}
```

To be able to use this event, you need to have the data stored somewhere so you can fill the data grid with it. Therefore, you need to **create another class that will act as the data manager**. This means you have to create a new package be.flexpert.contact.managers and create a PersonManager class inside of it. In this class, you define a private variable to hold the list of persons retrieved from the database. Of course, you must then create the getter method to access the property. Make sure you make the getter method [Bindable] so the list automatically reacts to the changes that have been made to this property when you use a binding expression on the data grid. Setting the value is done by calling a public method on the instance from within the EventMap, which you'll be creating later on. So, add a storeList method that takes an ArrayCollection as a parameter and saves it in the private class member. And that's all you need to do for this manager class, which you can find at **be ➤ flexpert ➤ contact ➤ managers ➤ PersonManager.as**.

Let's move on to the next piece of the puzzle. This piece is another separate class, but this one is the ServiceManager. It will hold the different services with their initial configuration so you just have to use them later on in the EventMap. You could also choose to define the services straight away in this EventMap component, but I find it better to keep the definitions completely separate. Why? For example, you can have multiple EventMap components that use the same RemoteObject definition. By extracting the definitions and basic setup of the RemoteObject into a separate class, you can reuse that class. Moreover, you would only need to modify it in one single location in case something needs to be altered

Within the ServiceManager **class, you need to create a private property** _personServices **of the type** RemoteObject. In the constructor, you instantiate it and refer to the destination you can find in the LiveCycle Data Services configuration files. All you need to do now is **create a public accessor** method to retrieve the service instance for future reference. You don't create the setter method, since the service instance itself will not be manipulated outside of this class.

Now that you have the data, the events, and the service defined, **let's bring it all together in the** EventMap **component**. As I've mentioned before, you can have multiple EventMap components, which can be quite useful when you're working with dynamically loaded modules, for example. But in this small application, I'll stick to just one single component. So, go ahead and create the package be.flexpert.contact.maps. This one will contain the EventMap component called MainEventMap. This is an MXML component, so you'll have to create it differently than the last couple of files you created. When you create the MXML component, you should base it on the EventMap component from the Mate framework, but since you can't select it from the list of base components, you **accept the default settings for now**. Just remove the width and height properties because this isn't going to be a visual component. Once you've created this file, you have to change the root tag into <mate:EventMap> and add the proper namespace for the Mate framework code to it.

In that component, you define four <EventHandlers> tags, one for each CRUD operation. **For each tag, you specify the event to which it should react** by using the constants that you have defined earlier in the PersonEvent class. Each of those four EventHandlers is going to use the same RemoteObject instance, so to access it, just define an instance of the ServiceManager in this component as well. Now you can refer to the RemoteObject instance of that class to call the back end methods. For the READ event, you call the getAllPersons method of the RemoteObject instance using the <RemoteObjectInvoker> tag from the framework. You don't need to provide any parameters to this method. As a result handler, you call the storeList method that you created earlier in the PersonManager class by means of the <MethodInvoker> tag. This will save the result in that class instance, triggering the binding on the data grid. In case of a fault, you just throw the fault back to the calling component through the `<CallBack>` tag to call a method on that component. Your first event handler should look like this now:

Excerpt from be ➤ flexpert ➤ contact ➤ maps ➤ MainEventMap.mxml

```
<mate:EventHandlers type="{PersonEvent.READ}">
  <mate:RemoteObjectInvoker instance="{services.personService}"
                            method="getAllPersons">
    <mate:resultHandlers>
      <mate:MethodInvoker generator="{PersonManager}"
                          method="storeList"
                          arguments="{resultObject}"/>
    </mate:resultHandlers>

    <mate:faultHandlers>
      <mate:CallBack method="faultHandler" arguments="{fault}"/>
    </mate:faultHandlers>
  </mate:RemoteObjectInvoker>
</mate:EventHandlers>
```

This `getAllPersons` **operation will return a list of persons from the database, which should update the data grid in the view, so it needs to update the** `PersonManager` **class instance.** But the other operations are all going to be modifying the database. That means that when they return successfully, they should call this `getAllPersons` method as well to update the view. So, the content of these `EventHandlers` blocks are going to be slightly different. **To start the fetch operation upon a successful execution, you should just dispatch the proper event again and let the framework handle how the data is retrieved.** That way, if the method name should ever change or the parameter list be altered, you only have to change it in one location. Instead of the `<MethodInvoker>` tag, you now need to use the `<EventAnnouncer>` tag to start the fetch operation. It should look like this:

Excerpt from be ➤ flexpert ➤ contact ➤ maps ➤ MainEventMap.mxml

```
<mate:resultHandlers>
  <mate:EventAnnouncer generator="{PersonEvent}"
                       type="{PersonEvent.READ}"/>
</mate:resultHandlers>
```

Of course, when you call the `createPerson` method for the `CREATE` event, you have to provide an additional parameter to this method; it is located in the `event` parameter you receive in this event handler. However, the handling of faults remains the same for all operations as it will execute a general fault handler in the calling view component. So, **copy this code block for the other events and adjust the event names and called back end methods accordingly**.

You still need to get the retrieved data back in the view. This is done by using a `<PropertyInjector>` tag, as shown:

Excerpt from be ➤ flexpert ➤ contact ➤ maps ➤ MainEventMap.mxml

```
<mate:Injectors target="{Contacts}">
  <mate:PropertyInjector targetKey="personsList"
                         source="{PersonManager}" sourceKey="personsList"/>
</mate:Injectors>
```

This statement will inject the property you have filled out in the result handler into the `Contacts` component and assign it to the `personsList` property. This injector will only work if the binding is triggered on the property you're trying to inject. Thus, you will have to adjust the `PersonManager` a little bit, because **having a read-only property doesn't trigger the binding properly**. When you set the value to this class instance, you have to trigger the binding manually by dispatching a custom notification event that will trigger the binding on that property. The finalized `PersonManager` class should look like this:

Excerpt from be ➤ flexpert ➤ contact ➤ managers ➤ PersonManager.as

```
public class PersonManager extends EventDispatcher {
  private var _personsList:ArrayCollection;

  public function PersonManager() {
  }

  [Bindable(event="listUpdated") ]
  public function get personsList():ArrayCollection {
    return _personsList;
  }

  public function storeList(value:ArrayCollection):void {
    _personsList = value;
    dispatchEvent(new Event("listUpdated", true));
  }
}
```

As a final step in implementing the framework for this application, you are going to have to make some serious adjustments to the main application. First of all, you should **turn the code in the current main application file into a view component**. In other words, you create a new com.projects. domain.views package and place the **Contacts.mxml** file inside of it. But this component should no longer be an application, so you need to adjust the `<s:Application>` root tag to an `<s:Group>` tag. Don't forget to rename the closing tag as well. The layout property remains the same, just as the rest of the code for now.

Before we dig into the rest of the changes, let's create a new application, since the project has none at the moment. You can do this by using the file creation wizards on the project and create a new **MXML Application**. In this main application, you have to define both the `EventMap` instance and the view to display the data. As a result, the code in this file is going to be quite small for this particular example:

Main.mxml

```
<?xml version="1.0" encoding="utf-8"?>
<s:Application xmlns:fx="http://ns.adobe.com/mxml/2009"
               xmlns:s="library://ns.adobe.com/flex/spark"
               xmlns:maps="be.flexpert.contact.maps.*"
               xmlns:views="be.flexpert.contact.views.*"
               minWidth="1024" minHeight="768">
  <s:layout>
    <s:VerticalLayout horizontalAlign="center"/>
  </s:layout>

  <fx:Declarations>
```

```
    <maps:MainEventMap/>
  </fx:Declarations>

  <views:Contacts/>
</s:Application>
```

If you leave the rest of the code as is and run the application at this point, you will see that it still works, because you're still just calling the `RemoteObject` service from within the `Contacts` component, and you handle the results there as well. But that's all about to change.

First of all, since the component is not an application anymore, you should **change the name of the event handler that reacts to the** `creationComplete` **event from** `initApp` **to just plain** `init`. And instead of calling the remote service directly, you are going to dispatch a custom event to initiate the READ operation through the framework. Make sure that you use the string constant defined in the `PersonEvent` class to define the event type to dispatch. The `btnDelete_clickHandler` and `btnSave_clickHandler` methods have to be adjusted in a similar fashion, so they are now dispatching events instead of directly calling the `RemoteObject` service instance.

Since the `_personsList` is a private variable, the value cannot be set by the property injector, so you will have to **define public accessor methods for this variable** to get this injection system to work. These accessor methods are also referred to as the *getters* and *setters* of a class. A final adjustment to this file can be found in the removal of the `fetchResultHandler`, because the result is now handled in the `MainEventMap`, and the adaptation of the `faultHandler` method. This method doesn't capture an event anymore, but rather the `Fault` object type, which means that you have to adjust the `Alert.show` statement in this method as well. The final ActionScript code for this component now looks like this:

Excerpt from be ➤ flexpert ➤ contact ➤ views ➤ Contacts.mxml

```
[Bindable]
private var _personsList:ArrayCollection;

[Bindable]
private var _selectedPerson:PersonDTO = null;

private function init():void {
  var event:PersonEvent = new PersonEvent(PersonEvent.READ);
  dispatchEvent(event);
}

protected function faultHandler(fault:Fault):void {
  Alert.show(fault.faultString, fault.faultCode);
}

protected function btnNew_clickHandler(event:MouseEvent):void {
  _selectedPerson = new PersonDTO();
  grid.selectedIndex = -1;
  fname.setFocus();
}

protected function btnDelete_clickHandler(event:MouseEvent):void {
```

```
    var personEvent:PersonEvent = new PersonEvent(PersonEvent.DELETE);
    personEvent.person = _selectedPerson;
    dispatchEvent(personEvent);
}

protected function btnSave_clickHandler(event:MouseEvent):void {
    var personEvent:PersonEvent;
    if(_selectedPerson.id == 0) {
        personEvent = new PersonEvent(PersonEvent.CREATE);
    } else {
        personEvent = new PersonEvent(PersonEvent.UPDATE);
    }
    personEvent.person = _selectedPerson;
    dispatchEvent(personEvent);
}

protected function grid_changeHandler(event:ListEvent):void {
    _selectedPerson = (grid.selectedItem as PersonDTO).clone();
}

public function get personsList():ArrayCollection {
    return _personsList;
}

public function set personsList(value:ArrayCollection):void {
    _personsList = value;
}
```

This finishes the implementation of the Mate framework. If you run the application now, you should see it working exactly the same as when you didn't use any framework.

Conclusion

I want to make it clear that in this particular example, **the usage of dependency injection doesn't seem logical since there is only one view that needs one piece of data. However, it does make more sense when you have a larger project with more views and more data** that needs to be distributed amongst multiple views. This way, you have one component taking care of the data lifecycle and multiple views using that data, without having to worry about how it's filled and when it is created or destroyed.

This framework is rather simple to understand, since **it uses basic Flex concepts and extends them.** However, there are a couple of usability issues, in my opinion:

- Because of the injection principle, there is no coupling between the `EventMap` and the actual view data. On the other hand, you are specifying the property that should be filled out as a fixed string. That means that **when the public accessors for the view property are not defined, you won't get any compilation errors**. But when you run the application, you get a runtime exception because the property doesn't exist. The downside of this is that a normal user with the release version of the Flash Player installed will not see this error at all. The application just doesn't work for him.

- Another disadvantage is that **you cannot change the constructor for the custom event classes when using those events** in an `<EventAnnouncer>` tag. For example, in this application you could have put the `PersonDTO` object in the parameter list of the constructor and you could have removed the `bubbles` parameter from the list, but that breaks the application (again, only at runtime) because the system expects the default constructor parameter list. I think it's a mistake, but maybe it can be fixed in future releases of the Mate framework.

On a positive note, Mate appears to be a lightweight framework; it only adds 25KB to the release version of the application, most of which is from the framework's SWC file being compiled in the resulting SWF application. Keep in mind that the bigger your project gets, the less impact this addition will have on the resulting application file size.

PureMVC

Whereas Mate is a framework designed specifically for Flex applications, PureMVC is not. It is an ActionScript framework that is completely based on the Model-View-Controller principle, which can be applied to not only Flex or AIR applications, but also to Flash applications. It even goes a step beyond that and states that it could be used for any programming environment, such as Java or PHP. (Note that if you are using this framework in languages other than ActionScript, it requires a port to be written for the framework components.)

PureMVC doesn't rely on Flex framework components to do its job, which means that it's going to be a completely different approach than the one you've just seen with Mate. Let's take a closer look at the framework diagram in Figure 8-3. As mentioned previously, you don't have to use each and every part of the framework, although some parts are mandatory. For example, the Command pattern isn't always necessary. In fact, unless I need undo/redo support in my applications, I hardly ever use it because of the additional complexity it adds to the code. However, the Command pattern is deeply rooted in the PureMVC framework, so extracting this design pattern is a little bit harder that with the Mate framework. It is not impossible, though, so I did it here in order to give you a better starting point from which to compare the frameworks.

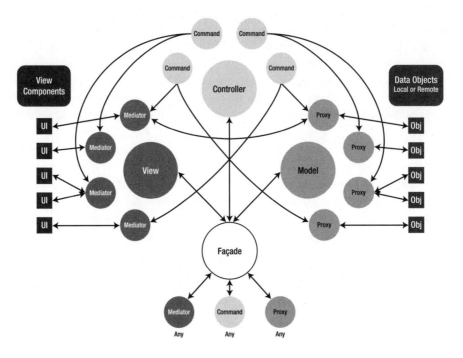

Figure 8-3: The PureMVC framework without the Command pattern in a diagram.

Let's walk through the workflow for this particular framework. Let's start with the Facade. This is a *singleton* class that links the mediators to the views and registers the proxies that will retrieve the data. A singleton is a class that can have only one single instance. Every time you access that singleton, you will actually retrieve and use that very same instance, no matter where you are in your application. We'll look this singleton principle in detail later in this chapter.

When you use the complete framework, you perform this registration process by calling one or more commands. Each command is linked to a custom event using the controller class. So calling a back end method starts with dispatching a custom event. Eventually a proxy class will then execute the requested operation on the back end data. When the operation returns, the data is stored and a notification is sent to the application. Each mediator will register itself to listen for certain notifications. Once such a notification is dispatched and an interested mediator is encountered, the message is handled and the view gets updated. That's briefly how the data gets called from the view and the result is put back in the view.

Again, this framework is event-based, but in this case, the events are also referred to as *notifications*. This means that, just as with Mate, the black box principle is applied, so the view doesn't care where the data comes from and the controller doesn't care how the data is displayed.

Before you can start using this particular framework, you have to download the framework library from `http://puremvc.org/pages/downloads/AS3/PureMVC_AS3.zip`. This ZIP file contains the latest version of the project including the sources. But the part we're interested in right now is the SWC library file, which you can find in the **bin** directory. Copy that file and place it in the **libs** folder of your Flex project, which will automatically add the library to the project. This project is, of course, another copy of the one without any framework and is aptly named **ContactsPureMVC**. Now you can use the framework components and you'll even get code completion on them.

The Code

The first thing to do to convert the application is to turn the main application file into a custom component again. To do so, create a new package be.flexpert.contact.views and create a custom component there. This component inherits from the Group container and then you move the remainder of the application file in that component. Just leave the code as is in that file for the moment. You will come back to it later to change the code to work with the framework. The main application file now needs to contain an instance of this newly created custom component to still display the data grid and form. Test your application and you'll see that it is still working as before.

For the next parts, I'm going to try to work from the inside out. Well, there is no real inside and outside to the framework, but I'm going to create the components before starting to use them, because it will make things easier for you to understand. So, **the first component you'll need to create is the** ContactProxy. Create this custom class in the be.flexpert.contact.proxies package and inherit from the PureMVC Proxy class while implementing the IProxy interface. Then you **define a bunch of static constants** that will be used to identify the service call that has to be made, like so:

be ➤ *flexpert* ➤ *contact* ➤ *proxies* ➤ *ContactProxy.as*

```
public class ContactProxy extends Proxy implements IProxy {
  public static const NAME:String = "ContactProxy";
  public static const READ_ALL_PERSONS:String = "readAllPerson";
  public static const CREATE_PERSON:String = "createPerson";
  public static const UPDATE_PERSON:String = "updatePerson";
  public static const DELETE_PERSON:String = "deletePerson";
  public static const READ_SUCCESS:String = "readSuccess";

  private var service:RemoteObject;
  private var responder:CallResponder;

  public function ContactProxy() {
    super(NAME, new Object());
    service = new RemoteObject("personServices");
    service.showBusyCursor = true;
    service.addEventListener(FaultEvent.FAULT, faultHandler);
    responder = new CallResponder();
    responder.addEventListener(ResultEvent.RESULT, ➡ resultHandler);
  }

  public function get person():PersonDTO {
    return data as PersonDTO;
  }

  public function getAllPersons():void {
    responder.token = service.getAllPersons();
    responder.token.action = READ_ALL_PERSONS;
  }
```

```
  public function createPerson(person:PersonDTO):void {
    responder.token = service.createPerson(person);
    responder.token.action = CREATE_PERSON;
  }

  public function updatePerson(person:PersonDTO):void {
    responder.token = service.updatePerson(person);
    responder.token.action = UPDATE_PERSON;
  }

  public function deletePerson(person:PersonDTO):void {
    responder.token = service.deletePerson(person);
    responder.token.action = DELETE_PERSON;
  }

  private function resultHandler(event:ResultEvent):void {
    switch(event.token.action) {
      case READ_ALL_PERSONS:
        sendNotification(READ_SUCCESS, event.result);
        break;
      case CREATE_PERSON:
      case UPDATE_PERSON:
      case DELETE_PERSON:
        getAllPersons();
        break;
    }
  }

  private function faultHandler(event:FaultEvent):void {
    Alert.show(event.fault.faultString, event.fault.faultCode);
  }
}
```

> The constant *NAME* in the list of contstants identifies the proxy itself and will be used for retrieving the proxy from the *Facade* later on.

Normally, this proxy class would trigger a few commands to fetch or update the data in the database, but since we're not going to use the command pattern, you're going to call the back end services directly from here. This means you have to **define a** `RemoteObject` **instance in this class** that refers to the `personServices` destination in the LiveCycle Data Services configuration files. And of course, you'll also need to respond to the results that are coming back, so **define an instance of the** `CallResponder` **class as well**. Initialize both instances in the constructor and attach the proper event listeners to them. Now you're all set up to start calling the back end methods.

Each back end service call will be triggered by a separate public method that also provides a custom token action to identify the call that is returned to the result handler. The result handler will then investigate the token and act appropriately according to the required functionality. Thus, the create, update and delete operations are just going to fetch the data again from the database, whereas the fetch operation itself will dispatch a notification letting the application know that the data has been retrieved successfully, as you can see in the code block above.

Of course, now that you have the proxy all set up, you still need to access it. This is done in the Mediator. This is **another class that you have to create**, but in the `be.flexpert.contact.mediators` package; it will act as the code behind for the `Contacts` view instead of having the code in there. This is part of the Model-View-Controller separation within the framework. **Extend the** `ContactMediator` **from the framework's** `Mediator` **class and implement the** `IMediator` **interface**. Then define a static constant NAME to identify this particular mediator.

In the constructor, you capture the view as a parameter and provide it, along with the mediator identification, to the super class. Next, you **add event listeners** for all the events that could be coming from the view component and that need to be addressed on this class. In this specific case, there are four events to capture:

- `ContactProxy.READ_ALL_PERSONS`
- `ContactProxy.CREATE_PERSON`
- `ContactProxy.UPDATE_PERSON`
- `ContactProxy.DELETE_PERSON`

Notice that in this example I'm reusing the constants from the proxy class you've just created. This is done just for convenience. In larger projects, this could lead to trouble because using the same names for notifications and custom events can be confusing when you try to figure out why a certain part of the code is executed when it shouldn't be, for example. In small application, the overview can still be kept and usage is limited.

To see what I mean, just take a look at the `ContactMediator` *code and you'll see that the notifications are being caught by the* `handleNotification` *event handler. At the same time, the* `ContactMediator` *also captures the custom events dispatched by the* `Contacts` *view component. So, you actually have two distinct ways of potentially capturing the same event type using PureMVC.*

Each of these event handlers will have to be implemented in this class as well, so go ahead and create the four event handlers. Within each event handler **you will have to access the** `ContactProxy`, which will do the actual back end call. To be able to access this proxy, you have to retrieve it from the Facade. This is accessible though the `facade` instance variable in the Mediator super class. Making it point to the proper facade in the application is done by registering the mediator with that facade. You will do this later on in the exercise. **Once you have access to that proxy instance, you simply call the proper method to perform the requested task.**

Another task this mediator has to do is update the view when the data has successfully been retrieved. You have seen that **the** `ContactProxy` **sends out a notification** to alert the application of this event. Now you have to capture that notification in the `ContactMediator` to react to it. **To capture that notification you have to implement two methods.** The first one is called `listNotificationInterests` and returns a list of notifications this mediator is interested in. the second one is called `handleNotification`. This one will take care of the functionality that should be executed when a notification of interest has been sent.

It is in this last method that you have to update the view with the retrieved data that is sent along with that notification, like so:

be ➤ flexpert ➤ contact ➤ mediators ➤ ContactMediator.as

```
public class ContactMediator extends Mediator implements IMediator {
  public static const NAME:String = "ContactMediator";

  public function ContactMediator(viewComponent:Contacts) {
    super(ContactMediator.NAME, viewComponent);
    viewComponent.addEventListener(ContactProxy.READ_ALL_PERSONS, getAllPersons);
    viewComponent.addEventListener(ContactProxy.CREATE_PERSON, createPerson);
    viewComponent.addEventListener(ContactProxy.UPDATE_PERSON, updatePerson);
    viewComponent.addEventListener(ContactProxy.DELETE_PERSON, deletePerson);
  }

  override public function listNotificationInterests():Array {
    return [ContactProxy.READ_SUCCESS];
  }

  override public function handleNotification(notification:INotification):void {
    switch(notification.getName()) {
      case ContactProxy.READ_SUCCESS:
        contactsView.personsList = notification.getBody() as ArrayCollection;
        break;
    }
  }

  private function get contactsView():Contacts {
    return viewComponent as Contacts;
  }

  private function getAllPersons(event:Event):void {
    var proxy:ContactProxy = facade.retrieveProxy(ContactProxy.NAME) ➥
as ContactProxy;
    proxy.getAllPersons();
  }

  private function createPerson(event:PersonEvent):void {
    var proxy:ContactProxy = facade.retrieveProxy(ContactProxy.NAME) ➥
as ContactProxy;
    proxy.createPerson(event.person);
  }

  private function updatePerson(event:PersonEvent):void {
    var proxy:ContactProxy = facade.retrieveProxy(ContactProxy.NAME) ➥
as ContactProxy;
    proxy.updatePerson(event.person);
  }
```

```
   private function deletePerson(event:PersonEvent):void {
     var proxy:ContactProxy = facade.retrieveProxy(ContactProxy.NAME) ➥
as ContactProxy;
     proxy.deletePerson(event.person);
   }
}
```

You may have noticed in the code above that there is also a `PersonEvent` type being used, and you haven't yet created that event. So, that's the next step in this exercise. **Create a new package** `be.flexpert.contact.events` **and create a custom** `PersonEvent` **class inside of it.** This class will extend the basic `flash.events.Event` class. Unlike with the custom events in Mate, you can now choose to include the `PersonDTO` instance in the parameter list of the constructor. Within that constructor, you have to retain that parameter for future reference. Of course, you should remember to include the `clone` method as well, because you'll need it when bubbling the event to higher levels in your application. Leave the return type for the clone method set to `Event`, because the method overrides the existing one in the basic `Event` class.

Next, you are going to **bind everything together by creating and instantiating the** `Facade` **instance**. This `Facade` is going to be a singleton—only one instance can ever exist in the application. One option would be to agree amongst your fellow developers that you should instantiate this component more than once in the application. But there is nothing that will prevent this. That's where the singleton pattern comes into play. There are several ways of creating a singleton in ActionScript, but I try to live by the motto *"Buggy code shouldn't compile!"* That's why I prefer a method that generates a compilation error when used incorrectly. **The key to creating a singleton class in other programming languages is making the constructor private so it can never be called directly from the outside. However, in ActionScript 3 it is not possible to make the constructor private.** A way to get around this problem is by creating an internal class that can only be accessed within the same class file, so only the standard static `getInstance` method can create an instance of the class. This may sound complicated, but the code below shows you how to do it:

Excerpt from be ➤ flexpert ➤ contact ➤ ApplicationFacade.as

```
package be.flexpert.contact {
  ...
  public class ApplicationFacade extends Facade implements IFacade {

    private static var _instance:ApplicationFacade = null;

    public function ApplicationFacade(sb:SingletonBlocker) {
      if(sb == null) {
        Alert.show("You should not create an instance of ApplicationFacade ➥
directly."
                  + "Use the getInstance method instead.",
                    "Singleton violation");
      } else {
        super();
      }
    }

    public static function getInstance():ApplicationFacade {
```

```
    if(_instance == null) {
      _instance = new ApplicationFacade(new SingletonBlocker());
    }

    return _instance;
  }
 }
}
```

```
internal class SingletonBlocker {}
```

I've highlighted the parts that ensure that your application will throw a compilation error. For this system to work, it is imperative that the `SingletonBlocker` class resides outside the package definition. Granted, the system isn't bulletproof, because you can still create an instance of this class by providing `null` as a parameter. That's why there is still a small chance that you have to prevent incorrect use in another way. If you let the application throw a runtime exception, only the people that have a debug player installed will be able to see that something is wrong. Normally, every developer should have that one installed. But unfortunately, you still come across runtime exceptions in applications that have been deployed in their production environment. That's why I prefer to display an alert box in this event: everyone gets to see it, and it renders your application pretty useless. **The** `ApplicationFacade` **also needs to initialize a couple of things.** It needs to register the mediators with the views and the proxies that will retrieve the actual data. Therefore, you need to **create a** `startup` **method** that does exactly this. The method receives the `Contacts` view as a parameter, which will be used to create the mediator. The complete method looks like this:

Excerpt from be ➤ flexpert ➤ contact ➤ ApplicationFacade.as

```
public function startup(view:Contacts):void {
  registerMediator(new ContactMediator(view));
  registerProxy(new ContactProxy());
}
```

This concludes the `ApplicationFacade` class. You still need to instantiate it in the application. **Open the main application file** and add an `<fx:Script>` block. Inside the block. **define a private variable** `facade` **of the** `ApplicationFacade` **type, and instantiate it immediately by retrieving the instance. Then, create an** `initApp` **method that you call upon** `creationComplete` **of the application.** Within that method, call the `startup` method of the facade instance to register the mediator and proxy class instances. Also, initialize the `Contacts` view by calling its `init` method which you will be creating in just a moment. The finished main application file should now look like this:

Main.mxml

```
<?xml version="1.0" encoding="utf-8"?>
<s:Application xmlns:fx="http://ns.adobe.com/mxml/2009"
               xmlns:s="library://ns.adobe.com/flex/spark"
               xmlns:mx="library://ns.adobe.com/flex/mx"
               xmlns:views="be.flexpert.contact.views.*"
               minWidth="1024" minHeight="768"
               creationComplete="initApp()">

  <s:layout>
    <s:VerticalLayout horizontalAlign="center"/>
```

```
    </s:layout>

    <fx:Script>
      <![CDATA[
        import be.flexpert.contact.ApplicationFacade;
        import be.flexpert.contact.proxies.ContactProxy;

        private var facade:ApplicationFacade = ApplicationFacade.getInstance();

        private function initApp():void {
          facade.startup(contacts);
          contacts.init();
        }
      ]]>
    </fx:Script>

    <views:Contacts id="contacts"/>
</s:Application>
```

The final part of this exercise is to alter the ActionScript code in the `Contacts` view so it doesn't fetch the data itself anymore, but rather lets the framework's proxy and mediator class handle it. First, you have to **rename the** `initApp` **method to just plain** `init`. **The method is also not going to call the** `RemoteObject` **anymore. Instead, it just dispatches the** `READ_ALL_PERSONS` **event** to trigger the fetch operation in the `ContactMediator` instance. This also means you don't need the `<fx:Declarations>` block anymore, so you can just delete it entirely. You can also completely **remove the two result handlers** you can find at the bottom of the `<fx:Script>` block. The last thing you need to do is to **find the existing service calls** to the `services` `RemoteObject` instance for creating, updating, and deleting a person in the database; **convert those calls to statements that dispatch the proper events**. Each event that is dispatched will be initialized with the `_selectedPerson` property to provide the proper data to the back end call in the `ContactProxy` class instance.

This concludes the changes to implement the PureMVC framework for this particular exercise. Again, bear in mind that the Command pattern is not implemented in order to give you a better chance of comparing this framework with the others. In reality, you will often implement this design pattern as it facilitates reuse and a more general handling of calling the back end methods. But if you run the application right now, you should again see it working exactly the same as the version without any framework implemented.

Conclusion

I know some people dislike the PureMVC framework because it uses singleton classes. Keeping things in one single location facilitates certain tasks such as retrieving data from the model. **You know there's only one model, so you don't have to pass around a certain data object from component to component, making them all strongly bound to each other.** So, I don't think that's a good reason to dismiss the framework all together.

A plus is that the framework has been used extensively in small and large projects, both in Flex and plain ActionScript projects, so **it's a proven methodology**. Furthermore, it only adds about 5KB to the resulting SWF file, so its footprint is smaller than that of the Mate framework. This is mainly because the library SWC file that is embedded in the SWF file is a lot smaller than the Mate library file.

The downside of this framework is that it is somewhat more complex than Mate to implement. Using the declarative syntax is easier to understand, but you have more control over things (when they are constructed and added to the other components, for example) **when using ActionScript**. However, as I've said, it makes thing more complex and that is certainly off-putting to certain people. Using the singleton pattern also make the application harder to unit test, because of the dependency between the singleton class and the components that use it.

Swiz

The last framework I will discuss in this chapter is *Swiz*. This framework is not quite as old as PureMVC; it is closer in age to Mate. It borrows some concepts from other application frameworks, but gives them a fresh approach for implementing them in a Flex application. Here are some of the features it provides:

- Inversion of Control
- Dependency injection
- Event handling and mediation
- A simple lifecycle for asynchronous remote methods
- A framework that is decoupled from your application code

Don't be alarmed by the (possibly) mystical terms here. You may find these terms in many of the frameworks, but the principles behind them are usually pretty straightforward. In fact, you are probably even using some of these principles without realizing it.

This looks all very promising. A major advantage with this framework is that you don't have to extend any specific framework classes to use it. Remember that when using PureMVC, you had to extend the `Facade`, `Mediator` and `Proxy` classes, for example. However, it does not mean that you don't have to use a specific library, because you do. You can download the latest version of the application framework at `http://code.google.com/p/swizframework/downloads/list`.

There are a few familiar things about this particular framework: it uses the Model-View-Controller concept, and it uses the event dispatching mechanism you are probably accustomed to when writing Flex applications. Now, let's take a look at the framework workflow, as shown in Figure 8-4.

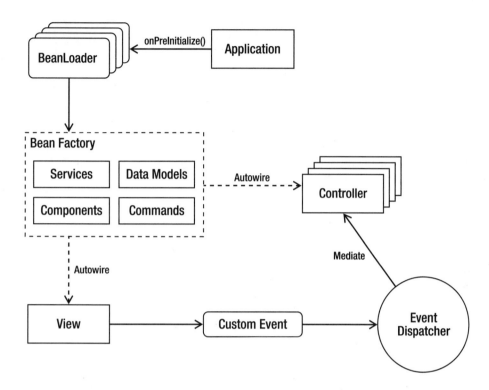

Figure 8-4: The Swiz framework workflow

Allow me to once again briefly explain the way this framework works. Before you can use this framework, you have to configure it by initializing one or more BeanLoader instances. Each one of those instances contains the non-visual components, such as the controllers, data models, services and commands (if you use the command pattern, which I did not in this example). The view then dispatches a custom event using the standard event dispatching system of the Flex framework. Because of the BeanLoader classes, this event then reaches the controller class because this class has [Mediate] metadata tags placed on the methods to be executed as a reaction to a particular event being thrown. The controller will execute the back end methods and will also fill out the local model. This local model is linked to the one in the BeanLoader using the [Autowire] metadata tag. This same system of autowiring is also used to get the model into the view. Since this model in the view will be made [Bindable], the view components are then automatically updated. This ends my brief explanation of how the Swiz framework handles your back end calls. (There is some more to it when using the command pattern, but as with the other frameworks, I've deliberately chosen not to implement it.)

The Swiz framework is known for being extremely lightweight, so let's find out if it is really true. Before you can get cracking at the code, you have to create a new copy of the application without any framework. In this ContactsSwiz project, place the downloaded framework SWC file in the libs folder to automatically include it in the application. This is necessary in order to use the framework-specific code and syntax. Once you've prepared your project for use with the Swiz framework, you can get started on adjusting bits and pieces of the code to get the application working with that framework.

> This time, you're going to use a top-down approach to make the necessary changes. In other words, you are going to be using references to components that haven't yet been created. But rest assured, everything will work perfectly in the end. It's going to be simpler to understand the framework if you implement it this way for the first time.

The Code

Since you will start with the main application file and, just like with the other examples, the current application will become a view component, you start by creating a new Flex application. In this new file, you're going to **add a** `SwizConfig` **tag to your application file**. This tag does not just configure your application for using the Swiz framework, it also allows you to configure exactly how the framework is implemented. Let's assume that you add the following tag configuration:

Excerpt from Main.mxml

```
<fx:Declarations>
  <swiz:SwizConfig strict="true"
                   eventPackages="be.flexpert.contact.events"
                   mediateBubbledEvents="true"
                   viewPackages="be.flexpert.contact.views"
                   beanLoaders="{[Beans]}"
                   serviceCallFaultHandler="{generalFaultHandler}"
                   logEventLevel="{LogEventLevel.WARN}"/>
</fx:Declarations>
```

Of course, the `swiz` namespace needs to refer to the framework components and will get the value of `http://swiz.swizframework.org`, which refers to the framework's manifest file. Now, let's take a closer look at these attributes and what they mean. The first one is quite puzzling. **What does this** `strict` **attribute mean? Well, this attribute is actually closely related to the** `eventPackages` **attribute.** When you set `strict` to `true`, the framework will make sure that the events defined in the `[Mediator]` metadata tags are verified at runtime, allowing you to use string constants to define the different event types. So, the package that you define in the `eventPackages` attribute will contain the custom events for your application. At this point, it would be a good idea to create that specific package.

Setting the `mediateBubbledEvents` **to** `true` **allows you to use the Flex framework dispatcher** instead of having to use Swiz framework specific event handling components. That makes the framework less dependent on itself. This may sound a little odd, but it is actually an advantage because you don't have to write any additional event dispatching and handling code. It also means that you can refrain from using the framework earlier as well (should you choose to do so), because the project contains less framework-dependent code. **The** `viewPackages` **attribute defines the package name where the application's views will be located.** Defining this location allows the framework to inspect the views inside of that package for `[AutoWire]` and `[Mediate]` metadata using the introspection feature of the Swiz framework. This would also be a good time to **create that package in your project structure and place the** `Contacts` **view inside of it**. You'll need to adjust the view so that it no longer inherits from `<s:Application>`, but rather from `<s:Group>`.

The `beanLoaders` **attribute** defines the components that use the Inversion of Control (IoC) design pattern in your application. Thus, **inside the component you will define the components that are not going to be placed on screen—not all components in your application are visual components**. Usually that means the models, controls, delegates and the services.

The `serviceCallFaultHandler` **allows you to specify a general fault handler** for all the back end calls that have been executed through the `executeServiceCall` method. Of course, you will also be able to define more custom and call-specific fault handlers. You then also create an `<fx:Script>` block to implement a standard fault event handler. **The final attribute defines the level of logging you wish to use.** The default is set to `WARN`, which means the warning level is used.

You have defined the `BeanLoader` class instance, but you still have to create it. This will be your next task. Since you didn't provide any package information regarding this class, you'll have to **create a new MXML component on the application level**. This component needs to have the same name as the one you've specified in the `beanLoaders` attribute of the `SwizConfig` tag in your main application file. When you create this component, just leave the default base class, but remove the size attributes all together. Once you've created it, **adjust the root tag of the component into** `<swiz:BeanLoader>`. Everything you define in this component should be placed inside of the `<fx:Declarations>` tag, because none of the items in here will be placed on screen.

As mentioned before, the BeanLoader component contains your non-visual components. This means that **you need to define your model in here**. So, go ahead and create an instance of the `ContactModel` class inside of the `<fx:Declarations>` tag. **It also needs to contain the controller** that will start up the back end methods for the application. This means you need to manually set the `ContactController` instance, because at this point you haven't yet created that class. You'll do that right after you're done with this file.

The last item to put in this file is the `RemoteObject` **instance** that refers to the `personServices` destination in the LiveCycle Data Services configuration files. You don't specify any result or fault handler here in this component. These will be defined in the controller in just a minute.

If you were to work with an additional presentation layer in this framework, you would also have the option to prototype the presentation model to be a singleton instance by using the following line of code:

```
<swiz:Prototype id="contactPresentationModel"
        classReference="{ContactPresentationModel}"
        constructorArguments="{person}"
        singleton="true"/>
```

This is not really necessary at this point, because you only have one view and one model, so I'll skip this part all together. I just wanted to let you that this framework can also work with singleton models, just like PureMVC.

This concludes the BeanLoader instance, and now you can start working on the controller and model classes. Let's create the model class first. **Create yet another package** `be.flexpert.contact.models` **and add the** `ContactModel` **ActionScript class inside of it.** Normally, such a model class would contain multiple class members, each one containing specific data. But in your application, you only need to **define one property** and that is an `ArrayCollection` of `personDTO` objects. Make sure that the property is made `[Bindable]` because you are going to use it in a binding expression later on inside of the view.

The controller class will also reside in its own package. Go ahead and **create the package** `be.flexpert.contact.controllers`. **The actual controller class** `ContactController` could be extending the `AbstractController` class of the Swiz framework. But this is only necessary when you want to use the executeServiceCall method. This method is used when working with Delegate classes to access your back end. Since I'm trying to compare the different frameworks without any additional design patterns such as delegates and commands, I'm not going to use it in this particular example. However, it also means that your controller class will also take care of the back end calls.

The ContactController **class contains three properties**:

- The service
- The model
- The responder

The first two properties need to be public and they also need to have the [Autowire] **property set.** This is part of the dependency injection design pattern, and it will link this property to the one that you have defined in the BeanLoader component. They must be defined public in order to get the dependency injection system to work; it does not work when the properties are set to private. Since the [Autowire] system will link the properties based on their type, you can make it easy on yourself here by not defining the specific property to bind to and let the framework sort it out. You can read up on the other possible properties for this metadata tag at http://swizframework.org/docs/dependency-injection/.

In the controller's constructor, you instantiate the responder and attach an event listener that listens for the ResultEvent.RESULT event. This event is triggered when the back end method returns successfully. You don't need to attach an event listener for the FaultEvent.FAULT event because you've already set the general fault handler in the main application file when you placed the SwizConfig tag in there.

Next, **define the methods that will actually execute the back end calls** for the RemoteObject instance that you have defined in the BeanLoader component and that is linked to the service property using the [Autowire] metadata tag. Each one of these methods is going to react to a custom event that is dispatched from the Contacts view component. **To make sure that the methods actually react to these custom events, you have to provide a** [Mediate] **metadata tag for them.** For each [Mediate] tag you have to specify the exact event to which the method should react. And even then there are still some options. One is to just define the event, which is what you are going to do with the getAllPersons method, because it doesn't require a specific property in order to do its job; it just needs to call the getAllPersons method from the service class instance. The second option is to add the properties that it requires from the custom event. If you do this, you are no longer capturing the custom event. Instead, the parameter for the method will be the property itself. This is what you are going to do for the create, update and delete methods. The prototype definitions for these methods will look like this:

Excerpt from be ➤ flexpert ➤ contact ➤ controllers ➤ ContactController.as

```
[Mediate(event="PersonEvent.READ")]
public function getAllPersons(event:PersonEvent):void {
}

[Mediate(event="PersonEvent.CREATE", properties="person")]
public function createPerson(person:PersonDTO):void {
}

[Mediate(event="PersonEvent.UPDATE", properties="person")]
public function updatePerson(person:PersonDTO):void {
}

[Mediate(event="PersonEvent.DELETE", properties="person")]
```

```
public function deletePerson(person:PersonDTO):void {
}
```

You can clearly see in this code excerpt that the `person` property is placed in the method's parameter list. Now, the Swiz framework will automatically grab the `person` property from the custom event and use that as the parameter for the method instead of just the custom event.

The final method for this controller class is the result handler. This method is triggered whenever one of the back end methods is executed successfully. Each service call also has a custom `action` property containing the name of the call so you can distinguish between the different calls in a single result handler instead of wiring up multiple responders and result handlers (which would be an equally valid way of working, of course). By examining this `action` property, you can now either fill up the model with the retrieved data or start the fetch operation from within the controller itself. The finished controller should now look like this:

be ➤ *flexpert* ➤ *contact* ➤ *controllers* ➤ *ContactController.as*

```
public class ContactController {

  [Autowire]
  public var service:RemoteObject;

  [Autowire]
  public var model:ContactModel;

  private var _responder:CallResponder;

  public function ContactController() {
    _responder = new CallResponder();
    _responder.addEventListener(ResultEvent.RESULT, resultHandler);
  }

  [Mediate(event="PersonEvent.READ")]
  public function getAllPersons(event:PersonEvent):void {
    retrieveContactsList();
  }

  private function retrieveContactsList():void {
    _responder.token = service.getAllPersons();
    _responder.token.action = PersonEvent.READ;
  }

  [Mediate(event="PersonEvent.CREATE", properties="person")]
  public function createPerson(person:PersonDTO):void {
    _responder.token = service.createPerson(person);
    _responder.token.action = PersonEvent.CREATE;
  }

  [Mediate(event="PersonEvent.UPDATE", properties="person")]
  public function updatePerson(person:PersonDTO):void {
    _responder.token = service.updatePerson(person);
```

```
      _responder.token.action = PersonEvent.UPDATE;
    }

    [Mediate(event="PersonEvent.DELETE", properties="person")]
    public function deletePerson(person:PersonDTO):void {
      _responder.token = service.deletePerson(person);
      _responder.token.action = PersonEvent.DELETE;
    }

    private function resultHandler(event:ResultEvent):void {
      switch(event.token.action) {
        case PersonEvent.READ:
          model.personsList = event.result as ArrayCollection;
          break;
        case PersonEvent.CREATE:
        case PersonEvent.UPDATE:
        case PersonEvent.DELETE:
          retrieveContactsList();
          break;
      }
    }
}
```

The final adjustments that you have to make to get this application to work with the Swiz framework can be compared with the adjustments you had to make when using the PureMVC framework: you have to go back to the Contacts view component. First of all, this component also needs some dependency injection for the list of persons. So, remove the _personsList property and replace it with the following:

```
[Bindable]
[Autowire]
public var model:ContactModel;
```

This will wire up the property to use the model instance that has been defined in the BeanLoader component. As a result of this modification, you have to modify the DataGrid control, so that the dataProvider now takes its data from the new model instance instead of getting it directly from the local _personsList property.

As you know by now, the service calls are actually made by the ContactController component, so you shouldn't be calling the RemoteObject instance anymore in this view component. This means you can **completely remove the** <fx:Declarations> **tag. You also need to remove the result and fault handlers,** as they are no longer used.

Of course, you still need to adjust the way that the back end methods are being called. At the moment, the CRUD methods are still referring to the service that you've just removed. As I've explained when creating the ContactController class and also when defining the SwizConfig tag in the main application file, the CRUD methods in that class are triggered by simple standard events that have been set to bubble. As a result, you need to **replace those service calls with** dispatchEvent **statements** that dispatch PersonEvent types using the proper string constants defined inside of that custom event class, like so:

Note that you need to provide null as the second parameter of the constructor of the PersonEvent class when simply retrieving all the items in the database. This is necessary because that specific method call doesn't require a parameter, and you didn't provide a default value for that parameter in the custom event class.

Excerpt from be ➤ flexpert ➤ contact ➤ views ➤ Contacts.mxml

```
[Bindable]
[Autowire]
public var model:ContactModel;

[Bindable]
private var _selectedPerson:PersonDTO;

private function init():void {
  dispatchEvent(new PersonEvent(PersonEvent.READ, null));
}

protected function btnNew_clickHandler(event:MouseEvent):void {
  _selectedPerson = new PersonDTO();
  grid.selectedIndex = -1;
  fname.setFocus();
}

protected function btnDelete_clickHandler(event:MouseEvent):void {
  dispatchEvent(new PersonEvent(PersonEvent.DELETE, _selectedPerson));
}

protected function btnSave_clickHandler(event:MouseEvent):void {
  var personEvent:PersonEvent;
  if(_selectedPerson.id == 0) {
    personEvent = new PersonEvent(PersonEvent.CREATE, _selectedPerson);
  } else {
    personEvent = new PersonEvent(PersonEvent.UPDATE, _selectedPerson);
  }
  dispatchEvent(personEvent);
}

protected function grid_changeHandler(event:ListEvent):void {
  _selectedPerson = (grid.selectedItem as PersonDTO).clone();
}
```

This concludes the process of making this application work using the Swiz application framework. When you run the application now, you'll see it working exactly the same as when you didn't use any application.

Conclusion

The Swiz footprint ends up being about 13KB, making it larger than PureMVC, but smaller than Mate. Get the library linked at runtime instead of compiling it into the application and you'll get rid of this disadvantage altogether, because then the library is downloaded only once, since these Runtime Shared Libraries are being cached in the browser cache. This is fundamentally different from the Flex framework caching, since that specific RSL is cached in the Flash Player cache instead, which is not affected by clearing the browser cache.

This is the obvious disadvantage. But there are other things that I'm not quite comfortable with. For instance, **when using the** [Autowire] **metadata tag, you need to make that property publicly accessible. This is a result of using the dependency injection system, but it is against the Object Oriented concept rules of encapsulation.** It's a shame that the framework documentation doesn't address this issue and provide you with a solution to still use encapsulation.

There is a solution for this problem, however. In ActionScript, the encapsulation using getter and setter methods is quite similar to just using public variables. It is not exactly the same, because with encapsulation you can still perform additional calculations, string conversions, etc. when assigning a value. But you can [Autowire] these methods as well. Thus, with encapsulation enabled, the ContactController*'s service reference would look like this:*

private var _service:RemoteObject;

public function get service():RemoteObject {

return _service;

}

[Autowire]
public function set service(value:RemoteObject):void {

_service = value;

}

Now you can perform extra functionality while simply using the dot notation for your service. Naturally, this also applies for the other "autowired" properties. So, you can still adhere to the Object Oriented concepts using this framework.

However, the fact that this framework uses dependency injection makes it very loosely coupled in its structure. The controller does not know about the view and the view does not know about the controller. And that's a good thing. When comparing this system to the one that Mate is using, I find this Swiz one better because you can implement it the other way around. **In Mate, you need to have knowledge of the property names of all the child components that you want to inject a certain property. In Swiz, however, every child component just needs to know the model or service name in the** BeanLoader **class when using the** [Autowire] **metadata tag.** This makes it less intrusive in view of the black box principle. When you add another component, chances are slim that the BeanLoader instance is going to have to be altered. And that is certainly not the case when using Mate.

Another great thing about this framework is that it uses the already existing Flex event dispatching mechanism to trigger the controller's functionality. So you don't need to learn a whole new rule set to get your first application working.

Summary

The Swiz framework is yet another approach to creating a uniform way of working with Flex applications. But how does it fair when comparing it to the other frameworks? Well, it shares a couple of features with the other frameworks such as dependency injection with Mate and the use of standard custom events. Personally, I like the dependency injection system of Swiz more than the one used with Mate because it has more familiarities with your existing framework-less code.

All three frameworks have a rather small footprint on your code, so using one of them does not really affect the initial loading performance. However, Mate has the nice option of using the Flex modules and making use of that system to only initialize the necessary components when they are actually requested. This might give you a very small advantage in memory footprint when running the application. On the other hand, having the models and controllers ready for use from the moment the application starts up can save you some precious waiting time when moving from one screen to another.

When deciding which framework to implement, it is crucial to remember that nothing in this world is perfect and nothing is flawless. Every framework has its advantages and disadvantages. However, I do think that you need to implement a decent framework when working with other people on Flex applications. At first, it may seem like you're making things harder on yourself by having to adhere to a whole set of programming and structural rules, but it will definitely pay off during the course of the project. This is also the reason why implementing frameworks is definitely on my list of best practices.

As for other best practices, in the next chapter I'll give you an extensive list of the ones I find important, ranging from simple naming conventions to performance improving tidbits. Once you get accustomed to them, you'll perform them automatically, allowing you to write better code with barely any extra effort.

Chapter 9

Best Practices

Up until now, I've taken you through the different aspects of creating Rich Internet Applications (RIAs) using new tools such as Flash Catalyst and Flash Builder. I've not just covered the technical details; I've also looked into the different collaboration workflows to help you determine the right tools for the job.

In this chapter, I'm going to take you through some of the best practices when creating RIA projects. Previously, I gave you some hints (does the phrase "application framework" ring a bell?) but there are many more. Some of them are officially promoted through the Adobe website. Others come from my own extensive development experience. I've had to learn the ropes without these guidelines, and I want to save you the trouble of learning the hard way. So here is the way to create better and more effective code with just some basic tips and tricks. Note that no matter which guidelines you set up for your team, the most important thing is to be consistent in applying them in all of your projects.

Some of the "best practices" on my list have been around for ages, so perhaps they will sound familiar to you. Maybe (and hopefully), you're already following these guidelines without even realizing it. I know that I was very happy to find out that my instincts were sound: upon discovering Sean Moore's guidelines a few years ago, I found that I was already using 90% of them (see `http://www.adobe.com/devnet/flex/articles/best_practices_pt1.html` and `http://www.adobe.com/devnet/flex/articles/best_practices_pt2.html`). I hope you feel the same when you read through the list in this chapter.

Project Setup

This first section contains guidelines to help you get off to a good start. Having to recreate your project or rewrite part of your code because you didn't get the project set up correctly in the beginning will cost you precious time in meeting your deadline.

Use Workspaces

A workspace in Flash Builder is nothing more than a directory on your file system. This directory contains one or more projects. Grouping your projects in separate directories helps keep the development environment organized. For instance, I have a separate workspace for each client. It helps me keeping an overview of all the projects for that client. It also prevents the client from seeing information about your other customers or projects. NDAs (Non-Disclosure Agreements) can cost you serious money if a client finds out that other people have been looking at their project. Beware!

Determine the Target Platform

When you create your project the first time, consider the target platform. In other words, this is the time to decide whether you want to deploy an AIR application or just a simple web application. This choice is made in the project wizard, and it is stored in the project's settings. Similar to Flash Builder 4, you do have the option of altering this setting after you've created the project by choosing the proper option from the right-click popup menu on the project (see Figure 9-1); however, certain functionality will not be interchangeable between the platforms, including mass storage detection, the automatic update framework, or the local SQLite database. Therefore, altering the project type should be avoided.

Figure 9-1. Flash Builder allows you to change the application type after the project was created.

Determine the Back End Technology

Even though you can also alter the back end technology post-creation, it's a best practice to decide on the technology up front. You want to avoid having to rewrite the entire back end if the original technology and the new one differ from each other. When using remoting, you can change the technology fairly easy, because it is configured in external XML files and you don't have to alter the Flex application much. However, when you change the way you call the back end, you do have some work rewriting the service layer on the Flex side as well.

Deploy Release Builds

When you're working with Flash Builder to create you applications, you are going to run and debug the application from within the IDE (Integrated Development Environment) . Doing so will always start up the debug version of your SWF file, even when you're not debugging. This version contains lots of additional information to help debug your code. It contains extra code for when you want to use the memory profiler, and trace statements are compiled into the SWF file to allow you to write something to the output console in debug mode. When you choose `Export Release Build...` from the `Project` menu, all this extra information will be stripped from the code. The resulting SWF file will be much smaller and therefore much more efficient.

Place External Libraries in the `libs` Folder

Often you will be using one or more external libraries to assist you in creating the proper custom components for your application. When you need to compile these libraries into your SWF file, you should place them inside of the `libs` folder of your project. That way, you don't have to change anything in the project settings, and the libraries are automatically linked to the project. Another advantage of placing the libraries in the `libs` folder is that when you hand the project over to another (external) developer, he has all the necessary libraries and they are all correctly linked, because they are in exactly the same place.

However, sometimes you need to refer to your own libraries. These may be located in some central location, like a separate server. In this case, you can make an exception and link directly to the centralized server to make sure that with every build you get the latest version compiled into your code. You do need to be careful that a new version doesn't give you unexpected results, so additional testing is required in this case.

Use Runtime Shared Libraries

Linking SWC files to be compiled into your code ensures that it is available to your application. However, this also increases your SWF file size, especially when using multiple libraries, which will affect the initial startup time of your application and impact the user experience. Runtime Shared Libraries (RSLs) are separate libraries that need to be placed on your web server or application server to be accessible. If you forget one, your application will throw runtime exceptions. That's the down side. On the bright side, RSLs are cached on the user's computer (in the browser cache), so as long as you don't need a newer version of the library and the user doesn't clear his cache, you only download this library once. Using RSLs improves startup times by having to download a smaller SWF file and loading it in memory. In this case, the rule for a better user experience is: less is more! You can find detailed information about creating and using RSLs at http://help.adobe.com/en_US/Flex/4.0/UsingSDK/WS2db454920e96a9e51e63e3d11c0bf674ba-7ff6.html.

Externalize the Flex framework

Ever since Flex 3, you have had the option to extract the Flex framework out of your SWF file. This created an additional RSL in your output directory that you had to place on the server as well. Did you ever wonder why this RSL was over 1MB in size, even though your compiled application was, let's say, only 300KB? It's because the compiler optimization only compiles the used components in the resulting SWF file. With the externalized framework, it is impossible to know which components are going to be used, so that RSL needs to contain every single component.

The large file size obviously makes for additional download time. However, this framework is also cached (in the Flash Player cache, which is not affected by clearing the browser cache). So, when you have multiple applications using the same Flex SDK, the framework RSL is downloaded only the first time, making for much faster download and startup times in your actual application in every subsequent visit to the application.

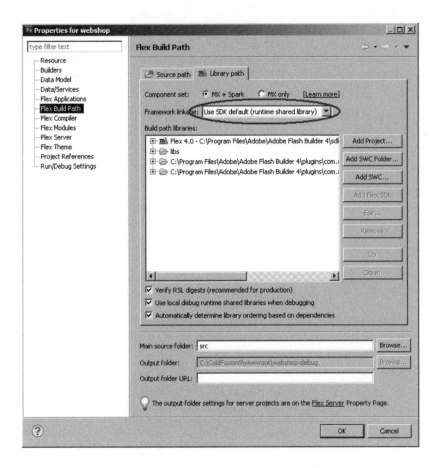

Figure 9-2. In Flex 4 projects, the framework is automatically linked as an RSL.

As you can see in Figure 9-2, in Flash Builder 4 and Flex 4, the option of externalizing the framework is automatically set—because the linkage settings are automatically set to detect whether or not the SDK supports this feature. If you want to compile the framework in your application for some reason, you can alter it in the Build Path section of the project's Properties dialog . However, I suggest you leave the default setting on this one.

Organize Code into Packages

Your project will probably contain many custom components, custom events, controllers, models and views. Don't throw them all into one or two packages. Instead, create a logical structure of packages to put them in. In Flex, a package is nothing more than a simple directory on your file system. This will help you organize your project, and it allows other developers to search through your project a lot easier. The use of packages is also part of the Object Oriented development approach.

Synchronize with Back End Packages

When you use a back end technology like Java, for instance, you are certainly going to create packages to keep your code structured and to adhere to the rules of certain application frameworks. Chances are that you are using the [RemoteObject] tag to map certain Data Transfer Objects or custom exceptions between Java and Flex. That metadata tag needs to contain the reference to the fully qualified class name of the Java class. To make it easy on yourself, you should keep the package structure in Java the same as in Flex. That way, when you want to look for a certain class that corresponds to the other side of the back end connection, you know in an instant where to look; you don't need to open the Flex class to get the reference to the remote class.

Note that this is only possible when you create both the front and back end of the application. When you use a pre-existing back end, you can, of course, create your own more logical package structure on the Flex side. So this guideline is not always applicable.

Plan the Illustrator/Photoshop File Structure

When it comes to designing your application, know that if you put too many things on a single layer, you make it harder for the interaction designer to create the correct view states or pages. States and pages are created by rendering certain design layers (in)visible. So, separate states should be designed in separate layers. All discrete items, such as buttons, list controls etc. need to be placed on separate layers and grouped in one or more layer folders. These layers are kept intact when you import the design into Flash Catalyst.

When using advanced design techniques in Photoshop, Illustrator or Fireworks, keep in mind that not all features (such as advanced gradients, layer masks, etc) will be available in Flash Catalyst. To get the design properly rendered in Flash Catalyst, you need to convert those layers into images by merging or rasterizing these layers. Text layers remain editable in Flash Catalyst, depending on the choice you've made when importing the design file, as you can see in Figure 9-3.

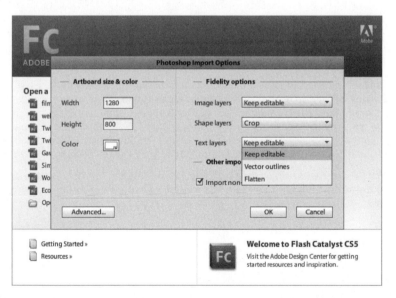

Figure 9-3. The Text layers conversion options when importing a design file in Flash Catalyst.

Use an Assets Directory

One of the common best practices is to create an "assets" directory in your src folder. This directory will contain all the different visual assets for your project, including:

- Pictures
- Icons
- Logos
- Skins
- Audio
- Video
- Fonts

If you place the assets folder inside of the src folder, this subfolder will automatically be placed in the bin-debug folder as well. This saves you the trouble of worrying if you have all the assets available when testing the application from within Flash Builder.

Organize Your Assets

Once you've created the assets folder, you should also organize your assets by putting them in subfolders. This will help you and the other developers keep track of the location for certain types of assets. This is especially useful when you have a lot of assets that are being used in your application. To improve the collaboration with other developers, you should also agree upon fixed names for the asset sub folders; also, these folders should have descriptive names to reflect what you can find inside. Examples could be:

- fonts
- images
- sounds
- skins

Use an XML File for the Parameters

Often, your applications will need to load some parameters at startup. These parameters are then used for example in calculations or for server and file locations, for example. There are a few ways to do this: you could place the parameters hardcoded in the application, but that would mean that whenever the parameters change, you would need to recompile the application; you could read the parameters from the database, but sometimes you need to make a parameter to determine which database you need to connect to; or you could use an external XML file and load it from a fixed location.

However, you might be confronted with a cross-domain issue, creating the need to use some kind of proxy service to load up the XML content. If you use this system, all you need to do is change a textual file to alter the parameters.

Coding and Naming Conventions

This second section contains globally accepted naming conventions. This will help you identify the purpose of certain parts of your code or components more easily, and it also allows other developers to find their way within your part of the code.

Don't Link to External Image Files

In team environments, you might need to pass your Illustrator file to an interaction designer to work on in Flash Catalyst. By placing images in Illustrator rather than linking to them, you can pass across a single Illustrator file and be assured that they will have all the assets they need to continue working on the project. Images and other assets in Illustrator will appear in the Library panel within Flash Catalyst.

After importing your images into Illustrator, use the `Object > Rasterize` option to optimize the image settings for screen resolution. In this dialog box, select 72 DPI for screen viewing and set the background as transparent.

I'm not saying you should never use linked images, because it will reduce file size and ensures that you always have the latest version of that image. However, to avoid broken links or missing images in Flash Catalyst, you should still include the images in the design file just before sending it to the interaction designer.

Name All Design Layers

When creating your design in Photoshop, Illustrator or Fireworks, you are creating a layer structure to group your component layers. All the design layers on every level should have proper names. These names are also brought into Flash Catalyst; the interaction designer will have an easier job constructing the proper custom components when the layer names give a hint as to what's inside of them. A layer name of "button hover" says a lot more than "Layer25."

Not only does it help the interaction designer to locate certain components, but it also avoids some layers being left out and thus creating a wrong component. The layer names are also retained in the resulting Flash Builder project, so the developer can also benefit from these layer names to better understand the design.

Design Only One Item for a Data List Component

If your design requires a data list component, you should only define one item in that list. Flash Catalyst is perfectly capable of creating an item renderer out of that single item and repeating it for every item in the list (see Figure 9-4). Even when you have design-time data that is static and doesn't require any back end support, you can simply define the number of items directly in Flash Catalyst and the designed item renderer will be repeated.

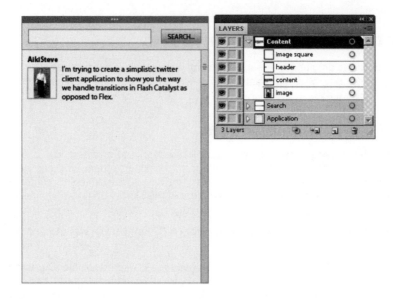

Figure 9-4. The Illustrator design file contains only one item of the data list component.

Of course, you may need to design multiple items in the list to get your design approved. In that case, you're better off creating the single item renderer and defining the other items in a different layer group, which you can easily remove from the design file before sending it to the interaction designer. Or you can tag that group layer to help the interaction designer understand that the layer is solely a design element and should not be converted into separate components.

Create Flash Catalyst Components Before Defining View States

When you create or alter custom components in Flash Catalyst, the changes only apply to the current view state. This is why you should first make the proper components and style adjustments before creating other view states. The following is a list of tasks to perform before creating the application's view states:

- Convert all artwork to components throughout the entire design (e.g. buttons, input fields, comboboxes, etc.).
- Create custom components that group design components (e.g. forms, etc.).
- Group remaining design components in logical layer groups.

Of course, this order does not only apply to the application level. It can also be applied recursively to any custom component that is a combination of other components. Just remember that when you don't respect this order, you can still apply the changes to all the states manually, as I've described in the Flash Catalyst chapter in this book.

Rename Flash Catalyst Components in the Library Panel

Just like state names, the names of the custom components are extensively used throughout a Flex project that is created using Flash Catalyst. Therefore, choose the component names wisely. Choosing the proper component names makes life easier for the developer to whom you're going to hand over the project.

When you create custom components in Flash Catalyst, they are automatically placed in the Library panel. They also automatically get a generic name. For instance, the first button you create will be named button1. The twenty-fifth button will be named button25. Similar naming rules apply for other components as well. For a developer (and even for yourself as an interaction designer), these types of names mean nothing. That's the reason why you should rename the custom components.

Figure 9-5. The Flash Catalyst Library panel contains components with proper names.

Reverse Engineer the Application's URL as a Package Structure

In Flex applications (as in other programming languages as well), it is common practice to structure your packages in such a fashion that the structure creates a world wide unique structure. This is achieved by reverse engineering the URL's domain where the application will reside and combine that with the application name. So, for example, if you have an application called "webshop" that resides at www.flexpert.be, you would create the package structure be.flexpert.webshop. It is from that point on that you create the packages for all the different types of components and classes in your project.

Use Plural Names for Packages

When creating packages, use plural names because packages contain more than one component or class. The package names should also be written in *titlecase* or *camelcase* (in other words, the names start with a lowercase letter and every part of the name that is a separate word begins with an uppercase character). Example package names are controllers, viewComponents, customEvents, valueObjects, etc.

Use Appropriate Package Names

Next to being plural, the package names should reflect what's inside. Note that there are a few names that are fixed in the sense that these package names have been widely adopted by the Flex community:

- events
- views
- itemRenderers
- valueObjects
- services

Use Singular Names for Classes

Class names should be singular, even when they contain one or more lists. The class just represents one object instance. Therefore, the class name should be kept in its singular form, preferably as a noun as well. Don't create class names as adverbs and choose a name that reflects its content. For example, don't create a class Smart to indicate a smart person. Instead, concatenate the adverb with a noun to create a composite class name such as SmartPerson.

Use Titlecase or Camelcase for Class Names

Class names and component names should be declared in camelcase or titlecase. Of course, class names cannot contain spaces, so that means that every separate word in the class name should start with a capital letter and all words are concatenated into one single word.

Append the Class Type to the Class Name

Since the class name should reflect its content, a good place to start is adding the class type to the name. Thus, when you're creating a custom event class, the name should end with "Event". If you create a special validator class, you append "Validator" to the class name. The same rule also applies for formatters, exceptions, skins, buttons and other class types. So this rule does not only apply to the classes that you create in Flash Builder; in Flash Catalyst, you also create components (which are also classes), and you should give those components proper names with the component type appended.

Consider Appending "Base" to Base Class Names

When you create an inheritance structure, consider appending "Base" at the end of the name of the base class. You can also find the naming convention in the Flex framework components (e.g. ListBase) and when you import WSDL files when using a web service. However, you should only do this when the base class is not supposed to be used directly in your code. So, you'll probably end up using this rule when creating custom library components.

Consider Appending "Abstract" to Abstract Class Names

Sometimes you will create *abstract classes*. This is a special class type in the sense that you will never instantiate an object of that particular class. Why create such a class? Well, in an abstract class, you can define the functionality that will have to be implemented in the classes that extend this abstract class.

For example, imagine you have two types of customers: an individual and a company. Both types of customers can be translated into two separate classes Individual and Customer. Each class will have different properties. For example, the `Company` class will have a `VAT` and the `Individual` class will not. However, both classes will have similar properties, such as an `address`. These common properties can be placed in a `Customer` base class, along with the behavior that is common for both types of customers, such as the `order`, `purchase` and `pay` methods.

However, there is one slight problem with this setup and it is that you can create an instance of the Customer, which in essence creates a customer that is neither an individual, nor a company. To prevent this, you have to convert the Customer base class into an abstract class. The class definition will look like this:

```
public class CustomerAbstract {...}
```

This definition has changed the class name, but it doesn't enforce the class to be abstract and doesn't prevent instances of this class type being created. This is because in ActionScript abstract classes are not part of the language features. Fortunately, there's a work-around for it, based on the concept of the Singleton class pattern I discussed in the previous chapter. You can find the full explanation of this work-around at `joshblog.net/2007/08/19/enforcing-abstract-classes-at-runtime-in-actionscript-3/`.

Maintain Order in Your Classes

In theory, it doesn't really matter what order you place your variables and methods inside your class definition, but it's always a good idea to get some logic in there, especially when you're creating extensive classes with a couple of hundred lines of code. You have two methods for maintaining order. The first option would be to place them all in an alphabetical order. The advantage of using this option is the fact that you can easily retrieve a certain method. It even makes it easier when you use the `Outline` panel, because the methods are depicted in that panel in the same order as in the actual file.

The second option is to create a logical structure in the placement of variables and methods. This is the one that is most commonly used:

- Class constants
- Static variables
    - Public
    - Protected
- Instance variables
    - Public
    - Protected
    - Private
- Constructor method
- Implicit getters and setters
- Methods
    - Public static methods
    - Public override methods
    - Public instance methods
    - Protected static methods
    - Protected override methods
    - Protected instance methods
    - Private instance methods

Use Uppercase for Constants

This guideline does not only apply to ActionScript or Flex project but to almost any other programming language. Constants should always be declared in uppercase (e.g. `SOME_CONSTANT`). Since you cannot use uppercase and lowercase letters to distinguish between words in a single constant, you use an underscore between every word that makes up the constant's name. This allows the developers to easily distinguish between a constant and an ordinary variable and is especially handy when using the code completion feature of the Flex Builder IDE (or any other IDE that has code completion for that matter).

Use Camelcase/Titlecase for Variables

To make sure the difference between constants and variables is clear enough, the variables should be declared using camelcase/titlecase with a lowercase first letter. This means that every variable that consists of multiple words will be written as one single term, with each word beginning with a capital (e.g. `someVariable`, `selectedPersonId`, etc.)

Give Variables Proper Names

When creating variables inside your class, they should be meaningful. This means you should avoid using exotic abbreviations and variable names that are less than three characters long. Exceptions to this rule are temporary variables with names that all programming languages have been using for ages. Here are some of those exceptions:

- i and j are used for index variables in `for`, `while` and `do…while` loops.
- `tmp` can point to a temporary variable inside of a method, but never as a class member or property.
- `str` can point to a temporary `String` inside of a method, but never as a class or instance variable.
- e can be used to designate a new custom event instance to dispatch when creating an event handler and "event" is already taken by the handlers parameter.

Put an Underscore in Front of Private Variables

This rule is actually a remnant from the previous versions of ActionScript. The concept of `public` and `private` was introduced into ActionScript 3. Before that, the same concept was not enforced by the compiler, but rather by means of naming conventions. Putting an underscore in front of a variable was agreed upon to indicate that the variable should not be used directly, but rather though some kind of method or other reference. The same naming conventions still live on in the current version of ActionScript.

Use Implicit Getters and Setters

In ActionScript 3, there is a concept called implicit getters and setters. This is fairly unique to the language and offers some great benefits. When you create `private` variables in other programming languages and want to make them accessible to the outside world, you would create what is called explicit getters and setters. You can do the same in ActionScript as well. Suppose you have a `private` variable `_someProperty` of the `String` type. The explicit getter and setter would look like this.

Example code for the explicit getter and setter methods

```
public function getSomeProperty():String {
  return _someProperty;
```

```
}
public function setSomeProperty(value:String):void {
  _someProperty = value;
}
```

This would work well, except, in this case, you can never set the property value from within MXML code because MXML notation only allows to set property values by using the property name directly. That means that your properties should be declared `public`, which is in violation of the Object Oriented coding principle of encapsulation.

The implicit getters and setters are the answer to this problem. When you create such methods, you will still be able to use the dot-notation on class instances and access the properties in MXML code as if they were `public` properties. But in essence, you're executing a method that will fill up the `private` variable, which means that you can perform some additional functionality when setting or getting the property value. The syntax for the implicit getter and setter of this property is the following:

Example code for the implicit getter and setter methods

```
public function get someProperty():String {
  return _someProperty;
}
public function set someProperty(value:String):void {
  _someProperty = value;
}
```

Name Implicit Getters and Setters according to the Property

When creating the getter and setter methods in your class, give the proper names. You should name them exactly the same as the property they are setting or returning, except for the underscore in front of the variable name. This makes it easier to understand what property value will be set using a specific implicit setter. Imagine you have a private property called "company" and you need to be able to access it from outside the class. The variable and accessor definitions will look like this:

Example code for the getter and setter naming convention

```
private var _company:String;

public function get company():String {
  return _company;
}

public function set company(value:String):void {
  _company = value;
}
```

As you can see in this small code example, the name of the getter and setter methods is the same as the name of the property, but without the underscore in front of it.

Use Implicit Getters and Setters Internally

You should also use the implicit getter and setter methods internally in your class. Since you are effectively executing a method to set or get a value from your class, some additional functionality may need to be applied to get or set the proper value. Therefore, you should also use these methods when referring to those properties inside of class. Naturally, there are some exceptions to avoid infinite loops in your code execution. For example, if you use the implicit getter inside of the implicit getter implementation, as shown below, you'll end up in an infinite loop:

Example code demonstrating an infinite loop

```
public function get someProperty():String {
  var random:Number = Math.round(Math.random() * 100);
  return someProperty + random;
}
```

Set Argument Types and Return Types Strictly

Because of the upcasting principle of Object Oriented programming, you can always capture or send a particular class instance as an instance of its parent type. For example, you can capture any event in a result handler using the `flash.events.Event` type as the parameter type.

The problem in this case is that you do not have access to the specific properties for the actual class type (e.g. `MouseEvent`, `KeyboardEvent`, `FlexEvent`, etc.) without any type casting being applied. Also, the Flex framework will have to check at runtime if the parameter is, in fact, a subclass of the actual parameter class type.

Also, setting the types as strict as possible will generate a compilation error in case you would try to throw or capture the wrong event type. This is also part of my motto: buggy code shouldn't compile!

Always Name the Argument of Event Handlers "Event"

This will help you distinguish the event handler from other methods in your code. This name also matches the name that is used by the Flex framework. Additionally, you should always capture the event parameter in event handlers, even if you're capturing the event directly from within MXML. This ensures that event handlers are always in the same format; it doesn't matter whether you're using the MXML capturing notation or just the `addEventListener` method to capture the event.

Use a Verb in the Method Name

Because a method executes some code part in reaction to something, you could also call it an action. Since actions are always active, you should use a verb in the name of the method (e.g. `doSomething`, `getAllPatients`, `updateTable`, etc.) to better understand the nature of the code inside of that method.

In case of event handlers it is also a best practice to use the present tense for actions that are going to happen and the past tense for actions that have already happened. For example, if you react to the `preinitialize` event of an application, you should name that event handler something like `initializeApplication`. However, when you react to the `creationComplete` event, the application has been initialized completely and your event handler should be named `applicationInitialized`, for example.

Override the `Clone()` Method for Custom Events

When you create a custom event class to use the Flex event handling system for communicating between components while maintaining the black box principle, you have to adhere to a couple of rules. The first one is that you have to inherit from the `flash.events.Event` class. That's quite obvious. However, something that is often forgotten in custom event classes is the fact that you should also override the `clone` method.

The reason for this can be found in the DOM level 3 event model (`www.w3.org/TR/DOM-Level-3-Events/#event-flow`) that is used. This event handling system has three stages: capture, target, and bubbling (Figure 9-6). It is during this bubbling phase that each event handler receives its own copy of the event object that has been dispatched (but only if the event is set to actually bubble). This is why it is important to override this `clone` method, because otherwise you won't be getting the proper values filled out in the custom properties of the event class.

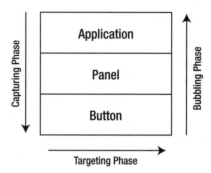

Figure 9-6. The DOM level 3 event model

Keep Order in Your MXML Files

An MXML file is simply an ActionScript class that has been written in an XML-based language. This notation facilitates the creation of visual layouts. But it also allows you to instantiate service classes such as HTTPService, RemoteObject and DataService. And naturally, you can write your ActionScript controller code in the file as well.

You've already seen in your ActionScript classes that there's a certain order you should apply when defining constants, variables and methods. Well, for an MXML file there's a similar rule to apply in order to make it easier on everyone to find the code part they need. This structure order is not strictly necessary, but it is already being followed by many Flex developers all over the world and you will recognize it in the code examples you can find online. The structure looks like this:

- `<fx:MetaData>`
- `<fx:Style>`
- `<fx:Script>`
- `<fx:Declarations>`
- `<fx:states>`
- `<fx:transitions>`
- Design code

Not all of these tags need to be present in the MXML file, but the order should still be applied when some tags are left out.

Use Whitespace

Another best practice that helps you keep your code clean and readable is the usage of whitespace to structure your file. Whitespace is completely optional and does not harm the code in any way if it is present, so, why not make use of it? Whether you're working on a controller class, a custom event or an MXML component and even in the main application file, you can clarify things a lot by putting blank lines in between code blocks.

In an ActionScript class, that does not only mean between the constants, variables and method code blocks, but also between every single method of that class. The same principle also applies to MXML components, where you should also put black lines between the different tag blocks. This allows other developers to recognize the different parts when they skim through the file.

Format Your Code

To improve the readability of your code, it is not only important that you write comments. The code itself should be structured as well. Therefore, every new level of your code should be indented by four spaces or a single tab. Again, this helps you and other developers find the code blocks within the method, allowing you to understand the process flow more easily.

For MXML files, formatting tags is a little different. Instead, all tag attributes begin at the same position, like so:

Example code for layout of MXML attributes on a single tag

```
<s:List id="photoList"
        skinClass="components.PhotoList"
        x.Closed="-544" x.Open="108" x.OpenAction="108" x.Settings="108"
        y="57"
        d:userLabel="Data List"
        dataProvider="{_listItems}"
        change="photoList_changeHandler(event)"/>
```

Every Visual Component Should Have an `id` Attribute

Every single tag that contains a visual element that will be put on screen should have an id attribute. Of course, there are other tags such as services and responders that need an id as well to be able to refer to later elsewhere in the code. Functionally speaking, it is not strictly necessary to have an id for each tag, because if you don't specify one yourself, the Flex compiler will create a generic one for you. However, it is that id that is going to be used in testing tools such as Mercury QuickTest Professional and FlexMonkey to determine which button has been clicked and which input field has gotten a value. Since you can edit the scenarios behind those tests and write checks on the calculated values to test the workings of your interface, it's easier to look for an input field called "firstnameInput" then having to look for "inputField72".

Set the `id` Attribute as the First One in an MXML Tag

To make it easier to find the id of a certain component in your MXML code, you should place this attribute as the first one in the list. That way, you immediately know where to look and you don't have to go through the entire list of attributes to find the one you will use the most in your ActionScript code or binding expressions.

Group MXML Tag Attributes on One Line

When you write the MXML attributes for a tag, use multiple lines to declare them all. Also, group associated attributes on the same line (e.g. `left` and `right`, `width` and `height`, etc.), like so:

Example code grouping tag attributes

```
<s:Panel id="myPanel"
         left="20" right="50"
         title="My Custom Panel"/>
```

Again, it improves readability, and it makes the easier to see all of the attributes at play and their effect on one another.

Use an External CSS File

When creating applications, you should minimize the use of inline or embedded CSS style declarations. An inline style is when you set the attribute directly on the MXML tag. The styles applied by this type of style declarations only apply to a single component instance. Thus, this styling will not be applied to other components of the same type.

Embedding CSS is done by making use of the `<fx:Style>` tag at the top of your component. The styles defined in this code block will apply to every instance of that component, but placing this markup code in the component itself will scatter the style declarations all over the application, making it harder to look for all of the styles to make sure that the inheritance tree is correct and styles are not overwritten when they shouldn't be.

Declaring all of your styles in one or more external CSS files groups them together, facilitating the overview of all the style elements in your application.

Maintain Order in Your CSS File

In some applications, the CSS styling is rather limited, and style declarations are kept to a minimum. In that case, you won't really have any trouble finding the proper declaration and adjusting it or adding a new one without having to wonder that maybe it has already been defined.

In applications that are heavily styled, chances are that the CSS file is quite large and all selector types are just planted somewhere within the file. This makes it hard to keep an overview of what's already been declared and what's hasn't. Therefore, you should keep a certain order in your CSS file in order to search for which styles are applied to a certain component.

In my opinion, there are two ways of structuring your selectors. The first one is just organizing them alphabetically, ignoring the non-alphabetical characters at the beginning of the selector type (e.g. the dot for class selectors and the hash for id selectors). This structuring method makes it very easy to search for a certain selector or for adding a new selector in the proper location. But it is a little harder to see which styling is applied to a certain component, because they are all over the place.

The second structuring method is done by grouping selectors logically. In other words, group all styles that apply to buttons together (type selectors, class selectors, etc.). This way, it is a bit harder to find the proper location to add a new CSS selector, but at least you have all the styles for a certain component grouped together. Within these logical groups you should also follow the CSS priority, which means you'll end up with groups of the following structure:

- Type selector
- Class selector
- Id selector
- Pseudo selector (for view states)
- Universal selector (for all child components)
- Descendant selector (for specific child components)

Both methods are valid options and have advantages and disadvantages. Pick one and stick with it amongst your entire development team. You can find an explanation of these selector types in the Flex 4 SDK overview chapter of his book.

Be Consistent in Naming Styles

In Flex (or ActionScript), there are two ways of defining a certain style. The first one is by using camelcase/titlecase and the second one is by using the same hyphenated system as in regular HTML styling. The first option exists because ActionScript (or any other programming language) does not support hyphens within variable names. The hyphen is also the minus operator, so that would cause one hell of a compiler issue mixing those two. But you do need to be able to define the style attributes for use in both the MXML notation and the `getStyle` and `setStyle` methods in ActionScript. However, you can also use this notation in both the embedded `<fx:Style>` blocks and the external CSS file. In the example code below you see the ActionScript style notation to embed a font using CSS:

Example for CSS code using ActionScript-style notation

```
@font-face
{
  fontFamily: Garamond;
  fontWeight: bold;
  src: url("C:\WINDOWS\Fonts\GARABD.TTF");
  embedAsCFF: true;
}
```

The hyphenated notation is more familiar because you use it in regular HTML files. However, you can only use this notation in the embedded style blocks and external CSS file. Otherwise, the style is treated similarly to a property, which could lead to this issue I've just explained. The good thing about this hyphenated style definition is that it is also used in the code completion feature. So, if you're keen on using that for your styles, you are automatically going to be getting this notation. The disadvantage of this notation is that when you occasionally need to define a certain style in ActionScript, you will have two different ways of defining your style. You could need this when creating custom components completely in ActionScript, with conditional styling applied depending on, for example, a certain selection in that component.

Limit the Number of CSS Files

Just like with HTML you can define your CSS style declarations in multiple external CSS files. These files can then all be applied to the application by declaring multiple `<fx:Style>` blocks. However, you have to be careful when declaring multiple style blocks, since the styles in a certain CSS file will potentially overwrite a style that has been declared in a previous style sheet. That means that you have to choose the order carefully so you won't mess up the styles accidentally. That is also the reason why you shouldn't use too many different CSS files.

Define the CSS Files in the Main Application File

You should also declare your CSS files in the main application file. The reason for this can be found in the way components are initialized in your application. In fact, not all components are initialized upon startup. Declaring the style sheet in a part of the application that is only initialized at a later stage will give you unexpected results, since the styles will initially not be applied. Therefore, make sure your style sheets are read and applied in the beginning of the application. And what better place to do that that in the main application file? And as an additional bonus, everyone knows where to look for which CSS files are being used in the application.

Collaboration

This section contains some guidelines that will help you collaborate more easily with other developers and designers. Most of the time, you will not be the only one working on a project. In the previous chapter, I covered the idea of using frameworks, but there are other guidelines that will come in handy.

Talk to Each Other

I think this might be the single most important guideline when working in a team. In most project teams, there is ample documentation available to designers, interaction designers and developers. However, people tend to forget that certain aspects are better conveyed personally.

You'd be amazed how many problems and bugs could have been avoided if only developers and designers talked to each other about what they are doing and what they are supposed to do.

Formalize Decisions

When working in larger project teams, not every single developer and designer needs to be at every single meeting. This would be counterproductive. However, all of those people do need to know what decisions have been made concerning the product development process. Formalizing these decisions by creating a meeting report and making it available to everyone involved is certainly a good thing to do. Be sure to notify those involved that the report is available and that they should read up on it because it contains important information for them.

Formal decisions also leave a paper trail. So when things get kind of fuzzy and people start to debate why a certain part is working in a certain way, you can take out those documents and solve the problem by looking at the decisions that have been made. Formal documents can be life savers at times.

Use a Source Versioning Tool

When working with multiple developers on the same project, a source versioning tool is imperative for keeping the changes in check. With a check-in/check-out system, only one developer at a time can make changes to a certain file, but multiple developers can lock multiple files. Examples of such tools are:

- SVN (Subversion)
- CVS (Concurrent Versioning System)
- VSS (Visual Source Safe)
- GIT

Using such a system is also a great way to create backups for your project. Taking snapshots or creating branches allows you to continue working on the project while a certain version is already being deployed.

Creating phased releases can be achieved in this fashion. Of course, you shouldn't neglect the fact that your versioning system also needs a backup.

Only Commit Code that Actually Works

Using a versioning system is a good thing, but you can use it the wrong way. The code you commit to the system should only be the code that has been tested and approved. When another developer gets the latest version of the project from the source control system, he will receive the code that you have submitted, so if your code contains a bug, it will be handed down to other developers who might get stuck with broken code. This only creates frustration amongst your colleagues; now they have to wait for the problem to be fixed before they can thoroughly test their own part.

Mark Duplicate Assets in Your Design

When you create a design for a certain project, you often have to create the same component is several pages. Just think about buttons, for example; only the label on the button changes. Although the design may feature many buttons, the interaction designer should not be turning all of those instances into separate components. Therefore, you need to indicate duplicate design layers, so it becomes obvious to the interaction designer which components should be reused instead of created.

You should choose some kind of naming convention to indicate these duplicate entries. Since Flash Catalyst is a new technology, common conventions have not yet been set. But placing an underscore in front of the (group) layer name should do the trick, as you keep the rest of the layer name exactly the same (see Figure 9-7).

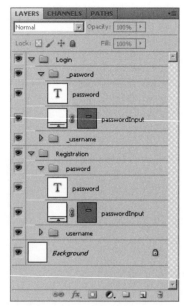

Figure 9-7. Duplicate layers are marked as such in the design file.

Design on a Single Artboard

Although this guideline only applies to Illustrator, it's necessary to clarify. Illustrator supports the use of multiple artboards in a single design file. However, Flash Catalyst does not support this feature. Therefore, you cannot import such a design file into Flash Catalyst; parts will be lost during the import operation.

Give Design Layers Proper Names

Naming design layers applies to Illustrator, Photoshop, Fireworks, *and* Flash Catalyst, since you can add and modify layers in there, too. Naming your layers with proper names helps other people involved in the creating of this application gain a better idea of what the layer contains, when it should be visible, and how it relates to the other layers. It is also very important to give proper names to the layers. When you have designed an input form, for example, just name that layer or layer group "inputForm".

When using layers in Flash Catalyst to create the pages or view states, the interaction designer needs to understand the relationship of a layer with other components in the application. Likewise, the layer names are also transmitted to Flash Builder when you import a Flash Catalyst project, and the developer needs to easily understand the importance and usage of the layer. A good name makes all of this possible.

Don't Define All Components in Your Design

When you create the design for your RIA in a tool such as Photoshop, Illustrator or Fireworks, you can import it in Flash Catalyst, as you've seen in the many examples throughout this book. However, that does not mean that you have to design every single pixel in those design tools. Flash Catalyst is very capable of creating its own components (see Figure 9-8). Only complex graphical representations with an exotic layout need to be created outside of Flash Catalyst.

Figure 9-8. Flash Catalyst is perfectly capable of creating basic custom components from scratch using both the drawing tools and the wireframe components.

Your design file should contain the necessary components that require extensive design. If the application just uses simple push buttons and default radio buttons, for example, there is no point in designing them. In other words, don't waste your time designing components that already exist.

Don't Define All Component States in Your Design

Although you can create all component states in your design tool, it is worth noting that Flash Catalyst is perfectly capable of creating custom component states by altering text properties, changing or adding gradient fills and strokes (see Figure 9-9). Creating these states in Photoshop, for example, will make the life of the interaction designer a lot easier, because then he only need to refer to the proper layers and render them (in)visible in the proper states.

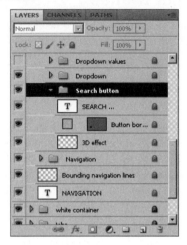

Figure 9-9. The `Search button` component only has the up and over state defined in the design file. The down state will be added in Flash Catalyst.

In a lot of designs, however, the same component states are used for multiple components; for example, the same color change in a certain state can be used in several components. In that case, if the interaction designer has sufficient information for the first component, he will be able to create the same or similar state for the other components.

Create Reusable "Black Box" Components

When you start working on Flex applications, initially you will be creating components within your project. By using the black box principle, you can make those components reusable, because they are not tied in to any other component by accessing their internal properties. For example, if you have a component that displays a list of objects, the component providing that list should not care how the component displays that data. It just provides it. The component could be using a `<mx:DataGrid>`, a `<s:ComboBox>`, a `<s:List>` or just a plain `<mx:Repeater>` tag to do that. Should the internal workings of that component change, it doesn't matter for the component that provides the data. Conversely, you are not going to access properties from the parent component or even from a sibling within your custom component, because that would make it dependent on the combination of those components.

Custom components should be able to be used in combination with any other component. For this purpose, you dispatch custom event classes. Whether or not other components in your application are going to do something with your data is of no interest to your component. It has done its job by gathering the data and making it available to the outside world. This is an object-oriented concept that is also referred to as *encapsulation*.

Consider Using Code Generation

In Flash Builder 4, Adobe offers new features that make life as a developer easier. One of the new features is the extensive code completion. Now you can have your event handlers automatically generated when you define them in MXML code. That saves you the trouble of having to write the function definitions over and over again. The second code generation feature is having the getter and setter methods generated for your private variables (see Figure 9-10). You can even turn a public variable into a private one at the same time.

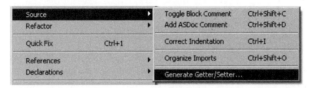

Figure 9-10. Flash Builder 4 can generate the getter and setter method for a variable automatically.

The feature can be found in the popup menu when you right-click on the private property in the source code. Unfortunately, at this writing, you can only generate the getter and setter for one variable at a time. This means you may have to repeat the process several times to generate all accessor methods for a certain class or component.

Create Library Projects

This guideline applies to both Flash Catalyst and Flash Builder. Once you start developing these RIAs or desktop applications, you are going to be creating custom components. As pointed out in the previous guideline, these components should be reusable. To distribute such components, place them in a separate project and turn them into library components. In Flash Catalyst, you have the export option. This will create a separate FXPL file, which you can import again in other projects. Here, you actually copy the content of the library project in your own project, as I showed you in the chapter on Flash Catalyst.

In Flash Builder, however, you need to create a separate project to have a library project, or you can import the FXPL file to create such a library project from your Flash Catalyst library. Either way, the result will be a SWC file that you can link to other projects by placing it in the `libs` folder.

Create a Manifest File for Your Library

When creating libraries, you are still going to use a logical package structure to organize your components. However, this would mean you would have to create a separate namespace for each and every package inside of the library project. It would also mean that you'd have to know the package structure of a project you didn't create. You shouldn't be bothered with that. Therefore, you can create a `manifest.xml` file similar to the one that the Flex framework uses. Such a manifest file would look like this:

Excerpt from the Flex framework's Spark manifest file.

```
<componentPackage>
  ...
  <component id="RadioButtonGroup" class="spark.components.RadioButtonGroup"/>
  <component id="Range" class="spark.components.supportClasses.Range"/>
  <component id="Rect" class="spark.primitives.Rect"/>
  <component id="RemoveAction" class="spark.effects.RemoveAction"/>
```

```
<component id="Resize" class="spark.effects.Resize"/>
...
</componentPackage>
```

In this manifest file, you define all the components that are contained within your library and link them to the proper fully qualified class name of the component. In that way, you only need to define one single namespace for the library in your project, and you can access all of the components in there. Just think of all the components you can access using the mx or s namespace prefixes for the Halo and Spark components, respectively. Creating such a file makes the life of developers using your library a lot easier.

Test, Test, Test

Testing the application is something most developers are not keen on. They wrote the code and verified that it works, and that's it. You'd be amazed how many Flash/Flex applications that are online generate runtime exceptions. In most cases, users have the release version of the Flash Player installed and they do not see these errors. Still, these applications should be thoroughly tested and fixed, because for the users that do have the debug player installed find this very annoying.

But runtime exceptions are not the only thing going wrong here. Since you, as a developer, know what the code is supposed to do, you are tempted to test that scenario and leave it at that: it works. But what if certain values go outside of the limits or a user does not fill out the input fields in the order that seems logical to you? Maybe you'll get a wrong result in your calculations. It may even be that you'll be inputting the wrong data in a database to which other applications are also connecting to retrieve that data.

Testing is something that should not be taken lightly. Don't just test to see if your part of the code is working. Be absolutely sure that you handle the situations that do not fall within the ordinary process flow. This ensures that the code delivered to the end users is of a higher quality, contains less bugs and therefore, it will not frustrate the end user!

Use Different Deployment Levels

If you've already been working on a project in a business environment, you're probably familiar with the concept of different deployment levels. If not, then let me explain it. Normally, a project goes through different stages before it is accepted for production. These different stages are all separate environments with separate versions of the application (both front end and back end) and separate database instances behind it. A typical stage hierarchy looks like this:

- Local
- Development
- Testing
- Acceptance
- Production

The further down the hierarchy you go, the less volatile the environment becomes. It's obvious that in your local environment you are going to be changing quite a lot quite often. After all, you're constantly developing and testing the features.

The development environment is where all the committed code from all the developers is combined into the latest version of the application. This is also the reason why you should only commit code that actually works. When you start working on a new feature, your local environment should be the same as the development environment. This level is also used for testing by the developers and project managers.

The next level is testing. This level contains features that have been validated by the developers and are considered ready to be tested in the greater picture. In this environment, you first test the application in conjunction with a working version of other applications that it needs to communicate with, for example. This is also referred to as "integration testing."

The acceptance level is where the end users come into play. A selected group of end users will test the application in its daily routine. They are the ones that report bugs and make feature requests that come back down to the developers, interaction designers, and sometimes even the designers. And then the cycle starts all over again.

Once the acceptance level has been thoroughly tested and validated, and the small group of test users has given the "go" on that version of the application, you can put it into production where every single user will have access to the new and improved features. Keep in mind that, in the mean time, other versions are making their way up the hierarchy. the entire process is always iterative.

Set Up a Bug Reporting/Change Request Environment

One thing you can hardly get around is bug fixing. We're all bound to make mistakes. So, bugs inevitably make their way to the test users. These users must have some way of letting you know what exactly has gone wrong and how it should actually work. This latter one is more appropriate when it concerns faulty functionality or a change request. Making a phone call or sending an email would be a start, but that's not nearly enough. Eventually, someone has to fix the problem and let the person who raised the problem know that it is fixed and ready to be tested again.

That is where this piece of software comes into play. Now, there are a lot of players on the market when it concerns bug reporting or change request handling. These are only a few of them:

- Sharepoint (`sharepoint.microsoft.com/`)
- JIRA (`www.atlassian.com/software/jira/`)
- Bugzilla (`www.bugzilla.org/`)
- Mantis Bug tracker (`www.mantisbt.org/`)

Some are licensed software, others are freeware. My personal favorite is still JIRA, mainly because I've used it for a couple of years and Adobe uses this as their internal bug tracking system software.

The important thing is that you have a system where users can log bugs and change requests, and where they can follow up on its status (whether someone is working on it, it's been dismissed as a non-issue, it's solved, it's been moved to a next release, etc.). You need to keep your test users in the loop of what you're doing with their feedback.

Use a Unit Testing Framework

Creating unit tests can help you achieve better functional code quality. There are a couple of frameworks available for testing Flex applications, such as ASUnit and FlexUnit. The latter is officially supported in Flash Builder 4. For those of you who have experience with JUnit as a unit testing tool for Java programs, FlexUnit works in exactly the same way. You create test suites that contain one or more tests. Tests check certain small parts of the application. Many tests combined will verify the workings of the application for the biggest part. Whenever you change something in the code and want to commit it, you run the unit tests and you instantly know whether your changes have affected the functionality elsewhere in the application.

However, do not get tricked into relying solely on unit tests to test your application. You cannot and should not write unit test for every possible situation your application might encounter. Taking care of the most obvious ones like the normal process flow and the most common mistakes can save you a lot of time. But you always have to test your application manually as well to check if unexpected behavior is countered properly. And of course, there is always the chance that your unit tests have not yet been adjusted to a certain change request and fail, but actually shouldn't fail. So for all the developers out there who hate testing: I'm sorry, but you'll still have to do it....

Use an Application Framework

I've already discussed some frameworks in the previous chapter. Together with this explanation I've also explained why using a framework is important. It provides you with a fixed structure and process flow. That means that when you work with other developers on the same project, everyone knows exactly how it is constructed and therefore they all know where to look for certain parts of the code.

It doesn't really matter what framework you use. Every one of them has advantages and disadvantages; no single framework is perfect. The choice has to be made based on previous experiences with other programming languages, the technology you use, whether or not you are connecting to a back end technology, and most importantly, what framework you and your team members feel comfortable with. However, don't use the same framework for years on end. New frameworks emerge regularly and they do so because developers get other insights and may have figured out a better way to tackle a certain kind of application. Don't be afraid of change; embrace it.

Know When Not to Use an Application Framework

As important as it is to use some kind of framework in your application, it is also important to know when not to use a framework. Sometimes using a framework makes your application unnecessary complicated. The added value of adding a framework to a very small application is virtually nil.

Perform Code Reviews

When you're working on a project with other developers and/or designers, some practical arrangements are made as to how to program or design the application, such as which framework to use, what to call your design layers, and when to make layer groups, for example. But these are just some rules that you agree upon, not something that will give you compilation errors or a faulty design. These rules are not enforced in any way, so there has to be a way to check whether or not you applied those rules. Letting someone else review your code is one of the things you can do. You can be so caught up in what you are programming or designing that you forget to apply these rules. When another developer looks at your code or another designer looks at your design structure, he might discover some violations of these rules. Again, that doesn't mean that your application will not work perfectly, but the rules should be obeyed to make it easier on everyone when they have to make changes on some part of the code or the design that they didn't do.

Comment Your Code

One of the most important things you should always do is comment your code. It's not a lot of work to do while you're coding, but it's one awful job if you need to do it afterwards. Commenting your code helps other developers understand what a certain class or method is intended to do without having to interpret the actual code. This can save a lot of time when you need to work on somebody else's code and you're trying to figure out what exactly a certain part of code is doing.

There are two ways you can comment your code and both of them should be used extensively. The first method is using inline comments. You use this within the method's body to clarify certain code parts that are not so obvious or to explain the process flow within that method. The second way of commenting your code is using the JavaDoc style notation, which is aptly named ASDoc for ActionScript projects. You can find the information about this documentation style at `help.adobe.com/en_US/Flex/4.0/html/WSd0ded3821e0d52fe1e63e3d11c2f44bc36-7ff6.html`.

You put this type of documentation in front of classes, methods and variables. The great thing about this documentation style is that it allows you to automatically generate the documentation for your classes and display it in a similar fashion as the official *livedocs*, which is the main source of documentation for the Flex framework classes. Instead of using the command line tool to generate this documentation, you can also use the *ASDocr* AIR tool by Grant Skinner. ASDocr provides a GUI for working with ASDoc to make generating documentation for AS3 classes easy. At the time of writing, the original post with the explanation of this tool could be found at `www.gskinner.com/blog/archives/2010/01/asdocr_simple_a.html`.

Validate Input Before Sending It to the Back End

In my career, I've worked on a few projects where you had the concept of server side validation implemented. For example, a form is filled out on the client side and sent to the back end, where it is validated before inserting the data in the database. When that validation fails, an error is sent back to the client, and the client displays a nice error message on screen. But some validations can be done easily on the client side, triggering a much faster response and also generating a lot less network traffic, the latter being important when you have a lot of simultaneous connections and a lot of validations, causing an increase in your server load as well.

I'm not saying that you should move all validation to the front end and not perform any validation in the back end. This would pose a serious risk in the long run: perhaps one day you want to replace your front end technology with something else; or the back end is also used by another application; or you want to open up your back end to the outside world by means of a web service. In that case, you cannot assume that the data being sent to you is going to be correct. Therefore, you should always check the input on the back end side as well. The front end validation is there to make sure that unnecessary requests (because they will fail anyway) are kept to a minimum.

Use the Same Local Server Settings For Everyone

Since the server configuration of your project is also going to be stored in the project settings, it is strongly recommended that every developer on the team have the same setup on his own machine. The project settings are kept in a file which is also stored in the source control system and therefore it is also set to the same settings for every developer.

It's not impossible to have a separate development environment with separate server settings, but in my opinion, that's just asking for trouble. First of all, you have to merge and override the default project settings every time you get the latest version and something has changed. But secondly, and maybe more important, when you have developed a certain part of the project that seems to be working and that part doesn't seem to be working with other developers, who's to say it's not because you have a different setup? If everyone works in the same way, the same code should work exactly the same for every developer.

Configure Your Application Externally

A lot of applications have some form of parameters applied to them. These parameters are subject to change; some more than others. Here are some examples:

- An annual index value
- A URL that needs to be triggered

- The server location
- A certain folder location
- ...

These parameters are best placed in an external XML file, rather than being incorporated directly into the code. The biggest issue with embedding the values in the code is that when they change, you need to recompile the application again. And then you're off for another round of testing on all platforms, because you never know if you've broken something in the code because of that recompilation.

Example of an XML configuration file

```
<?xml version='1.0' encoding='utf-8'?>
<Application>
  <urls>
    <uploadFile>http://www.flexpert.be/processFileUpload.php</uploadFile>
    <downloadScriptUrl>http://www.flexpert.be/download.php</downloadScriptUrl>
  </urls>
  <folders>
    <root>\\someServer\Application/</root>
    <imagesFolder>images/</imagesFolder>
  </folders>
  <thumbnails>
    <root>http://www.flexpert.be/</root>
    <folder>application/thumbnails/</folder>
    <maxWidth>150</maxWidth>
    <maxHeight>150</maxHeight>
  </thumbnails>
  <email>
    <support>steven@flexpert.be</support>
  </email>
</Application>
```

Placing the parameters in an external file allows you to change the values in a much easier way, without having to recompile the application. There are two types of parameter files for a Flex or AIR application. The first one contains basic elements such as index values, URLs and file locations. This file can easily be adjusted by the people who work with these applications when something needs to be changed. The second type of parameter files contains more static data, such as server locations and channel definitions. Just think of the services-config.xml file for the LiveCycle Data Services. The added value here is that in an external version, some of the values are being filled out dynamically, depending on which server the file is located on. Practically speaking, you can take your development version, leave the configuration file as is, and deploy it on the testing acceptance and production environment, and it still keeps working on all of these different environments. It even adjusts itself to the new locations and will automatically connect to the different versions of the back end.

So, all in all, placing parameters and your application's back end configuration in a separate external XML file provides you with a large degree of flexibility to modify your application's inner workings without having to recompile it for every little change.

Summary

In this final chapter I provided an extensive list of guidelines and best practices when working on RIA projects. These are only guidelines, not real obligations. They have been passed on from developer to developer and have proven their use in all sorts of application types. They should help you create better and more reliable code, and they will facilitate the collaboration with your other team members, which is also very important to deliver high quality products. The most important thing is that you are consistent in the guidelines you set up throughout all of your projects!

Index

Generate Details Form option, 87
generation of getter and setter methods, 78
generic component, 163–164, 208
get method, 78
get property( ) method, 9
getAllPersons( ) method, 12, 33, 90, 93,
    264–265, 282
getAllPhotos( ) method, 224, 232
getInstance method, 275
getProperty( ) method, 9
getSolarData file, 181
getStyle method, 306
getter methods, 80, 221, 225–226, 228, 256,
    264, 286, 311
getUser( ) method, 223
GIF (Graphics Interchange Format), 2, 107
global selector, 60–61, 86
Glow efect, 56
Glow filter, 117
Go To URL action, 112–113
Goralski, Greg, 101
GPU (Graphics Processing Unit), 54
gradient color property, 194, 201
gradient fill color, 196
gradient fills, 310
gradient focus color property, 209
gradient hover layer, 211
gradient opacity fill, 200
gradient selection overlay layer, 207
GraniteDS (Granite Data Services), 28–31
_graphData property, 175
Graphical User Interface (GUI), 2, 315
graphics, editing in Illustrator, 126–127
Graphics Interchange Format (GIF), 2
graphics primitives, 42
Graphics Processing Unit (GPU), 54
graphs, mortgage simulator application,
    175–176
Group class, 40
Group container, 271
group folders, 104
group layer, list component, 200, 296
Group layout component, 40
GUI (Graphical User Interface), 2, 315

H

Halo button, 57
Halo components, 39, 53, 57, 73, 312
Halo namespace, 142
Halo theme, 74
hand cursor, 229, 238
handleNotification event handler, 273
handleNotification method, 273

hashing methods, 218
hashing systems, 238
HBox class, 40
headerText property, 86
Heads-Up Display (HUD), 109–111, 169, 204,
    207–211
height parameter, 147
height property, 138, 141–142, 146–147
helicopter view, 187–188
Hibernate framework, 18, 28, 220–222
High setting, 118
high-level modules, 261
highlight overlay layer, 212
Hit count property, 95
Home button, 213
Home menu item, 213–214
Home page, in e-commerce site case study,
    198–213
Home sublayer group, 213
Homepage page, 229
Homepage state, 213, 217
Horizontal layout, 211
horizontal spacing, 211
horizontalCenter property, 52, 86, 143, 183
hover color property, 206–207, 210
hover menu item layer, 204
hover state, 196
htdocs folder, 92
HTML (HyperText Markup Language), 5–6, 31,
    56, 58, 60, 201, 203, 229, 306
HTTP (HyperText Transfer Protocol), 25–26, 28,
    36–37, 90, 181
HTTPS (HyperText Transfer Protocol Secure),
    26
HTTPService class, 182
HTTPService definition, 155
HTTPService object, 180
HTTPService service, 155, 176
HUD (Heads-Up Display), 109–111, 169, 204,
    207–211
HyperText Markup Language (HTML), 5–6, 31,
    56, 58, 60, 201, 203, 229, 306
Hypertext Preprocessor (PHP), 7–8, 10–12, 31,
    92, 181–182, 259, 269
HyperText Transfer Protocol (HTTP), 25–26, 28,
    36, 181
HyperText Transfer Protocol Secure (HTTPS),
    26
hyphenated style definition, 306

I

id attribute, 304
ID selector, 61–63

S

You Need the Companion eBook

Your purchase of this book entitles you to buy the companion PDF-version eBook for only $10. Take the weightless companion with you anywhere.

We believe this Apress title will prove so indispensable that you'll want to carry it with you everywhere, which is why we are offering the companion eBook (in PDF format) for $10 to customers who purchase this book now. Convenient and fully searchable, the PDF version of any content-rich, page-heavy Apress book makes a valuable addition to your programming library. You can easily find and copy code—or perform examples by quickly toggling between instructions and the application. Even simultaneously tackling a donut, diet soda, and complex code becomes simplified with hands-free eBooks!

Once you purchase your book, getting the $10 companion eBook is simple:

❶ Visit **www.apress.com/promo/tendollars/**.

❷ Complete a basic registration form to receive a randomly generated question about this title.

❸ Answer the question correctly in 60 seconds, and you will receive a promotional code to redeem for the $10.00 eBook.

eBookshop

233 Spring Street, New York, NY 10013

Offer valid through 11/10.